The Nietzsche Dictionary

BLOOMSBURY PHILOSOPHY DICTIONARIES

The *Bloomsbury Philosophy Dictionaries* offer clear and accessible guides to the work of some of the more challenging thinkers in the history of philosophy. A-Z entries provide clear definitions of key terminology, synopses of key works, and details of each thinker's major themes, ideas and philosophical influences. The *Dictionaries* are the ideal resource for anyone reading or studying these key philosophers.

Titles available in the series:

The Deleuze and Guattari Dictionary, Eugene B. Young with Gary Genosko and Janell Watson

The Derrida Dictionary, Simon Morgan Wortham

The Descartes Dictionary, Kurt Smith

The Gadamer Dictionary, Chris Lawn and Niall Keane

The Hegel Dictionary, Glenn Alexander Magee

The Heidegger Dictionary, Daniel O. Dahlstrom

The Husserl Dictionary, Dermot Moran and Joseph Cohen

The Kant Dictionary, Lucas Thorpe

The Marx Dictionary, Ian Fraser and Lawrence Wilde

The Merleau-Ponty Dictionary, Donald A. Landes

The Sartre Dictionary, Gary Cox

BLOOMSBURY PHILOSOPHY DICTIONARIES

The Nietzsche Dictionary

DOUGLAS BURNHAM

BLOOMSBURY

LONDON • NEW DELHI • NEW YORK • SYDNEY

Bloomsbury Academic
An imprint of Bloomsbury Publishing Plc

50 Bedford Square   1385 Broadway
London   New York
WC1B 3DP   NY 10018
UK   USA

www.bloomsbury.com

Bloomsbury is a registered trade mark of Bloomsbury Publishing Plc

First published 2015

British Library Cataloguing-in-Publication Data
A catalogue record for this book is available from the British Library.

ISBN: HB: 978-1-44116-200-7
PB: 978-1-44116-075-1
ePDF: 978-1-44114-940-4
ePub: 978-1-44118-114-5

Library of Congress Cataloging-in-Publication Data
Burnham, Douglas.
The Nietzsche Dictionary / Douglas Burnham.
pages cm. – (Bloomsbury philosophy dictionaries)
Includes bibliographical references.
ISBN 978–1-4411–6075–1 (paperback) – ISBN 978–1-4411–6200–7 (hardback) –
ISBN 978-1-4411–8114–5 (epub) 1. Nietzsche, Friedrich Wilhelm, 1844–1900 –
Dictionaries. I. Title.
B3311.B87 2015
193–dc23
2014013107

Typeset by Newgen Knowledge Works (P) Ltd., Chennai, India
Printed and bound in India

For Eleanor and Catherine

CONTENTS

ACKNOWLEDGEMENTS

Many thanks to David Webb and Martin Jesinghausen; also to many PhD students over the years, but most recently and helpfully Jon Egan, Georgios Papandreopoulos and Brian Pines.

How to use this book

It is necessary to produce an index and not a critical dictionary, for that my powers are utterly insufficient.
NIETZSCHE, LETTER TO HERMANN MUSHACKE,
NOVEMBER 1866

1   With a few exceptions, Nietzsche does not employ a technical vocabulary, like say Aristotle or Kant. Nor does he always use the same words or phrases to designate concepts. Moreover, concepts are developed through the use of imagery and symbolism. It's probably best to think of this book as a guide to Nietzsche's philosophical language. Following cross-referencing will be important in obtaining a more complete picture.

2   For similar reasons, if you cannot find what you are looking for, please use the index.

3   Many compromises had to be made for reasons of space. If any important ideas have been omitted, an aspect left undiscussed, or a key reference missed, please contact me in the furtherance of a 2nd edition.

4   To save space, the following abbreviations will be used. In this table, 'n' stands for the number of the section, aphorism chapter or volume (e.g. H3.101); P for preface (e.g. GMP3); and there may be an abbreviation of a section title (e.g. EHWise4). Notebooks are by year, volume, entry (e.g. 1875.3.63); letters by addressee and date; some miscellaneous essays are by a title, perhaps shortened (e.g. 'On Truth and Lies').

Beyond Good and Evil	BGEn
Birth of Tragedy	BTn
Daybreak	Dn
Ecce Homo	EHabbreviationn
Human, All Too Human	Hn.n
On the Genealogy of Morality	GMn.n
Philosophy in the Tragic Age of the Greeks	PTGn
The Antichrist	ACn
The Gay Science	GSn
Thus Spoke Zarathustra, sections are numbered	Zn.n
Twilight of the Idols	Tlabbreviationn
Untimely Meditations	UMn.n
The Wagner Case	WCn

Nietzsche's life

Friedrich Nietzsche was born in 1844 in Prussia. His father, a minister, dies in 1849 and his baby brother in 1850; after which the family moves to Naumburg where N and his sister Elisabeth grow up. N graduates from the Schulpforta in 1864 and attends the University of Bonn as a student of theology. The next year he transfers his studies to Leipzig and changes his subject to philology. So impressive is his early work that he is appointed professor of classical philology at Basle in 1869 – at which time he also gives up his Prussian citizenship. In the meantime he has been reading philosophy (especially Schopenhauer and Lange), become friends with Richard Wagner, and has started independent reading in science. In 1870, N is developing his ideas on Greek tragedy and in the summer serves briefly as a medic in the Franco-Prussian war. His first book *The Birth of Tragedy* is ready by 1871 but published in 1872; its unconventional approach to philology – it is more philosophical and poetic – badly damages N's reputation in his field. This is followed by four *Untimely Meditations*, which focus on culture and cultural themes – and in particular are deeply critical and confrontational on the subject of German culture.

In 1878, N published *Human, All Too Human* which marks a break both with the art and culture-oriented early work, in favour of a more positivist conception of thought, and also with Wagner, whom N believed had sold out to modernity and the German state. By the late 1870s N was on more or less perpetual sick leave from the University and would shortly retire altogether. He begins a kind of nomadic life, living in various rented accommodation in Switzerland, France and Italy, rarely for more than a few months at a time. *Assorted Opinions and Maxims*, *The Wanderer and His Shadow* (both of which are then later bound together with *Human, All Too Human* in a single volume) and *Daybreak* are produced over the next three years. In 1882, he published *The Gay Science* which inaugurates a new phase in his thought; in this year also, his friendship with Paul Rée and his quasi-love affair with Lou Salomé both break down in recriminations – also, N would never forgive his sister for her role in this. From 1883 to 1884, he published the three public parts of *Thus Spoke Zarathustra*, and a privately circulated fourth part follows in 1885. The next three years are furious activity: *Beyond Good and Evil* is published in 1886, *The Genealogy of Morality* in 1887 and four short books are written in 1888 (*The Anti-Christ, Ecce Homo, Nietzsche contra Wagner,* and *Twilight of the Idols*) – and in between these, he finds time for a number of other projects, including adding a fifth book to the original edition of *The Gay Science*, new prefaces to several earlier books and assembling a collection of his poetry. At the beginning of 1889, N collapses on the streets of Turin, and rarely writes or speaks again through to his death in 1900. He is cared for first by his mother, and then by his sister, who also gains control of his literary estate (including unpublished books, essays and a vast number of notebooks).

Just before his breakdown, N was beginning to attract attention from intellectuals across Europe. By the time he died, he was a celebrity and well on the way to becoming the focal point of a whole industry of cultural and scholarly work. N's views on race and breeding were magnified and distorted by eugenicists and anti-Semites (with some encouragement from his sister) and eventually he became an important point of reference for the Nazis. This harmed his reputation across Europe, and it was only in the 1960s that interest in N again rocketed. He has since become a canonical figure in the history of thought.

The A–Z dictionary

abstraction

In the early 1870s, one of N's projects was an account of the development of *concepts* and *language* from out of the flux of stimuli. Abstraction is one of the achievements of this development (1872.19.217): one term stands for a number of particulars. However, N is suspicious of directly using 'abstraction' as a way of understanding the process itself. Abstraction, N speculates, is in turn founded upon the trope of metonymy (1872.19.204, 215), designating the whole of something by a particular thing closely associated with it. Selection and reflection are still 'a long way' from abstraction (1872.19.78); indeed, concepts are not abstractions but 'relations' (1872.19.43), that is the relation of similarity or association, or also the relation between some particular and its utility for a people ('On Truth and Lies'1). In the later work, 'abstraction' is rarely used, except to designate the flight from reality (AC11), or similarly the 'grey sky' of metaphysical concepts (1884.26.384, 1885.40.6, WC1). Also relevant to N is a Hegelian analysis of abstraction: it is a mistake to believe that things are best understood in themselves and in isolation from their concrete situation (see for example TIMorality6: 'the individual is a piece of fate'; also see the analysis of nutrition, location and climate at EHClever1–2). Accordingly, N's frequent metaphor of viewing things from a height is not akin to abstraction. Rather, such height allows one to see the network of power relationships, to observe things and their development in their concreteness.

abyss

Abgrund. Literally, 'that which has no end, limit or (especially) bottom'. Thus the 'abyss of being' or 'abyss of things' (BT21,

PTA10) to describe the lack of anything fixed and thing-like in the *Dionysian* conception of the real, which is thought of as underlying the realm of apparent things (and see also Z2.1). '*Grund*' in German also means 'ground' in the sense of 'reason' (as in 'what are your grounds for claiming that?'); therefore '*Abgrund*' can mean a lack of justification, legitimacy or sense. Thus also 'abyss of reason' (1870.7.123) especially in connection with Kant. N often associates the abyss with the Sphinx, who killed herself by throwing herself from a high place after Oedipus successfully answered the riddle (1881.13.22, BVN-1885, 599, 1885.2.13). The idea seems to be that certain questions, or certain paths of philosophical enquiry, are themselves abysses because they cause one to leave any solid intellectual or moral footing behind, and thus represent some kind of *danger* (e.g. the 'abyss of savagery' described in 'Homer's Contest', GSVorspiel27, BGE289, the abyss of 'scientific conscience' at GM3.23, and see EHClever4). The idea of *eternal recurrence* is an 'abyss-deep thought' (Z3.3, 3.13.1), representing a danger of self-destruction; likewise, the thought of the death of God is such an abyss (Z4.13.2), or the temptation to *pity* and thus to the abandonment of one's ideals (Z3.2.1).

This is why, when one looks into the abyss, the abyss looks back (BGE146) – that is to say, one's response to the abyss is all important. Does one view the abyss with pride (Z4.13.4), are the abyss and one's summit as one (Z3.1)? That is, can one view the recognition of the abyss and its *affirmation* as an achievement?

action

An action, considered on its own is *Handlung;* being active is *tätig,* as in 'the active person'. The most obvious but not perhaps the most important issues here are the old philosophical problems of whether my will, or my actions, are free (e.g. H18, 106); can they ever be unegoistic (H37); and what does it mean to subject them to universal rules (H25). Perhaps action is only possible under the illusion of freedom, or through a kind of deliberate ignorance, because knowledge kills action (BT7, and UM2.1). All our actions live on through an endless chain of consequences, and are thus eternalized (H208). Nietzsche's accounts of such problems tend to employ something akin to a deterministic metaphysics. Once

N develops the notion of will to power, the concept of action is included under it: for example, neither the fact nor expectation of happiness (at least in an ordinary sense of this term) is at the ground of action; rather, the ground is an expression of and a feeling of power (GM3.7). In general N is less interested in the resolution of such traditional philosophical problems than in the origin and meaning of our belief in certain concepts such as freedom. One reason for this is that noble morality is concerned with the value of human beings, a 'triumphant yes-saying to oneself' (GM1.10), and not with the features of actions (neither their conformity to laws, or their utility) (BGE260, 287).

N distinguishes frequently between the life of action and the life of contemplation; Napoleon is one of his foremost examples of the former. Likewise Prometheus (see BT9) and Faust (in Goethe). The latter is the man of endless striving, of acting to change, obtain or achieve things. When Faust attains a moment of contemplative happiness, he dies and Mephistopheles moves in to claim his prize. Faust's endless striving is both his downfall and his salvation, since his striving is ultimately more akin to the creativity of God than to the negation or nothingness of Mephistopheles. More particularly, it is the 'eternal feminine' that saves Faust (see entry on *feminine*). Not surprisingly, N generally stresses the importance of action, of the deed; knowledge has meaning only if fulfilled in action (UM2F, D20). This idea frames N's critique of the historical sciences of his day which accumulated only facts, and likewise science more generally which conceives of the intellect as a passive or at least a dispassionate spectator (see entries on *science* and *spirit*). Indeed, the very notion of a 'doer' distinct from any deed is nonsense related to ideas of substance (GM1.13); a 'quantum of power' is not distinct from will and effecting. It follows also that there is both an error and something ignoble in 'disowning' one's actions by feeling the pang of a guilty conscience. Actions are necessary expressions of an identity; to feel guilt (the criminal who has become 'pale') is to apply an external criteria based upon consequences, and to falsely imagine that one's identity is not what it is (Z1.6, TIArrows10, EHClever1); a further aspect to this concept is the cultivation of the capacity to be responsible (see GM2.2, and see entry on *conscience*).

Action has no necessary relation to our knowledge or beliefs, as Socrates and Plato thought (D22, D116). Active people do not act out of self-knowledge, but rather act so as thereby to *form* a self (H2.366). Only the doer learns (Z4.7). That is, first of all, being a disciple of Zarathustra is not about knowing or understanding, but about action (see EHZ6). Second, the disciple is about *discipline*. However, both active and contemplative forms of life are necessary, perhaps in alternation within a single life (H3.308). The comprehensive 'new philosopher' that N envisages, then, would be neither simply the person of action nor the contemplative person. The contemplative life in its best sense should not be understood as an escape, but as a choice made from understanding (D440), as the proper mode of one's contribution to the growth of culture. Indeed, such contemplation can be creative in a way that action can not (GS301 – the idea is similar to the relation of lion and child at Z1.1).

This creativity is to be distinguished from another: the *ressentiment* of the slave revolt is prevented from straight-forward activity, and thus becomes creative at the level of values (GM1.10 and see 2.22); this is an 'imaginary revenge'. This repressed or sublimated 'activity' is always only 'reaction', commencing always as the rejection of some external value (compare GM2.18). Often, when N writes of a 'yes-saying' or affirmative mode of life, it is such creative, positive action that he has in mind (e.g. GS377).

actor

Schauspieler. In the evolution of the form of Greek tragedy, as N describes it in BT, the addition of actors to the original chorus is a symptom of an increasing lack of faith in, or misunderstanding, of the nature of tragedy (BT12); it is a move towards realism (see also BT5). Instead of permitting mythic figures to appear, the actor pretends to be them; it is to this pretence that (N imagines) Socrates and Plato objected. (See entry on *appearance*.)

Thus, much more generally 'actor' can be used as a term of abuse: e.g. UM1.10 or the sorcerer [Wagner] in Z4.5.2. The actor is a fake, one whose power and need is to represent something, perhaps not even having an identity in him or herself, and also needing for others to have a need to watch them (thus vanity: Z2.21, see WC11). The talent for acting is bred in certain classes or peoples by virtue of a requirement of constant adaptation (D306, GS356, 361). However, the D passage just cited contains something different: the idea of Odysseus' self-possession. This is the idea of one who wears many masks without having 'faith' in them, where this 'faith' is how the GS passage defines the later Greeks. The actor may be the right conceptual model also for the 'artist' (N uses inverted commas here at GS361 to indicate he is discussing a degenerate mode of artist, for which he sometimes uses the word 'artiste', for example at GS356; see a parallel discussion at Z2.17). Those who are called 'great' are often actors, because they are incapable of willing greatness (Z4.13.8, and see TISkirmishes11). N uses the phrase 'actors of the spirit' (GM3.8, and similarly at Z1.12 and 2.21) in this way. Such an actor makes others believe he or she has a capacity for envisioning great things and carrying out great action, and demands an over-dramatic setting. The actor may seek to transform what is around in his or her own (false) image (thus the Stoics at BGE9, and see the 'martyr' to truth at BGE25). The concept of actor obviously has links to N's concepts of *mask* and *honesty*. Finally, one should compare this notion of actor to N's portrayal of Dionysian intoxication at TISkirmishes10.

actuality

Wirklichkeit, Realität. Both of these are often translated as 'reality'. *Wirklichkeit* is the most common German translation of the Latin *actualis*, and in turn Aristotle's Greek *energeia*, and thus refers to the real of events or their results; *Realität* has its etymology ultimately in the Latin *res* meaning 'thing' – and is thus the reality of things, objects or materials.

While these etymological considerations may be significant at times, frequently enough N uses the terms more or less interchangeably (e.g. BT7 and 8, or GM3.4). N sometimes adopts Schopenhauer's reasoning that that which is phenomenally real is that which acts or has effects (*Wirken*) in space and time, and thus the term '*Wirklichkeit*' is to be preferred for such phenomenal reality (PTAG5), with respect to which *Realität* is the true, underlying world (e.g. PTAG12).

Alongside the above runs a different meaning. Already in BT7, N finds himself agreeing with Schiller that the chorus protects the space of tragedy against the intrusions of everyday, present reality (see 'tyranny of the actual' at UM2.8). Here, the actual comprises the innumerable, profoundly petty and short-sighted concerns of 'today' – including, for example, the *'realpolitik'* of Bismarck, and even forms of 'idealism' (EHClever1). Tragic experience and genuine culture require turning away from this actuality. This is another expression of the theme of *untimeliness*. The concept of actuality as the concerns of the present occurs again at Z2.14: Zarathustra calls it 'infertile' and 'without prophetic dreams' – that is without the capacity to create, long for and pursue ideals. This is all an allusion to Hegel's concept of actuality, perhaps as mediated through David Strauss (see UM1.2): 'What is rational is actual, and what is actual is rational.' The actual is that which, through a process of becoming, has attained to its full essence: in Hegel's case the concretization of the Absolute idea.

Untimeliness may involve a turning away from the actual in the above sense of 'todayness', but certainly not in a more general sense. For, a certain hatred of or fleeing from reality characterizes early Christian (and not only Christian) thought (AC29–30). This hatred in turn branches out into (i) the elevation of Jesus to divinity as an act of *ressentiment* against those who crucified him (AC40), (ii) the notions of guilt before God, and judgement (AC41–2) and so forth. Other examples of hatred of reality include despising the body and all that is associated with the body (e.g. sexuality), plus the corresponding elevation in value of the fiction that is 'soul' (see for example Z1.3, 4 and the entry for *body*). Likewise, modern science involves a flight from the actual, for it relies upon ideal fictions such as the atom (or some other version of substance), number, pure observation and law. Reality thus requires redemption (GM2.24 and see entry on *redemption*; similarly, Zarathustra's plea to be 'true to the earth' at ZP3). What is this 'redeemed' reality? Not some renewed naïve metaphysical faith in exterior substance or matter, for example (see GS57–8). It can only mean recognizing (not as mere knowledge, but as an alignment) reality as will to power and perspective (e.g. EHDestiny5).

Aeschylus

The first, and to N's mind, the most pure of the Greek tragic poets. See especially the contrast of the artistic activity of Aeschylus' *Prometheus* with the saint-like passivity of Sophocles' *Oedipus* at BT9.

aesthetics

The philosophical treatment of art and related concepts (such as beauty). See *art*.

affect

Affekt, Gefühl, Pathos. States of mind (or reports of states of mind) that include an immediate evaluation of the state or its object, such as pain, *pleasure* or the emotions (at BGE284, N seems to define 'affect' as one's 'for and against'). Moreover, these states assign objects as causes or locations (*this* is painful, *that* makes *me* angry, etc.). All these words could also be translated as either 'emotion' (though few would call pleasure or pain an emotion) or more commonly 'feeling'. In both English and German, feeling can seem to be a value-neutral report of a factual state ('The stone feels rough', 'I feel sad'). However, N describes feeling as always interpretation (D35, GM3.16), bringing the concept of feeling in line with that of affect – that is, a feeling is an evaluation of some physiological state. The feelings N discusses most often – such as pity or pleasure – are equally appropriately called affects. The German term *Empfindung* can also mean 'feeling' in this sense – but we will discuss it under the heading of *sensation*.

Pathos is a Greek word, either meaning a specific state of suffering, or more generally the idea of emotion, and perhaps an even better translation would be 'mood'. In Aristotle's *Rhetoric* pathos is one of the three means of successful persuasion (along with *logos* [reasoning and truth], and *ethos* [way of life or character, and more specifically wisdom and virtue]). For Aristotle, pathos means understanding how emotions lead to judgements and actions. As suggested by 'mood', though, N generally uses pathos to mean a more lasting state, one that accompanies and is perhaps a chief characteristic of a way of life (see GS317). This idea is particularly pertinent in the most famous use of the term pathos, in N's expression 'pathos of distance' (see *distance*).

The concept of *Affekt* is employed but relatively rarely discussed until around 1880. Roughly at the time of working on *Daybreak*, the problem of the affects – their origin and role in human action, and particularly the relationship to morality – becomes prominent (e.g. 1880.6.444). Christianity rescues affects from the idea of disinterest, but only if their object is transferred to God (D58, and see BGE198); affects are not primarily individual, but socially conditioned (1881.11.82). Affects arise in part also because of basic intellectual operations such as imagination (1881.11.301). A parallel discussion denies that the affects as ordinarily understood are a fundamental feature of organisms; this amounts to a rejection of certain psychological ideas that understand human behaviour through, for example, pain or pleasure (including N's own work in *Human, All Too Human*). Rather, there is a physiological basis of the affects in assimilation, transformation, excretion, etc. (e.g. 1881.11.128 and 241, 1883.24.20, BGE230). The compound word '*Machtgefühl*' [feeling of power] is used frequently (D112 is typical – see entry on *power*). Such discussions culminate in the thought experiment concerning the *will to power* (see especially BGE36). Will to power is a primitive world of affects. In turn the affects play a role in perception, avoiding or selecting (BGE192, GM3.12) – this infects even apparently neutral scientific claims (GM1.13, 2.11) or if reason in some way masters the affects, then this has been achieved by a long process of cruel discipline (GM2.3).

Moral judgements are a sublimated (i.e. diverted so as to be in some way more acceptable) way of discharging affects (1880.3.51, and see 1881.11.103). A revaluation of values would have to include a revaluation of affects. Certain affects, such as lust for example, need to be redeemed as valuable for the overall health and growth of the human organism (e.g. 1881.11.73, Z3.10, BGE23, GM2.11). Others, including those that are a product of *ressentiment* and comprise a sublimation of and release of *ressentiment*, should be revalued as modes of sickness (e.g. GM3.15). A necessary part of such a revaluation, though, is to have an effect on the domain of affects – and not just, for example, to change our conscious or intellectual view of things. In other words, new values change the way we feel (D103), and are incorporated into the body (e.g. 1881.11.141).

Near the end of his career, N characterizes the Dionysian state as a total stimulation of the affective system, transforming itself through and into all affects (even those that are apparently self-contradictory) (TISkirmishes10, and Ancients5). This idea is also found, nearly two decades previously, in N's early work on tragedy ('Dionysian World View'1). As N puts it at EHDestiny5, the great human who can redeem reality does so by immersion, even identification, with it.

affirmation

N uses a number of terms, including *Bejahung* and *jasagen*. Affirmation is a yes-saying in two senses. First of all, a yes-saying to life, to fate, and to all the suffering or senseless destruction they in fact do and must contain (UM3.3, EHBT2, and at EHZ1 such affirmation is called 'tragic'). N remarks that even those 'beneath' us are necessary for the perfection of the world (AC57). This first idea of affirmation is linked to the notions of *amor fati* and *eternal recurrence*. Second, affirmation specifies a mode of life the values and actions of which are positive and healthy expressions of that life. That is, values and actions are not derived by or reaction against or even sublimation of other values. These two senses are closely related; indeed, they both describe aspects of an ascending and healthy mode of life (see for example EHBT2 where N brings them together). The first concerns the embracing of the whole system of life and one's place within it; the second more focused on ideas of creativity and autonomy.

To the first sense of affirmation, the contrasting idea is that the histories of philosophy, morality and religion are histories essentially formed out of an impossible rejection or revenge. Now, being able to say 'no' to certain kinds of things is indeed important. 'All life is a disputing about taste' says Zarathustra (Z1.13 and see for example TIAncients1); that is to say, life involves struggle, attempting to overcome one thing in favour of another. However, such saying 'no' is predicated upon a prior 'yes'; one accepts the existence of that which is rejected. Indeed, insofar as rejecting it is part of my identity – 'I affirm myself as the one who in this case says no' – I am *grateful* for its existence although I reject it (see GS276–7, 'he is a principle of selection' at EHWise2, and the notion of *amor fati*; also GM3.7, EHZ6). N also argues that affirmation is conditional upon 'no'-saying insofar as those values that have come to dominate culture (and, through the internalization of culture, the self) must be overturned if that form of life capable of affirmation is to develop (EHDestiny4); no saying becomes an instrument or an aspect of method. My 'no' is the expression of an evaluation that belongs *within* the system of power relations and perspectives that make up life or the real. On N's analysis a religious system like Christianity, a philosophical system like Platonism, or a political system like socialism is precisely the impossible rejection of the system of life itself. Affirmation, thus, cannot generate universal laws (see TIMorality6).

Affirmation is tested by eternal recurrence. On a literal interpretation of eternal recurrence, every detail in the sequence of events and things repeats itself in a huge, cosmic cycle. This thought becomes a test of the capacity of an individual to affirm the course of their life (GS341). However, more broadly, eternal recurrence means at least that the system of life – founded upon the struggle of affects and values, complete with wastefulness, indifference, long periods of degeneracy – is inescapable. It will never be a system without these features. Affirmation is not just the acceptance of such a system (a pessimist's response) but gratitude and love towards it.

Notice that in such affirmation in the first sense (a yes-saying to eternity), affirmation in the second sense must also occur: for, thereby also one claims responsibility for one's life and all that conditioned it, *as if* the whole were willed by their creative will. Eternal recurrence is thus the dangerous solution to the problem of the redemption of time posed at the end of Z2 (Z2.20). The two senses of affirmation are sometimes symbolized as *feminine* (the first sense) and masculine (the second) – thus the imagery of Z3.15.

agon

Greek word, meaning 'contest', 'competition', 'strife' or 'struggle'. N uses the Greek term or derivatives occasionally, but more often discusses the concept under the headings of words such as '*Streit*' (fight or battle), '*Kampf*' (contest or struggle). N's thought here comes under a number of influences, let us mention just four. First, *Heraclitus*. N interprets Heraclitus as positing 'strife' as the basic principle behind the famous notion of continual flux. Second, Greek cultural life was, N believed, agonistic through and through, to the extent that competitors who were too powerful were ostracized (see 'Homer's Contest'). Third, the real Zarathustra, the ancient Persian religious figure, conceived of the cosmos as a battle between good and evil forces. Fourth, there are later philosophers or scientists who, in one way or another, posit conflict at the root of human or animal action. These would include Hobbes (who conceived of human nature as essentially incapable of peace, and state power as the mechanism for controlling this nature, see UM1.7), Schopenhauer and Darwin (the struggle for existence being a basic condition for natural selection). There is a key difference among these influences: on the Greek conception (and arguably also in Darwin), strife and contest are positive, generating in Heraclitus a cosmic sense of justice, in Greek culture generally pushing humans towards greatness (see PTAG5, H2.222), and in Darwinian thought struggle is a key feature of the mechanism of natural selection and the development of species. On N's analysis, though, this struggle for limited resources is not the chief characteristic of the overall 'economy' of life (see BGE13, TISkirmishes14).

Examples of concepts in N that involve a conflict (especially one that is productive) abound: the mythic-symbolic figures of Apollo and Dionysus (BT1); cultural advancement N often argues happens through conflict (UM4.9, H1.158, 170 and see 276); likewise, the history of scientific development (H1.634) and the development of dialectic in philosophy and ultimately of logic ('Socrates and Tragedy', 1872.19.43, TIPS8, Skirmishes23); the best friendship is not agreement but antagonism: 'let us be enemies too, my friends!' (Z2.7), and similarly a good enemy is an asset (D192, 431, Z1.10, TIMorality3); man and woman are said to be locked in antagonism (BGE238); likewise the masculine and feminine, by means of which agon is symbolized erotically; Wisdom 'loves only a warrior' is a metaphorical evocation of agon in philosophical overcoming (Z1.7, and see GM3). The instinct for struggle is not always productive, however, and must be contained or discharged in a way that does not threaten. This, N argues in a manner akin to Hobbes, was the role of of the Greek state (H3.226, 1872.21.14). In other words, the proper function of the state is to harness the agon.

Struggle is either among those of equal power, or unequal. The former may yield enhancement (perhaps for both parties). One reason why struggle may not be productive is that it is not among equals (see H3.226): to war against an inferior is ignoble or shameful, to war against a superior is irreverent. Agon is productive, then, only if it recognizes differences, rather than collapses them.

Thus, N's concept of the agon is also part of his critique of 'modern ideas' such as equality, democracy or socialism. Similarly, tyranny is a monopoly of power that collapses power towards an individual (thus N's analysis of ostracism in 'Homer's Contest'; likewise, his critique of Bismarck).

The above examples are mostly external – for example, the struggle among agents within a social group. Struggle is also internal, however: since the individual self is comprised of a multiplicity of drives, an agonistic 'society' is also found within the self. Thus, for example, the ascetic struggles to repress certain drives, or against enervation (e.g. H1.141). Likewise, self-overcoming is figured in terms of struggle (e.g. Z2.7, 2.12); thus to Zarathustra, the spirit of gravity is an 'arch-enemy' (Z3.11.1, 4.17.1). N sometimes uses the figure of the 'hero' to designate one whose agon is not external and thus not on display before others (H3.337, and similarly EHClever9).

Alexander

'the Great'. King of Macedonia and famously conqueror of the known world from Greece east to India by the age of 32. Alexander disseminated Greek culture throughout the ancient world, and also brought Eastern culture West. When, in BT, N writes of 'Alexandrian' culture, this is a reference to wide dissemination, but also to the attendant, Socratic turn of cultural scholarship to the mere accumulation of information (symbolized by the library at Alexandria). Thus, N speculates at UM4.4, what are needed now are a series of 'anti-Alexanders' who concentrate and purify. Alexander is, for N, already a caricature of early Greek civilization, exaggerated and simplified (1871.16.43), although still displaying their deep rooted cruelty ('Homer's Contest', see EHWise3). The story of Alexander cutting the Gordian knot is a commonly used image (e.g. D547).

allegory

N does use the word *Allegorie*, but only very rarely. Much more common is *Gleichnis*, which occurs in some contexts where the only reasonable translation is 'allegory' or 'parable'. *Gleichnis* can also refer to the literary trope of simile (N seems to have this specifically in mind at BGE202 and 244), and for this please see the entry under *metaphor*. An allegory is an image (visual or perhaps described in language) that has a certain coherence on its own terms (is for example, a recognizable thing, a character, a narrative) but carries also a symbolic meaning. For example, N ends UM2.10 by using the Delphic Oracle as an allegory to sum up his prescription for how history should be used. This is fairly conventional. For a few additional examples, see H1.278, GS28, Z4.4, BGE209. Allegory can be termed 'ironic' when the allegorical vehicle already has a symbolic meaning of its own, but something else is meant. An example of this would be N's use of the image of the heavens (Z3.4). The heavens become a symbol of the *absence* of providence. Similarly, Zarathustra gathers disciples, but urges them to betray and deny him (Z1.22).

Philosophical thinking about the nature of allegory begins early. At BT6, while music is understood to be directly symbolic of the original unity of things (the idea is Schopenhauer's), lyric poetry employs allegories to attempt the same symbolic work. The same point is made concerning the allegorical nature of myth at BT21. The pure musical route, though, is untranslatable or incommunicable, and thus is not anything like an insight into or *wisdom* concerning the original unity. Thus, while Apollonian images are appearances – and thus, it would seem something like the opposite of knowledge (certainly, that is how Socrates interpreted such images) – when they function as allegories, they are in fact an important mechanism of wisdom.

Let us take Z1.20 as an example of a later use of allegory. N writes that 'even your best love is only a rapturous allegory'. Here we have a factual state of affairs (love or marriage) carrying symbolic meaning for those involved in that state of affairs and perhaps for others. This is a case of a concrete image (real marriage) that symbolizes an ideal, but also serve as a set of practices or institutions that may inspire one to understand or pursue that ideal. (In this case, the ideal is the role of masculine and feminine drives within the total health of both organism and culture.) There is a similar use of the concept of allegory at Z22.1 and 3.10.2 (arguably also at EHClever8 and EHBT2). In all these cases, N is describing particular human practices or institutions that may have utility on their own terms, but which gain much of their significance from their allegorical meaning.

Twice in Z2 it is repeated that all permanence is a poet's allegory, and the poets lie too much (Z2.2, Z2.17 – the first point being an inversion of the last lines of Goethe's *Faust:* 'All that is transient is merely allegory'). 'Poet' here does not only mean an artist in verse, but also anyone who posits permanence (the metaphysics of substance, or the theology of a god), since that is only a poetic device. Such lying allegories are not contrasted to any direct, non-poetic statement of facts. A model of language that values clarity, directness and the absence of imagery is even further from the capacity to speak the truths of, say, will to power (H1.217). Instead, the contrast is with 'higher' allegories of time and becoming – N likely has eternal recurrence in mind here. N writes, concerning Zarathustra's homecoming: 'Here, on every allegory you ride to every truth' (Z3.9 – the passage is further discussed at EHZ3). Similarly, N writes 'Only in dance can I tell the allegory of the highest things' (Z2.11). Something like 'inspiration' (EHZ6), then, is required for such images to cease being a lie and attain to their proper symbolic functioning.

alternate

See *cycle, opposite.*

altruism

See *egoism.*

amor fati

The love of one's fate, specifically a *gratitude* towards all that makes up the situation that I inhabit, and which has produced me in the way that I am. The root of the idea is found in the notion of 'antiquarian history' at UM2.3. Given that N often stresses the interconnectedness of all things and events, this 'all' is effectively the whole course of history – see for example GS337 – insofar as that history 'passes', in part, through an individual. *Amor fati* is a 'formula for greatness' (EHClever10). My love or gratitude comes from the fact that this fate produces me, and does so as the being capable of affirming myself, and also capable of having a *creative* role into the future (see H1.208 or GS337). The phrase itself is relatively rare (cognate discussions of gratitude or *affirmation* are more common), and first appears in notebook entries in 1881 and then GS276. However, similar concepts can be found earlier, e.g. at H292 and UM3.3.

The idea is closely allied to that of affirmation more generally: to say yes to this situation is the only way of saying yes to oneself, and *vice versa*. In particular, it is related to the affirmation of *eternal recurrence*. Only an individual who (a) embodied a *healthy* and *ascending* life, (b) was *spiritually* attuned to such life (e.g. not deceived about themselves) and (c) could 'redeem' the past and present as if it were a product of their will, could genuinely love one's fate. As such, accident or *chance* (in any ordinary sense) is not relevant (GS377, Z3.1). Likewise, necessity is no cause for distress (EHWC4), for nothing can befall the lover of fate that is not also a product of the creative will (Z2.2). See *becoming what one is.*

anarchism

A term describing any number of thinkers, who argued that any hierarchical framework of political, economic, legal or social power must be harmful to human beings, and also revolutionary figures and groups in the nineteenth century and beyond, who believed that political institutions could not be reformed, but had to be dismantled. Although Rousseau was not an anarchist, certain elements of his thinking were important for later anarchist thought. Bakunin, whom Wagner knew in Dresden, was a leading figure in European anarchism movement. Through the First International movement, anarchism had a (deeply uneasy and brief) association with socialism and with Marx.

For N, anarchism, although it appears to be intellectually opposed to other modern ideas such as democracy, equality or even socialism, is in fact of a piece with them. Anarchism is founded on reaction and *ressentiment* (GS370, GM2.11, letter to Ernst Schmeitzner 2 April 1883), remains moralistic (DP3), expresses a fundamental belief in the value of pity, or rather a fundamental inability not to feel pity, and finally evidences a desire for the herd (BGE202). Early Christians were anarchistic (AC57–8); likewise, emancipated women (EHBooks5). Some anarchists are individuals of great power, but that power expresses itself in self-denial and in simple destruction (D184, GS370).

animal

Tier, and with different connotations, *Bestie.* In general, N joins a long tradition which uses the figure of animality to describe aspects of the human, for example virtues, vices, drives or types. Much of N's uses of animal imagery is conventional. This is mainly because N is alluding to this long tradition (e.g. Greek, Northern European or Indian mythology; the Bible and other religious texts; Plato among other philosophers). Sometimes, however, there will be a characteristic twist or inversion of meanings or values. The snake is a good example in N of a conventional image with altered meanings. See entries under individual animals (lion, ass, snake, etc.).

However, N does not only talk about types of animals, but animality more generally. Here there are several relevant meanings. First, the animal stands for a conception of humanity that attempts to reintegrate the human into the broader natural world. N proposes such a conception, Darwinism is another, both Hobbes and Rousseau can be understood in this direction. (See *nature.*) For N, the human has been falsely differentiated (in Christianity, and elsewhere). He counters with an 'honest', even scientific, characterization of the human animal (e.g. D26, Z2.3, GM3.25, AC14). Second, the animal is the figure of that creature guided by *instinct* rather than by *reason* or *conscious* deliberation, and thus also whose instincts may be *healthy* rather than repressed or distorted through *domestication* or *guilt* before God (e.g. GM2.22 and 23, AC14, TIIH2). Third, and most conventionally, the animal can mean that aspect of the human which does or should cause shame, which has not attained to that type of nobility that is distinctively human (e.g. Z4.13.13, BGE60).

Finally, the animal kingdom is one where differences (such as those along the food chain) are an integral part of a healthy system

(N no doubt has passages such as Isaiah 11 in mind). In N, this is a commentary on the necessity in human affairs of *class* or caste; and ultimately also a claim about the will to power as a fundamental description of life. *The notion of the beast of prey*, or the infamous image of the 'blond beast' belongs here (e.g. BGE257, GM2.17). Notice that the beast of prey image is by no means always a positive one: on what and how it preys, and with what good *conscience*, is the difference (see Z12.22, GM3.15). While culture and the state begins with the 'blond beast', the further development of the human type will occur through 'bad conscience' – a phenomenon utterly impossible for that beast (compare GM2.17 with 24).

ant

Ameise. Symbol of work, especially industrial, as part of a homogeneous group (e.g. D206). In this, akin to the *bee*. Also, small, incremental and in-themselves blind contributions (H2.186) and likewise a necessarily limited or *fragmentary* view of *purposes* or projects (H3.14, 16, 189). Tellingly, at 1886.5.81 N links this to the failure of *Bildung*, and to the necessity of his concept of *synthesis* or *comprehensiveness*.

anthropomorphism

This means to impose the form or qualities of the human onto something. N is tireless in exposing the innumerable ways in which the histories of science, philosophy or religion have involved anthropomorphism (PTAG4, 11, 'Truth and Lies'1, UM1.7). A key example is the concept of cause and effect in nature: N argues that this separation of cause and effect is an anthropomorphism, founded upon what is already a false characterization of human action in terms of will (e.g. TIFGE3). Generally, the whole of our knowledge of the world (including human beings) is anthropomorphic.

On the one hand, then, these anthropomorphisms are illegitimate (they are, essentially, 'lies'), despite their enormous utility for human beings. Early in his career, N ascribes to Kant especially the credit for a critical philosophy capable of uncovering these anthropomorphisms (PTAG11). On the other hand, there remains a danger of the destruction of culture through the overemphasis on critique (historicism, specialization, etc.). The generation of greatness, the flourishing and advancement of the human depend upon such 'lies' being productive in the realm of culture (1872.19.35, 180 – but the point is made often elsewhere, for example the last few sections of BT, or in the first two UM).

anti-Semitism

N expresses revulsion at the rise of anti-Semitism in Europe. He sees it as a symptom of a weak and defensive culture (BGE251), of *ressentiment* (GM2.11), of nationalism and also of a form of asceticism that demands stimulation (GM3.26). Significant figures in his life were pronounced anti-Semites, including his sister *Elisabeth,* her husband and *Wagner.* The mistaken opinion that N himself held anti-Semitic views was common for some time, and was reinforced by three key factors. First, his literary remains (after his mental collapse) were selectively edited by his sister. Second, N's own repeated stress on *race* and *breeding* played into the hands of later figures (including eugenicists and some within Nazism). Third, N's attacks on *Christianity* also dealt with its origin in *Judaism,* particularly the notions of monotheism and the origin of the priestly class.

Antichrist, The

One of N's last publications, written in 1888, but not published until after his mental collapse. The title should be understood more as 'Anti-Christian'. A brief book, but tightly focused on the psychological and physiological meanings of the advent, growth and triumph of *Christianity*, in comparison especially with *Buddhism*. Notable for a sustained, speculative and positive psychological interpretation of Jesus, as akin to a Buddhist. The book revolves around the contrast between this Jesus and the Christ figure disastrously generated by the Church Fathers, especially *Paul.*

ape (also monkey, etc.)

Affe. Seeing primates as akin to the animal aspect of humans (thus, for example, the climbers at Z1.11) pre-dates Darwin; with Darwin though arises the notion of a common evolutionary ancestor. The ape, then, is either an origin or disfigured mirror-image, of which we are ashamed (ZP3). The ape is a imitator, unaware even of being an imitator, and which brings disrepute to the imitated (TIArrows39, Z3.7). Nietzsche is concerned with being understood, or being misunderstood – one of the explicit reasons behind the writing of *Ecce Homo* (EHP1).

aphorism

Aphorismus. A brief, self-contained and striking piece of writing, usually gathered together in sequences. Aphoristic writing was common in ancient literature, and was employed by many authors of whom N was fond, such as Montaigne, La Rochefoucauld, Goethe and N's close intellectual partner for a period in the 1870s, Paul Rée. N's anti-systematic use of aphorisms also owes much to German romantics such as Novalis or Schlegel (see *irony*). N writes aphoristically in two distinct ways: first, an (apparently) random series of very brief sayings or epigrams (e.g. the fourth chapter of BGE), and second a series of longer pieces, each like a short study (e.g. the first five chapters of H1). There are a number of additional possible variations. For example, in H1 and in later work (much of BGE, AC and TI after the first chapter), the series may have explicit overarching themes, while at other times N will string out the aphorisms so as to make any overall interpretation bewildering (chapter four of BGE, chapter one of TI). Likewise, and regardless of the presence of an overarching theme to the series, aphorisms can speak to each other, as if they were short segments of a continuous piece of writing (e.g. the comments on pity D132–40). Almost all of N's middle and late books are written aphoristically, and although Z is a quite different stylistic experiment, it too has elements of the aphorism (e.g. Z3.12, and even within otherwise continuous sections such as Z1.7). Of the later work, only GM is almost entirely non-aphoristic.

The different rhythms of these various ways of writing, and the different interpretative demands they make on readers, are important elements of N's writing strategy. N describes the function of such writing as fully developed thoughts (H2.127) with either maximally compressed, or fragmentary, expression and an 'immortal' perfection of form (TISUM51, and see D506); aphorisms serve as a kind of test of readers (Z1.7); or an interpretative task set to readers (GMP8), perhaps because the expression is deliberately incomplete (H1.178, 199, 207). See *irony*.

Apollonian

Named after the Greek god Apollo, this is one of three *drives* that, in BT, N identifies as key to understanding culture production and cultural change, from the ancient Greek world on. The other two are *Dionysian* and *Socratic*. A brief period in which the Apollonian and Dionysian work together produces ancient *tragedy*. The Apollonian is the origin of those cultural forms where *beauty* and clarity of *form* are emphasized (examples would be *epic* poetry, architecture and sculpture), and the affects of calm or *cheerfulness*. As a drive, N argues that it implicitly carries with it a metaphysical view concerning reality, which he identifies with *Schopenhauer's* principle of individuation – that is, the belief that individual entities are ontologically original. Importantly, though, the Apollonian is also characterized by an awareness that these valued forms are an *illusion* with respect to a Dionysian view of existence (N compares this to a *dream* in which we are aware we are dreaming). Thus, the Apollonian should *not* be understood as a kind of self-deception or turning away from the real (that would be more akin to the Socratic). In his later work, the Apollonian is no longer thought of as a competing, brother drive to the Dionysian, but rather as a moment (of calm, stillness, beauty, image, etc.) within the latter. This is implicitly acknowledged at GM3.25, when N claims that the 'complete and authentic antagonism' is between Homer and Plato: the former the deifier of life, the latter its 'slanderer'.

appearance

Erscheinung. Schein. Early in his career, under the influence of *Schopenhauer*, N held that the fundamental characteristic of things as they appear to us, including our own selves and bodies, is their givenness as individual *form*. This is Schopenhauer's *principium individuationis* and *veil of Maya*. Schopenhauer, in turn, was trying to interpret *Kant's* distinction between appearances and things-in-themselves (see for example H1.16), and also incorporate ideas from Eastern thought. 'Behind' appearances, so to speak, is the will, continually striving and *becoming*, in itself without form. This distinction allows N in BT to formulate his concepts of the basic cultural *drives* (Apollonian, Dionysian, Socratic), and to arrive at a broad theory of the significance of *art*. Here, an important distinction arises between two senses of appearance: appearance as symbolic image in genuine art, versus appearance as mere copy, and thus as possibly deceptive (see BT12). N characterizes Socratic thought as the forgetting of the first possibility of appearance, and thus also as the advent of a certain *modern* faith in *science*, broadly speaking. This theme continues throughout his career, and involves analyses of how that which merely appears is denigrated with respect to some 'beyond' or 'behind'. See *allegory*.

Appearance has an important role within N's theory of the *utility* of falsehoods (starting in the short, unpublished essay 'On Truth and Lies', and continuing in H). The point is that human perception is, from the ground up, a simplification of the world in order that it appears as intelligible, predictable, available for human beings to use. The ultimate motive behind this is utility: without such interpretations, human beings could not survive. Moreover, different *peoples* interpret things according to their specific situation (e.g. *climate*, resources, their *enemies*) and thus differences in understanding the world arise, mainly in terms of what is *valued* (and ultimately, what is approved or disapproved of *morally*).

Later, the notion of value becomes fundamental. If one rigorously rejects the hypothesis of a world, god or life that is somehow not here but 'beyond', then ultimately one also has to rigorously reject the notion of appearance itself (TIFable). Appearance only makes sense with respect to something 'behind' or 'beyond' it. The notion of appearance becomes transformed into the notion of *perspective* or interpretation. A world understood as will to power is neither something in-itself, nor is it appearance, but is perspectival and evaluating (e.g. GM3.12). The building blocks of nature, so to speak, and very much including the human, are perspectives or values – in other words, relations of *will to power*. See *Bachofen*.

Ariadne

Ariadne is a common point of reference in later N. In Greek mythology, Ariadne was the Cretan princess who aids the Athenian Theseus in defeating the Minotaur in the *labyrinth*. Ariadne was the subtlety to Theseus' destructive power. According to some versions of the story, Theseus promises to marry her, but then abandons her on Naxos. There, the god *Dionysus* becomes her lover. For N, Theseus abandoning Ariadne is humanity abandoning its possibilities of *growth* and *health*, in favour of the turn towards European modernity; and an abandonment of the mythic *feminine* in favour of a misunderstood masculine. Ariadne thus stands as a representative of the specific greatness of Greek humanity, desirous of the Dionysian. (This is true as early as BT7.) The poem from Z4.5 [entitled 'Ariadne's Lament' when N uses it in *The Dionysian Dithyrambs*] portrays this desire for the Dionysian, as does Z3.14. We moderns may have more scientific knowledge, but it has not made us greater beings (1885.37.4), quite the contrary – our subtle knowledge, N has Ariadne say to him in rebuke, is 'snout philosophy!'. Thus, only in giving up a narrow conception of the utility of knowledge, of progress as preservation and the alleviation of suffering, and other such 'heroic' modern achievements, will growth and beauty of the human be possible again (Z2.13). (See also BGE296, TISUM19, EHZ8 [in which Z2.9 is discussed].) In a famous letter from January 1889, N seems to reimagine himself as Dionysus, Cosima Wagner as Ariadne, and therefore Richard Wagner as Theseus.

aristocracy

See *noble*.

Aristotle

To a great extent, N's engagement with Aristotle is by way of the latter's account of tragedy (and to a lesser extent, rhetoric). So, N disagrees with Aristotle's account of the relation of tragedy to the chorus in 'Greek Music Drama' and again at BT7 and 14; likewise with the famous idea of the catharsis of pity and fear (BT22, GS80, TIAncients5, EHBT3, but see AC7). N sees Aristotle as a product of the decay of Greek culture: thus, despite his careful consideration of earlier philosophers, he has no real understanding of their greatness (H1.261); likewise, Aristotle as both 'powerful and harmless' is exemplary of the man of science (D424 and see PTAG3). Other themes in Aristotle include the account of *time* in terms of *number*, and the notion of *energeia* (see *actuality*).

art

Kunst, although this word can mean anything 'made', and not just the 'fine' arts. The category of 'art' covers the visual and musical arts most centrally, but also includes literature. The concept of art is used also in a broader sense, beyond its meaning as a particular cultural practice: thus, the necessary lies that are discussed in 'On Truth and Lies', and much later life's healing instinct (GM3.16), are both termed 'artistic'.

Generally speaking, Nietzsche's philosophy of art goes through three phases. First, an early period, represented by BT and UM4. Here, N is under the influence of the aesthetics of Schopenhauer and Wagner. True art is both token and saviour of authentically unified culture – by a way of discovery and employment of the myths that unify a people (BT23, UM4.8). Art is also the destination of post-Enlightenment *critical science* (BT17). In the first phase, everything revolves around *tragedy*, which N sees as the pinnacle of ancient *Greek culture*, as a mechanism for achieving insight into psychological and metaphysical realities, and also sees as the means of rehabilitation of *modernity*. Analyses of other genres, such as *lyric* poetry, *epic*, or modern opera, are all treated as contributing to the understanding of tragedy. Likewise, if art in modernity deviates from the Greek conception, it serves only as a *narcotic* (UM4.6), at best a temporary relief from the *fragmentation* of culture and artistic forms (BT18). This duality of true (Greek or tragic) art – and the wider culture that goes with it – and a degenerate, modern art, is a key theme of all of UM.

In the second phase we find a sceptical or even damning view taken – partly no doubt in response to N's disappointment with the directions Wagner was taking in the mid and late 1870s (see, for example, the comments about 'degeneration' at H1.158; this is frequently echoed even later, for example GM3.25). The age of art is over, once and for all. Particularly in H, N sets art and science in a different opposition and order of priority (D433). Art is not a route to insight or knowledge (e.g. H1.29, 151, 160, 164), and indeed depends upon a certain ignorance or positing of metaphysical falsehoods (H1.220, 222). The notion that art protects or soothes remains, but this is not understood as culturally productive; instead it is a dangerous *narcotic* (H1.108, 148). N now rejects the *Schopenhauer/Wagner* conception of music as the direct expression of feeling or *will* (and also Schopenhauer's positing of art as a means to the quieting of the will, likewise Kant's account of *disinterest*). Instead, N discusses the development in *modernity* of *symbolic* and de-*sensualized* media (H1, 215–18), which development affects both art and its audiences (cf D191). One reason for the decline of art is the thinking of the artist as the *individual* and the *genius*, rather than as essentially an artisan (H163) and in *contest* with others (H158, 170).

The Gay Science GS is an important turning point for the third phase. Again we find the distinction between true art and degraded art (the later N is no less sceptical about artists and art, especially in modernity, thus for example the parody of Wagner in the figure of the sorcerer in Z). However, he has returned enthusiastically to his earlier understanding of art (and again, especially, tragic art) as a means to a new *ideal*. One must be the poet of oneself – to live as a work of art (GS78, 299). Art allows us to treat ourselves as phenomena, not taking ourselves and our truths too seriously (GS107). In general, in N's later work, art is a mode of the growth of will to power (GM2.17), *instinctive* and involuntary (BGE213, GM3.4), associated with *overfullness* and *perfection* (TISUM8–11, 19), and *pregnancy* (GM3.4). Art is the transformation of one's environment into an image of one's own beauty – it is a *magnanimous gift*. Likewise, art *can* be a tool combating the *ascetic* ideal (GM3.5). An 'art of life' is a key characteristic of great peoples, too (AC56, GM2.17); similarly, N talks about art without artists, by which he means certain kinds of institutions (1885.2.114 – the idea is similar to the manner in which culture drives work *through* individuals in BT).

ascent

The symbols of height and ascending play an important role in N, understandably associated with for example *mountains*, *birds*, lightness (as opposed to *heaviness*), the sky (e.g. *astronomical* references), *cold* and *overcoming*. To some extent, N's use of such symbols follows deep conventions within philosophy (Plato's philosopher climbs up from the cave) and culture more widely (God and heaven above us, elevated moods, high priests, etc.). Above all, the symbol stands for the increase of an individual's (or a people's) *power* and *health*, and thus also for the increase in their capacity for *beauty*, great projects, or rule. For example, at TISocrates11, N claims that both an anarchy of the instincts and a need to fight the instincts, are symptoms of decadence, explaining that for ascending *life*, happiness and instinct are equivalent.

Ascent is relative to flatness or descent; and ascending generally implicates the reverse movement of descending. Thus, Zarathustra must 'go under', that is return from the mountains down to humans (ZP1) in the flatlands; psychology must descend to depths not in the sense of being profound or fundamental, but in the sense of investigating the most repellent cases and problems (BGE23); and thinking pessimism to its depths might lead to the opposite, highest ideal (BGE56). This is part of the concept of *cycles*. Also, ascent and height are relative in that one can look down, have things beneath one: height represents a *comprehensive* view that is not *abstract*, and a pride that is *honest* and not condescending. Again, though, every ascent must also lead to a going-under, lest height be a form of fleeing (BGE41).

asceticism

Asceticism refers to a life practice that involves a deliberate denial to oneself of certain pleasures or activities, perhaps in the belief that this will enhance other things (e.g. one's virtue, or closeness to

God). It is a common practice across many religions. N's interest in the concept comes partly from trying to understand why it is so widespread – that is, what more general purposes does it serve? Equally important is the idea that the influence of asceticism did not disappear with certain ancient and medieval practices, but remains surreptitiously pervasive and influential in modernity. N's work on the subject culminates in the long and famous third Treatise of GM, but in fact asceticism is a theme found throughout his work. H contains a sustained discussion of asceticism (H1.136–44); in accordance with the general strategy of that book, N attempts to break down the various factors in asceticism and show how they all involve *pleasure*. Key to this is the setting up of a moral ideal that involves an impossible suppression of the body – that is, an ideal impossible to attain. In that way, the aim is not to become moral, but to feel as sinful as possible, so as to perpetuate the ascetic condition. Although the explanatory tool N employs changes from the psychology of pleasure and pain to the will to power, many of these same analyses are found, in modified form, in his later work. D113 emphasizes the quality of spectacle: the ascetic wanted to demonstrate his power in the sight of non-believers (barbarians), and ultimately he himself is both spectacle and spectator.

GM3 begins, unusually, with a precis of the argument to come, which shows N's ambition to demonstrate ascetic ideals' pervasiveness across many aspects of human life. The chief purpose of the Treatise is not about the ascetic ideal per se, but rather either demonstrating the inescapable nature of will to power (which is what GM3.1 says) or demonstrating the art of interpretation (GMP8). The various analyses of the ascetic ideal simply provide evidence for these. The Treatise then comprises a series of studies of the meaning of the ascetic ideal in artists, philosophers, the weak and ill and in priests. The discussion of the philosopher is significant, for here the ascetic ideal shows its often overlooked positive aspect, as the search for the conditions of spiritual growth and elevation (and see GM3.11), like the abstinence and careful mode of life of an athlete in training. (See also entry on *discipline*.) The topic of the priest, and his relation to the weak and ill, arrives with GM3.11, and N reaches the nub of the problem. Asceticism seems to be a way of diverting the course of one's life onto the right path, the path that leads to another world or after-life. This means, though, that asceticism is a mode of life that seeks to cancel out life – but that is a contradiction, and (at least at the physiological level) must be only an appearance (GM3.13). That is, the ascetic ideal must be somehow a way of a degenerated life preserving itself at all costs. The priest is a kind of 'doctor' to the sick, serving to change the direction of their *ressentiment* so as to render it harmless (GM3.15–16). Instruments to this end are described from sections 17 to 20. This institutionalization of the sick and weak, is also a valuable separation of them from the healthy (GM3.16). Both science and historiography (history understood as a scientific undertaking) are complicit in the ascetic ideal (GM3.24–6); likewise, atheism which remains ascetic in its will to truth (GM3.27). In the end, the ascetic ideal means that the will to power can will anything (even nothingness), but cannot not will (GM3.28) – that is to say, the ascetic ideal is the last recourse of a diseased form of life attempting to prevent itself falling into a 'suicidal nihilism'. How the dangerous aspects of the ascetic ideal are to be overcome is not focused on here. There are two clues: first, through comedy, that is through a light-footed, mocking irreverence; second, through the will to truth coming to consciousness not as principle but as problem (GM3.27). See also 1887.9.93 at which N claims to want to make asceticism natural, that is a return to the original Greek concept of *askesis* (training), a discipline of improving strength and health.

Asia

When N writes of 'Asia' or the 'East' he generally has one of the following in mind: (i) Russia as a great rival to European power (BGE208, TISkirmishes39), or as a key origin for *nihilism* and *anarchism*; (ii) culture, social systems or philosophical systems in India or China, founded on Hinduism or Buddhism (BGE56); (iii) relatedly, China in reference to its capacity for an industrious class without resentment (D206); (iv) the area to the east of Greek civilization, particularly as the 'prehistory' of the Dionysian (BT1).

ass

Esel. As in English, ass can be a general term of abuse, connoting above all stupidity and dullness or slowness (e.g. BGE8 and 283); thus N jokingly calls himself the 'anti-ass' (EHBooks2). All humans, from a higher perspective, are asinine (TISkirmishes19). The characteristic braying is 'i-a' in N's German, thus '*ja*' or yes – the ass stands for indiscriminate *affirmation*, lack of *taste* (Z3.11.2, and in Z4). Such meanings are sometimes replaced by the ass as stubborn, enduring (Z1.7, BGE284), and even *clever* (Z2.8); as a weight-bearing creature, the figure of the ass sometimes overlaps with the more familiar image of the camel (TwilightArrows11). The festival of the ass (Z4.17–18) is akin to one aspect of the Greek 'Dionysian' festival – the suspension of cultural and social order (see BT4); likewise, there are Medieval traditions with a similar theme. Also, the ass is made sacred in some myths of Dionysus. Moreover, worshipping the ass is akin to the final *nihilistic* stages of religion (see BGE55), but here in a *joyous* and *festive* spirit.

assimilation

See *incorporation*.

astronomy, references to

N's works contain many allusions to astronomy and indeed relatively recent discoveries. His knowledge came from popular or semi-popular books such as Zöllner's *On the Nature of Comets*. N evidently found a modern conception of space – the vast, largely empty and cold distances between stars or planets – an excellent symbolic vehicle for his conceptions of the *pathos of distance* ('too distant star': D548), the infrequent appearance of greatness (image of the comet at PTAG1), *nobility, friendship* (GS279), *solitude* (the image of the star emitting light into the darkness at Z2.9, notice also the allusion to solar flares) or *untimeliness* ('the light of the stars needs time' at GS125 and BGE285, or relative stellar motion at BGE243). Likewise, it serves to convey the cosmic insignificance of human beings ('On Truth and Lies', H3.14), and even the chaotic nature of reality overall (irregular galaxies at GS109, 322). Likewise, even the methods of astronomy are employed: not seeing the stars as 'above you' (BGE71 – that is not transcendent in nature – see also the references to Copernicus at BGE12, GM3.25), or the indirect inferences of 'dark bodies' (BGE196).

atheism

In its basic sense, atheism is the positive assertion of the non-existence of anything like a god. N's position on atheism is complex. To be sure, nothing like a god exists as either an independent physical or a transcendent entity. If gods are symbolic expressions of human ideals, however, then N's atheism in this basic sense is modified by his commitment to the Dionysian ideal (see BGE295 and entry on *Dionysus*).

Abandoning a belief in a transcendent God is clearly a step forward culturally (D96). However, in general, the issue of a god's existence is far from the most important issue (Z3.8.2, AC47). More significant are questions like the following: (i) what does the need to posit a god's existence say about the believer? N asks such a question frequently about *Wagner*, for example. (ii) What does atheistic questioning say about the *metaphysical* commitments of the questioner? So, for example, N writes that atheism 'today' remains in the tradition of the *ascetic* ideal (GM3.27). Likewise, the hidden implication of theism with science, language or morality means that atheism is often blind to its causes and consequences (GS125, TIReason5). (iii) What *ideals* are posited in a belief, or despite a lack of belief, in a god? The arising of a Christian idea of God is discussed at AC16, insofar as Christianity is not the function of the survival, much less the growth, of a people (and see AC51). Moreover, Christianity is not *just* a theism, nor just *any* theism, and therefore atheism is not necessarily anti-Christian. Nineteenth-century English moral philosophy, for example, remains Christian even if it rejects theism (TISkirmishes5 and see BGE252).

atom/atomism

Atomism is a theory of nature that posits as the ultimate constituent parts of nature small, indivisible particles that move, collide and combine in empty space. The theory begins with Democritus, and becomes an important part of Epicureanism. It is revived in the early modern period as the basis of many philosophical materialisms and mechanistic accounts of physics. In the eighteenth and nineteenth centuries, atomism received a boost because of the success of the science of chemistry, and likewise its role in models of themodynamics. As a comprehensive account of nature, atomism always had certain weaknesses, such as its difficulty in understanding the action at a distance that is gravity or magnetism, the often wave-like properties of light, and the whiff of metaphysics that hangs around concepts like indivisibility, indestructability or pure substance.

N's account of atomism has several roots. First, his reading of eighteenth-century physicist Boscovich, from whom he gets an account of the effect of matter based upon forces – that is, without requiring an underlying positing of matter (BGE12). Second, a Neo-Kantian (and Schopenhauerian) critique of the nature of matter considered as a substantial thing-in-itself (i.e. to say, an attack on the notion of permanence). Third, the claim that atoms are a hypostatization of a certain illegitimate concept of the separability and separate identifiability of cause and effect (GM1.13), which is ultimately a psychological concept (TIErrors3). Fourth, and closely related, the atom is a projection into the inorganic of a metaphysical conception of the self or soul understood as subject of its affects or experiences, and initiator of its actions (BGE17), and this conception itself may arise from linguistic habit (TIReason5). The metaphysical question of whether atoms are real is supplanted by the question of what lies behind the belief in atoms (the 'atomistic need' BGE12): namely a moral commitment to notions of stability, order, responsibility and freedom.

Bachofen, Johann Jakob

One source for N's account of Dionysian and Apollonian as basic cultural forms is the work of Bachofen, a Swiss anthropologist and legal historian who lived a generation prior to N. Bachofen is a prominent example of the attempt to read mythology as encoded history or anthropology; a trend N continues and which is influential to this day. Bachofen in *Mother Right* assembled evidence for an original, matriarchal origin of human societies and institutions, one that was superseded by a transitional 'Dionysian' stage, and then a fully patriarchal stage that Bachofen called 'Apollonian'. Obviously, N's account differs greatly. He does not see the Apollonian and Dionysian as historical stages of culture, but rather as drives within all cultures. For further discussion, see *feminine and masculine*.

Bakunin

See *anarchism*.

barbarism

A word from Greek, referring to the unintelligible sounds of non-Greek languages and thus effectively meaning 'non-Greek' (BT2). There are two phases to N's use of the term. Early in his career, N primarily uses the word to mean lacking in any authentic culture (UM1.1, GS99), particularly where the idea is that such culture has been lost or undone (as at BT22, UM3.4, H1.251, H3.279). To be sure, this meaning continues in later work (e.g. GS120, AC41). Later, however, N does question the viability of such a simply-made distinction. The history of culture could be written as the turning inwards, onto oneself, of the instincts of domination of the barbarian (D113). The democratic mixing of races and cultures in Europe has led to a 'semi-barbarism', but this provides it also with its 'historical sense' (BGE224). Every higher culture begins because of the dominance of a 'barbarian' class, who are more natural, whole, animal and without impaired instincts (BGE257, GM1.11, see entry on *nobility*).

barrel organ

Leierkasten, or similar. A mechanical musical instrument. N uses it as a metaphor: music, repetitious and without soul, is a culture without life (UM3.4), or something merely repeated without genuine understanding (H2.155, Z3.13).

beast of prey

See *animal*.

beauty

Schönheit, Schöne. N's treatment of beauty obviously has a connection with his account of art, and many of the same influences. However, beauty is both a narrower and a wider concept: narrower, because not all art has being beautiful as its aim or effect; wider, because not all that is encountered as beautiful is art. In N's early account of tragedy, beauty plays a particular role as the healing quality of the Apollonian illusion, which both protects us from but also permits some access to wisdom concerning the true nature of the world. This means also that the primary distinction among aesthetic categories is not between beauty and sublimity (Homeric epic is an important category within the Apollonian; and see H3.295), but rather between both together and a third: the Dionysian effect that properly belongs to music (BT16, 19). (N develops a new conception of the sublime and heroic at Z2.13.) See also, for example, N's discussion of architecture at H2.218, where beauty is said to be a late innovation, masking the shudder in the presence of the divine. Later in his career, this concept of Apollonian beauty remains a reference point (e.g. BGE59) but becomes only a part of a richer account of beauty.

Beauty has a decisive relationship to knowledge (see also *allegory*). Nothing is beautiful in itself, but only because it is known (D550); likewise, the origin of beauty may be ugliness coming to an awareness of itself (GM2.18). Because knowledge always involves projection of human values onto its object (TISkirmishes19), and could only be knowledge of *being*, it is thus illusion. N's point is that the portrayal of knowledge, insofar as it must involve metaphysical error, is beautiful; and the progress of knowledge is the transformation of the ugly into the beautiful. A key reference point for N is Plato's *Symposium* 206–10, which metaphorically describes philosophical reflection in terms of procreation and childbirth: the philosopher is pregnant with wisdom, and requires a beautiful soul (Socrates) as midwife to bring this wisdom to term. The lover does not pursue beauty per se, but gives birth 'in beauty'. Thus, for example, history must be 'overcome' and 'bathed in beauty' in order for genius to be born (1872.19.10, 152, and see UM2.6). Beauty urges one towards procreation (either sexually or spiritually) (TISkirmishes21). The influence of Plato also contributes towards N generally thinking of beauty as feminine. Above all, this feminine beauty means protective, preserving, approximating to being (i.e. relatively unchanging) (D25, GS24). The feminine and masculine become moments in an account of *creativity*. Similarly, beauty arises under constraint or *discipline* (H3.159, and see TISkirmishes47). All of these instances are further evolutions of the original idea of Apollonian beauty as healing, but also as allegory a form of indirect wisdom. For further discussion, see the entry under *feminine*. However, the beautiful can also be 'wild' (e.g. the 'beast-of-prey beauty' of the sea at H2.49, the beauty of wickedness at D468 or noble passion at D502). This reiterates the lack of a profound contrast to the sublime as conventionally thought, the fact the calmness of protective beauty is a symbol and not a straight-forward property, and ultimately that beauty is only part of a concept of life, which also involves creation and destruction (thus, for example, 'struggle and inequality are present even in beauty', Z2.7).

Beauty is a quality of the ideal (e.g. the gods) that a human value sets for itself ; thus, beauty is a human measure, 'given' to the world, by means of which it *affirms* or even worships itself (TISkirmishes19). Thus the metaphor of everything being a mirror to one's beauty (Z2.13). The spectacle of *ascending* life is beautiful; degeneration is ugliness (TISkirmishes20, and see Z4.1, 11). As again in Plato, beauty in itself is not the goal or endpoint, but rather either a sign of *health* (e.g. GS105), or that which 'lures' one towards further creation (the soft voice of beauty at Z2.5, wisdom and life personified at Z2.7). Thus, for example, life is the seductress, teasing with beauty, at GS339; or beauty is a culture's imagined happiness (D433); likewise, the beauty of the overhuman (Z2.2). N often criticizes the notion of disinterest in Kant's account of beauty – which is also in Schopenhauer as the quieting of the will. Such disinterest is both physiologically impossible (or at least unlikely), but more importantly also a perverse conception of what is beautiful (thus, Z2.15 and 'immaculate perception'; TISkirmishes22, GM3.6–7). Instead, what is given up for the sake of beauty is only the 'hero's will' (Z2.13), and this leads not to disinterest, but to 'godlike' (rather than heroic) 'desires'. See also the 'transfiguration' of the sensual at GM3.8. In other words, disinterest is at best a stage, an overcoming of what is merely a fragment of the whole will towards the overhuman.

becoming

Werden. N's concept of becoming falls under two main headings: historical analysis and metaphysics. By the first is meant an exploration of the origin and development of beliefs, values, institutions or other forms of life. For example, at H1.145, N proposes a 'science of art' that investigates the becoming of supposedly miraculous works. This basic move is found frequently, and is reflected in the title of the second chapter of H1, the fifth chapter of BGE, and of course the whole title of GM. N is, broadly speaking, following a trend in historical analysis that received a powerful impetus from Hegel and from biological science (Darwin and similar thinkers). The significance of this kind of investigation lies in the fact that many *values* (moral values in particular, but by no means exclusively) receive part of their value from the assumption that they are eternal, perhaps God given, or at least natural laws (see Z3.12.8, TIReason4). Questioning this is part of questioning the value itself. Moreover, the historical investigation often shows that a given value has its origin in its opposite, and thus involves a kind of practical contradiction – so, for example, N attempts to show that Christian morality arises from out of affects that it itself would consider 'evil': namely, envy and revenge (this is part of the purpose of GM1). Finally, such historical analysis is valuable because it opens up new possibilities for values – so, for example, N's investigation of the historical *self-overcoming* of religion then culminates in the discovery of an 'opposite ideal' (BGE56). See *genealogy, history.*

The metaphysical sense of becoming involves an attempt to investigate the nature of the real. N's account of becoming is heavily influenced by Heraclitus (N even frequently employs Heraclitus' famous example of the river, for example at Z2.12). There is also a significant influence from out of the tradition of Hume and then Kant (which in turn is radicalized by Schopenhauer) which asserted that, at the level of sense at least, there is only constant, disordered change. Becoming can be understood in at least three fundamental ways: first, that what is real is a chaos, without form or order. The problem with this first view is that it provides no explanation of why the appearance of form or order occurs. Moreover, N argues that the dissolution of contemporary culture (for example) into its historical becoming produces a kind of cultural paralysis (UM2.1, and see the end of UM3.4), one that perhaps leads to pessimism or nihilism. Second, that what is real is something like a process, that produces and then modifies various forms, with some overall sense of direction or an end-point. This conception of becoming is a view that many of N's contemporaries get from Hegel, and which N criticizes at UM2.9, 3.4, and ZP5. N also finds analogous ways of thinking in several Darwinian thinkers, such as Spencer. Similarly, a traditional account of the freedom of the will robs becoming of its 'innocence' (TIErrors7, 8 and Z3.4).

The third possibility is that what is real are, again, something like processes, but which interact and produce temporary forms only to dissolve them again. Here there is no overall coordination of these processes, no 'purpose' or 'end', except perhaps for what human beings posit for themselves as purposes. There is indeed constant change, without stable entities (i.e. without being, such as atoms or substances), but through process forms are realized only to then be replaced by new forms. This notion will serve as a first approximation to N's preferred view (and also his preferred interpretation of both Heraclitus and Epicurus). AT UM2.9, he pronounces such an idea true, but very dangerous. At the time of BT, the key processes N studied were the 'cultural drives' that he calls Apollonian, Dionysian or Socratic. Later, in H, N seems to attempt a psychology founded upon the interactions of sensations (especially pleasure and pain), and the striving for pleasure and pain (see for example H1.18). Later still, from around 1880 onwards, a dynamic network of power and power-relations – that is to say, life considered as the *will to power* (together with the feeling of growing or diminishing power) – is the preferred explanatory instrument. Implications include, first, that knowledge itself is not knowledge *of* this network, as if from an independent vantage point, but rather a part within it; thus the notion of *perspective*. Second, all unities are actually multiplicities (e.g. the soul is akin to a society of drives: BGE19). Third, insofar as the concept of cause and effect involves the positing of separable unities (that which is the cause, that which is the effect), it is an illegitimate concept, meaning also that necessity and calculability have to be understood differently. A fourth consequence concerns N's famous idea of 'becoming what you are' (see separate entry). Fifth, just as the becoming (in the narrower sense of historical analysis) poses a challenge to values that presented themselves as unchanging, so the metaphysical sense of becoming poses a challenge to all values, to value as such. It is thus one factor contributing to *nihilism*; and a form of life that can experience joy in becoming is an important new ideal (see Z2.2).

Sixth, there are several fragmentary attempts from the mid-1880s on to produce a metaphysical argument that relates N's conception of becoming to *eternal recurrence*. At least, eternal recurrence is a way of thinking about value in a world characterized by becoming, and thus by the critique of values mentioned above. A life that could be willed eternally would be the only possible remaining criterion of value – it would be an approximation to being (1886.7.54) – and yet such a life would also have to be understood as healthy and ascending. This is the 'opposite ideal' to the pessimistic or indeed nihilistic state (BGE55–6).

Becoming oneself

The phrase 'to become who or what one is' is an adaptation of a line from Pindar's *Second Pythian Ode*. It is something of a refrain in N, from GS on (see GS335, Z4.1, EHClever9, as well as the subtitle of the latter book). The individual is a 'piece of fate' (TIMorality6), meaning it cannot be fundamentally recast in the image of some external (i.e. moral) value. To do so would be a dishonest betrayal of oneself, a deviation or distortion of the life one is, resulting in all kinds of physical or spiritual degeneration. See for example the account of bad conscience at GM2.16–22 (although then N also calls this a 'pregnancy' at GM2.19); likewise GM3.14 or TIImproving2. Nor is it a question of choosing to fashion oneself in any way – for the individual does not have that freedom of will. In some sense, then, the individual already is what it is, or at least is already *pregnant* with itself. This idea of being pregnant with oneself is probably a reference to Plato's *Symposium* (see entry on beauty), and also to Leibniz (who uses this metaphor frequently himself; see his *Monadology*). In EH, N somewhat disingenuously talks about needing to get out of one's way, to not try to find out about oneself, and not to struggle, while the 'governing idea' within one grows (EHClever9). This idea of not knowing oneself – in contradiction to the Socratic maxim – is also found at GMP1. This not struggling, though, ultimately means to align oneself with the fate of oneself – and this in turn requires a certain *honesty* (although not necessarily a *conscious* one). This honesty will involve, if not self-knowledge, then at least the *strength* for truth more generally; also a certain act of *creation* (GS335), a questioning or critical attitude towards one's age, and a refusal of external models of living (external to one's alignment to fate), in favour of an internal adaptation (see note 1885.2.175). For this reason, also, Zarathustra requests that his disciples do not think of him as offering a way of life ('guard yourself against Zarathustra' he says at Z1.22.3).

bee

Biene. Symbol of *industry* (thus akin to *ant*), building (OTL1, 2) or swarming (H1.285). Bees creating *honey* is a symbol of patiently extracting, accumulating and concentrating (H2.179, Z2.11, ZP1), indeed committed to such accumulation and unaware of anything else (GMP1). Gathering of honey is related to autumnal *ripening* or *pregnancy.*

Beer

Bier. For N, beer is particularly associated with Germany (along with *newspapers* and *Wagnerian* music); beer thus becomes a symbol of a particularly German way of *narcotizing* (H2.324, BGE244, GM3.26).

being

Sein. N uses the concept of being in a way akin to Parmenides or Plato: true being is that which is, eternally, and does not become (see Z2.2, TIReason4). Moreover, even with respect to everyday entities (things that we know are not truly permanent or self-identical) we still employ the concepts of being, *as if* they were true being (TIReason5). Belief in the existence of being is a key feature of metaphysics, and also carries a moral value. See *becoming.*

belief (opinion)

Belief [*Glaube*] has two different meanings in both English and German. (i) Belief in the sense of opinion, the largely unjustified or careless views that someone or a group happens to have. N will often use *Meinung* rather than *Glaube* for this (e.g. GS345). (ii) Belief in the sense of faith, often now in a religious sense. A religious sceptic would claim there is very little difference between them, but in many philosophical traditions (including the Kantian) there *is* an important difference: one can acquire evidence such that opinion becomes knowledge; but the object of faith could not in principle be an object of knowledge. N frequently takes up a position of the religious sceptic (e.g. UM1.3, H2.225). The notions of a *disciple* (e.g. Z1.22.3, TIAncients5), or of the 'love of man for the sake of God' (BGE60) should be understood as ways of rethinking the notion of religious faith in the absence of a transcendent or impossible object.

N also often (it is a particularly common theme in GM) writes about *metaphysical* or religious concepts as being objects of 'faith' – for example GM1.13, 3.20. He suggests that these individual items of belief are part of a system which serves one dominant faith, around which one builds a form of life. In this case, it is the faith of the weak that they someday will be the masters (GM1.15). Because these concepts are abstract, not the concrete expression of the life of a *people*, this kind of faith is universalizing and arises from *ressentiment*. It refuses on principle to tolerate any other faith (or form of life). At GM2.21, N puns on *Glaube* (belief) and *Gläubiger* (a creditor, who is ultimately God). (See also the 'unconditional' universality of the faith in the ascetic ideal at GM3.23.)

However, N also argues that opinions and beliefs are legitimated by the kind of person who holds them. At H2.325, he differentiates between the opinions of 'most people' and those of 'exceptional men'. The idea is elaborated at Z2.14: those who live in the land of culture (modern Germans) have no beliefs, but this is because they are 'unworthy of belief'. But a people capable of creating must have a prophetic belief in their future. Towards the end of BGE, N contrasts the South with the German North by saying the former have an existence that believes in itself (BGE255); something similar is said of the 'masters' at 260, and again of the noble at 287.

benevolence (or goodwill)

Wohlwollen. Primarily in H, benevolence is considered by N to be a key *virtue*, although not one well understood previously. At H1.49, N praises the small acts of benevolence that people show to each other every day, and counts the sum total of little pleasures they evoke as, collectively, enormous (see also H1.111). This effect arises despite the fact that benevolence is not unegoistic, and indeed founded upon a feeling of superiority (H1.509). In the next section (H1.50), he contrasts this with *pity*, which he considers a form of malice. Likewise, at H2.196, in a reference to Plato's metaphor of the chariot in the *Phaedrus*, he contrasts benevolence as a virtue associated with clear thinking and restraint, with the ruthlessness often attached to unclear thinking and sentimentality. In D, N also insists that benevolence must also be founded on a benevolent inclination towards the self (D516) – this anticipates several key later ideas, such as the notion of a reactive *will to power* that is founded on *ressentiment*, or the idea that the *noble* has self-*veneration*. By GS, N's analysis of certain moral *affects* in terms of will to power is well advanced. Benevolence is traced back to the enhancement of power (GS13 and 118). After this point, benevolence drops out of view, to be replaced by other notions of virtue, notably *veneration* and *magnanimity*. At EHWagner4, he implicitly contrasts his own 'humanity' [*Humanität*] with the cynical benevolence of others.

Beyond Good and Evil

Written 1885–6, published 1886. In letters, N claims it is a restatement of Z, albeit in a dramatically different style (e.g. Letter to Burckhardt, September, 1886); while at EHBGE, N claims that this book was written as the negative, critical side of his thought, after the *affirmation* of Z. Written in an *aphoristic* style, this book gathers the aphorisms under a series of thematic chapters, rather like H. The work is notable for a more explicit discussion than is generally found outside his notebooks of the *metaphysics* that seems to underlie N's reflections on morality and *religion* (e.g. the concept of the *will to power*). There are also nicely focused chapters on religion and on *virtue*. The book ends with an important evocation of the figure of *Dionysus*, and one of N's finest poems.

Bible, the

The Old Testament N argues is one of the greatest, certainly the most sublime, pieces of literature (BGE52), and the record of a great people (GM3.22). He finds the New Testament a distasteful account of a catastrophic turn in European history. *Luther's* translation of the Bible into German is one of the key events of the reformation, and had a huge formative effect upon the history of German. Thus, N's comments about Luther are often in terms of *style* (e.g. BGE 247). N's works are full of references to biblical events and persons, either for the purposes of direct discussion (i.e. the account of Jesus and Paul in AC) or metaphorically (i.e. the images of love, gift and sacrifice in ZP are allusions to the life of Christ). See *Jesus, Paul, creation, sacrifice, cruelty, religion, Christianity, Judaism*.

Bildung

See *culture*.

bird

Vogel. The bird is a symbol of rapid *ascent* (BT20, H1.168, Z2.2), of something that needs and desires to be ahead of its time, to exhibit spiritual *growth*. Birds must also be *light*, able to throw off burdens. The bird is thus in opposition to the *spirit of heaviness* (Z3.11). The flock of doves at the end of Z4 is chosen precisely because it is a conventional symbol of gentleness and peace, but combined with the bird's lightness and need for ascent, and thus is unlike a herd of sheep or cows, say. The dove image also has important biblical echoes – Gen. 8.11 and Lk. 3.22.

The eagle (*Adler*) is the most common bird mentioned in N. The most famous use of the eagle is as one of Zarathustra's animals, where it is the symbol of a healthy and honest *pride* (ZP10,

1882.2.7). The eagle can view things as beneath it; this is both a certain kind of *comprehensive* sight which is not *abstraction*, and also an *honest* pride (see also *pathos of distance*). The *snake* is *cleverness*. The combination of these animals (the eagle carrying the snake: ZP10 and Z4.11) is something rare: those who have pride generally do not understand themselves; those who are clever tend to be self-loathing. It seems likely that they also represent two great mythic and cultural inputs into Europe, the eagle as the masculine Greek, the serpent as the feminine Judaic (see also BT9); their union is an expression of an as yet unrealized 'wholeness' of the human. The eagle is a bird of prey. Birds generally, and especially the eagle, thus also stand for a particular kind of *strength* (GS314). Its happiness lies in relishing the terror of the great *heights* and the *abyss* (Z2.8), rather than in ignorance of that terror. Moreover, the eagle's hunt is direct, straight down; it is thus, considered on its own, a *noble* 'stupidity' (1885.2.20). It is nourished on *innocence*, it both loves and hates the lamb (Z4.14.3) – thus mirroring N and Zarathustra's relationship to the human, which is loved because of its as yet unspoiled *possibilities* (e.g. ZP4). In his correspondence to and about Lou Salomé, he compares her to an eagle both in her keen physical and spiritual perception, and in terms of her being to him a 'sign' (as the eagle was to Zeus before the battle with the Titans) (e.g. to Köselitz July 13th and Aug 4th, 1882).

Birth of Tragedy, The

N's first book, written 1870–1 and published in 1872. This book, with its lack of scholarly apparatus, energetic and figure-laden prose, philosophical and psychological speculation, and mixture of ancient and modern contexts, was not what the philological community expected. It was promoted by Wagner, but attacked by fellow philologist Wilamowitz-Moellendorf, and this badly damaged N's academic career.

The book has three main purposes and correspondingly divides into three sections: first, to elaborate a theory of ancient Greek *tragedy* as a synthesis of two metaphysically understood cultural *drives* (*Apollonian* and *Dionysian*). In this way N solves in an original manner the relationship between *cheerfulness* and pessimism: how could the Greeks, with their deep knowledge of suffering and futility, have remained cheerful? Second, BT traces the reasons for the decline of tragedy to a third drive, the *Socratic*, which is also the advent of *science* and *modernity*. Third, the book seeks to understand what it would mean, and what it would take, for tragedy to be reborn in the present. The account of culture is thus revealed to be a general one, and not specific to Greece. The book is heavily influenced (although not entirely uncritically) by *Schopenhauer*, and especially in its third part plays homage to *Wagner*. In 1886 the book was reissued with a new, self-critical preface.

Bismarck

Otto von Bismarck was the chief political figure in Germany from the 1860s to 1890. Bismarck provoked wars (especially with France in 1870–1) that in turn led to the unification of Germany around Prussian leadership. His brand of pragmatic and power politics, and his *nationalism*, made him for N a symbol of all that was wrong with modern Germany. Passages alluding clearly to Bismarck are common, such as BGE241. See *politics*.

blond beast

See *animal*.

blood

N employs *Blut* (blood) as a metaphor. As a metaphor it has to do life, obviously – and is thus a key symbol in Christianity for a life made eternal by being cleansed of sin (Mt. 26.28, Jn 6.53–4). Particularly: (i) Blood stands for the specific mode of life of an individual or group (thus history transformed into blood: UM2.1; morals part of our 'flesh and blood': BGE24). Blood is accumulated and passed down, forming peoples, types or families (BGE213, 261, Z2.4; *Geblüt* means belonging to an aristocratic family line). (ii) Blood is that which makes one strong and capable of creation. Thus we have the vampire or leech images N employs to describe the life-draining of certain ideas or practices (e.g. GS372, Z4.4), revenge (Z1.12), or asceticism or nihilism (Z3.5). (iii) At Z1.7, Zarthustra loves things that are written 'with blood'. This seems to have several meanings. One must write sparingly because blood is precious, thus the mention there of aphorisms and of things written in blood being an effort to read. Blood is also courage and the love of danger (see entry on *spirit*), so that which is written in blood will take risks, and those who read it to take risks with themselves (in Goethe's *Faust*, the pact with Mephistopheles is signed in blood). (iv) Blood is sacrifice or martyrdom, as towards the end of Z2.4. This idea is related to Christian symbolism, but also to Bismarck's famous speech in 1862, where he uses the phrase 'iron and blood' to describe a nationalistic foreign policy not afraid to risk warfare (see BGE254).

body

Leib. By body N usually means the human body (as opposed to just any material object). If one rejects dualism – an account of the mind or soul as essentially different from, perhaps even separable from, the body – then bodily states are sensations, appetites, passions and so on, and *also* thought and reason. In turn, this means that the one set of processes (those traditionally associated with body) and the other (those traditionally associated with mind) will require a similar set of explanatory accounts. Many of N's contemporaries found this joint explanatory account in a *materialistic* account of *physiology*. N was influenced by this work, but goes what he believes is a step further: in the second half of his career, the *will to power* seems to provide such an account that does not involve the metaphysical commitments of materialism. Moreover, these two sets must also influence each other (indeed overlap or coincide) much more than is generally thought. Importantly, the individual body is not necessarily the primary object of enquiry – N treats groups (based on gender, class or race) as effectively one body (e.g. BGE259, TISkirmishes47). That is, certain groups are effectively a single organism. For example, the mobility and intermarriage of various human types vertically across classes, and geographically across Europe and beyond, has created mixed physiologies and thus also new types of *cultural* forces or possibilities (BGE224).

Similarly, this account of the body explains N's concern with the concept of health or growth in both physical and spiritual ways, and with practices like diet, cleanliness or discipline. Through such practices, bodies can be developed (or made ill) through what N sometimes calls internalization (TISkirmishes47) or *incorporation*.

N goes so far as to say that the sickness of the body, and a misunderstanding of this sickness, comprises the whole of philosophy (GSP2). The most obvious example of this is the denigration of the body and what are taken to be its characteristics: sex, desire, *sensuality*, violent *affects* of all kinds. From this denigration arise certain *ascetic* practices that seek to repress the body (Z1.3–4, GM3.11, EHDestiny7). To this N counterpoises a 'deification of the body', the 'development of a higher body' (1883.24.16), or a state in which sensuality and spirit are 'at home' together (1885.41.6). Part of the *redemption* of the body, then, is a redemption, or revaluation, of the value of those denigrated characteristics (see for example Z3.10 'On the Three Evils').

Boscovich

See *senses, atomism.*

breeding

Züchten among other terms. To breed means to select reproductive pairs in order to emphasize or eliminate certain inherited traits. N seems to believe that acquired characteristics can be inherited, which is an outdated concept of biological inheritance. If we think of breeding in a wider sense, as the inheriting of selected values by way of institutions (such as education or church), then N's analysis is more plausible. A school 'breeds' in the sense that it values and passes on certain characteristics. N uses the concept in both a negative and positive sense. In a negative sense, Christianity in particular is a procedure for breeding herdlike features, and physical and psychological illnesses, into populations (e.g. GM3.21–2, or BGE199). In TIImproving2–5, Nietzsche distinguishes the domestication aimed at by Christianity from the breeding (in a strict sense) aimed at in Hindu culture, but the process is not dissimilar. In a positive sense, breeding is how *peoples* came to be, by favouring those characteristics that enabled survival under difficult conditions (BGE262), which then became *virtues*. Likewise, breeding is the taking charge of human development, rather than leaving it to lucky accidents (BGE61, 203, 213, AC3).

bridge

Brücke. N's use of the image of a bridge in his later work is fairly conventional: it is an opportunity for overcoming (for growth, development, progress of some type), and it has value for that reason alone. Thus, Zarathustra tells us that the human is a bridge and not a goal (ZP4, and similarly at Z2.7, 4.11, GM2.16). Thus also, the passage called 'On Redemption' takes place on a 'great bridge' (Z2.20). The *ascetic* ideal is, for a philosophy, a unique bridge to his or her conditions of growth (GM3.7 – a similar notion is found at UM3.1). The priests are scolded for believing that there is 'but one bridge' (i.e. a universalizing morality and monotheism, Z2.4; and see GM3.11), and the tyrant believes all history has been a bridge to him (Z3.12.11). A more complex analogy of a bridge is used at UM2.9 to discuss the idea of the Republic of Genius, which is understood as a goal.

Buddhism

This is an ancient Asian nontheistic religion. Along with Vedanta it had a significant influence on European thought from the late eighteenth century on, albeit probably accompanied by a number of misunderstandings. Schopenhauer was an enthusiastic reader, and this is one key source for N. Schopenhauer finds in the accounts of *dukkha* (suffering) and the meaninglessness of action support for his own pessimism; likewise, in Buddhism he finds the 'solution' to suffering in the renunciation of will. From this it follows that N's critique of Schopenhauer will also be a critique of Buddhism (BGE56 is particularly revealing). Buddhism is to be praised for its lack of theism and pursuit of the otherworldly, and for its freedom from *ressentiment* (e.g. EHEHWise6 – notice that the late N has changed his mind on the moral content of Buddhism). On both these grounds, N describes the historical Jesus as Buddhistic in AC. Nevertheless, it has to be judged a passive *nihilistic* form of life (GMP5 and 1.6, 1887.9.35 and 11.411).

buildings (also foundations, architecture, ruins, etc.)

There are a whole host of symbols here, involving the building of, living in, decay or demolition of built structures. Most of these symbols are fairly conventional and not difficult to understand. Nice examples are found at H2.172 or GS358 (ruins), DP2 (undermining foundations), UM2.6 ('architect of the future', and see Z2.22), 'On Truth and Lies' (architect with concepts). See also *nook*. N also talks about architecture occasionally in a literal manner. Highlights include H1.218 (regarding our diminished sense of the symbolic nature of building), TISkirmishes11 (architecture as will to power), and the observations about city architecture at GS280, 291 and GM3.8.

Burckhardt, Jacob

Burckhardt was an important scholar of the *Renaissance*, and a senior colleague of N's at Basel. The two shared an interest in Schopenhauer. Particularly important ideas for N were (i) Burckhardt's portrayal of the Renaissance as a turbulent and dynamic cultural environment; (ii) Burckhardt's historical approach which viewed as potentially important all aspects of culture; (iii) Burckhardt's 'aristocratic' critique of what N called 'modern ideas', particularly the commercialization of culture, the consolidation of political power in a militaristic state and the reduction in the diversity of social strata.

burden

See *weight*.

butterfly

Schmetterling. The butterfly is an important image for N, with far-reaching but not always evident implications. Broadly, he uses the image in a negative though also in a positive way. The key meaning of the former is thoughtless living in and for the present (BT20, Z3.9, Z4.9). The butterfly is thus *modern* humanity with its newspapers and petty politics. There are two aspects to the positive meaning. First, the butterfly is *childlike, innocent* (H1.207, H3.51) and thus able to relate to its world without the heaviness of values. Second, the butterfly represents a healthy mode of existence, lightly and laughingly affirming of its conditions and its fate (D553, Z1.7). The butterfly in this sense is perhaps also eager for growth (H1.107). At Z2.19 the butterfly is used in this sense, but now with an emphasis on the difficult sacrifices that are the precondition of such growth. N uses the idea of cocoon to talk about the Apollonian cultural drive being forced to disguise itself as mania for dialectic, but re-emerging in modernity (BT14, 25).

Caesar

Roman general, politician and then 'dictator' of Rome. N often mentions Caesar and Napoleon together as instances of something exceptionally *free*, characterized by *scepticism* and the throwing off of faiths (1887.9.157), a brief moment of *beauty* and *genius* (1888.14.133). Caesar the tyrant is thus also an example of the opportunities and dangers of *decadence* (GS23, 98), for the highest type is always 'five paces from tyranny' (TISkirmishes38). It is precisely that danger which is their condition of growth.

camel

Kamel. The camel is the first of the three 'transformations of the spirit' at Z1.1. Importantly, the *spirit* as camel is *already* a transformation (perhaps a first stage for those who would be Zarathustra's disciples), and not a default position of the human. N elaborates on this symbol also at Z3.11.2. The camel wishes to bear as heavy a burden as possible, to feel its own strength and test that strength. The burdens N has in mind are those of the deliberate assumption of humility and self-mockery, confining oneself to a specialization, discovering dangerous or unpleasant truths, rejecting the pity of others and overcoming one's overcomings (i.e. departing a cause when it is victorious). In other words, the camel is the *free spirit* insofar as he or she (i) recognizes these states as burdens and (ii) exhibits 'veneration' towards the burdens, that is interprets them as valuable; and (iii) knows him or herself to be strong enough to bear them.

capital punishment

See *punishment*.

Case of Wagner, The

Short book written early in 1888, which attempts to assess both *Wagner*'s career, contribution and more importantly the significance and danger of his *decadence*. Later that year, N also assembled *Nietzsche contra Wagner*, a collection of excerpts from his writings over the previous decade.

cat

Katze. N uses many images from the cat family, from domestic cats to tigers and lions.

The lion stands for great *strength*, ravenous desire, healthy *will to power* (ZP3, Z2.8), but is primarily destructive and only prefiguring creation (Z1.1). The figure of the lion is a echo of Plato's analogy at *Republic* 588b–589b, where the lion stands for the *thumos* element of the soul (usually translated 'spiritedness'). The lion figures prominently in Nietzsche's plans for Z3 and Z4 from late 1883 on. Z4 ends with the appearance of the *laughing* lion with a flock of doves: the sign that Zarathustra's days of loneliness are over, and his true children approach. In a note N discusses this symbol as combining power with gentleness (1883.21.2). Moreover, the image is akin both to the sphinx, and the symbol of St Mark, the 'lion of Venice' – a winged lion. (The 'Lion of Venice' is N's suggested title for an opera written by N's friend Peter Gast.) With eagle, serpent and doves, the lion makes four animal companions for Zarathustra (1883.21.2, 1884.29.26) – possibly a reference to the four animals in *Rev.* 4.7. The lion frightening the 'higher men' is a reference to the tale of *Dionysus* on the ship of the pirates.

The tiger is one of the animals associated in mythology with *Dionysus*, which fact N explicitly refers to at for example BT1, 2, and 1883.13.1. The tiger's wildness is not tamed by, but rather simply not opposed to Dionysus' needs or purposes. As one lush growth of the tropical *south*, the tiger is a symbol of wanton and sudden *destructiveness* (always about to leap) and over-abundance ('Homer's Contest', H1.236, Z2.21). Thus also the tiger is the figure of that sudden urge to traitorous injustice among the Greeks (D199) which requires the *state* to keep it in check. This tension can be seen negatively as unresolved, lacking perfection or direction (Z2.13). Late in Z, the 'higher men' are compared to a tiger that has failed in its leap (Z4.13.14) – that is, *ashamed* of their *action*, and not accepting the role of *chance* in the growth of the human.

In general, the cat is an incompletely domesticated animal: it appears peaceful (BGE131), loves comfort (Z3.12.17), but has a residual wildness, remains akin to a beast of prey and is mischievous or wilful (1880.4.268, 1884.28.21, 1884.31.31, Z4.14.3). At Z3.4, the clouds are cats, incapable of decision. In much of the above, and elsewhere, N associates the cat above all with the figure of *woman* (see also for example BGE239). N uses cat imagery often towards the bitter end of his correspondence with Lou Salomé (e.g. 'mid-Dec., 1882). Here the cat is incapable of giving, reciprocity or love. (See also 1882.1.30 and 1882.3.1.184; although, see Z4.13.17.) In this, it is the polar opposite of the *dog* (1884.25.516). Over several years, N experiments in his notebooks with images of granite statues of cats, standing for ancient values, heavy and unmovable (e.g. 1884.32.9).

categorical imperative

See *Kant*.

category

The notion of 'category' has a long history within philosophy, commencing with Aristotle; however, it is Kant whom N generally has in mind when he discusses this notion. In Kant, the categories form a set of 12 absolutely basic and a priori concepts under which all experience falls. They thus describe the structure of experience and its limits, but also provide a transcendental account of how experience is possible in the first place. N ridicules Kant's pride in his 'table of categories' at BGE11, but at the same time accepts Kant as an important philosophical worker at BGE44, 211. For further discussion, see *Kant*.

causality

Kausalität, or *Ursache* and *Wirkung* (cause and effect). N's analysis of causality is one of his key physical and *metaphysical* lines of thought. There are several aspects. First and fundamentally, there is a critique of any simple account of cause and effect. The critique begins early on in N's career, using some of the same concepts as 'On Truth and Lies' (see for example 1872.19.209–10). Although useful as a kind of shorthand for describing and predicting, the concepts of cause and effect require us to posit the cause and the effect as separable and identifiable; that is, each has to be a stable entity. 'In truth', N writes, 'a continuum faces us' (GS112) and every causal event is actually an 'infinite number of processes'. Cause and effect thus offers no real understanding or explanation. This simplifying treatment of cause and effect is founded upon a natural, but mistaken, analysis of *will* (GS127, TIErrors3) – our apparent willing and effecting becomes a model for natural processes. Cause and effect does not follow 'laws' – this notion of natural law as something that 'governs' also is an illegitimate application of our (mistaken) notion of willing according to a maxim. The critique of causality also amounts to a critique of mechanical thought (all nature consists of pushing and pulling entities) (BGE21). N replaces natural causality with his concept of a network of forces – that is with the *will to power.* Among other things, this new concept demands (as against mechanism) 'action at a distance' (1885.34.247). Importantly, N's analysis of this concept of cause and effect includes a diagnosis of the psychological needs that might explain its adoption (e.g. BGE21, TIErrors5).

Second, clearly there are some natural processes at work that are gestured towards by the concept of cause and effect. This whole natural realm N contrasts with an unnatural or anti-natural sense of cause and effect: the concept of a sin against God for example (AC25, TIErrors6), 'spiritual causality' (AC39), or the *causa sui* (cause of itself) that is both an account of God but also a model of free will (BGE21, and see TIReason4). In all these cases, a cause is posited that lies outside the natural order.

A third strand of thought concerning causality is the notion of *sublimation*, in which a force or desire has its 'direction' changed – that is, its mode of discharge – by a second force or desire. This is part of the meaning of GS360 (and likewise H2.394). There, N distinguishes between a vast quantum of force, and a smaller trigger, that serves to give the former direction. The latter would be the ends we set ourselves for tasks or for our lives. But these are, N insists, more often than not 'beautifying pretexts' – the real function of the discharge is hidden from us.

cave

Höhle. Although N will sometimes use the figure of the cave in other writings, its most obvious appearance is as the dwelling place of Zarathustra in Z. There are many caves in Greek mythology, the three most obviously pertinent to Zarathustra – because they serve as symbolic sources or amplifications of Zarathustra's traits – are (i) the Diktaean Cave where the infant Zeus was born and hidden away from his father Chronos (time); (ii) the cave near Mount Kyllene where Maia gave birth to Hermes (god of travel and herald of the gods), son of Zeus; (iii) and the cave near Mount Nysa where *Dionysus* (another son of Zeus) was raised by nymphs, hidden from Hera's jealousy.

The other main classical source for the image of cave is, of course, Plato. In *The Republic*, Plato uses the 'allegory of the cave' to describe the journey of the philosopher, who flees the illusory images in the cave (appearances), up to the sunlight (the forms as genuine entities illuminated by genuine light), and then back again to aid others in escaping. N here inverts Plato. Zarathustra's cave, rather than being a dark place of illusion, represents depth (in the sense of profundity) but is also elevated in the mountains (see entry on *height*). When, in ZP1, he steps out before the sun, it is not to gain insight, but to bestow it on others. Similarly, at UM3.3, N uses the figure of a cave to talk about the solitude of the free spirit; at UM4.6, the cave is the depths of insight compared to the superficial daylight of modernity. Finally, at BGE289, N claims that the philosopher-hermit does not ever have 'ultimate and real opinions', that for every cave there is 'another, deeper cave'.

Chaldini, Ernst

One of N's favourite scientific demonstrations is Chaldini's sound figures, which used the patterns formed by sand on a vibrating plate to visualize resonance. N saw this as illustrating a translation from vibration to image, but (metaphorically) a translation that is in no way obvious, and thus does not allow us easily to reverse the translation back to the vibration (see especially 'On Truth and Lies' and 1872.19.237).

chance (or accident)

Zufall. N's concern with the notion of chance is not, as one might have expected, primarily in the context of a discussion of physics or metaphysics. For example, N has little time for the idea of '*clinamen*' (swerve) in Epicurianism, or for any other discussion of the role of a conventional concept of chance in nature or free will. In these contexts, the much more common problem is the relationship between law, calculability and *necessity*.

Chance plays only a modest role in N's earlier thought. Even there, though, the concept reveals an important ambiguity. On the one hand, history broadly and the life of an individual are subject to chance, meaning that there is no visible or comprehensible necessity, and no repetition of events (e.g. the dice game at UM2.2). Moreover, existence is characterized by chance in a grander sense: without overall or original purpose or meaning (GS109, Z3.4). Thus even necessity has a chance-like character to it, since that necessity is not *willed*. Where its highest *values* are concerned, human cognition cannot accept chance; thus the simplifying operation of cognition (see entries *interpretation, metaphor, perspective, truth*) makes such chance appear as necessity and subjection to natural law, or alternatively as purpose or will (UM2.6, 3.1, D130, and see AC40). This simplification has moral consequences: the famous idea of the *innocence* of chance is found at D13 in the context of a discussion of punishment (and see Z3.6, AC25). So, for example, simple mistakes are counted as crimes against God or justice, while the happy accident which is a great human being is accounted evil. Indeed, even the origin of those mental functions by which we think necessity (knowledge, reason, logic) lies in chance (1872.19.179, 248, Z1.16), that is in some fortunate event of prehistory in which a useful new characteristic or technique was stumbled upon. Likewise, the relationship between a genuine culture and the philosopher (PTAG1): without such a culture, the philosopher is a chance appearance like a 'comet'. Moreover, without that culture – that is to say, in most times and places – the great human is likely crushed by chance (UM4.6, BGE62, and see AC4) and this tempts one to *pity* (e.g. BGE41). Nevertheless, love and gratitude towards such chance are required (Z3.6, and see *amor fati*).

On the other hand, there is a necessity (or a fate) at work in cultural production, particularly art and philosophy. Here, chance is defined against some underlying necessity, one that may be a willed achievement. For example, the rhetoric of the New Testament is not an 'accident' but is an intensification of a characteristic of the Jewish people (AC44). Again, the advent of Wagner could not be chance (UM4.5 and 6). Especially in the sphere of culture, greatness means allowing an underlying necessity, rather than incidental chances or irrelevant details, to guide one's hand (UM4.1, H1.624, Z3.1 – this latter passage is Epicurean in tone). Similarly, what is chance is fragmentary, aimless or stunted; the response of *health* to this is a synthetic, compositional activity, making whole out of what is in itself only chance, and giving it a goal (GS277, Z2.20, 3.5.3, BGE274, TISkirmishes47). The one with a long and unbroken will has the strength to will into the future, whatever may chance to interfere (GM2.2). The human must be liberated from chance as from priests (EHDaybreak2); that is, liberated from either a pessimistic assessment of human possibilities, from the endless diversion of the aimless and incidental (e.g. D150, AC58), or from the rule of chance in human evolution (H1.24).

chaos

Chaos, among other terms. Chaos is a significant ancient concept. The earth is 'formless and empty' prior to God's creation at Gen. 1.2. Similar ideas are common in other accounts of creation, such as Hesiod for whom Chaos was the first primordial deity. Eighteenth and nineteenth-century anthropology discovered that this myth pattern frequently took the form of a struggle against chaos, which was often represented by a serpent or dragon (e.g. Zeus' battle with Typhon). The notion of chaos is used at UM2.9–10 but is inverted: on its own, scientific knowledge is a destruction of human nature and a descent to chaos. One of the meanings of the 'evil' principle in Zoroastrianism is 'chaos'. In Z1.1, however, the struggle against the dragon is a struggle against a fixed order, and *for* chaos. Thus, at ZP5, we find 'one must have chaos within one still, in order to give birth to a dancing star'. Here, chaos is not the enemy of but rather the principle of *creation* (N implies a similar notion at H2.119).

Chaos is a basic character of the real (GS109). By this N means that the real has no intrinsic order, and thus also no meaning, purpose, wisdom or beauty. Zarathustra claims to have liberated things from their bondage under purposes (Z3.4). The idea is that all of the various ways in which the real is supposed to have a pre-given order are anthropomorphic and in fact moral in character – restoring their chaos means restoring their *innocence*. Such an idea of the real as 'chaos' has a long philosophical tradition, stretching back to Heraclitus who argued that change was the only constant. The atomists (including the Epicureans) argue that chaos is the natural state of things, and the formation of entities is both contingent and temporary. In both Hume and Kant, and subsequently Schophenhauer, the order in experience is not found but constructed (although for Kant, at least, this certainly did not entail that the thing in itself was chaos). Broadly speaking, N follows this line and thus he talks about naming and concept formation in 'On Truth and Lies'. At this point, N is also influenced by more recent trends in nineteenth-century thought such as *positivism* or neo-Kantianism. See *interpretation, truth, names.*

character

Charakter. By 'character' is meant either the 'nature' or 'essence' of something (N will also use the term '*Wesen*' for this) or, those patterns of behaviour that are distinctive of an individual, group or type. Here we will discuss only this second meaning. Under the heading of character we will find the concepts such as *customs* or habits, *virtues* or vices, roles and drives. The notions are important for N through his career, but discussions of the notion of 'character' per se are clustered in the late 1870s and early 1880s.

There are two important strands to N's thought here. The first is the notion of the unchangeability of character, an idea important to Schopenhauer. N finds this notion metaphysically implausible (because of the continual *becoming* of underlying drives; see D560 and GS307: 'you are always another person'). More importantly, it is also suspect in its *value*. The *free spirit* and 'seeker after knowledge' must be able to 'declare himself *against* his previous opinion' (GS296 and see H1.464, D56). Importantly, this does not mean conceiving of one's character and opinions as somehow arbitrary or disorderly (GS290), nor being an 'apostate' of the free spirit (D56, see Z3.8). The other strand of N's thought here involves the creation of character. Characterization in art and especially in drama is always superficial, because it can only present an image of the inner necessity in the life of an actual human being (H1.160). A similar point is made at H1.228, where people of 'strong character' are created through education in just this way, to be more like art than life and thus to be useful to their community. The genuinely stronger *spirit*, however will 'give style' to their character, force it under one 'taste', and indeed take pleasure in this self-imposed law (GS290). Likewise, higher spirits of this type will create a 'role' – a simplified version of themselves – as an instrument of communication or rule (GS235–6, D182, and see GS356).

cheerfulness

Heiterkeit, most often, but the concept shades into other words that might otherwise be translated as *happiness* or joyfulness. One way N framed the project of BT was in terms of the nature of Greek 'cheerfulness' or 'serenity', a topic on which he found himself in profound disagreement with much of classical scholarship (on which see UM3.2, D329). In the period of BT, N's argument is that cheerfulness cannot be a consequence of a lack of awareness of pain, cruelty or destructiveness – because this was the people that invented tragedy and celebrated the wisdom of Silenus (BT3) – nor could it be a consequence of 'unendangered ease and comfort' (BT9), or simple sensuality (PTAG1), because then philosophy would never have arisen. Instead this cheerfulness or serenity arises because of the healing effects of *Apollonian* beauty, and because on its own terms the immersion into the *Dionysian* is experienced as 'the eternal lust and delight of existence' (BT17). That is to say, the Greeks were much more aware of the true nature of existence than we moderns, but had developed a *culture* in which existence is justified as an aesthetic phenomenon (BT5). This degenerates after the death of tragedy into the 'cheerfulness of slaves' without responsibility (BT11).

The concept continues to be used intermittently in later periods of N's work. Broadly speaking there are three meanings. First, cheerfulness as blissful ignorance (e.g. GS53); second, cheerfulness as a disguise, a way of appearing to be different from, and be misunderstood by, others (D201, BGE270). Third, and most importantly, cheerfulness is part of the ideal of a new form of life that does not suffer from the defining features of modernity (UM2.1, 9). This last idea is, in part, an updating of the Apollonian concept from the period of BT (and see BGE24 and 269); in part it is a new analysis of the perils of an over-historicized culture (see *historical sense*). Cheerfulness is thought of as an affect of the exercise of power (D251), or of one who exhibits an excess of strength (TIPreface). Likewise it is a characteristic of someone who has found their proper element, the role most aligned to their character (D440, GS169). Thus, the highest human beings of the present will be both 'cheerful' and also 'live dangerously' (GS283). Taking the questioning of morality seriously has, as a kind of reward, cheerfulness – or the 'gay science' (GMP7). In other words, there is a stage of nausea or nihilism in the confrontation with the genealogy of values (TIPreface), but this stage overcomes itself in cheerfulness. In Z, Zarathustra feels distress at the thought of eternal recurrence, but after his convalescence, the thought is joyful;

and see also the 'heaven-cheerfulness' at Z3.4. The significance of cheerfulness for N's thought is emphasized by its employment in the opening remarks of TI: cheerfulness as in a necessary *cycle* with serious intellectual labour, as a form of *convalescence* (TIP). Likewise, N introduces the newly added book five of GS with an account of cheerfulness rather than nihilism (GS343). See also *laughter*.

child

Kind. As a symbol, the child has two conventional meanings, either that age of humanity which is *innocent*, or that which is most animal-like and dominated by *instinct* and passion. In N these are not incompatible, though he tends to emphasize innocence. For examples, see UM2.1, H1.124, H2.270, BGE57, AC32. In association with this innocence, the child figure is capable of genuine creation (Z1.1, GSP4), or more commonly, the child is synonymous with genuine creation and a healthy relationship to the future (so, Zarathustra's 'children' at Z2.14, 3.3). It is thus appropriate that the grotesque distortions being made of Zarathustra's teachings should be revealed by a child (Z2.1, and see Z2.16, 4.11) For these reasons also, we find many images of pregnancy in Z, and the devotion of a mother (UM4.10). Similarly, those who are contemplating marriage should ask themselves 'have you the right to wish for a child' (Z1.20, and see BGE194).

At H2.270 or BGE57, N evokes the notion of the 'eternal child'. This is an allusion to Ovid's account of Iacchus (associated with Dionysus, particularly in the notion of perpetual rebirth). The idea also contains a reference to Heraclitus, who wrote that time, or the creator, is a child building with, then scattering, his playthings. Mozart was often called an 'eternal child'. N's point is two-fold. First, that psychologically there is no sharp divide between childhood and adulthood, and to believe there is shows an unhealthy devotion to seriousness. Second, that in the 'genuine man, a child is hidden: it wants to play' (Z1.18) – that is, the higher human will embrace the concepts of play, toys, laughter or fantasy (see also BGE57, H2.270, GSP4). Thus, if knowledge removes its playthings, it will have to create others in a perpetual *cycle*. See also *education, feminine and masculine*.

Chinese

N's way of thinking about China and the Chinese has two aspects. First, his interest in Asian thought which was inspired at least in part by Schopenhauer (see entry on *Buddhism*). Second, his sense that the Chinese have a quite different form of life, to the extent that the Chinese represent a distinct type of human being. This is particularly manifested in their valuation of work (see D206), and in attributes of the great age of their civilization (BGE 267, GM1.12).

Christianity

Broadly speaking, there are three aspects to N's account of Christianity. First, and famously, there is N's often bitter attack on Christianity and especially its effects on *modernity* (as evident in the title of AC). Christianity is responsible for *breeding* (or domesticating) human beings into a *herd* animal (TIImproving2); Christianity espouses a hatred of rationality (D58), but also of the *body* and any bodily *passion* (i.e. one not directed towards God) (D76, Z1.4); more generally, it is in part responsible for the prevalence of the *ascetic* ideal and the practices it devises (GM3.17–18), which in turn has ruined the *health* and *taste* of modern Europe and continues in disguised form in morality and science; it is responsible for a whole host of moral concepts but especially that of *pity*; in its denigration of *becoming* with respect to true being, it is in part responsible for the cultural paralysis induced by the *historical sense* (UM2.8); Christianity involves the destruction of the ability to read *philologically* (D84); finally, it has waged war upon the *noble*, healthy and powerful (the 'slave revolt' GM1.7), and in the end broken most of the *great* (e.g. Wagner) before the cross (BGE256). Much of this damage is historical; however, importantly, many of these values or practices continue surreptitiously, even without their basis intact (D57; see entry on *atheism*). N's attack is directed primarily towards Christianity because of its dominant position within the European history and present, but some of these points are also (N argues) valid concerning other religions (especially Judaism) or philosophies (especially Platonism).

Second, Christianity is a frequent object of *genealogical* analysis – that is, a historical account of the origin and development of concepts, values or practices. This way of thinking obviously overlaps with the first, above. Here we will provide just a few examples. N characterizes Jesus as a kind of Buddhist, whose teachings were catastrophically misinterpreted by *Paul*. Paul's notion of the impossibility of virtue and his need for revenge against the law are found at D68 and 87. N returns to this topic in more detail starting at AC37 (see especially 42–4). N provides various accounts of the origin of the concept of sin (e.g. GS135); similarly, the concept of debt or guilt when raised to its highest point, practically necessitated Christianity's stroke of genius: the God sacrificed (GM2.21).

Third, N discusses the positive contribution that Christianity – generally despite its explicit aims – has had. Christianity, N argues, involves a powerful cultural drive for the production of greatness in the form of the saint (although this was corrupted by its association with the modern state: UM3.6). Similarly, Christianity produced human beauty and refinement (D60). In France, the Christian realized itself as the great human being – and thus also this is the place where great *free spirits* could arise, since they needed 'perfect opponents' (D192). Christianity has taught us moral scepticism (GS122). Christianity rescued the ancient world from its *decadence*, and in some way preserved it (H2.224). Christian practices, including especially the ascetic, have produced an agile intellect capable of understanding *perspective* (GM3.12). Likewise, Christian values and institutions can now be understood as tools for the advantage of a higher nobility (BGE61).

city

Stadt. N's own migratory life took him to a number of cities, especially in Italy, but he had an uncomfortable relation to the idea of cities in general. Epicurus left the city behind, in favour of his walled garden and circle of friends – N essentially approves. So, Zarathustra has little luck teaching in the marketplace (ZP3, and see Z1.12, H2.386) and although he rejects as impotent negativity a description of the 'great city', nevertheless does not enter it (Z3.7). That notion of impotence is found also in N's account of 'antiquarian' history (UM2.3) which is associated particularly with cities. Such history at best serves life simply as preservation and not creation but, at worst, 'mummifies' life. The city is also associated with the 'mob' (H2.386 – see entry on *herd*). It is thus a place where wisdom is all but impossible. N thus calls for a revision to the standard architecture of large cities, ensuring 'places for reflection' (GS280). The city becomes a metaphor for a desire to depict, even in art, the ugly side of life (as the 'sewers' at H2.111).

See also *building, garden*.

class/caste

Stand, Klasse, Kaste. N uses the terms 'classes' or 'castes' to mean recognized and persistent differences between whole sections of a society in terms of political, economic or social value and power, and attendant behaviours. There are two broad ways of analysing class: either it arises because of extrinsic circumstance, or because of intrinsic nature. Liberals and socialists tend to take the former view: in themselves, all human beings are of *equal* value and approximately equal ability, but historical accidents left one group with certain privileges and characteristics. In socialism, this situation is deemed essentially unjust and is to be set right through revolution. The key figures here are obviously Marx and Engels. For liberalism, the given situation may be deemed acceptable provided reforms yield 'equality of opportunity'. Key historical figures here are Hobbes, *Rousseau* and Mill. Insofar as the *Reformation* involved criticism of the grip of the priestly class over the religious life of all humans, who are in themselves equal before God, then *Luther* too should be mentioned. The intrinsic view, on the other hand, claims that there are real differences between individuals and groups and these mean that the existing class order is broadly natural and beneficial. These differences may be supposed to have arisen historically, biologically or be divinely sanctioned, among other explanations. Key figures would include Burke and *Carlyle*, as well as Catholic defenders of church hierarchy.

On N's analysis early in his career, two elements of which modernity is most proud are incompatible. *Science* and *culture* require a 'scholarly' or 'aristocratic' class which has leisure. This leisure can only arise at the expense of a 'slave' class, and this is in direct contradiction of the dominant modern belief in liberal values of equality and *democracy* (BT18, 'The Greek State', BGE257). Thus also at H1.439 N argues for class mobility to ensure that the function of class is not ossified. Given the degeneracy of modern culture, though, early N sometimes sides with Wagner's revolutionary vision and argues that it is the working classes that offer the greatest hope for the formation of a genuine *people* (see for example 1873.29.220).

As is typical of N, he rejects the above distinction between extrinsic and intrinsic analyses of class. He recasts the problem in a different light. Both biological types and historical circumstances are temporary *instruments* available to a people – and behind any people, *life* itself – to further those ends necessary to the people or to life. These ends include survival, no doubt, but more importantly the enhancement and expression of *power*. A class system is just, then, for as long as it serves these ends – regardless of whether its origin happens to be intrinsic or extrinsic (AC57, TIImprove3, GS40). Historically, from out of these hierarchies, *moral values* and *religious ideals* were developed, either as images of the distinctive *virtues* of the various classes, especially the highest – or in reaction against them (the *slave revolt* in morality) (see GM1, and H1.45, 114). Thus, any deliberate attempt at the creation of new morals must involve a change of class structure (1884.25.107, AC26, 42). Often, a system of values will outlive the class structure from which it arose (e.g. UM2.8). N anticipates a future in which the necessity of class differences will be appreciated and welcomed, and a new 'caste' of cultural leaders will emerge (BGE208, 251). The existence of such healthy differences among individuals or groups is felt as the *pathos of distance*.

clean(-liness) and its opposites

Reinlichkeit and less often, *Sauberkeit*. Any number of other symbols may refer to this concept as well, such as fresh air, clarity, brightness, health, nakedness. Cleanliness is obviously opposed to filth, dirt, murky waters, etc. It should be noted that *Reinlichkeit* has the same root as *rein* or *Reinheit* (pure, purity) and these concepts have something of a moral and religious connotation.

N writes, 'Cleanly, to be sure. – One who dresses in clean-washed rags dresses cleanly, to be sure, but still raggedly' (H3.199). N had been playing with this aphorism for at least five years (its first draft is 1873.27.72). Its point is to distinguish between a literal and figurative meaning of cleanliness – the latter corresponds to something like *nobility* (similarly see H1.479). In other words, a condition of possibility of nobility is not wealth, but freedom from abject poverty. Analogously, the cleanliness of a child 'transforms' itself into something more spiritual later (H2.288), including 'purity'. Whether it is exaggerated or not, N discusses his own fastidiousness at EHWise8, and does so in terms of a *cycle* between social engagement and solitude as *convalescence*.

Another aspect of the symbolic meaning is *honesty* (GS99, 293, BGE210). That is, cleanliness now refers to a set of intellectual practices that refuse unclear thought practices, particularly those that defer to a metaphysical beyond (e.g. religious institutions and the beliefs they embody). The notion that religion (Christianity in particular) is not clean enough for the spirit is made again at Z4.18.1 and BGE58. This functions as a kind of summary of N's critique of Christianity. Particularly pertinent to this image is N's analysis of Christianity in terms of its darkness or murkiness, that is its willingness to be dishonest (see AC46, 52). Also bound up in the image of uncleanliness is Christianity's association with the herd or slaves; its attempt to crush nobility; its moral attitudes are often masking lecherous desires (Z1.13); its contempt for the *body* creates filth (e.g. in sexuality) – indeed, even cleanliness is seen as sensuousness, that is as filth (AC21). Cleanliness as *innocence* is, of course, also a reference to the blood of Christ as cleansing one of sin (e.g. Jn 1.7); N's ironic point is that the Christian idea of sin is what creates the 'dirt' in the first place.

However, as N asserts elsewhere, that type of uncleanliness is not the worst thing; the worst thing is shallowness (Z1.13, EHWagner3). This he finds a typical characteristic of modernity, especially in Germany. It is the product of a democratic community. The point concerns what N calls *distance*; that is, a herd is defined not by numbers, or cleanliness in an ordinary sense, but by thinking, speaking and acting as one, and by assuming *equality* (e.g. touching). This is unclean in a spiritual sense because it must involve falsifications or simplifications, passivity and weakness, and because it leads to a stagnation of the human. Thus, what is unclean is 'common' (see BGE284). Once a work has been produced (e.g. an act done, a book published) then it is in the common sphere; if observed at all, it becomes common. Nobility cannot be judged, then, by acts or works (BGE287). This is part of the reasoning behind N's melancholic tone in BGE, from BGE277 to the end. Only a noble reserve, *solitude* and self-respect could maintain its spiritual cleanliness.

cleverness

The German word *Klugheit* receives a number of different English translations: cleverness, shrewdness or prudence being the most common. In N's typical usage, the emphasis is on both a patient caution and also on a subtle, surreptitious and often inventive calculation bent upon reaping rewards. Clear if distasteful examples are found at H1.412, 415, BGE232. The concept contrasts both with the 'human of intuition' in his or her exuberance and beauty ('On Truth and Lies' 2), with wisdom (implicit at BT11, explicit at UM2.9) and with a noble foolishness (GS20). This cleverness, seen as a characteristic of modernity (with particular reference to education, business or industry, scholarship and utilitarian morality), is a constant throughout N's career (see for example UM2.9, Z3.5.3 or 4.13.3, GM1.2). Likewise, at GM2.15 cleverness is analysed as a consequence of the taming of the human through institutions of punishment.

Cleverness also describes those subtle tactics designed to influence moral feelings (e.g. H1.117, BGE198) or maintain religious practices or ideas (prayer at H3.74, revelation at AC55). Likewise, it is priestly shrewdness that organized the weak into the herd by means of which the will to power is, in a small way, stimulated to life (GM3.18). Not all usages have these moral overtones, though. Cleverness lies at the origin or maintenance of the state and state institutions (H1.472, H3.26, D112), and the agonistic institutions of Greece at H3.226. Likewise, through the discipline of manners, a shrewdness even in the body can be cultivated (H1.250). This cleverness is an element in those virtues that N traces back to the animal (e.g. D26).

This cleverness takes on an important role in Z: Zarathustra has two animals, the eagle is pride and the serpent is cleverness. In the

Prologue, Zarathustra has not been clever enough: his first strategies for speaking to the people were a disaster. At ZP10 he thus indicates that these two are symbols of his own as-yet incomplete virtues. EH contains a chapter entitled 'Why I am so Clever': here N discusses his diet, the places and climates in which he chooses to live, how he manages his illnesses and convalescences. The aim, he says is a certain kind of self-preservation or selfishness, although one that leads to *becoming who you are* (EHClever8–9). Z4.15 is particularly significant: the whole prehistory of the human is, Zarathustra says, 'courage', which has become refined as (among other things) 'serpent cleverness'. In other words, the caution that may make up part of cleverness is not a primary characteristic, but merely a strategy in the service of courage and experimentation (see also BGE45). In the next line, though, the Sorcerer's speech (which apparently makes Zarathustra angry) is described as 'clever'. This is perhaps explained by the distinction N makes at GM1.10: shrewdness is honoured both by the noble and by those of *ressentiment* but for different reasons. Only for the latter is it a condition of existence, of preservation (see comments on utility at GM1.2). These notions of caution and *ressentiment* allow us to distinguish between lower and higher concept of cleverness (Z2.21).

climate

See *closest things*.

cloak

See *mask*.

closest things

N calls for us to be 'good neighbours to the closest things' (H3.16, and see for example EHZ6). While the philosophical tradition tends to chase after the big and most distant questions of existence, and particularly of other transcendent or ideal existences, N argues that we should pay attention to this world and life. Because of continuous becoming, not only are these big questions hopelessly unsolvable, but even the ways of life typical of only a few generations previous may be antiquated. Therefore, philosophy needs to refocus on issues of health, mode of life, the small-scale sociology of friendships, the family and other inter-personal relations, the role of architecture, educational institutions, etc. These *conditions* must eventually have an impact upon thought, and upon the capacity of thought to be critical or creative with respect to values. This list very much includes the everyday things around us: for example, our daily habits, our diet, and where (e.g. climate, city, town or country) and in what we live (see especially EHClever, AC20–1 or Z3.6). Similar reflections are found at Z3.6 and GS295. Note the contrast to the Christian notion of the *neighbour.*

cloud

Wolke. In N, the cloud has no one symbolic meaning. In BT25, N argues that if the Dionysian has reappeared in modernity, then the Greek sense of the Apollonian must also have appeared. There he alludes to the theatrical practice of disguising behind a 'cloud' the ropes and pulleys of stage apparatus by which things (e.g. a character representing a god) are made to appear. This is known as the *deus ex machina.* However, this cloud is also an allusion to N's idea in BT14 that the Apollonian 'cocooned itself away'; this cloud is also a cocoon. In addition, the cloud is that which obscures, or which is neither one thing nor another (UM4.4, Z3.4). The cloud is also, of course, the source of lightning either because it is elevated (H3.284, Z3.16.1 – and see entry on 'pregnancy') or because it is interpreted as fearful (H3.16, Z1.7).

comfort, solace

Bequemlichkeit, Beruhigung, Trost. To comfort is to ease suffering, whether physical or spiritual. It is a key idea in BT. Tragedy presents suffering in a way such that we are protected by the Apollonian image (what we might call artistic comfort), and also that we understand that beneath suffering is an unbreakable unity and continuity of life (what N calls 'metaphysical comfort') (BT7,

18). Later, N regrets the second of these ideas (BTAttempt7). It is *romantic* pessimism, or practical *nihilism*, and already half-way to religious faith. The desire to relieve suffering is also part of the notion of *pity*. Further non-metaphysical notions of comforting are provided at H3.7, with explicit reference to *Epicurus*. Christianity is 'a great treasure of the most ingenious means for comforting' (GM3.17). The Christian *ascetic* priest cannot attack the underlying sickness that causes suffering (indeed, he makes it worse), but can combat its symptoms. Because it only targets the symptoms, N contrasts comforting with *convalescence*.

communication

The basic condition of communication for N is the sharing of a *language* – a system of signs and significations. But what is signified is by no means either 'raw' (i.e. uninterpreted) experiences or things in the world; rather, these significations are modified by *values* (see 'Truth and Lies'). Therefore having a language in common is dependent upon also sharing a set of values (GS354, BGE268, EHBooks4). It follows that communication of thoughts that depend upon a new set of values, or those values themselves, is the most difficult. This is why Zarathustra is so comprehensively misunderstood and laughed at in ZP. Moreover, one's values are a product of one's constitution – for example various inheritances from the past, including both cultural and genetic, the habits that comprise a particular mode of life, etc. So, to communicate genuinely new thoughts or values would be to transform the listener (thus Z1.7). In ZP, Zarathustra thus decides that he cannot communicate directly to the people. Instead, he needs to gather disciples, by which is meant those who in some way already possess some of these new values (see also GSP1, H2P6). There is the same problem with interpreting or understanding ancient cultures. Particularly with respect to the ancient Greeks, N often claims that there is an alienness that is difficult and perhaps impossible to bridge ('Homer's Contest', TIAncients2); or, alternatively, if it can be bridged, would result in a transformation of the present – this for example is the reason N repeatedly emphasizes the Greek sense of religion (H1.114, BGE49, GM2.23 – and see H2.218).

This 'pessimistic' view of language is not the final word, however. That which is *noble* will have both a need and even an ability to communicate singular values 'to men and things' (GS55, 'genius of communication': TISkirmishes24). Notice in these passages that the idea is expressed in terms of an overflowing of fullness; see *gift*. There is likely an echo in that passage of Kant's notion of genius as having (among other things) the capacity to hit upon a communicative vehicle for an idea that, in other ways, is inexpressible. N echoes this idea in saying that the purpose of *style* is to communicate states (EHBooks4) – and if N has new states, then he will require a new style: 'I was the first to discover the *great* rhythm, the *great style* of the period' (and see H3.88).

In his early work, N employed the concept of *mythic symbols* as the mechanism by which culture might be unified, and thus share the basis for communication concerning that which is genuinely significant. From his early work on, N also identified concepts of metaphor, symbol and allegory as mechanisms by which communication might be able to surpass its apparently built-in limits. So, for example, the 'man of intuition' discussed at the end of 'Truth and Lies' occupies a world where things are liberated from their bondage under utilitarian needs and accompanying values. Later, N sometimes talks about the Dionysian in this fashion (see TISkirmishes10, and EHZ3). This 'inspired' state is thus key to the noble attempt to communicate to and transform others. Sometimes, however, the free spirit needs to avoid communication even to his or her closest friends, either to protect the self and its ideals, or them – see GS381, BGE40 and *masks*. A similar idea is found at TISkirmishes26, although N in the last sentence turns the idea into a satire.

A common observation N makes, often in the form of a joke, is just how bad a communicator God is (Z4.6, BGE53). The joke is at the expense of religious controversy which was often over points of interpretation, and also the recently developed science of biblical hermeneutics, the purpose of which was to apply the rigorous methods of philology and history to sacred texts. This bad communication leads to scepticism and ultimately to atheism; it is thus part of N's account of the death of God.

community (*Gemeinschaft*)

See *communication, people*.

compassion

See *pity*.

complex

See *multiple*.

comprehensiveness

This is a concept without a single term to name it. Comprehensiveness describes an individual who encompasses and is able to employ a variety of different states, drives or types of knowledge. Thus, comprehensiveness stands especially in contrast to the *specialization* typical of modern intellectual life (BGE205, and see UM3.3). It is clearly related to the idea of the *multiple* (the human soul is multiple), and to the *wanderer* (who has no fixed cultural home and observes and participates in much). D43 describes the various abilities, all separately developed in human prehistory, that needed to come together to make the thinker. Analogously, BGE262 analyses the emergence of the comprehensive 'individual' who is able to live 'beyond' the morality of some old, decaying culture (see also H1.632, and cosmopolitanism at H2.204). The philosopher must be able to see with many eyes, to view things from many *perspectives* (UM4.7, GS249, GM3.12); to develop this ability N suggests 'brief habits' (GS295). Similarly, the ability to function with respect to both science and other aspects of culture (1872.19.172, the 'double brain' at H1.251).

Comprehensiveness is thus a feature of a future philosophical *nobility*, to be distinguished from the nobility of a narrowly perfected culture, as well as from the anti-culture of the *historical sense* (BGE224). (The historical sense is a kind of comprehensiveness but without discrimination, without any setting of limits.) Such an ideal requires dangerous experiences to enable judgements about the value of modes of life (BGE205). Greatness is judged in fact by the capacity for comprehensiveness (BGE212). Comprehensiveness thus describes a height that is not that of abstraction (BGE257), and describes an overall responsibility for the development of the human, and which is able to use a wide variety of cultural forms and institutions as tools (BGE61). Such responsibility will be able to take on all the hopes and disasters of the past and present, and still rise joyfully to greet the dawn (GS337). Thus, comprehensiveness is also related to the ideas of *the gift* and *pregnancy* (Z3.14).

Comte

See *Positivism*.

concept

Begriff. Generally, when talking about concepts, N means philosophical concepts or the key concepts of a religion or culture: so, for example, substance, cause, virtue, sin. Any discussion of concepts therefore will also be a discussion of *philosophy*, *metaphysics*, *religion* etc. Concepts form a *system* (BGE20, TISkirmishes5) – that is, individual concepts cannot be isolated but must be understood as a whole way of thinking (and ultimately also living and evaluating), and likewise studied in their historically developing and repeating interconnection. For N, philosophical concepts are subsequent and dependent upon the underlying values that produce language – see entry on *language*. Thus, for example, philosophical concepts are largely governed or produced by grammar (BGE20, TIReason5). Even the belief in the validity of concept-formation has philosophical implications (H3.11). Concepts may also be able to influence those values (see *spirit*). When, under pressure of new discoveries or critique, a concept gives way the result is memorably described by N as a 'concept-quake' (UM2.10).

conditions

Bedingung. It is N's broad contention that nothing is isolated, simple or unconditional. That is, everything is only properly understood in its concrete context and by understanding the various 'conditions' under which it developed and continues to develop. By 'conditions' are meant historical period, culture, values, language, psychological or psychological forces, or education and other institutions. So, for example, Zarathustra often criticizes those who are 'unconditional' – that is, take their values to be simple and eternal (Z1.12, Z4.13.16, BGE46 or 221). Pity – in the form of protective institutions like hospitals, or the various other instruments in the hands of the ascetic priest (GM3.17–9) – becomes a mechanism for preserving suffering and decadent forms of life from the conditions that otherwise might destroy them. By way of contrast, N analyses the broadly ascetic practices – selective withdrawal from certain present conditions – as themselves a condition of a philosopher's development (GM3.7). Similarly, he discusses the conditions under which new and enhanced forms of the human might arise (BGE62, 203) – and specifying these conditions is the content of N's treatments of institutions like education or marriage. Likewise, he describes the conditions that would permit a reader to understand him (ACP). Thus also, sometimes what N recounts is the struggle to remain 'on course' despite the conditions one finds oneself in (e.g. Wagner at UM4.3, or GS338). Likewise, many affects that have traditionally been devalued (such as lust or envy) are nevertheless not merely necessary aspects of life, but even necessary conditions of it (BGE23, Z3.10). A similar point is made about even the 'rabble' (Z2.6). The highest form of life would be one that has the strength to remain devoted to the ascending movement of life regardless of conditions. N refuses the theory of the all-determining effects of milieu (a sociological concept prominent in nineteenth-century France) in favour of an account of successful or unsuccessful adaptation (1885.2.175, 1887.9.178, 1888.15.106, TISkirmishes55, and see BGE242), where 'adaptation' may mean wearing a mask so as to appear adapted. Conditions become not irrelevant but interpreted and *affirmed* as exactly what was required for this ascent to happen. Zarathustra, who has sought to affirm the whole course of life in its becoming up to and through himself, says 'The time has flowed past when accidents could still befall me' (Z2.1). This is an early statement of the notion of *amor fati*.

conscience

Gewissen. Conscience is one's sense that what one is doing is the 'right' or 'wrong' thing; the concept applies whatever the sphere of action is (intellectual, practical, moral) and whatever standard of right or wrong is relevant. For example, despite temptations, the rigorous seeker after truth cannot return to romanticism or Christianity without 'dirtying' his or her intellectual conscience (H1.109, DP4). Conscience can be individual, or some group can act as the conscience of an age (e.g. H2P6, WCP). Not surprisingly, conscience is often associated with *honesty* (BGE5, 32, AC54, but see TISkirmishes18). The idea seems to be that a good conscience is the alignment of the maxims of one's action with the growth of higher culture, of the feeling of power or of the human type. N admits that this notion of conscience is rather an old-fashioned one (BGE214).

To not adopt a questioning attitude especially with respect to moral questions, to not even be interested, demonstrates neither a good or bad conscience but a lack of conscience (GS2. Z3.8.2). Similarly, at TISkirmishes18, N observes his contemporaries as too 'comfortable' to have resolute beliefs, and thus happily chop and change their beliefs. They are incapable even of hypocrisy or bad intellectual conscience (see also UM4.6). Z1.12 contains another example of a lack of conscience: the play-actor only believes in what he can convince others of. His beliefs are thus reactive, and changeable depending upon the audience. The philosopher who seeks to find reasons for what he or she already believes would have a bad conscience, if a conscience at all (BGE5).

It is possible for conscience to be corrupted: for example, through a morality of custom, creativity acquires a bad conscience – that is to say, the conscience of the social group as a whole has been internalized. Similarly, habits of obedience in a people can lead to even the commanders having a bad conscience at having to command, and perhaps masking this by pretending to follow still higher rules (BGE199). At GS297, N describes the opposite movement, namely the acquisition of the ability to contradict established customs with a good conscience (and see Z1.17). Thus, N introduces the concept of the 'intellectual conscience', defined at GS335 as the 'conscience behind your "conscience"', and which is precisely the ability to question one's habits, and the customs or beliefs of one's age.

In the middle Treatise of GM is found N's most sustained treatment of the theme of the genesis of conscience. The ultimate aim evidently is to explore the sovereign individual, with 'power over oneself and fate' (GM2.2). This idea of having a 'long, unbreakable will' relates to N's frequent criticism of bad conscience in the sense of regretting an action (see Z1.6, EHClever1, TIArrows10, and the entry on *action*). But this is a 'late' fruit (GM2.3) and much of the treatise concerns preliminary stages: the breeding of the concepts of guilt and punishment from out of the debt of legal subjects and the cruelty involved in the redemption of debt. On N's account, bad conscience is initially the state of the higher human being – one whose animal part has not been entirely bred out – in society, when no outlet for his or her instincts remains. It is defined as a directing against oneself of these higher instincts and desire for power; equivalently, it is a joy in the *disciplined* formation of oneself. Here it is not the result of an internalization of external values, but rather a sense that one's own being is in some way defective with respect to one's ideal. From this bad conscience arises ultimately a sense of debt to God, a debt that could never be repaid except by a sacrifice of God on the cross (GM3.21). N claims that this bad conscience is both a 'sickness' and also 'full of future' (GM2.16). That is, bad conscience is a product of a culture that has reached a plateau point of peace and prosperity, but is also the mechanism by which that culture, grown stagnant, is eventually undone through the creation of individuals. The sovereign individual, however, is not yet the one who can 'reverse' bad conscience (GM2.24, and see the similar phrasing at BGE56). That would demand that the sense of guilt would lie precisely in any positing of a God, or a beyond, and any denigration of the natural instincts. Guilt would be directed at anything that remains within one that is yet unaligned to, or hostile to, life. Such a new form of 'conscience' would belong to the 'great health' (GM3.24).

consciousness

Bewusstsein. A traditional definition of consciousness is that part or function of us that not only thinks, feels and acts but is aware of itself doing so, and can perhaps reflect upon it. Because of that awareness, consciousness generally also implies the ability to *will* its thinking, acting and even to some extent its feeling. Accordingly, tied up with N's account of consciousness is his critique of will, and his critique of the human subject as a *causal* agent. For the most part, N is simply not interested in consciousness; he thus also argues that the emphasis placed on consciousness within modern thought (Descartes, Kant and German Idealism) is an enormous error (GS11). N often cites Leibniz as an exception, since the latter posited unconscious *petites perceptions* as an important factor in human identity and motivation. On N's account, the human being is an ensemble of *drives* in competition with each other (i.e. *will to power*). These drives, their competition and any subsequent effects are mostly unconscious (in the sense that they never enter consciousness) – see for example D119, GS333, BGE3. Or, if some do become conscious, they are transformed (by pre-existing values or perspectives) and thus what we are aware of is by no means an unmediated or even reliable source of data about ourselves ('the phenomenality of the inner world': 1887.11.113). For this reason, N's *psychology* is generally concerned with the observation of others, and not introspection. N speculates that consciousness is collective and not individual: only what is 'common' becomes conscious (GS354, see BGE268).

On the other hand, there is in N something that looks like a traditional view of consciousness as the becoming aware and taking charge of something. So, at UM3.6 and H1.24, N talks about no longer leaving culture and human development to chance, but consciously willing it. This idea is echoed much later when N writes that 'in us this will to truth has come to a consciousness of itself *as a problem*' (GM3.27). Likewise, he writes 'what would be "beautiful" if contradiction had not first come to a consciousness of itself, if the ugly had not first said to itself "I am ugly"?' (GM2.18). Here, consciousness is not a goal in and of itself, but a means – namely a means of positing new ideals and the task of overcoming those errors that have become instinctive in us. The development of consciousness is a way – albeit an enormously wasteful way – of trying to correct an organism that has gone wrong. Being conscious indicates imperfection (AC14). The goal – even the goal of knowledge itself – is not consciousness, but rather the rectification of the *instincts* (see AC57, TISkirmishes41).

consolation

See *comfort*.

constraint

See *discipline*.

contemplation

During his middle period, from the mid-1870s to the early 1880s, a common theme in N's writings was the contrast between the *vita contemplativa* and the *vita activa* (or *vita practica*) – between the life of contemplation and that of *action*. By the former, N means those whose dispositions take them to religion, art, philosophy and science (D41). In 1875, he suggests that this is in fact a false distinction and that the 'Greeks knew better' (1875.6.17). The two modes are two halves of a whole, action seeking itself in the future, contemplation in the past (H2.366). Although there are certainly spirits that are merely reactive – whose values are always generated from out of a hatred of the values of others, or whose highest state is to serve – the *vita contemplativa* can and should be a kind of action ('thinking well . . . *is* an action': 1888.14.107). This action may involve leadership or creativity in the realm of ideas, or perhaps instances of self-overcoming (GS301). It is not simply renunciation (D440). *Luther's* Reformation was a hatred of contemplative types (1880.4.132). Precisely because of this rejection, the Reformation was a historical disaster. In the accelerating tempo of *modern* life, contemplation is virtually impossible (H1.282, GS329, GM3.8). N's task, then, is to rescue contemplation from the Church (GS280), to revalue the concept away from traditional forms (GM3.10), for example making it contemplation on the *closest things*.

contentment

Throughout his career, N treats 'contentment' – in the sense of a cosy and safe relationship with one's existing mode of life – with scorn. Examples would include the contentment [*Behagen*] with one's limitations and narrow-mindedness found in the 'cultural philistine' (UM1.2), and the 'wretched contentment' of the 'last humans' described by Zarathustra at ZP3 (and see Z3.5). On the other hand, contentment as an occasional refuge for those with difficult tasks or who suffer, is described at UM2.3 and BGE61. N's attitude clearly depends upon whether this contentment is an end in itself, or an instrument within the task of the furtherance of life.

contingency

See *chance*.

continuum

N continues the kinds of analysis found in Epicurus or Kant (who writes 'a manifold's combination (*conjunctio*) as such can never come to us through the senses' – *Critique of Pure Reason* B129). On N's analysis, whatever it is that is originally given (sensation, nervous stimulation, etc.) is characterized by a continuous flow, and not by discrete and stable qualities and quantities. In other words, individual things are not originally given, but our cognition of them is a product of the action of cognition (*interpretation*). Likewise, our analysis of *causes* and effects has to first separate and make discrete that which is cause and that which is effect, from out of a continuum. See for example H3.11, GS112.

control (and self-control)

Beherrschung, among others. The idea of having control, especially over the self, is an important source of the feeling of power (D65). This can be in an *ascetic* sense, involving subordination of the self to an impossible or metaphysical ideal (e.g. H137–8). Or it can be in the sense of a productive subtlety in the war against oneself (BGE200, see *self-overcoming*). Self-control can also be associated with courage or strength. For example, N contrasts Thucydides's courage for the real with Plato's cowardice at TIAncients2. Similarly, he describes Zarathustra as having control over his 'great disgust' (EHZ8 – see entry on nausea), and thus able to employ people as materials.

convalescence

Genesung. N was an ill man, suffering from crippling fatigue, eyesight problems, nausea and headaches for much of his adult life. Thus, he tried to discover what diet, patterns of life or places to live would help him to convalesce from bouts of this illness. His concern with the *closest things* has this practical issue as one of its sources. However, N believed that he was ill (in a sense that is by no means entirely metaphorical) also from culture. That is, ideas, beliefs, values, or modes of life that he has inherited and with which he is surrounded. For the most part, when N writes about 'convalescence' he has this second kind of illness, and its overcoming, in mind. Good examples are H2.349, BGE255, Z3.13 (Zarathustra convalescing from the nausea induced by the thought of eternal recurrence), TIP. N particularly thinks of his writings around the time of H in this way (H1P1 and EHHuman4). Convalescence as an overcoming is thus contrasted to *comforting* as a relieving of suffering. Convalescence is also part of the *cycle* of creative states, linked to exhaustion and wthe need for *repose* (EHBGE2). See *health*.

convention

See *tradition*.

conviction

Überzeugung. A conviction is a belief, held stubbornly to be 'unqualified truth'. N provides an analysis of the dangers and origin of conviction at H1.629–38, developing the notion there that one must be a 'noble traitor' to one's convictions. Convictions are opposed by both the genius of science and of *justice*. The chapter and book end with the notion of the *wanderer*, a thinker who has no home or 'final destination' (both understood as convictions). This analysis is alluded to again at AC54.

corruption

See *decadence*.

courage, bravery

Mut. An ancient virtue that N seeks to appreciate and revalue. Courage is the capacity to stick resolutely to life and the real, and not to borrow one's beliefs and values from imaginary other worlds or modes of life (TIAncients2). Likewise, it is courage not to manufacture one's beliefs and values by a fearful negation of becoming, uncertainty and suffering, which are the conditions of life and the real. N finds such courage in the type represented by Epictetus (the Stoic philosopher who had been a slave), and contrasts it with the Christian slave characterized by faith and hope in a different life (D546). A few sections later, courage is proclaimed as a key 'future virtue': the arrogance to understand and not be afraid of the world, a courage that is not dissimilar to generosity (D551, and see Z4.15). Thus, at BGE230, N discusses the courageous type of thinker who is aware of the 'cruelty of the intellectual conscience', which does not simplify but insists upon multiplicity and *perspective*. Such courage is ultimately a form of self-overcoming. At Z3.8, Zarathustra talks about those among his disciples who are too cowardly to change the direction of their willing and thus soon abandon him in favour of their contentment. Likewise, it is Zarathustra's courage that tells the Spirit of Gravity to get off his back at Z3.2.

COW

Kuh. Happy because unconcerned with past or future (UM2.1), or not stricken by *heavy* thoughts (Z4.8) (here, chewing the cud means focused in the present moment, not prone to *nausea*). The cow is also patient and observing (GS351), and thus a metaphor for *reading* and *interpretation* as an art lost in *modernity* (GMP8); rumination means to consider and *contemplate* without hurry. The cow is trusting, not slighted by *distance* or change; warm and reassuring like a true companion (EHZ5, Z4.8). The cow of course is an important religious symbol in many Eastern religions: the 'voluntary beggar' in Z4.8, learning contentment from a herd of cows, is a portrait of *Jesus* as a displaced and misunderstood Eastern sage. A similar portrayal of Jesus is found in AC. The cow's calm is a possible and worthy response to *nihilism* and the degeneration of humanity (cf. 1887.11.297).

creation, creativity

There are two different German words here that get translated as creation: *Schöpfung* and more commonly, *Schaffen*. The former is the religious or theological term, but its use is not confined to such contexts; the latter is a slightly more 'ordinary' term, not far from concepts such as 'making', 'crafting' or 'producing'. We will refer to these as creation1 and creation2.

In BT, there is creation1 but it does not belong to us as individuals; rather, we are a 'channel' through which the Will is the creator1 of art (BT5). This concept comes ultimately from Kant – the artistic genius how nature gives the rule to art – but by way of a Schopenhauerian conception of the Will. In general, then, creation1 is used when it is a question of the artist being a vehicle in this sense; or at any rate having reached a victorious pinnacle of achievement that is miraculous with respect to other artistic or cultural efforts (UM4.4, and compare EHZ3). Significantly, this creation1 is associated with the production of a new *future* (UM4.9, 10), an idea that definitely carries on into his later work. After this point, N becomes sceptical of the concept of creation1. At H2.172, he contrasts contemporary artists with the Greeks who were 'creators of men' (and see H3.150). (Likewise, creation in Greece is not understood in a trivial sense as 'originality': H3.122, D544.) By the time of D, this scepticism has extended further: creation1 generally is a product of human thought or development. However, it seems to be a miracle and is thus assigned to the influence of the divine (D62). In general, N almost stops using the term in a sense that would distinguish it from creation2. Thus, for example, at the end of GS335, the two words are used interchangeably.

Let us turn, then, to creation2 which, as we noted above, is a distinct word but – after the late 1870s – not a distinct concept. Indeed, to the extent that creation2 might carry something of the meaning of creation1, N dismisses its validity (D552). So, we will now drop the numerical suffix. In that passage, significantly, he dismisses creation in favour of the notion of *pregnancy*. The association of pregnancy or procreation with creation is common (e.g. Z2.2). This gives us a clue to N's late notion of creation: it is to be understood as creation from out of oneself, of what is in some sense already there. One important analogy, borrowed from

Michelangelo's sonnets, is with the sculptor 'releasing' the sculpture from out of the stone (Z2.2; Leibniz uses the notion similarly in the Preface to his *New Essays*). Only under relatively rare historical conditions is creation primarily or initially an *external* giving of form, for example the formation of a new state (GM2.17). Thus, at GS335, creating oneself is associated with 'becoming who you are'. Only in this way could one 'create beyond oneself' (a common phrase in Z: for example Z1.4, Z2.15). The idea is that becoming aligned to and *affirmative* of one's place in the development of life and the human, is already to create beyond oneself; moreover, in so doing, one brings closer a future of still greater development. Such creation involves generating need or distress within oneself (GS56, GM2.16).

A second aspect of creation is that the primary act of creation is in the domain of *values*. 'Things' – what is encountered or experienced – are objects for an act of naming or valuing (GS58, Z1.15). So, for example, N talks about creating a new medical responsibility (TISkirmishes36). This is not an ordinary nominalism – where things are assigned names without reference to any essence. Thus, to create new values means to create new things. Likewise, at BGE211, N writes of future philosophers: 'their "knowing" is creating'. The formation of a people and its culture comprise the first acts of creation; later, in the context of the decadence of the former, creation becomes the provenance of a great individual (Z1.15). It is the right of the *noble* or the masters to give names, to make values (BGE261); GM1.2 claims that this right to create values or give names is taken from the *pathos of distance*. The projection of these values in the highest degree forms an ideal – creates a 'god' in the sense of Greek religion (see BT3, GS143) or the overhuman (Z2.2). Analogously, creating creates creators (ZP9, Z1.16).

A third aspect is that all creation must involve destruction (GS58). For example, the lion stage which cannot create values, but can create the freedom to create (Z1.1). This means both that creating from out of oneself entails a rejection or an overcoming of one's previous state (e.g. Z1.17), and that creation through values necessarily means withdrawing other values (and thus other things constituted through those values). Fourth, all creation is directed towards the future, not in the trivial sense of a sequence of time, but in the sense of the growth of life, health or power; indeed, those who cannot create have no future, they are the 'last human' (ZP5). It is only through creation (in all the senses discussed here) that a future of new possibilities can open, and the human type can develop. See, for example, Z2.14, 3.12.3 and 26, and also the comments on marriage and children at Z1.20.

criminal

Most often *Verbrecher*. A criminal is a lawbreaker, someone who acts against accepted traditions. There are three important ideas that N develops in this connection. First of all, the observation that changes or developments in laws are made, often enough, because of law breakers (D20, GS4, TISkirmishes45). The 'free-doer' and the criminal will at one stage be subjected to the same defamation. Second, N offers a critique of the concept of punishment. At GM2.9, he derives the notion of punishment from the fact that someone outside the social contract is effectively at war with that society; punishment is thus the criminal expelled. This notion is pursued also at D202, where N argues that our behaviour towards the criminal should not be founded on revenge, but rather rehabilitation or healing from an illness. Punishment is a means of maintaining power, by possessing the right to find guilty and impose the law (GM2, TIErrors7). Third, N analyses the psychology of *responsibility*, in particular the state of having the strength to act but not having the strength later to affirm the act. Thus the portrait of the pale criminal (Z1.6). This idea is related to N's own perseverance or courage in passages such as EHClever1. There is also a line of thought – an endpoint of what N calls the softening of morality – that denies all responsibility, and for that reason treats the criminal very differently. N develops such a thought (founded upon his account of responsibility) as H1.70, 105, and then criticizes its excessiveness at BGE21, 201.

critique

The concept of critique has both a broader and a narrower meaning. The broad sense of critique is to approach an object (especially some cultural object, such as a historical text) objectively and without pre-conceptions, in order to understand it or evaluate it. Thus, today, we might talk about a literary critic or film critic, and a philosophy student might be asked to 'critically appraise' an idea. An important historical influence here is 'critical hermeneutics', an eighteenth and nineteenth century mode of study that viewed biblical texts as historical objects rather than as revelation (or, at least, not as pure revelation). N's discipline of philology was to a considerable degree influenced by early hermeneutics.

The narrower concept of critique stems primarily from Kant, where it has a specific philosophical meaning. For Kant, 'critique' means to investigate the basis of any particular human ability (e.g. understanding, judgement, reason) so as to discover both its fundamental, a priori principles and its limits. The principles are what gives that ability its legitimacy, which is to say a guarantee of its value with respect to certain goals (e.g. the principles of the understand make possible knowledge of the natural world); the limits define possible usages of the ability which are illegitimate (e.g. knowledge of a supernatural world).

N takes over something like this Kantian sense of critique. For example, it seems to be at stake in his analysis of Socrates at BT13 – Socrates was incapable of turning the logical drive against itself (this is also a reference to the *Ouroboros*, see BT15 and *snake*). N introduces his new, modified sense of critique in discussing University philosophy and its association with the state, at UM3.8. Here, he proposes an *experimental* type of critique. One cannot critique words with words – because of the account of the origin of words as described, for example in 'On Truth and Lies' – instead life supplies the principle, and the possibility of living in accordance with a philosophy is its legitimacy (see also the first Preface to PTAG). A similar point is made at greater length years later at BGE210. The philosopher of the future is 'critic in body and soul', although this is still, like the sceptic, only part of the *comprehensive* sense of the philosopher. At GM2.24, N again proposes that truth needs an experimental form of critique; in the next section he adds that this is not the 'self-critique' of knowledge (the critique of words with words) which remains within the orbit of the ascetic ideal.

cruelty

Usually *Grausamkeit*. Traditionally, *pity* or 'love of the neighbour' distinguish the human being from the *animal* or 'cruel and playful' nature (1872.19.50, H1.233 and see 101). More importantly, such moral practices are often themselves cruel or even founded upon cruelty, to the point that cruelty to oneself (asceticism) is accounted a virtue (D18). This point is made generally at GM3.21 concerning the reactive values of Christian thought. This artificial contrast between the human and nature leads N often to emphasize the role of cruelty in human affairs. N reminds us that 'cruelty is one of the oldest festive joys of mankind', and we deceive ourselves if we think this has been left behind. Rather, 'every smallest step in the field of free thought . . .' involves cruelty, generally towards oneself (D18, GM2.6). A similar idea, that in late stages of culture 'cruelty now *refines* itself' is found at GS23, and the point is made in more detail at BGE229. More generally still, N asserts that life means 'being cruel . . . toward anything that is growing weak and old in us' (GS26, Z3.12.20); likewise, greatness means the ability to inflict great pain (GS325). In other words, cruelty is necessary for life; but not *all* cruelty – specifically, the cruelty often found in moral practices is 'anti-life'.

At Z3.13, Zarathustra calls humans 'the cruellest beast', and brings together several forms of cruelty: the pleasure at the suffering of others, the pleasure involved in the ascetic denigration of life and the cruelty in self-overcoming. The final item on this list certainly includes the cruelty to one's intellectual conscience involved in the pursuit of knowledge (BGE229–30). The point is elaborated at GM3.10: having internalized existing values and traditions, the philosopher (discoverer of knowledge or creator of values) must be first cruel against him or herself. All these forms of cruelty, from the passive to the reactive, and on to the most active and internal, bring with them a feeling of power. These types of cruelty return more explicitly as the three stages of 'religious cruelty' at BGE55, culminating in *nihilism* – the sacrifice of God 'for nothing'. Importantly, though, in the next section N makes it clear that by pursuing such cruelty to its conclusion that an 'opposite ideal' can reveal itself: namely, that form of human being who can joyously affirm his or her existence (BGE56).

culture

Kultur. By 'culture' N means a form of life that a *people* has established for itself. This culture encapsulates their *values*, is what allows a people both to have an identity and to reproduce and perhaps reinforce that identity over time (1878.32.24), and which also allows a people to produce excellence or greatness. This latter point is what N uses to distinguish culture from *Bildung* (often translated as 'culture', but sometimes also as 'education') – indeed, he sometimes conceives of them virtually as opposites (although see 'The Greek State'). The concept of culture can be used broadly, to designate types of culture that span dozens of nations and hundreds of years (e.g. 'Alexandrian' or 'Hellenic': BT18); or narrowly, to discuss individual peoples or sub-groups (such as 'noble culture' (D201), and see H3.188). Culture includes everything from mundane practices (e.g. diet, daily routines), through institutions (church, military, education) up to 'high' culture (literature and art) (see H2.186).

N's early work can be interpreted as all about the nature of culture; in this he was motivated in part by his contemporary Germany, which was a new state formed in nationalism and militarism, and the culture of which was still being formed. (See N's comments on the relation of state and culture at H1.474, and again at TIGermans4.) Culture is thought of as the variety of ways that the underlying *Will* has of keeping a people alive, and especially stimulating or tricking 'nobler natures' who feel the burden of being (BT18). In this period also, N distinguishes between an authentic and an inauthentic (or dispersed) culture, and similarly between lower and higher (see the chapter in H, and GS99). Authentic culture can be defined as one that is unified, and which still serves a key purpose of all culture, which is to produce genius or greatness (BT23, 'The Greek State', UM3.5, 4.4). The dispersion of culture happens through the influence of the drive for knowledge, especially historical knowledge (1882.19.27, UM2.4, H1.249), which eventually turns a culture into a mere patchwork of styles or practices borrowed randomly from the past (UM1.1), and without the dynamism to take on future projects (see *historical sense*). The Socratic drive for knowledge cannot be simply eliminated; rather, the task of culture is to incorporate it into a unity (thus the 'music-making Socrates' theme in BT, and see H1.251 or 281). This concern with understanding the unity of a culture, and perhaps aiding its development in modernity (1873.28.2, H1.245), animates much of N's early work (see PTAG1).

In later work, the concept of culture becomes aligned to N's conception of *power* (e.g. D23, 201) but remains similar in important respects. Higher culture comprises the feeling of power and of the growth of power; indeed, higher culture always begins with barbarians, perhaps with a contempt for and the destruction of a previous decadent culture, but in any case with the 'lust for power' and cruelty with a good conscience (BGE257, GM2.6). Cultural advances depend upon power differences and the 'pathos of distance' (AC43); in turn this means that culture is a 'pyramid' with a wide base of workers (AC57). Contrasted to higher culture is one based on various forms of physical or spiritual *narcotization* or making ill (GS86, GM1.11, the 'madhouses of culture' at GM3.14; also see how N describes the 3rd and 4th UM at EHUntimely1). Moreover, we find a similar analysis of the over-historicized, patchwork culture to the one that N made a decade earlier, and the same contrast of authentic or noble culture to *Bildung* (Z2.14; see the 'backwards glancing tiredness' at GMP5). Ultimately, it is this lack of a future, a lack of awareness that there could or should be future possibilities, that disturbs N (see ZP5, Z2.14, AC58).

cunning

The two German words under consideration here (*List, Schlauheit*) are often found associated (e.g. right at the beginning of N's career, in 'Socrates and Tragedy'). In the first half of his career, N's use of these terms is fairly conventional. It is not until the mid-1880s, that N begins to use these terms in more interesting ways. At the beginning of Z4, Zarathustra calls himself 'cunning' when he refuses to reveal that he is using the honey as bait for the higher men (Z4.1). Such cunning, that is, has entered the philosopher's 'fishing tackle' as serving his or her comprehensive responsibility for the development of humans into the future. This becomes explicit at BGE39 – where 'perhaps' cunning provides more favourable conditions than scholarship for the development of the philosopher – and again the following section where cunning is the 'kindness' behind the mask. (See also AC16, TISkirmishes14.)

Cunning is also associated with the ability to find a way to preserve a diseased or decadent life (Socrates at BTA1, the priest at GM3.15, metaphysicians at BGE10). These two usages are not in contradiction, but are a recognition of the amoral truth that not all battles can be fought in the open, with displays of force.

custom

See *habit*.

cycle

In a number of different areas, N sees a cyclical or alternating pattern. Obviously, there is the idea of *eternal recurrence*. Also, on a broad *historical* scale there are repeated patterns of the formation of cultural forms of life, their *corruption*, the emergence of *individuals* and perhaps a *slave revolution* (see 1885.34.179; N is influenced here by the Italian historian Vico). In the life of the philosopher, there is a cycle of *creative* overflowing, followed by a period of *exhaustion* or *convalescence*; or, similarly, the investigation of dangerous and ugly topics, followed by 'running out into the sunlight' (TIP); likewise, Zarathustra repeatedly goes down and then up to his mountains. N also uses the symbols of *feminine and masculine* as a means of exploring this idea. Finally, religious fervor is identified with *folie circulaire* – Falret's phrase for what is now called manic depression or bipolar disorder – in its alternation of feelings of ecstatic redemption followed by severe penitence (see AC51, EHDestiny8). Metaphorically, N employs night and day, the seasons of the year, and the life cycle of organisms (the cycle of growth and reproduction, or of life and death) to illustrate such cycles – along with associated mythical allusions, such as the life of *Dionysus*.

dance

Tanz. Dance is defined by N quite early as a display of strength and agility, but one that is graceful, as if only a sign of still further reserves of strength and agility (BT9, H1.278, GS381). (This

description could also be of the *noble*.) The ancient Greeks lived
dancelike in this sense; and dialogue in Sophocles has this character.
Dance thus serves as an analogy for Dionysian insight apprehended
calmly in an Apollonian vision (UM4.7); for the overcoming of
shame in the healthy and beautiful body (Z3.12.2); likewise, for
N's conception of freedom of will as self-determination, taking
leave of certainty and dancing beside the abyss (GS347 – this
notion should recall the tight rope 'dancer' in ZP); and generally as
the ideal of philosophy, which needs to be able to work with both
science and art, accomplished in both but constrained by neither
(H1.278, GM3.8), even though this means a certain inevitable
scientific ignorance (GS381). N criticizes German philosophers, for
whom thinking is nothing like dancing (TIGermans7), struggling
without a 'finger for nuance'. Wagner is identified – and also
implicitly criticized – for moving music away from dance (H2.134)
and its ideal of self-possession even amidst emotional enthusiasm
(and see Z2.11).

Zarathustra walks like a dancer at ZP2, an indication of the
self-overcoming during his long sojourn in the mountains (and see
Z1.3). 'The Dance Song' (Z2.10) is explicitly there to advocate
against the 'spirit of gravity', the enemy of anyone who would seek
to overcome such burdens. In accord with this conception of dance,
we have the famous lines 'one must have chaos within one still so as
to give birth to a dancing star' (ZP5), and 'I would only believe in
a God who knew how to dance' (Z1.7). To the latter is contrasted
the discontented God who created an 'eternally imperfect' world –
that is a world characterized by illusion, suffering and dependence
(Z1.3). Such a god suffers and, in revenge, wants to make suffer. The
dancing god, on the other hand, is *Dionysus*. Both are projections
of human *ideals*, but the latter is of a healthy form of human life
and one aligned to the nature of life as *will to power*.

danger

N employs the idea of *danger* in several interconnected ways.
First, danger is the 'mother of morality' (BGE262, and 198).
That is, moral systems and other forms of values arise to fix in
place a working social arrangement, one that offers stability and
security to the group. Second, though, this same stability itself
endangers the health or growth of life. So, the priestly type is 'an

essentially dangerous form of human existence' (GM1.6), and likewise the good and righteous are the 'greatest danger to all human future' (Z3.12.26). Third, N discuses those factors that are a specific danger to the development of a philosopher (BGE205: specialization, intellectual conscience or the need to revalue those values assigned to life). For an earlier example see also the 'three dangers' that confronted Schopenhauer (UM3.3). Similarly, there is the danger attached to philosophical knowledge itself (H1.109), such that N frequently: asks how much of the truth can you endure? (e.g. BGE39). That is, if certain falsehoods or simplifications are a condition of life, then bringing these into question will be a danger both to the questioner and to existing forms of human life. Accordingly, the passage to the 'overhuman' will be a 'dangerous across', and Zarathustra praises the tight-rope walker for making 'danger your vocation' (ZP4, 6). The image of the tight-rope walker brings us to the fourth meaning: danger as a duty. N exhorts us to 'live dangerously!' (H1.283, BGE224), risking and ultimately having to lose ourselves and our current way of life. Regarding Zarathustra's inability to express the idea of eternal recurrence, his conscience chides him 'What do you matter? Speak your word and break!' (Z2.22, see also GS233, 341). More generally, Zarathustra talks about courage and the seeking out of dangers as the main characteristic of the growth of the human (Z4.15).

Darwin

See *evolution*.

day

See *night*.

Daybreak: Thoughts on the Prejudices of Morality

Written 1880–1 and published in 1881 in five books of aphorisms; reissued with a new Preface in 1886. Daybreak represents a subtle move away from the 'positivism' of *Human, All Too Human*. The book begins by returning to the origin of morality, though with a modified model that has more emphasis on *evaluation* and the *drives* as origins, and *custom* as mechanism. There is an extended discussion of early *Christianity* in this light. It then turns to contemporary moral practices and social institutions (*marriage*, *education*, etc.). By the end of the book, N offers exhortations to a new, and *future*, way of living and thinking.

de la Rochefoucauld, Francois

Seventeenth-century French author, much admired by N both for the aphoristic form of his *Maxims* as for the sceptical and even cynical psychological observations about human behaviour and moral values that they contain.

death

Tod. There are three key aspects to N's thinking about death. The first and most obvious revolves around those values or beliefs that involve a denigration or even rejection of life – either *this* life (as opposed to the 'afterlife') or aspects associated with the living body (sex, passion, pleasure, etc.). A key passage in this regard would be Zarathustra on the 'preachers of death' (Z1.9); likewise, N's interpretation of the death of Socrates (TISocrates12). The rejection of life on the part of the *ascetic* priest is only apparent; such asceticism is really a means to carry on living despite suffering and degeneration (GM3). A related idea is the danger that the philosopher will encounter in his or her attempt to *overcome* values. The death of the tight-rope walker, who made *danger* his 'vocation', is an example (ZP6). Finally, metaphysics will, on N's account, often involve a conceptual rejection of becoming, or a positing of facts and values as eternal. This N often describes with metaphors of death: for example, the 'mummified concepts' at TIReason1.

The 'death of God' (e.g. GS125, ZP2) is a second notion. Belief in God – and the values that go with such belief – is no longer possible or relevant within modernity. This is both a liberation but also a crushing blow (for it means that the burden of creating and justifying values falls upon the human). Here, 'death' means old, weak, irrelevant, but also historical, transient and certainly not eternal. Z4 contains several discussions of the meaning and reasons for the death of God (see Z4.6 and 7).

The third concerns either the notion of euthanasia, or the relation of life to the thought of mortality. Some of N's most beautiful passages are pleas for a 'rational' or 'free' death, one that precisely from out of 'love of life' does not allow the body entirely to outlive its usefulness and capacity for action (see H3.185, TISkirmishes36, Z1.21). The thought of death should mix a drop of 'foolishness' into life (H3.322), rather than gloom; this is partly because, without the need to come rapidly to a judgement about the big issues for the sake of one's eternal soul, the thought of our mortality frees us to have time for experimentation, and even for mistakes (D501, GS152). N desires to provide people more reasons to focus on life and joy in life, rather than death (GS278).

decadence

There are a whole set of terms here that N uses in waves throughout his career. Decadence [almost always the French word *décadence*] is probably the most famous of them, and it is if anything overused in N's last writings. Terms with similar meanings include 'degeneration' [*Entartung* or sometimes *Degenerescenz*] and 'corruption' [*Corruption* or *Verderbniss*].

'Decadent' was a term of abuse used by French neo-classical or conservative critics against the romanticism of painters like Delacroix or novelists such as Hugo. Later, writers like Baudelaire adopted the term as their own, using it to express scepticism towards many dominant moral or political values. N picks up the term late in 1883–4 (concepts of corruption, decline or degeneration date from much earlier). By 1887–8 it is one of his key concepts. Baudelaire is termed 'a typical decadent' by N (EHClever5), and almost all references to him associate him with Wagner (Baudelaire was one of Wagner's champions in France). So, by 'decadence' N means any period of cultural history – or any state of the human organism – which has lost its good taste and value judgement (thus it is associated with pity at AC7 and TISkirmishes37; with Kantian duty at AC11; with Schopenhauer's quieting of the will at TIMorality5), health and sureness of instinct (AC6 and see the discussions of post-Hellenic Greek culture at TISocrates4, 11, Ancients2 and 1888.14.111), discipline and sense of a future. It is to be associated either with the decline of old cultures, or with moral revolutions.

The Kantian and Platonic-Christian metaphysical distinction between appearance and 'true world' is termed a 'sign of decadence' (TIReason6). For all these reasons at AC19–20 Christianity is called a 'monster of decadence'. Decadent cultures are exhausted cultures, such cultures often exhibit a pathological over-sensitivity; indeed, often an inability not to respond, lacking the strength simply to inhibit one's passions (TIMorality6, 1888.14.157, 1888.17.6; see however the description of Dionysian intoxication at TISkirmishes10). Alternatively, the decadent culture can manifest itself as a craving for stimulation (for the voluptuous, the exotic, the dangerous). Importantly, this desire for stimulation is a symptom and not a cause – as those who react ascetically against such stimulation believe. Thus, decadence in the form of a culture of exhaustion that needs stimulation often precipitates a reaction, which is the 'gathering gloom of the religious-moral pathos' (1887.11.375, and see 1887.10.119).

Most of the above could serve as an account of the notion of degeneration or corruption also. Degeneration, however, is used by N throughout his career (for early examples, see BT17 and 24). If there is a distinction to be drawn from decadence, degeneration tends to have a stronger physiological emphasis (see the comments about beer at TIGermans2), and is used more often in specific cases (e.g. the instincts of the criminal at TISkirmishes45, or the degeneration of individual philosophers at BGE25), and is sometimes associated particularly with an increasing homogeneity of society (thus 'herd animal' at BGE203). Corruption, on the other hand, tends in the opposite direction, and is associated with the spiritual ('the corruption of reason' at TIErrors1) and with the decline of the higher strata of a society (BGE257, AC27, 44).

At BGE262, an aging and over-comfortable society produces either a 'variation' [*Abartung*] into something higher, or a degeneration [*Entartung*] and monstrosity. At GS23, corruption is a term applied to the 'autumn' of all societies, and the time of the rise of individuals 'the seed-bearers of the future'. In other words, broadly speaking, decadence is a watershed moment of great danger and promise. Human forms of life can either exhaust themselves and degenerate into a herd or mob, or the corruption can blossom into new forms of life and values can be created.

deception, dissimulation

At a stage of human development prior to the formation of any social order, the primary function of the intellect is deception ('On Truth and Lies'). Only within a social order is truth-telling or honesty valued. Moreover, the foundation of knowledge lies in a set of simplifications or 'basic errors' (GS110), embedded in our lives as its condition. Therefore, the greatest of philosophers have always had to deceive themselves about both the nature of things and the nature of life (similarly, see GS344). Analogously, at the origin of virtue lies a long period of dissimulation of virtue – this eventually *sublimates* itself and produces virtue. Similar points are made about social relations and friendship at H1.293 and 376. In all these various ways, then, N speculates that deception is the real foundation of what is normally called *virtue*. The idea is generalized as the production of states from their opposites at BGE2. Nevertheless, *honesty* understood rather differently is an important concept for N (see separate entry). See also entry on *masks*.

degeneration

See *decadence*.

democracy

N understands the notion of democracy very broadly, as any mode of thought that ascribes homogeneity or uniformity to the real. In political thought, therefore, democracy involves the passing of power to the masses, and generally also conceptions such as equality of rights or of moral value. N's critique of political conceptions of democracy parallel his accounts of herd morality and of nobility. There was a period during the writing of H3 that

N seems to have embraced the concept of democracy, at least as a provisional instrument for stability and for the overcoming of militarized nationalism (H3.275, 289). He discusses a 'future democracy' characterized by independence of opinion, and modes of life and employment (H3.293). This future form is distinguished from current forms, such as parliamentarianism (GS174). The democratic idea is also discussed in the fifth book of GS as that which breaks up rigid class hierarchies and thus liberates individual ambition (GS348, GS356), although at the cost of a coordinated and enduring sense of the future, of the organizational power of the group (TISkirmishes39), and of productive differences (BGE242, TIGermans5). Democracy produces a people incapable of command (BGE199), and is in danger of falling prey to a tyrant.

Importantly, though, that first broad definition of democracy means that it has influence in non-political domains. For example, the 'democracy of concepts' whereby modernity regards anyone as ill who is single-minded (H3.230); the democratic notion of universal natural law (BGE22); or the democratic prejudice that now pervades science and eliminates one of the basic concepts of life, genuine activity (GM2.12).

Democritus

See *atomism*.

depth

Tiefe. Depth plays several roles in N. First, depth describes the more interesting or revealing rule (i.e. those who are not among the *great* and *noble*), as opposed to the *exception*. So, N's many studies of *actors, slaves, priests, scholars*, etc. Second, that which is 'below' the *superficial*, especially conventional interpretations of psychological phenomena (e.g. GM3.15). Third, similarly, some people or peoples are 'profound' as opposed to those who are only superficial (see BGE244, EHCase3). Partly because interesting and revealing, depth is often the necessary precondition or accompaniment of height and *ascent* (DP1–2, H1.291–2).

Descartes

Seventeenth-century French philosopher. N sees his importance as being first in the line of 'modern' philosophers who offer a critique of the Christian concept of soul (BGE54, but see 191). Similarly, N praises Descartes' idea that animals are biological machines (AC14), as well as Descartes as a psychologist (EHWC3). Nevertheless, Descartes' faith in the immediate veracity of self-reflection is a frequent target (he ironically twists the *cogito* at GS276, and see GS357, BGE2, 16–17).

desert

Wüste. A common symbol in N, the desert generally stands for some mode of life or method of enquiry that is characterized by solitary suffering, wandering or uncertainty, and thus also possible temptation (perhaps a mirage or an oasis). The story of the Israelites wandering in the desert (Exodus) or the temptation of Jesus in the desert (Matthew 4 and Luke 4) are unavoidable allusions; likewise anthropological accounts of nomadic peoples in Arabia. For clear examples, see H2.31, Z1.1 (the camel tests its strength in the desert, the lion becomes lord of its own desert), BGE12, GM3.17. Z4.16 presents a comic song of moral and sexual temptation in an oasis. This symbol relates closely to a number of others, including the *south* and *wandering*.

desire

See *longing*.

despising (or hatred, contempt)

There are a number of related concepts here. Probably the most important is *Verachtung* (usually translated as 'despising'), which represents an important theme in Z. Four different broad uses can be identified.

The despising of the self. Christian self-despising arises, N argues, from out of the impossibility of living up to the ideal of selfless acts, especially in the 'brilliant mirror' that is God's selflessness (H1.132); similarly, in order to feel contented with some aspect of him or herself, the Christian must despise some other part (*asceticism*, H1.137). The consequences of this self-contempt are explored frequently, for example at D411, GM3.14. Such self-hatred creates an *artistic* 'need' of a lower kind: a *narcotic* to disguise one's discontentment (H2.169). Hatred for the self can be externalized in an act (real or imaginary) of revenge (e.g. Paul's revenge against the impossible Jewish law: D68). In that passage, N claims Luther had the same psychological movement. In contrast, N argues, it is essential to be 'well disposed' towards oneself in order to avoid one's actions being determined by reaction or *ressentiment* (see D79, 516, GS290); reverence for the self is thus a *noble* trait.

The despising of the master. In a psychological inversion that N calls '*ressentiment*', those individuals or peoples who were enslaved (literally or metaphorically) created a value system from out of their hatred of their masters. Whatever characteristics the masters possessed, these would now be called 'evil'; the characteristics of the slaves (meekness, poverty, etc.) would be called 'good'. See BGE195 and the whole of GM1. Thus for example the inversion of the ancient view that *work* is contemptible (GS329). Significantly, GM1.10 contains a clear distinction between the 'hatred' of the slaves, and the 'despising' of the noble class. At the root of the latter is the 'feeling of happiness in oneself'. This is the same distinction as found at GS379 (and compare to Pascal at D63).

The 'great despising'. This is a recurring phrase in Z. The idea is that the human being, insofar as of fixed character and resistant to becoming and growth, must be judged despicable from the perspective of life, or of future human possibilities. The 'great despising' then is this judgement conceived of as generally applicable (i.e. to humanity as a whole), as a primary affect associated with our individual philosophical development (ZP3), and as productive with respect to the future of the human. An important passage is Z1.4 'On the despisers of the body'. The argument is that these despisers' despising is worthy of respect. However, they are still in some way reactive, or incapable of 'creating beyond themselves'; their despising is a negation and thus not productive. That is to say, it is not a 'loving despising' (Z3.14). Similarly, Zarathustra says to the 'ape' who warns him about the great city 'I despise your despising' (Z3.7) for it is founded upon impotent rage and revenge. An earlier version of this idea is found at H1.40, which is intriguingly entitled 'The overanimal'. N picks up the theme of despising again at BGE216, which should be understood as a revaluation of the Christian theme of loving one's enemies (Mt. 5.44). See also the 'redeeming human of the great love and despising' at GM2.24.

Contempt as a feeling of power. To have contempt for something – that is, for one's negative value judgement to achieve the level of a passion – is a mode of feeling power-over. It is, therefore, a basic drive. See, for example, H1.62, or likewise the modern feeling that freedom is an absence of discipline (H1.221). Equally importantly, the feeling of power is a key part of N's analysis of *pity* (e.g. H3.50, D135). N alternatively suggests that self-contempt is found in pity, insofar as one projects one's suffering onto others (BGE223).

destiny

See *fate*.

detour (digression)

See *wanderer*.

devil

Teufel. The devil has three main meanings in N. First, it represents common fears and traditional conceptions of evil, especially so that N or Zarathustra can belittle them (Z2.21). Second, the devil may represent certain temptations, through which one might deviate from or be held down from one's path of growth. Zarathustra's own devil is the 'spirit of gravity' (Z1.7 or Z3.2), while the Sorcerer's is 'spirit of melancholy' (Z4.15, gravity and melancholy are both variations on the word '*schwer*' which means 'heavy'). Third, the devil indicates the interconnection of the good and the bad, the positive and negative (i.e. the notion that opposites are not really opposite) – so, for example, N describes BGE as the 'no-saying, no-doing' half of his project, after the affirmative stance of Z. Thus he writes: 'The devil is just God's leisure every seventh day . . .' (EHBGE1–2).

dialectic

Although in philosophical history the notion of dialectic has other reference points than this (Kant and Hegel, particularly), N's use of the term is more or less exclusively in reference to Socrates (and by extension Plato). See *Socrates*.

diet

N is convinced that what one habitually eats and drinks has a relationship to one's spiritual life – that is, on what we think and how we value. N thus frequently discusses the traditional diets of various nations, the religious practice of fasting or the role of beer in German culture (e.g. Z4.12, WC5, BGE47, 234, GM3.17, TIErrors1, TIGermans2). More generally, this is part of N's concern with the *'closest things'*: the spiritual significance of the patterns of life that are usually overlooked by philosophers on the hunt of 'big' issues. See H3.5–16 and EHClever. N's interest in diet also has a more or less metaphorical counterpoint in the idea of *'incorporation'*: the manner in which the will to power absorbs, digests, makes its own other powers, values or ideas (e.g. D171).

digestion (bowels, (stomach, etc.)

Digestion, broadly speaking, has several meanings in N. First, literally, N is convinced that philosophers have always chased after the big issues and ignored the *closest things*, such as the food we eat. His discussions of digestion, intestines or stomachs are thus meant to be suggestions as to how certain daily life practices affect the spiritual domain of beliefs and ideas. See GS366, GM3.16, EHBooks3. Second, digestion is a metaphor for the ability of an individual or group to live with certain facts or conditions, thus at UM2.9 N talks about those who find life indigestible, and therefore desire its end. This idea returns at Z3.12.16 ('their spirit is an upset stomach', see BGE230). At BGE244, N says of the Germans that they are incapable of digesting, meaning they are stuck at a certain point, unable to move on (the idea is repeated at EHClever1).

Similarly, he calls human beings in the modern period *homo pamphagus* because they seem to be able to consume everything, indiscriminately, without benefit and without decision (D171, and see UM2.10, EHWagner1 – see *historical sense*). In contrast, the 'coming philosophers' will have 'teeth and stomachs for the most indigestible' (BGE44), meaning will be able to deal with – and indeed form a new mode of life out of – dangerous truths. Excrement, the end product of digestion, is an important metaphor also. Pessimists only view the world's 'backside', Zarathustra says at Z3.12.14. N claims that writing is a necessity, like having to relieve oneself (GS93) – which is a joking elaboration of the idea that 'my writings speak only of my overcomings' (H2P1). Third, to consume or digest means to make something one's own, and thereby have power over something (e.g. BGE230); for this, see *incorporation*.

Dionysus

Greek deity, after whom N names the Dionysian, a concept that undergoes profound change from N's early to later work, but remains central throughout. N employs many features of the myths and cultural practices associated with Dionysus, either as anthropological reference points, or as symbols: the association with grape vines, wine and intoxication; the association both with harvest and with spring, and thus both with plenty and with sexuality; the fact that the tragedy and comedy competition was held at a festival to Dionysus; that Dionysus' mortal mother made Zeus reveal his full divinity, and was killed by Zeus' lightning; that as a child he was hidden and protected in a cave by nymphs; that, in some tales, he is torn apart but then reborn; that Dionysus marries Ariadne, after she was abandoned by Theseus; that he is represented both as kind and generous, though also cruel to his enemies; his association with lions and dolphins, as well as minor mythic creatures such as satyrs or nymphs; the reported savagely destructive behaviour of devotees during certain religious rites; and in general the association of Dionysus with joy and with release from labour or care.

The Dionysian is one of the three cultural drives in *The Birth of Tragedy*, along with the *Apollonian* and *Socratic*. The Dionysian is there associated with *intoxication*, ecstasy (literally, being-outside-of-oneself), and thus with cultural productions such as *lyric* poetry and many aspects of music (especially harmony). This cultural drive implicitly contains a metaphysics (i.e. a way of understanding the nature of reality), which N identifies with Schopenhauer's conception of the dynamic *Will* that underlies *appearance*. The coming together of Dionysian and Apollonian drives into a singular cultural production is N's account of the nature of ancient *tragedy*.

In TI, N appears to contrast his earlier concepts of both Dionysian and Apollonian with a third art drive (represented by architecture) (TISkirmishes10–11). This then allows N later in the book to formulate a new, much broader concept of the Dionysian (TIAncients4–5). The new concept is central in N's later writings. Dionysus becomes a key figure, a god who tempts or seduces humanity to growth and health (e.g. BGE295). The original concepts of Apollonian and Dionysian, rather than distinct drives, are thought of as moments within the overall *creative* and destructive cycle of Dionysus. Growth, and in particular a growth in the expression and feeling of power, requires both creativity (the devising of new life practices and values) and destruction (of existing practices and values, including those in the self). Creativity, in turn, requires both the dynamism of longing for and pursuing a future and also the attaining of a height or plateau (described as a quiet beauty or perfection, an image of *eternity*, for example at Z3.3,4 and 4.10); while destruction requires both scholarly or scientific attention and a 'cruel' will to overcome. The ability simultaneously and joyfully to affirm all the aspects of Dionysian reality is what is at stake in *eternal recurrence* (thus N stresses 'eternity' at TIAncients 4–5 and EHZ6). N illustrates the necessity of both the creative and destructive at Z1.1 and 2.13. If N can be considered a theological thinker, Dionysus is his god (N calls himself a '*disciple*' – for example TIAncients5). Regardless, we should think of Dionysus as an ideal, or personification, of the *longing* humanity should feel for its own growth and overcoming, as well as the longing of life for the *health* of its highest products. Therefore, *Ariadne* is the figurehead (and mother) of the humanity that so longs. In EH, N claims that the character of Zarathustra is effectively a portrait of this Dionysian ideal (EHZ6). See also entries on *Bachofen, feminine and masculine, pregnancy, beauty.*

Dionysus Dithyrambs

A collection of his poetry that N prepared for publication towards the end of 1888, some with slight modifications and new titles. Most of the pieces were written earlier, including a few that had appeared in *Thus Spoke Zarathustra*.

dirt

See *cleanliness*.

disciple

Jünger. The allusion to the disciples of Jesus is unavoidable. In ZP, Zarathustra decides the appropriate strategy would be to acquire 'disciples'. At GS32 N laments disciples who do not have adequate strength (and see Z1.8); indeed, the best kind of disciple is one who can remain 'faithful' to him or herself (GS99) and even attack an idea so as to make it stronger (GS106, and see Z1.22.3). N calls himself a 'disciple' of Dionysus (BGE295, EHP2), which is a way of thinking about one's relationship to an *ideal*.

discipline

Zucht. Certain kinds of growth or creativity only take place under strict rules, or generally harsh conditions (e.g. UM2.3). Where *creativity* is an *overcoming*, creativity needs opposition *(agon)*. If external resistance is not to be found – a rival or enemy, a precarious situation – one must impose such resistances upon oneself. A favourite example is in literature, where N contrasts the tight formal and narrative constraint of some authors (particularly the Greeks H3.127, 140) with the looseness of others (notably Shakespeare: see H1.221). Likewise, in modern music after Wagner (H2.134). A related notion is that of the discipline involved in method, such as the 'discipline of spirit' (AC36); likewise, the 'rigorous self-discipline' and thus 'liberation' that

N attributes to his writing of H (EHH1, 5); or the discipline of logic that is akin to *dance* (TIGermans7). The connection made just there between logic and dance suggests that discipline fails unless directed first and foremost at the body (TISkirmishes47); it must be a training at the level of physiology if it is to have any effect. Discipline in this sense of rigorous training is the meaning of the Greek term *askesis* (see *ascetic*). 'Discipline' also describes the task of those comprehensive 'new philosophers' to redeem the creation of human greatness from the 'nonsense and accident' of history (BGE203).

The word *Zucht* is the same as that which is translated 'breeding' – and indeed the concepts are related, since in both there is deliberate selection and likely also harsh pruning. Likewise, the concept of education is often discussed in this connection (1872.19.299). At the same time, discipline without the accompaniment of nobility or good taste, can be a disaster (e.g. WC11, TIGermans5). Accordingly, discipline as the turning of one's cruel instincts onto oneself is a key aspect of N's description of the origin of 'bad conscience' (GM2.16).

Disgust

See *nausea*.

distance

Ferne or *Distanz*. 'Distance' designates the separation or independence of things. So, at ZP7, Zarathustra is still 'distant' from the people in the market place, for they do not understand him; again, if he has *pity*, then it is 'from a distance' (Z2.3) so as not to bring shame on the pitied. An associated idea is that distance characterizes a longing for *ideals* that lie beyond the currently existing forms of the human (e.g. 'Too long have I . . . looked into the distance' Z2.1). In a manner akin to Buddhism, Jesus refuses to place happiness or the ideal at a distance – that is in a transcendent deity or an unfulfilable promise (AC29, 32).

The most famous usage of the metaphor of distance is in the expression 'pathos of distance' (see BGE257, GM1.2, GM3.14,

AC43, 57, TISkirmishes37). It should be noted that N uses *Distanz* here; indeed, N seem to imply a distinction between *Distanz* and the more general *Ferne,* employing the former when he wants to draw attention primarily to 'rank' (e.g. GS15, 60). The relevant sense of distance is that of insisting upon real distinctions among individuals or groups (mainly between types or classes), and the value of these for the health and growth of human life (it is thus related to *height* or 'separation' [e.g. BGE270]). Even among his or her peers, even in acts of obedience, the noble person remains independent, not forming part of a 'herd'. This distance is not just a state, but a 'pathos' – that is, a kind of *affect.* An affect is a state of mind that includes an evaluation of its object and perhaps leads to judgement or action. Pathos falls under this category, but is not something that could be called incidental or fleeting; by 'pathos' N means an affect that is a defining characteristic of a way of life. Pathos of distance, therefore, stands for a defining characteristic of the noble, part and parcel of his or her self-respect and sense of right. Likewise, some things should be apprehended only from a distance, because then their image can inspire (D485, GS15 – and see the entry on *friend*). N defends such a pathos against, primarily, Christianity, which abolishes distances (except for the absurd distance of transcendence), making everyone equal, eliminating any possibility of *reverence* among humans (AC43). In addition, N sometimes writes that the pathos of distance is significant because it represents a condition of health in the human which in turn makes possible a 'more mysterious pathos', namely for new possibilities of human life and growth (BGE257, and see BGE57). Likewise, those noble types who feel the pathos of distance have an overall responsibility for the future (GM3.14).

distress

Not. As a noun, this term is usually rendered as 'distress' or sometimes as 'need', but it should be noted that the word is identical to 'necessary' (as in 'it is now necessary to . . .'). So, distress is an affective state experienced as an emergency: something vitally important is (or will be) wrong or missing. N uses the term frequently enough in a straight-forward way to describe conditions of suffering or poverty. Its philosophical significance lies in N's conception that certain instances of distress are required in order for life to overcome itself. The narrative of Z4 begins when Zarathustra hears a 'cry of distress', and is tempted by pity for the higher humans (and see GS325). For the recognition of, and responding to, distress lies at the origin of the common or ordinary (BGE268). Likewise, in BGEP, N observes a 'magnificent tension of the spirit' (N probably has nihilism in mind here) which is experienced as distress. Rather than anaesthetizing that distress, N's aim is to release the tension in pursuit of new forms of human life. Other relevant passages elaborating on this idea include: the 'highly spiritual' will feel a delight over and above all the distress of a problem (GSP3), psychology must overcome distress – an 'unconscious resistance' – to ideas of the reciprocal dependence of good and wicked (BGE23), or celebrated Greek characteristics were not 'natural', but products of a need (TIAncients3). Three times in Z, N repeats the expression 'turning of need' (Z1.21.1, 3.12.30, 3.14, and see 3.16.3). Turning is presumably a reference to eternal recurrence, as well as meaning 'transforming' (it may also be an allusion to spiritual orientation in Plato and especially Plotinus). So, N seems to be arguing that, for a being capable of aligning itself with the will to power and incorporating the notion of *eternal recurrence*, distress is transformed into necessity, into a joyful affirmation of one's self and one's world. See also *amor fati*.

dithyramb

The dithyramb was in ancient Greek literature a choral hymn to Dionysus, set to music and dance. The dithyramb, N believes (following Aristotle) was thus the original form of Greek tragedy (see BT5 and 8). Only fragments of dithyrambs survive, along with observations concerning characteristic rhythmic, formal and narrative qualities, but without any clear evidence as to how they were performed. N thus sees himself and Wagner as reinventing the form (Wagner is the 'dithrambic dramatist' at UM4.7). N attempts to recreate the dithyramb as a literary form (albeit without music) in Z. In EH, N draws particular attention to Z2.9 and Z3.4 as his finest examples (see EHZ7). Near the end of his working life, he prepared for publication a set of poems with the title *Dionysus Dithyrambs*.

dog

Hund. A dog is a domesticated, and degraded, beast of prey. Thus, it is both suddenly aggressive, and also contemptible in its display of cowardliness (D135), distress (1883.7.42, Z4.19.8) or anger (1885.38.20, GM3.14, WCPostscript1). Having been a slave, it has become nothing other than a slave (H3.closing dialogue). Thus, the dog is an important analogy for *internalization,* the opinions of or relationships to others becoming part of one's identity. The dog's famous loyalty is nothing more than submission, and it is thus no more capable of love, but for a different reason, than the *cat* (1882.1.30). This submission is akin to a human's religious feeling (1885.34.141) – obedience out of fear, or long discipline. The dog is something that is supposed to be wretched, so that its owner can feel important or powerful (D369, and see GS312). The sheepdog is an obvious metaphor for those who devote themselves to the protection of the herd (ZP9, Z4.7). The firedog in Z (a volcano) is noisy, spectacular, but ultimately irrelevant (Z2.18, 1883.10.28) – and thus like the socialist revolution and similar events. The truly important moments are quiet creatings of values. In Z4, Zarathustra tells the story of a traveller accidentally stepping on a sleeping dog, making enemies of those who could be friends (Z4.4 – but N worked on this passage in many notebook entries); the meaning is similar to the story of the adder at Z1.19.

dove

See *bird.*

dragon

See *snake, chaos.*

dream

Traum. Early in his career, N uses the dream to characterize the *Apollonian.* The key distinction there is not between dreaming and being awake; the dream is employed to understand a certain domain of culture, and particularly of art. The dream is a self-created world, one that is created to be aligned with our instincts of preservation and our need to justify our existence and our values. The dream is *not* simply illusion – we can be aware of ourselves dreaming – but the validity of the beautiful forms that we dream are derived from their role in our health and our preservation, and not in their truth strictly speaking. This is the account throughout BT, and is found again at UM4.4. In H, N attempts a general psychology of the dream, particularly the manner in which dreams make sense of stimuli through a retrospective ascription of causation. But this is precisely how, for the most part, we live our waking lives also (H1.13). At D119, the analysis changes focus, to dreams as the space in which our drives act or realize themselves; again, this is not different to waking life. Such ideas were important for Freud.

Later, N explores the idea that not only is waking life not a great deal different from dreams but that, to extent that we insist on it being so, this is a sign of weakness or degeneracy. Waking life is the domain in which our instincts or drives are despised, but the values expressed, and developed, in my dreams will inevitably find their way into waking life (BGE193). Likewise, the degeneration of the will means that we moderns do not understand the 'freedom of the will' even in our dreams (BGE208). At GS54, N suggests that 'ancient humanity' continues in me, in both waking life and in dream. He asks 'what is "appearance" to me now? Certainly not the opposite of some essence' – that is, appearance, even dream appearance, is again not contrasted to some straight-forward relationship to that which is true. Rather, 'appearance is the acting and living itself' – adjectives without an 'x' that they are adjectives of. Dream thus becomes an important element within N's analysis of the 'true world' (TITrueworld). At Z3.10, it is in a dream that Zarathustra does the impossible, which is to stand 'beyond' the world and 'weigh' it; Zarathustra wants to learn from and imitate his dream in his waking life. The dream, that is, can teach waking life how to allow healthy, life-affirming values to develop new ways of life. Likewise, in Z4.10 a dream is the moment of perfection and stillness that Zarathustra experiences after his frantic search for the origin of the 'cry of distress'. Here, the dream serves as a first reminder to Zarathustra that his pity may be leading him astray, and thus that his waking life has lost something (compare

Z2.13). Sometimes, also, N uses dream or wakefulness in a fairly conventional sense, as at BGEP, where he quips that modern Europe has overcome the 'nightmare' of Platonic thought, it can now sleep easy.

drive

See *instinct*.

drunkedness/sobriety

See *intoxication, narcotic*.

Dühring

German realist or materialist philosopher whom N read avidly in the mid-1870s and again a decade later. Dühring is important for N in so far as he represents an attempt to (in N's language) *revalue* morally rejected affects; however, Dühring uses the term *ressentiment* to analyse the concept of justice (indeed, it is Dühring that N has in mind at the beginning of GM2.11). Dühring was a Wagnerite and anti-Semite, and thus N's break with Wagner was also a break with Dühring.

duty

Pflicht. In Kant, duty names a *moral* responsibility that is unconditional (i.e. without exceptions). N, obviously enough, rejects the universal and unconditional character of Kantian morality (e.g. D112, GS5, AC11), and also its express independence from any other motives (e.g. pleasure or fear, see D339). N analyses the development of the concept of duty at GM2.5–6. He does however use the notion of duty in a revalued manner. For example, as early as UM3.5, N discusses the duties that might arise from the ideal of the philosophical mode of life that he has found in Schopenhauer. Likewise, at H3.43, N explores the paradox that is the thinker's supposed 'duty' with respect to truth (and see the confessed 'joke' of a 'duty to suspicion' at BGE34). The notion of duty is used as part of the account of the 'free spirit' at BGE226 – and the very next section is about 'honesty'. At BGE260, N discusses the the deeply unKantian idea of a 'duty to one's peers'. N's revaluation of duty results in the notion of a future duty as one way of characterizing individual behaviours and the social structure as a whole, but one that is different for different levels of that structure, and moreover which is founded upon the need for human life to grow and develop.

dwarf

Zwerg. In Northern European mythology and folklore, dwarves make a common appearance as minor supernatural creatures. Although the tales vary, dwarves tend to be characterized by their dwelling place (underground or in mountains, and thus probably an association with death), occupation (industry and especially smithing), disposition (lust, greed, deviousness). Dwarves play an important role in Wagner's *Ring* cycle. In the symbol of the dwarf, N may also have had the Greek god Hephaestus in mind, who shares many of the above characteristics, and is also lame (as is the dwarf at Z3.2).

N uses the image of dwarf in two ways. First, more generally, as meaning a type of human who is ill, degenerate or weak – or who is in some other way of little cultural significance. For examples, see BT24 (and see EHBT1), UM2.9, H3.179 (the dwarf as a scholar), BGE58. N addresses explicitly the symbolism of dwarf at D130. Second, more specifically, the 'spirit of gravity' in Z is a 'dwarf' (see especially Z3.2 but also Z4.11). This is both because the spirit of gravity is Zarathustra's own internalization of the 'serious' values of the people (i.e. the dwarves in the first sense), and also in allusion to Wagner's narrative of the dwarf Alberich's curses – first of love and then of the possessor of the magic ring – that eventually brings about the downfall of heroes and gods alike.

earth

Erde. The stress N lays on 'earth' has the same meaning as the stress on 'this world'. Thus, earth means the whole of the real (including human beings), stripped of any metaphysical additions and values. Earth is opposed to that which is supposed to be transcendent to earth, superior to or 'above' earth. In comparison to these, the earth is traditionally slandered as something lowly, dirty (like the body: Z1.3), illusory (because characterized by matter and by change), perhaps dark and fallen. 'Earth', with its more direct connections to mythology, connotes these values much more readily than 'world'. Because of its alignment to reality and to life, the overhuman is the 'sense of the earth' (ZP3) and 'speaks from the heart of the earth' (Z2.18). Since earth is associated with matter (here understood in a metaphysical sense), N calls the 'atom' a 'earth-residue' at BGE12 – that is, the atom is the last hold-out of a metaphysical belief in material substance.

Sometimes, also, N uses 'the earth' as the proper country or nation (so to speak) of human beings, ignoring historically specific nations and peoples. Thus, the overhuman as the 'sense of the earth' means dominion over the whole earth. Because of its global reach, Christianity has been able to make the earth a 'madhouse' (GM2.22). Likewise, for example, N talks about free spirits taking on the task of the management 'of the earth as a whole' (H1.24–5, 472).

east

See *Asia*.

Ecce Homo

One of N's last works, written in 1888, but not published until 20 years later. It is an intellectual autobiography of infamous immodesty. Together with the prefaces N added to earlier books in 1887, EH gives us N's self-evaluation of the trajectory of his thought and the *conditions* under which this thought became possible. After the Preface, the book falls in two parts. The first (first two sections) concerns N's way of living (with a discussion of factors like *diet* and *climate*, and why these are important). Then, the next two sections provide a book-by-book commentary on his work, and then a summary of what he considers its greatest significance (namely 'the uncovering of Christian morality' (EHDestiny.7)).

economy

The literal meaning of the term in Greek is 'household', thus N's frequent use of the term '*Haushalt*'. Economy is one of N's most frequent concepts used to describe the interrelated, systematic nature of life (or, for example, the soul). It is suitable insofar as both are dynamic and relational. That is, for example, an economy must involve both those who buy and sell; analogously, the system of life will have to involve both active and passive, weak and strong moments of will to power. See for example BGE23, 40, TIMorality6.

education

Erziehung, Bildung. (The latter term, *Bildung*, has a wider meaning: *culture*, and thus the process of cultivation. However, it is frequently used as equivalent to *Erziehung*. We will discuss the distinctive meanings of *Bildung* in the entry on *culture*.) Education, and especially higher education, was a perennial theme for N. N wrote a series of lectures on 'The Future of our Educational Institutions' in 1872, and the third *Untimely Meditation* is much more concerned with the theme of education and culture than with Schopenhauer per se. Following reforms in the early nineteenth century, which were largely led by Humboldt, Prussia had one of the first 'modern' education systems in the world: publicly funded schools, teacher certification and further or higher education available based upon ability rather than class. Likewise, Humboldt had a major role in the creation of the modern university, enshrining principles like academic independence, general rather than vocational education, and the close relation between teaching and research.

On N's analysis, however, such reforms were counter-productive, being founded on a *Socratic* notion of science (BT15, 18) in which knowledge is understood as information rather than a way of living (BT20, D195, UM2.10), way of thinking (H1.265–6) or involving genuine insight (H2.181). The supposedly non-vocational system was, in fact, serving a different kind of vocation: creating servants of economy and state (Future1, H2.320), and simply reproducing or reinforcing the current system of values (UM2.10, H3.267,

BGE194). Moreover, without a cultivated grasp of German (Future2), a classical education is only 'a leap in the dark', and there is no possibility of a genuine or authentic culture. Education for culture is something different from education for economic social or political roles (Future4, and see PTAG1).

Modern education with its post-reform shape and universal franchise is an off-shoot of modern ideas of equality and democracy (Future3). Education, N argues, should be a privilege and not universal (Future1, 3), although this privilege should not be bound to class (Future4). Universities have become increasingly compartmentalized, with narrow specialization, a lack of vision and redundant experimentation (H1.242, TIGL3). Likewise, the *historical sense* pervades all education, including the teaching of language, taught as a dead object of study rather than a living practice, as 'living through' what one learns (PTAG1). In contrast, the philosopher must be self-educated after having passed through a variety of specializations, in order then to use them as instruments (H3.267, BGE211) – see *comprehensive*.

egoism (or selfishness)

On N's analysis, many moral systems make a basic distinction between egoistic (or selfish) motives or acts and those that are altruistic. Altruism refers to an act based entirely on concern for the welfare of others – thus, in certain moralities, it characterizes the highest of moral virtues, or indeed the basis of morality itself. N most often claims altruism is psychologically impossible (H1.133). That is, on a rough classification, N is a psychological egoist: all actions are motivated egoistically. Altruism, at best, is an ideal caused by suffering from a lack of love or care (1880.6.21, D147), a sacrifice of one aspect of the self for the egoism of another (H1.57, 455), to avoid a feeling of impotence (D133), or gain a feeling of power (D215), a desire for possession (1881.11.21), or an illusion propagated by those who see their self-interest in becoming a function of another, or of the whole (D516, GS119). At worst, it is a destructive and decadent ideal (see for example 1881.11.43). Indeed, altruism involves a contradiction: the moral demand for altruism for the sake of utility is, itself, not altruistic (GS21, 1883.17.81). The feeling for others, or for their state, by great humans is often misinterpreted as altruism (1884.25.335, 1887.9.156), when in fact it is an expression of power. Altruism is the key theme in N's occasional discussions of Spencer (e.g. TISkirmishes37).

N's argument is that the opposition between egoism and altruism is either a false distinction (i.e. there are only varieties of egoistic acts) or one which carries a negative value for life (i.e. an ideal of altruistic acts contributes to human weakness or degeneration). The removal of the distinction leads to a 'revaluation' of egoism (D148, GS328). The value of selfishness is measured by the value of the self, depending upon whether individuals represent 'the ascending or the descending line of life' (TISkirmishes33, 1884.25.287). There are, in other words, many types of selfishness or egoism which are 'despicable': see UM2.7, D105 (the 'phantom' ego), GS335 ('it is selfish to consider one's own judgement a universal law'), the 'tidal waves of selfishness' found in certain ages (BGE212), and likewise greed or lust (in unspiritualized senses). On the other hand, selfishness that is *noble* or aligned to life is a chief virtue for N, and the ground of much that one might want to call good: for example love and friendship (GS14), magnanimity (GS49, 55), likewise courage and trust (Z3.10).

There are two complications that should be added, however, to the above discussion. The first is that by selfishness in many such contexts N means selfishness with respect to an extended sense of self. For example, insofar as the *free spirit* has *comprehensive* responsibility for the human future, this future is an extension of his or her self (1887.9.7). N's favoured model for this is *pregnancy* – a mother's love and care for the offspring as an extension of her selfishness (D552, EHClever9). Similarly, N argues that future philosophers will understand that their 'destiny' is everything, and thus 'what do I matter?' (D547, see also Z2.22, BGE23). The second is that N has a conception of the ego as multiple; the simplicity or unity of the ego is yet another of the metaphysical or moral errors. As living beings, we comprise a social order of drives, all characterized by *will to power* (D115, 1885.40.21, BGE12, 16–17). Moreover, the notion of *will* here (the ego wills actions in its own interest) is no less mistaken (BGE19, TIErrors3). As a consequence, N is consistent in claiming that, strictly speaking, there are neither egoistic nor unegoistic acts (EHBooks5).

Emerson

Ralph Waldo Emerson was an influential American essayist and poet of the mid-nineteenth century. Nietzsche owned and repeatedly read many of Emerson's essays throughout his career, and references in his letters or notebooks are particularly frequent in the period from 1878 to 1884. The first edition of GS has a motto from Emerson concerning affirmation (but N removed it for the second edition). N was disenchanted with Emerson's later work. In Emerson, N finds a conception of the human relation to nature that is different from Schopenhauer, involving alignment to or identification with nature, and including a definite spiritual element: 'The happiest man is he who learns from nature the lesson of worship'. Emerson, in his description of the solitary and exceptional human who believes in his own thought, also gives N an element in the latter's concept of nobility or the overhuman. Other concepts with respect to which N feels some affinity with Emerson include the analysis of will and motive, the critique of consciousness as the core of human identity, the nature and importance of solitude, friendship, and the oversoul (in Emerson, a concept that is equal parts Neoplatonic and Vedanta).

empiricism

Empiricism is a type of epistemology that traces all knowledge back to data of the senses. Although the notion has strong roots in the ancient world, it is particularly associated with the British tradition of Locke and Hume, and French *positivism* in the nineteenth century. At first glance, N is an empiricist (see entry on *sensation*), complete with a scepticism akin to Hume's. However, there is also a strong neo-Kantian influence (see *Kant, Gerber, Spir*). Much of his epistemological analyses concern the cognitive processes that mediate or distort the data of the senses, and the interpretative 'errors' – most of which have moral values underpinning them – that make knowledge possible (see *truth*). In other words, on N's account there is no unmediated or simple access to the data of the senses, as would be required in a traditional empiricist epistemology.

enemy

See *friend*, *agon*.

energy

Energie. Although it is used primarily in N's favoured domains of individual or social psychology, the definition he seems to employ is broadly the accepted one within physics: energy is the ability to do work. It is a particularly common term in the period of H1. *Free spirits* tend to be relatively weak, by comparison with the energetic focus achieved by the unfree spirit (H1.228); so, how is it possible for the free spirit to have energy (H1.230) – to have what N in other contexts might call 'strength' and 'endurance'? The answers are given in subsequent sections: the struggle against unfavourable conditions (H1.231), or tapping into a cultural reserve of the 'accumulated energy of will' (H1.234–5). Within the social sphere, this notion of an 'accumulated' energy is important, and is associated with periods of *decadence* (see GS23, BGE212). In N's late notebooks, he employs the notion of energy frequently to explore aspects of *health* (relation to *exhaustion* at 1888.14.68; abrupt ability to defend or resist 1888.14.161, 211), and also the positive aspects of pessimism or *nihilism* (1887.9.123, 126). See also *power*.

Enlightenment

In the history of thought, the Enlightenment refers to eighteenth-century European thought, with an emphasis upon the use of a scientifically understood reason to solve political, philosophical, religious or moral problems, and a judicious scepticism in matters *metaphysical*. N originally dedicates H1 to Voltaire (it was published on the 100th anniversary of his death), but removes the dedication for the second edition. In N's middle period, then, he sees himself taking up the banner of Enlightenment ideas, especially to contrast the *romanticism* and nationalism of his own century. To be sure, he understands Enlightenment not as a single historical period, but as a broader tendency towards the overcoming of metaphysical and moral constraints. Moreover, even in H1, he argues that the Enlightenment was naïve about religious metaphysics (H1.26, 110), and that it had no inner relation to the French Revolution (H1.463). Later, Enlightenment is occasionally a name for N's own task (e.g. D197, GS5), however N's suspicions about the nature of science and reason have by then grown. This manifests itself particularly in the political sphere: N comes to see Enlightenment political ideals in their relationship to democracy (BGEP), and equality (BGE232).

Epicurus

Along with Heraclitus, Epicurus is the ancient Greek philosopher with whom N feels most affinity. Epicurus took the atomism of Democritus and extended it into an ethical philosophy that had great influence. Among the ideas which parallel, or influenced N are: (i) liberation from irrational fears (e.g. of the gods) leading to a sense of tranquillity as the aim of the good life (see for example H1.10, or the 'heroic-idyllic' at H3.295); in its extreme, this is a kind of self-hypnosis or deep sleep (GM3.17); (ii) similarly, liberation from desires that extend beyond one's capacity (see entry on *longing*). (iii) the ethical values of *friendship* and *solitude* (see *garden*); (iv) the gods are at least uninterested in human affairs, and indeed there is a hint in Epicurus that the *gods* are projections of human ethical values. In either case, it follows that the cosmos should be contemplated, but without fear, as chaotic and without purposes.

epigone

Someone who believes that all great striving or achievement is behind him or her. This is a feeling N ascribes to his contemporaries, victims of the *historical sense* (e.g. UM2.5).

equal/equality

Gleich. This concept is employed by N is several contexts. For example, just as he talks about strong or weak powers, he also explores the political implications of powers in equilibrium (see entry on *power*). However, N's primary use of equality is in discussing the moral/political notions associated with *democracy* or *class*.

error

See *truth*.

esprit

See *spirit*.

eternal recurrence

Ewige Wiederkunft, or similar expression. Eternal recurrence (or 'return') is among N's most famous and widely discussed concepts. Eternal recurrence makes its first appearance at the end of the first edition of GS (GS341), in 1882. However, N discusses related ideas earlier (UM2.2, 9) and also earlier in GS (GS285, 334). The concept plays a very important role in Z (at EHZ1, N claims it is the central thought of that book), and appears regularly in N's notebooks in 1885 and 1886. It gets a mention (albeit an important one) at BGE56. Thereafter, N gives less attention to the concept, although he does not disown it.

Generally speaking, there are two broad (and not mutually exclusive) ways of interpreting eternal recurrence. Either it is a metaphysical/cosmological claim concerning reality; or it is a test of – or element within – the highest affirmation of life. On the first of these interpretations, the whole of the real exhibits only so many possible combinations, which are interlinked and follow in a definite order. Thus in infinite time, the real must repeat itself in a vast 'year'. On each cycle, exactly the same entities and events occur. N discusses and attempts to demonstrate this cosmological view mainly in his notebooks (see 1884.26.284, 1885.36.15, 1886.35.54–5, 1886.5.6–7, 54, 1888.13.14 – most of these are collected together as the last chapter of *The Will to Power*). However, many of the presuppositions of the argument, such as a deterministic view of events, are also found in published writings. In published writings, N occasionally comes close to stating eternal recurrence in its cosmological sense (e.g. BGE56).

The second interpretation is more important, not least because on its own the first is irrelevant with respect to human *values* or behaviours. To affirm eternal recurrence means to exist in such a way as to celebrate eternal recurrence *as if* it were a cosmological truth, to *desire* its truth. Only that form of life that has (i) overcome *nihilism*, (ii) overcome also the temptation of *pity* for higher types that are incapable of further development, (iii) overcome likewise the *nausea* at the thought of the periods of history dominated by *ressentiment* or *degeneration*, and (iv) loves its fate (the notion of *amor fati*), would be able to affirm the eternal recurrence of all things. Nihilism must be overcome because the affirmation of eternal recurrence is an assigning of value, but one that is immanent, rather than founded upon some origin or *telos* (end or purpose). Pity must be overcome because to will eternal recurrence is also to will the destruction even of higher humans, and in general one must will the rule which is the triumph of the 'small'. Fate must be loved because the eternal recurrence demands a willing higher than just a reconciliation with or acceptance of fate (Z2.20, BGE56). That is, an *affirmation*, even a *longing* for (GS341). Moreover, affirmation of eternal recurrence is the love not only of the whole course of things, but specifically of my place within them. The love of fate must include gratitude towards the cruelty of accident and my own foolishnesses (i.e. the past must be redeemed), and desire for my own 'going under' (my self-overcoming so as to further the development of the human thereafter).

It might seem odd to talk about the development of the human in this context. That, though, is precisely the point: eternal recurrence demands that we free our thought from any false sense of purposes (i.e. from teleology) or origins. The 'year' has no beginning or end (or every moment is both beginning and end). What is important are moments of *beauty* and *perfection* in achievement, and moments of the feeling of the growth of *power*. The great human being *returns ascending*. Eternal recurrence is the affirmation of the moment, which is always in some sense the *kairos* (BGE274 – the right moment) and an opportunity to generate a future (the idea of a watershed, where things are delicately balanced and could go 'either way' – see Z4.1).

Likewise, it might seem odd to talk about eternal recurrence being some kind of test of one's health and affirmative strength, since my attitude towards eternal recurrence is among the things that recur. A first answer to this is that, again, this is part of the point: the love of fate is premised upon the notion that I must joyfully consider that which is no one's responsibility, not even my own, to be a product of my will. A second answer to this query requires that we distinguish between eternal recurrence as a view from outside of time (transcendent), and as a view from within (immanent). In Z3.2, when Zarathustra challenges that Spirit of Gravity, the latter jumps off and sits down on a rock – that is, sits by the *side of the path*, rather than on it. The dwarf is viewing eternal recurrence as if from the outside, and as if it did not contain the dwarf himself. That is, the dwarf is trying to think the whole thing as *merely* a cosmological truth claim. Viewed from the inside, eternal recurrence is not really about the deterministic repetition of things and events and associated metaphysical ideas. Rather, the thought pertains only to total affirmation of the moment. Accordingly, Z3 culminates in the various symbols of circularity becoming a wedding ring, symbolizing not a moving cycle so much as a bond of love (Z3.16). To be sure, in explicating the thought of eternal recurrence, it may be necessary to talk about circles of time, endless repetitions and so forth. Perhaps, however, this is necessary only as a first stage, and is not the core of the thought.

eternity

Ewigheit. In Christian thought, and in much of European metaphysics, 'eternity' is a transcendent feature of the divine with respect to the created, or of the genuinely real with respect to mere appearance. It means either timeless, or time itself without end. In either case, eternity relies upon an opposition to the transient, *becoming* character of appearances and the finite character of human lives. See for example Plato, *Timaeus* 37c where 'time' is the 'image of eternity'; *Republic* 608c; *John* 6:40 on 'eternal life'; and finally also see Kant's *The Critique of Pure Reason* where the form of time is unchanging but is not itself an object of experience (e.g. B224–5). N, however, rejects the distinction between apparent being and real being. Without a transcendent 'eternal' being, eternity is asserted to be a feature of the *same reality* as transience. Nor are these two 'features' of the real reliant upon two entirely different ways of thinking – for example Spinoza's *sub specie aeternitatis*, which is reality as viewed from eternity (i.e. as apprehended by God). Rather, N's idea is that becoming and eternity are not incompatible, such that we would need some transcendent viewpoint to reconcile them. Moments of still beauty and perfection like Z3.3 and Z4.10 are not illusions; rather, the world in its eternity is also profoundly tranquil (and see TISkirmishes49). Likewise, in contrast to Goethe's 'eternal feminine', N's eternity is characterized by the repetition or *cycle* of types of becoming (see TIAncients4), and in particular an alternation of destruction and creation.

'Repetition', as used above, is obviously a different, wider notion than 'recurrence'. Thus, although sometimes N seems to employ it to refer to eternal recurrence primarily, 'eternity' is likewise a wider concept. Metaphorically, at Z3.16, eternity is the object of longing, while recurrence is the 'nuptial ring'. Thus, I affirm the whole of what is and was, and my position within that whole, but that which seals this bond – demonstrating the profundity of my affirmation – is eternal recurrence. See also *Dionysus, wholeness, amor fati*.

Euripides

The last of the three great Greek tragedians, and the one whose changes to the form, style and content of tragedy N believed was the actual suicide of the art. He sees Euripides as heavily influenced by *Socratism*, and simply unable to understand tragedy as previously pursued by *Aeschylus* and *Sophocles*. In particular, according to N, Euripides made tragedy naturalistic (eliminating its symbolic power), and *optimistic* (knowledge and understanding of events is possible through *reason*) – see BT11–12.

Europe, Europeans

Very roughly speaking, the orbit of N's historical thought is the European continent. In several contexts, N evidently believes that there is sense in talking about Europe as a single entity, and the European as a single type (e.g. H3.215). (Also, for most purposes, the United States is considered to be an extension of Europe.) This is because of a shared set of language precursors as well as human sub-races, the cultural inheritance (e.g. in political institutions, modes of art or literature, etc.) of ancient Greece and Rome, and the broad Christianization of Europe (the influence of the 'ascetic priest' discussed at GM3.21). Other regions of human geography – India, Russia, China or Africa – are present in his writings either to talk about cultural cross-fertilization (thus also the figures of Zarathustra and Alexander), or for comparisons (Buddhism, or the Hindu caste system). So, when N discusses the history of the human, he is thinking mainly of Europe.

However, N does extensively treat of individual European nations or cultures – the distinction between South and North is common, as are character studies of the Germans, French, English, Italians and of course the Jews. From a European perspective, these are to be understood as the inevitable variety within the European type. This variation presents dangers – N is particularly concerned with the domination (whether political, military or cultural) by one variety. However, it also presents opportunities, with each variety contributing some piece of the overall puzzle that is an anticipated higher form of the European type (see for example H1.475, D272). On this basis, some individual figures are presented as 'European events' rather than national ones (GS357, TISkirmishes21). The 'Good European' is a familiar refrain in N. By this he means those who are unconcerned with national rivalries and, being 'heirs to Europe's longest and most courageous self-overcoming' (GS357, 377), take upon themselves the task of preparing for a European future. These ideas are the overarching theme of chapter 8 of BGE, entitled 'Peoples and Fatherlands' (see especially BGE256). N even speaks of a kind of quasi-political organization of the Good Europeans, across nations (D96).

evil

See *Good*.

evolution

N stands among a long line of philosophers and natural scientists who discuss in what way, and by way of what mechanisms, living creatures have developed. Hegel (see H1.238) and Schopenhauer – both of whom treat of the history of organic forms and the emergence of consciousness – are particularly important for N. Likewise, N was broadly familiar with the work of Charles Darwin and the British thinkers influenced by him such as Spencer. If any of these versions of human development is true, then many important consequences would follow: there was no (or no single) act of divine creation and in particular man is not made in the image of God; moreover the basic structures of cognition are not a priori (as per for example Kant); and it will be impossible to project backwards, anachronistically, onto history or prehistory the beliefs and values held today.

N's particular focus is the evolution of human *instincts* pertaining to cognition (i.e. how the world and knowledge are constituted) and morality (i.e. valuing of certain aspects of the human, culture or world). This development he ascribes both to a prehistorical period, and to the operations of culture within the historical period. Because cultural forces (beliefs, laws, practices, institutions) affect the body and the body's affects and health, the development of the human continues to be conditioned by cultural means. Thus it is not an entirely metaphorical usage when N claims that 'The scientific man is the further evolution of the artistic' (H1.222). For the most part, the development of the human has been a matter of accident. What modernity presents to us is an opportunity to take conscious control of the evolution of the human (UM3.6, H1.24, and see entry on *responsibility*). Although he was happy to use the term evolution, N refuses to be identified with Darwin (EHBooks1). Among the mechanisms N describes in his account of human development are *ressentiment, internalization, sublimation, form creation, incorporation* and *degeneration*.

Most of N's knowledge of Darwinism is second-hand, through German philosophers of biology. N objects to the Darwinian account on at least four points. (i) He argues that self-preservation (or adaptation) is not the dominant or most common of instincts; the basic will of all life is to express its power and form its environment thereby; (ii) that life is not characterized by scarcity but by plenitude, and that therefore struggle for survival is not the rule; (iii) the 'weak' have more spirit (are more clever, more similar, cooperative) and thus are more likely to survive; (iv) that each stage of evolutionary development comprises its own unique value (of 'happiness'), and thus one cannot get from evolution to the idea of *progress* (one or more of these is found at H1.224, D108, BGE13, GM2.12, TISkirmishes14).

exception

Ausnahme. The basic contrast here is between the rule – human beings whose values, beliefs and other qualities are broadly average or shared (the herd) – and the exceptions – those who have different values, greater will to power, etc. Those who are *noble* are exceptions (e.g. GS3). The exceptions are thus more significant for the health and development of a culture and, although in themselves representatives of strength, are in need of defending against the rule (GS76). However, philosophically, the rule is of greater interest (H2.362, D442, BGE26). This may be because there is little to be learned from exceptions – each being a singular instance – and thus insight into human beings, their drives, and the mechanisms of development or expression of those drives, are only to be found in the rule. The exception will 'overflow' in communication, and rather than slander the rule, will become the 'advocate of the rule' (GS55, 1887.10.175) – this is what N elsewhere calls *magnanimity*, and at an even higher stage, *amor fati*. If the exception defines himself against the group, then he or she is only an *individual* – a higher stage is reached insofar as exceptions find each other, work out a system of justice or mutual respect, and become a 'group' (e.g. 1887.10.82; see *genius*).

exhaustion, tiredness

Exhaustion is a characterization of a society (or perhaps an individual) that no longer has the capacity to create new forms. The idea is closely related to *decadence*. N observes that his great predecessors have come to a stop, ignobly, out of weariness (D575 – he likely has the aged Wagner in mind). More generally, beneath morality and highest values is the 'great exhaustion' (WCP). Its corresponding pleasure is sleep (Z1.2). Where this pleasure is generalized, asserted to be the only pleasure, then the result are the 'nihilistic religions and philosophies'. '[A]ll great religions' fight against the symptoms of tiredness and heaviness (GM3.17), employing stimulants to avoid a people grinding entirely to a halt – or, equally, to avoid them acting on just any accidental stimulus (1888.7.16). The wisest, exhausted from life, conclude pessimistically that life is without value; they are thus 'types of decline' (TISocrates1–2). Exhausted people or peoples choose things that harm them; including nervous stimulants (WC5, 1888.14.68). A legal system conceived of as a means of bringing struggle to an end would be a 'sign of weariness' (GM2.11). Scepticism is symptom of exhaustion from the clash of values and instincts created by cross-breeding (BGE20). Even for the free spirit, this is a danger: at GM1.12, N says that we are 'tired of man', of the sight of a culture going downhill, where 'nothing wishes to become greater'. The consequence of tiredness would again be *nihilism*. For a contrasting use of 'tiredness', see *repose*.

experience

Erfahrung, Erlebnis. Experience is the most familiar term for our encounters with the world around us, and with our own 'inner' world. Philosophical issues tend to centre upon how such experience relates to knowledge, and upon the conditions or processes by which experience comes to be. For N's analyses, see especially the entries on *value, perspective, sensation, Kant.* N's most distinctive use of the concept concerns the importance of first-hand experience for questions of rank – that is for the most important questions of value. Clear examples are found at BGE204 or GM3.24 ('does he know the Minotaur of this cave *from experience?*'). Similarly, he writes of Z 'to understand six sentences from it – that is to have *experienced* six sentences' would mean the transformation of the reader (EHBooks1). The point is a distinction between an understanding that operates at the level of concepts and words, and an understanding that is operating at the level of drives, the body and ways of life, and the transformation of these. This is a critique, then, of *abstraction.* See also UM2.10, H3.297–8.

experiment or attempt

Versuchen, Experiment. Versuchen means to try something, make an attempt at something – and also to tempt or be tempted. (Note that in German there is no common etymology to 'experiment' and 'experience', although for N the concepts are connected.) The nature of experimentation, and of the experimental method, is a key theme in the philosophy of science; N has very little interest in this (but see H1.242, TIGL3). Rather, N's experiments are (i) whether it is possible to live without some or all of those *metaphysical* errors that were originally a condition of the preservation of life, (ii) likewise, whether it is possible to live according to new beliefs or values and (iii) what new forms of life (habits, institutions, virtues) this might require. These questions cannot be addressed in advance or in the abstract; we must make an experiment out of ourselves. This is an important idea, especially from D onwards. Indeed, N even proposes 'experimenters' as a name for the free spirits or new philosophers (BGE42, Z3.2). For discussions, please see D432, GS7, 110 ('To what extent can truth stand to be incorporated . . . that is the experiment'), 324, Z1.22.2 ('experimenting with knowing, [the body] elevates itself'), BGE210, GM2.24, 3.24, AC57.

explosive

N was fond of the metaphor of explosion. In part, this is because of its association with war or with revolutionary activity. An explosive destroys an existing order, so as to make possible a new order; thus the association with nihilism and anarchism, but perhaps it serves some other creative purpose (BGE208, EHDestiny1). N employs the metaphor with respect to Schopenhauer at UM3.3 – but with associated imagery that anticipates the figure of Zarathustra. Less obvious but probably more important is the distinction between the explosive and the trigger. That is, between an enormous quantity of stored-up energy – usually some cultural energy that has been repressed for decades or centuries, but which lacks direction – and the trigger that is of incidental magnitude but gives the former direction, timing and sudden release (GS360). Other key examples would be BGE262, GM3.15 (the priest changes the direction of *ressentiment*), TIAncients3 (institutions protect against 'inner *explosives*'), TISkirmishes44 ('Great humans are like the dynamite of great ages', but it is an 'accidental stimulus' that brings them about), and EHDestiny1.

faith

See *Belief.*

fate/destiny

Schicksal. N argues that belief in fate is not optional (H2.363), for science in the broad sense demands it. Thus, the real question is how one responds to that belief. Is it with resignation, or with honesty and magnanimity? The response too is fate ('the soil upon which the seed has been scattered'). The former response sees fate as an escape (no one is in any way responsible) or a kind of pessimism (nothing matters and there is nothing to be done). Such a response is 'fatalism'. The latter response, however, is akin to *amor fati*: to love fate means both to have profound gratitude towards one's own conditions of existence (the past and present), to see oneself as a creative channel through which the future comes to be, and thus to accept responsibility towards the future. The different responses to fate are discussed also at H3.61 ('in you the whole future of the world of man is predetermined'), and see also the 'fatefulness' of the philosopher at BGE292. Wotan accepts the gods' fate in a similar manner: 'What once I resolved despairingly, torn by wild pain, now happily and joyfully I will bring to pass' (*Siegfried* 3.1). Significantly, N's concept of fate is not that of a 'mechanical' system of causes and effects, according to laws of nature (a common eighteenth- and nineteenth-century model) – see *causality.* Nor is it a fatalism in which the world is held under the *purposes* of its creator (i.e. God's plan).

At GM2.14, N treats of earlier conceptions of the notion of punishment which did without responsibility, and saw the criminal as a 'piece of fate'. The same expression is used about the individual at TIMorality6. The point is that responsibility in the sense of *free* will is an error, and the modern notion of criminal justice and punishment is built upon that error. Responsibility, however, in the sense described above – the future as, in some sense, 'one's work' – is both less of a metaphysical nonsense, and also a higher or *nobler* attitude. See, however, EHWise6 (and GM3.17) on what N there calls 'Russian fatalism', as a medicine for those who are spiritually sick, in order to avoid the reactive response of *ressentiment*.

fear

Furcht. Fear plays an important role in N's analysis of the development of culture. At GS355, N argues that what is taken to be knowledge is always a making familiar, and is a response to an 'instinct of fear'. Likewise at BGE201, N speculates that fear is the 'mother' of morality. Again, fear in religion is the preparatory ground of Christianity (BGE49), while fear of being insufficiently obedient to the ancestors raises them to gods (GM2.19); similarly with metaphysics (1888.18.16). D551 suggests that while fear was an essential ingredient within our primitive reverence towards nature and the gods, now our greater understanding has led us to lose that fear. However, the result of this lack of fear is a kind of diminishment of the dignity of the human. (This passage is likely a rebuttal to the tranquillity described by Epicurus.)

To this fear, N contrasts the Greek religion of gratitude (BGE49), and likewise the courage of those who have throughout the history of culture advanced it (this is Zarathustra's response to the 'conscientious of spirit' at Z4.15). N calls for a new courage that does not simply react to the fearful, or aspire to indifference. The fifth book of GS is entitled 'We Fearless Ones', and its first aphorism (343) argues that we are not afraid of the consequences of nihilistic modernity, because we have found a 'new happiness'. In contrast to Aristotle, who argued that pity and fear were the two emotions roused by tragedy, N discusses the 'fearlessness' of the tragic artist, who must be understood as celebratory (TISkirmishes24; it is worth comparing this passage to the account of Prometheus at BT9). See *experiment, danger*.

feeling

See *affect*.

feminine and masculine, women and men

N's writings on the subject of gender fall somewhat awkwardly into two sets. The first are the frequent well-known passages on biological gender (i.e. women and men), and psychological or sociological gender roles. All of N's books from H to BGE contain a sustained series of passages or aphorisms devoted to women (and, by extension, men). N's views often cross well into sexism or misogyny. In this, N is no doubt at least in part a product of his era – and in the first half of Z motivated also by the breakdown of his relationship with Lou Salomé. The second set of writings concern femininity or masculinity understood as symbols of differing drives, psychological states, cultures or peoples and ideals. The biological distinction is not the same as the symbolic one, although to be sure feminine and masculine do correspond roughly to a conservative nineteenth-century view of women and men. Thus, the difference between these two sets of writings is an 'awkward' one because, first of all, N does not himself draw it explicitly or follow it rigorously, and also because there is a considerable amount of conceptual cross-over from the one to the other.

The concept of the feminine in N has many sources; these three are the most prominent: Greek mythology and its interpretation; Plato's *Symposium* (for which, see *beauty*); and Goethe's *Faust*. In the Greek creation myth, as recounted by Hesiod, Gaia is the Earth, a female divinity who emerged into being just after Chaos. She produced, without a mate, Uranus (the heavens) as well as mountains and the sea. With Uranus as their father, she also gave birth to the race of gods. The myth of Demeter and Persephone is also a mother-divinity narrative. Accordingly, when Goethe (in *Faust*) and N (in BT16, 20) speak of the 'mothers of being' it is to this kind of mythological framework that they allude. Bachofen published in 1861 a famous and influential book of anthropology that argued that the earliest human societies were matriarchal, with divinities such as Gaia or Demeter, before being erased from history by patriarchal societies with divinities such as Dionysus and ultimately Apollo. N may not have accepted this account, but he was certainly engaged with its themes: the role of gender (both literally and symbolically) in the development of cultures and nations (a few early instances: 1870.7.31; 1871.9.6, 10.1, 16.3). In N's early notebooks, the figure of the Sphinx represents something like Bachofen's earlier stage superseded by science in the form of Oedipus answering the riddle (1870.7.22). Likewise at 1870.7.27, the sphinx is beauty, concealing the destructive truth. Notice that at BT9, N contrasts Semitic and Aryan myths as 'feminine' and 'masculine'. At BT21, N describes Apollo as a deity of the formation of States and the 'male lust for struggle'. Apollonian beauty is both feminine sphinx *and* masculine state-formation; the Dionysian both the ecstatic voice of the mothers of being *and* also male science penetrating illusion to its depths. In the early N, then, there is an attempt but one never fully worked out to integrate meditations of the Bachofen type with N's metaphysics, borrowed from Schopenhauer. In later work, N arrives at a solution.

Goethe's long dramatic poem *Faust* is another key influence on the early N's understanding of the concepts feminine and masculine. Faust is a figure of endless striving and thus also endless longing. However, by the end of Part Two of *Faust*, this striving is (primarily) directed to the happiness and well-being of others (as it was at the beginning, when Faust worked to cure a plague). Importantly his task at the end of the drama is a huge building project to reclaim fertile land from the sea – this is, as he says, the reconciliation of the feminine Earth with itself. This is *hubris*, to be sure, but nevertheless a worthy effort to achieve some kind of balance. Faust's masculine striving is in itself empty; it is the feminine that gives it direction, value and productivity. When Faust achieves a moment of still, contemplative happiness – he stops striving – he dies. Mephistopheles tries to claim him, but Faust is saved by angels. These last scenes are ironic, in the sense that Goethe is using a Medieval Christian theological language to say something about non-Christian spiritual forces in nature. Faust's salvation is the feminine, personified by *Mater Gloriosa* (the Virgin Mary, the 'Mother of God'). The eternal feminine is divine, but is not simply something transcendent to the world (for it is anticipated in the physical working of the Earth, and in the name Euphorion for Faust and Helen's child). The whole work ends with the famous stanza: All that is transient/is only allegory;/The uncompletable/Here it becomes event;/The indescribable/Here it is done;/The eternal feminine/Draws us up.

Goethe does not write this in a Platonic mind-set that all transient things are simply illusions, but rather are *allegories*. Faust's efforts to link masculine and feminine, albeit flawed (i.e. incomplete or tainted), nevertheless have spiritual meaning and value – and thus his salvation. See the entry on *allegory*. N refers to these lines often, but usually with at least a touch of scorn. This is because he sees the nineteenth century interpreting them mistakenly as the perfect excuse for the abandonment of masculine virtues in favour of an idealized feminine (e.g. DP4).

N employs the concepts of masculine and feminine as symbols for a wide range of topics, from human behaviours through to cultural acts or achievements (e.g. science, the state or music). To summarize the discussion of mythology, Plato and Goethe above, the feminine is the symbol of fertility, but in its protecting and preserving side (GS24 is particularly clear). That is, what in BT was the function of Apollonian beauty is a key characteristic of the feminine. The feminine can be activity and even heroic (see 1870.7.122, 1871.16.3 and H1.259), but is not directed outwards towards incorporation, but inwards towards consolidation. Thus, and not surprisingly, N describes the feminine type of genius (genuine creativity, great contributions to culture) with the metaphor *pregnancy* (BGE248); Greece and France, he says, were feminine cultures in this sense (at least with respect to other cultures; internally, Greece would be more 'masculine' – see H1.259). Likewise, the feminine is the symbol of something relatively constant and unchanging (Goethe's 'eternal', but also this is related to the preserving function). Accordingly, the feminine is associated with a kind of idealism, a rejection of the senses. The feminine beautiful is also something that seduces, creates longing – thus the many instances in N of tropes such as truth is a woman, a goddess, a beautiful girl, etc. (UM3.8, H1.257, GS339 and the famous opening of BGEP). 'Life' and 'Wild Wisdom' are figured as women in Zarathustra (Z2.10). However, in accordance with the analysis given by Plato, what is longed for here is not the beautiful itself but rather what could be attained *by way of* beauty. That attainment is, in both a sexual and spiritual sense, *children* (e.g. UM3.8). Finally, the feminine is the symbol of something valuable that has itself been attained – it is like a quiet plateau reached after a struggle, a deserved repose.

Morality and especially modern ideas concerning morality (democratic, socialist or utilitarian ideas and of course gender equality) are feminine. Such modern ideas seek the preservation or diminishment of the current state of the human and, specifically, certain weak or diseased segments of a society. Indeed, N's definition of 'feminism' ('*Femininismus*', for example GM3.19, EHBooks3) is precisely the feminine viewed as exclusive and a 'closed door' to 'daring knowledge'. N's objection to such 'feminism' is not an objection to the feminine, but to its being *exclusively* feminine, and thus 'weak' (in fact, symbolically infertile). This is akin to romanticism (GS371, BTP7). GS24 provides a similar account – N's critique of the 'as it were feminine' lies in its attempt to narcotize the masculine out of existence, as (he claims) in China.

In contrast, the masculine is associated with precisely struggle and war, or the desire to conquer and rule. Thus, for example, Napoleon ushered in a warlike, masculine era of European history (GS362). Accordingly, the masculine form of genius is that which seeks out and impregnates, 'in love and lusting after foreign races': N's examples are the Jews, Romans and (perhaps) Germans (BGE248). Moreover, the masculine involves destruction, including the risk of self-destruction. Finally, the masculine is connected to laws, constraints and discipline (e.g. training leading to improvement through narrow application of rules). These qualities are characteristic of the disposition to, and method of, the sciences (GS293); while music imitating but inferior to Wagner risks losing altogether the discipline of rhythm (H2.147, and see H2P3). At TIGermans1, N claims that the Germans possess the most masculine virtues in Europe, and yet this does not amount to noble taste or high culture; instead, power makes 'stupid'. There is a similar passage at BGE241 where N distinguishes between strength and 'greatness' in political action. Both of these are in their ways commentaries on the 'lion' stage of Z1.1 and also Z2.13. In the later passage the sublime hero of critique is restless, unproductive. For him 'the beautiful is of all things the most difficult'.

What is most important about these two symbols, however, is their interaction and indeed reciprocity. The feminine without the masculine is simply 'weak'; the masculine without the feminine is simply 'strong'. Neither on its own is productive or healthy (although see TISkirmishes38). In his early work, N employed the Apollonian and Dionysian as 'brother' drives that accounted for cultural change; later, because of his rejection of Schopenhauer's metaphysics, and his development of concepts like will to power, this account is modified. The concepts of feminine and masculine come to replace the Apollonian and Dionysian. The necessary dynamic between them can occur in the form of an *cycle*, which is how N views European history at GS24. This alternation is an important aspect of the rhythm of the narrative in Zarathustra. So, for example, the violent scenes of Z3.2 are followed by the meditative peacefulness of Z3.3. The latter ends with 'Happiness, however, is a woman.' A similar cycling occurs between Z4.2–9 and Z4.10. In both cases, notice that Zarathustra welcomes the calm happiness, but then also has to urge himself to reject it as an end in itself, and move on. The feminine–masculine dynamic can also be a synthesis: arguably, this is the meaning of the 'child' stage at Z1.1, or the transformation of the hero at the end of Z2.13. Again, the concept of the *agon* although certainly linked to war or conflict more generally cannot be simply masculine, since it demands the preservation of the enemy and thus of competition. N chooses the term *Versucher* as one of his key new names for future philosophers (e.g. BGE42). The word means both the one who tempts and also the one who *experiments*. This word is significant because it combines both the feminine (beauty, seduction) and the masculine (change, exploration). Dionysus is thus the experimenting/tempting god at BGE295 (and see EHBooks6): the ideal of a mode of life that integrates feminine and masculine principles.

N's views on women will appear to today's political and social consciousness as sexist (i.e. drawing moral or political conclusions based upon gender), occasionally even misogynist. Here, N is repeating the views of his era – indeed, of conservatives of his era. However, he is not doing so simply unreflectively. That is to say, more important and perhaps disturbing than his conclusions are the principles that seem to lead him there. These principles are the concepts of feminine and masculine discussed above. When these concepts are projected onto female or male human beings, the result is N's analysis of women and men. Thus, for example, the nature of feminine beauty as concerned with surface leads N to argue that women are incapable of science (BGE232). Again, the virtues required for preservation mean that women are clever and men stupid (H1.411, H3.273, EHBooks5). Finally, the feminine–masculine distinction is evident in N's account of women as an image of what has been attained in the human, and men as an image of the struggles in the past and which await in the future (H1.274).

One of the models for how to understand the respective natures of women and men, and their roles, is ancient Greece. Greek society represented for N a healthy balance between the feminine and masculine types of human life and culture; this balance found its way in to the social roles of women and men (H1.259, 1870.10.1). N thus argues that Plato's proposals in the *Republic* concerning marriage arrangements and the removal of children from their mothers are not bizarrely at odds with existing Greek culture, but just a kind of radicalization of it. The treatment of women in Greece, N argues, is *one* successful solution to the problem of the synthesis of feminine and masculine so as to create a healthy, dynamic culture, one that releases rather than inhibits the possibilities of the human. N's reflections on women and men in contemporary Europe begin from the need to discover a similarly successful solution (H1.424, Z1.18). These reflections concern especially the institutions of marriage and education. Any 'solution' to this cultural problem has to contend with what N at GS68 calls the 'corruption' of women by men, who create an image for women who in turn are doomed to follow it: woman as 'soul and form' (GS59), women as calmness (GS60), women as 'masters' (GS70). The masculine drive results in a denaturing of the feminine and, with it, women (GS361, BGE232, TIArrows13, Z2.10: 'you men always confer on us your own virtues'). One of N's accusations against his contemporary culture is a kind of inversion of this: so unmasculine are men that women have had to take their place (Z3.5.2, BGE239). Importantly, N would likely accept the charge of sexism, but reject misogyny. Our assumption that his descriptions of women are descriptions of something 'inferior' are, he might argue, the result of the projection of masculine values. The genuine subordination of women is their application to themselves of those beliefs that the masculine projects upon them (see for example EHBooks5).

On the other hand, if we believe that N's views about women and men are a grotesque mistake, then (working backwards) we must either reject the legitimacy of the concepts of the masculine and feminine, or we can reject the assumption that they necessarily inform biological gender. The former solution is, in effect, a rejection of N's philosophy because it involves rejecting his account of life in terms of competing drives and alternating states. The latter solution transforms N's observations from the biologically determined into a psychological or social analysis of cultural beliefs – that is the question is no longer what women and men *are*, but what they are believed to be (where those beliefs might also be embodied in institutions and everyday practices). Here, liberation is not a return to an essence, but rather a removal of limiting or degrading cultural constraints.

fertility (or fruitfulness, fecundity, etc.)

N employs a whole range of symbols that cluster around the idea of fertility. These serve to designate the manner in which the present has a future (often by way of the additional metaphor of *pregnancy* or procreation: Z4.13.2, TISkirmishes22, Ancients4) or the way in which an individual or group has the power to create new values (GM3.8, WC1). Conversely, the absence of these possibilities is symbolized by infertility or impotence (Z2.14, GM3.12). See also *feminine and masculine*.

festival

Fest. Broadly speaking, a festival is a celebratory occasion, held in the honour or reverent memory of something – a god or saint, perhaps, or an event (e.g. the arrival of spring). N takes it that festival is the event at which the underlying drives or *instincts* are most clearly displayed and in the highest way satisfied. Thus, he talks about Dionysian festivals at BT2, and the condemnation of lyric found at the Apollonian festivals (BT6). Religious festivals, then, are indirect ways of praising the humanity of the participants. Similarly, the 'festival of the ass' that Zarathustra's guests create (Z4.17–18) is a mockery of religious worship, but a celebration of the human capacity to be cheerful and even foolish. Zarathustra says, celebrate this festival 'for love of yourselves' and do it also 'in remembrance of me' (an echo of Lk. 22.19). A second important feature of festivals is genuine joy – joy in these drives and their expression, joy in being the people of this god, etc. Even the solemnity of some festivals is part of the 'happiness of Homer' (GS302). So, the 'consummating death' should be a matter of festival (Z1.21) – that is, the celebration of a life as a 'promise' to the future. The joy in passion is emphasized at H2.187 and 220.

This is incomprehensible to Christianity and its hatred of passion. More generally, modernity is characterized by its inability to understand the festival. At GS89, N writes 'What does all our art of making art matter, if we lose that higher art, the art of festivals!' The idea is that art is no longer a celebration of 'high and happy' moments, but rather merely a narcotic to help those who are sick or weak. (See the account of art and music festivals at UM1.3, and 3.4.) Likewise, Zarathustra finds play-actors at Christian festivals, where love of the neighbour is merely apparent (Z1.15 – compare GS353). In contrast, Zarathustra insists that the 'neighbour' be replaced by the *friend* who is a 'festival of the earth' (Z1.15).

A third feature of festival, which dates back to N's early treatment of tragic festivals and the Dionysian, is *cruelty*. At AC25, N argues that for the Israelites 'Yahweh expressed a consciousness of power'; therefore, their festivals were in gratitude for a 'magnificent elevation' over their difficulties or their enemies. Likewise, punishment represents a festival of cruel triumph, 'mocking and doing violence to a finally defeated enemy' (GM2.13 and see GM2.6–7). See *happiness*.

flee

See *solitude*.

food

See *diet*.

fool, foolishness, buffoon

Usually *Narr*. N uses the term in a quite conventional manner up in the early and middle writings, indicating something unequivocally stupid or wrong (e.g. 'only a fool would think that' at D103 or GS36; similarly, in later work at Z3.7, TISkirmishes40). There are a few instances earlier of a positive or finessed use, but these are rare: for example, the Shadow is called 'dear fool' (H3Dialogue), part of the value of art today is foolishness (D531), or the ambiguous dialogue between sage and fool staged at GS213.

It is in Z, though, that the fool becomes an important image in N. The historical sources of this new meaning are: the close relationship between tragedy and comedy (offered as a set at the Greek festivals), the generally comedic role of Vice in medieval mystery plays, the court jester in European history, and some of the important stock characters in Commedia dell'Arte and in Shakespeare. The fool is in fact the *wise* one, but seen from the perspective of those who are uncomprehending, ill or decadent (thus ZP5, Z1.9, Z1.18, or the poem 'To Goethe' at the end of GS). The opposition between fool and wise man is high on the list of false oppositions (Z3.12.20, Z4.19.10). The fool is thus seen as a bungler even in his or her writing (Z3.11.1, and the poem 'Fool in Despair' at the end of GS). This foolish perspective is made explicit at BGE2 and 30. Moreover, the philosopher is a product of this perspective, and so will feel him or herself to be a fool (BGE212). The new philosopher has to embrace and pursue this foolishness, despite his or her bad conscience (thus the anguish of 'only fool! only poet!' in the poem at Z4.11, and see GM2.16). The jester in ZP embodies something of this conscience, so Zarathustra is 'between fool and corpse' (ZP7). Foolishness is associated with poetry, and more generally with those states or modes of life that express health but in a manner distinct from philosophical seriousness and striving (Z4.6, 11). In Z2 and Z3, 'fool' is also used to describe Zarathustra's childishly innocent happiness (Z2.1) or his over-fondness for human beings (Z3.1, Z3.9). Thus, the fool (or foolishness) represents a kind of strategy or mask (or at any rate an indulgence) of Zarathustra when he is among others (see also BGE270).

force

See *energy, power*.

forget

Most often *vergessen*. The philosophical concept of forgetting plays an important role in N, especially in the early period. Let us list three key instances. First, part of the process of the formation of *concepts*, and the forging of things taken to be *truths*, must be a forgetting of their origins ('On Truth and Lies'). Other philosophers, such as Hume or Kant, stress the remembering of multiple instances of something, in order to construct an association independent of varying circumstances (see 1872.19.161). N stresses the forgetting of specificities and of metaphorical transformations. N similarly toys with Plato's concept of *anamnesis* (recollection). While for Plato we remember our acquaintance with the forms, and thus remember true knowledge, in N we should remember the artifice in the formation of knowledge, and thus become aware of the ubiquity of metaphysical errors (GS286). When philosophers work with concepts, it is indeed a recollection, but normally of some other part of the system of errors, without recognizing them as errors (BGE20).

Second, forgetting has a significant part to play in the formation of moral codes. So, at H3.40, N argues that, for a given people, those actions for which the original utilitarian motives are forgotten and replaced either by fear or by *habit*, are now called morality. We obey them because they exist as customs, not because of any awareness of their utility. This is a good example of a typical idea of N's, namely that concepts or values undergo surreptitious transformations or discontinuities (see *morality, history*).

Third, UM2 famously begins by arguing that forgetting is essential, because to remember everything is either impossible or disabling. The theme of UM2, then, is: how does one decide what to forget? That is to say, which strategies for forgetting serve the health and growth of *culture* (see also *festival*).This point is made again, much later, at GM2.1: active forgetfulness is part of the *health* of an organism, a shutting of 'doors and windows of consciousness', without which the *noble* and far-sighted functions of that organism would be disabled. Accordingly, forgetting is also part of the concept of *solitude* or of rest and *repose* (BGE269, EHHuman4, and compare Byron's *Manfred*, which N greatly admired). GM2 continues, again on analogy with UM2, with the development of a particular type of not-forgetting: namely, being able to promise. This new capacity ultimately leads to the 'sovereign individual' and the concept of conscience. At ZP4, Zarathustra describes someone whose soul is 'overfull' and who thus 'forgets himself'. The idea here is the development of a different type of *egoism*, which claims fate and future as its own, and forgets both its earlier, individual ego, and also its 'degrading selflessness' (EHHuman4). N returns to this concept at GM1.10, claiming it to be a characteristic of the noble type.

form, structure

The concept of form is used by N in two connected ways: (i) N investigates the nature and role of cognitive forms, as well as the forms ascribed to nature. The key reference points are Plato (the theory of forms or ideas) and Kant (space and time as forms of intuition; the categories as something like the forms of thought). So, for example, N's account of the concept of number in distinction from Plato and Pythagoras; or of concepts like substance or cause and effect as 'forms' falsifying experiences. (See also the wide-ranging meditations on form at 1872.19.140–53. The key metaphor there is the *mirror*.) These errors are conditions of the survival of human life, but have a more complex relationship to its health and development. The will to the imposition of form, even to the point of a kind of deliberate forgetfulness or stupidity, is a basic characteristic of *will to power* (BGE230). However, the will to the multiplicity of form is something different, N argues, and may be preparatory to the creation of new form (i.e. new values – see Z1.1). In other words, while the form-giving function of the will to power is basic (GM2.12), sometimes its strength needs to be renewed by way of a period of decadence (where the instinct for form is shrugged off for a time), scepticism, or critique.

(ii) N is also concerned with various types of cultural forms – ways of organizing material such as poetic or artistic form, institutions (such as the military or education) or morality. One basic philosophical distinction at play here is that between form and either material or content (Aristotle and again Kant are the key historical points of reference). N offers a critique of this distinction: form and style *are* a part of content. If an authentic culture is the unity of style of a people, then the sign of the inauthenticity of German culture is that it still depends upon forms borrowed from France (see UM1.1, 2.4, BGE254). Form-giving is an important mechanism in N's understanding of the development of cultures. On the one hand, such forms act as a set of constraints or *disciplines* that might produce greatness (see for example H1.221, H2.172, TIGermans7). On the other hand, such constraints might be a project for the 'taming' of the human, a making ill or degenerate (e.g. GM1.11, TIImproving). More interestingly, the imposition of form could be both, as in the case of the formation of bad conscience through 'internalization', which among other effects generates a humanity 'full of future' (GM2.16), and which is subsequent to the formation of the state and occurs through a form-giving tyranny directed inwards (GM2.17).

Förster-Nietzsche, Elisabeth

N's sister. N's relation with his sister was close in his younger years but often very tense later, as for example over his relationship with Lou Salome, and certainly over her marriage to Bernhard Förster, who had strong anti-Semitic views. In the 1890s, Elisabeth largely took over the custodianship of his estate from N's friends Overbeck and Gast, eventually creating the *Nietzsche Archive*. After 1897 she took over the physical care of her brother. For the next several decades, she helped construct a particular image of N as prophet of an anti-Semitic and nationalist German future.

fragment

See *aphorism*.

France, the French

Other than Germany, the French are the most often discussed people (or national type). From N's perspective, France was the home of two of the most important events of the previous 100 years: the Revolution (end result of the corruption of a previously great aristocracy, and the modern instance *par excellence* of the slave revolution: BGE45), and Napoleon (see for example GM1.16). Moreover, many of the figures most important to N – either as something like fellow free spirits, or as deeply corrupted greatness – were French: Montaigne, Voltaire, Rousseau, Pascal, Stendhal. N views the French as dominant in the domain of cultural forms (e.g. UM1.1, EHClever3); as having the highest exemplars of religious spirituality and therefore also producing the best modern instances of free spirits (D192; or, similarly, having a long and deep moral culture and thus not psychologically naïve about morality: BGE254); as the home of *esprit* (discussed in the entry on *spirit*); and also home to the most successful experiments in a fusion of

South and North, and thus also those comprehensive spirits who
are 'good Europeans' (BGE254).

free spirit

Freigeist or similar. The 'free spirit' is N's most common name for
members of that group of people in the contemporary world with
whom he feels some affinity, either because of their ideas, their
actions and modes of living, or because of their spiritual health.
The phrase 'free spirit' is based, in part, on the idea of the 'free
thinkers', which refers to a loose tradition of secular humanist
thought from the late Renaissance onwards, across Europe and in
the United States. To the extent that this tradition had any consistent
identity, it would be centred on atheism (or at least a radically
individual and anti-institutional religious belief), tolerance, human
rights and equality – in other words, what N calls 'modern ideas'.
N is generally critical of free thinkers, arguing that their moral and
political beliefs still reflect religious ideas, and thus the freedom of
their thought is both misunderstood and exaggerated (see BGE44,
EHUntimely2 – where N also states that UM1 introduced 'an
entirely *new* type of free-spiritedness').

H is subtitled 'A Book for Free Spirits', and the second chapter
of BGE is entitled 'The Free Spirit'. However, in the later Preface to
H, N admits that free spirits were his 'invention', for they 'do not
exist, did not exist' (H1P2). That is, N needed to frame the notion
as an imagined future community, so that he could contribute to
the rise of free spirits among his readers. Free spirits may be best
understood from the point of view of that from which they have
become free. So, for example, the free spirit is opposed to previous
versions of 'free thinking'; likewise, to Christian values especially
insofar as they denigrate higher or *noble values* (AC37); freedom
from faith, and from moral habits (H1.225), and thus if not having
the truth then at least inquiring (and note in the surrounding
passages the connection to *genius*); freedom from errors regarding
spirit itself (i.e. from humanist truths about freedom or reason –
H2.11); from serving the people, as do the 'famous wise men'
(Z2.8). Some positive characteristics of the free spirit are discussed
under separate entries: *courage* (GS347 – 'dancing beside abysses'),
honesty (H2.11, AC36); *solitude* (D562, BGE44); *wandering*
(H1.636–7, H2.211 'spiritual nomadism', and Z4.9).

Let us discuss in a little more detail two other characteristics:

(i) That the free spirit has *become* free. The phrase 'free spirits' is often replaced by some variation on 'we spirits who have become free' (e.g. EHHuman1; and see UM4.11). By this N means that becoming free has been a task and a victory. It is not just a question of recognizing that some ideas might be false or dangerous. Beliefs and ideas form a system; are embedded in language; are institutionalized in our culture, politics, etc.; inform our everyday habits; are 'incorporated' into the body. So, becoming free means an *overcoming* of something and ultimately an overcoming of oneself. Thus, as N remarks at AC13, a free spirit is, in his or her existence and mode of life, already a 'revaluation of all values'. Likewise, see N's praise of Goethe as a figure who 'made use of practical activity' to overcoming the eighteenth century, and who '*created* himself' (TISkirmishes49). The free spirit is thus a tragedy to those who love them (D562 – and this is beautifully described in the poem at the end of BGE).

(ii) The notion of the 'oligarchs of the spirit' (H1.261). N coins this phrase as a way of designating a future organization of free spirits, one that crosses nations and classes, or sets up little experimental states (D453). Its purpose is to create new values for the future both spiritually (i.e. as philosophers, scientists, etc.) and insofar as they employ existing beliefs and institutions as 'instruments' for their ends (H1.472, BGE61). Towards each other, the free spirits will behave according to the notion of *nobility*. The idea is discussed also at D96, 164, but is later largely subsumed under the 'good European'. It follows from such an idea that the free spirit is an intermediate stage; the philosopher of the future is something different again (BGE44).

freedom

Freiheit. There are at least three relevant senses of the word here. (i) The philosophical and moral concept of an agent capable of determining his or her own actions; (ii) freedom in N's distinctive sense, conceived of as a replacement for (i); (iii) freedom as a social or political notion – for a discussion, see entries under *class* and *slave*.

We will discuss the first and second of these ideas here. N offers a critique of free will along two lines. First, it involves a basic misunderstanding of the nature of *will* – treating it as a unity (BGE19) and ultimately as having a power akin to the *causa sui* (cause of itself: BGE21, 188, and see TIReason4). Will also involves a misunderstanding of the nature of *causality* – treating cause and effect as separable entities or events (e.g. H3.11). The second line of criticism is that free will leads to dangerous consequences, such as inappropriate and crippling *guilt* (H2.33), or a mistaken notion of *responsibility* and thus *punishment* (see for example H1.39, H3.23, GM1.13, TIErrors7).

N's own conception of freedom has four aspects. (i) N argues that the idea of free will is in fact based upon an *affect*, namely the affect of command, the situation of a drive having power over something (and similarly see H3.9). This affect is mistaken for a separable, abstract and illusory capacity called 'free will'. (ii) Freedom in N's sense is an achievement and not a gift. That is, one becomes free by an act of *overcoming* (see for example UM4.11; the camel and lion stages of the spirit at Z1.1; and see 1885.2.205 where freedom is described in terms often associated with N's concept of *innocence*). Someone that has become free N terms the *free spirit*. (iii) Moreover, freedom is not unconditional, but rather depends upon a whole series of delicately constructed circumstances – of education, economic and social independence, etc. (see UM3.8). What produces freedom is constraint, discipline and conflict (BGE188, TISkirmishes38). That is, freedom develops under those conditions that the 'modern' conception of freedom calls 'unfree'. (iv) N's sense of freedom is closely allied with his idea of the *noble*. It comprises recognition of the order of rank. That is, a veneration of one's peers, rather than the slave's longing to be free which is a revenge against the order of rank (BGE260, and see Z1.8). Above all, it involves a certain kind of responsibility for the future health and growth of human life (see Z1.17, TISkirmishes38–9). N's account of freedom centres upon one's alignment to and affirmation of life as *will to power* (in Z1.1, this is the innocence of the child).

friend

Freund. Within N's analysis of interpersonal relationships, friendship is a key concept. Insofar as a part of N's project is a recovery of great ancient virtues, friendship is high on this list (D503, GS61), in contrast to our modern virtue of spiritualized sexual *love* (but see entry on *marriage)*. Friendship is created not by egoism in a narrow sense, nor by mutual aid the aim of which is preservation or the relief of suffering (e.g. *pity* – see also Z2.3). Rather, N defines friendship in terms of a bond created by a 'shared higher thirst for an ideal above them' (GS14), two who 'share not pain, but joy' (GS338). For this reason, the friend should also be the 'best enemy' (Z1.14), generating the *agonistic* relationship that is instrumental to human growth. The friend is in fact the 'third', creating a healthy agonistic relationship when the internal dynamics of the solitary ('I and me': Z1.14) become destructive. Friendship, that is, helps one to give some type of hierarchical unity to the multiplicity of the drives found in any individual (and see H1.491, and see Z1.16). Friendship is characterized by *veneration*, that is to say by respect for what is high or *noble* in the other, but also by a sense of shame. Therefore, one must be well 'adorned' (Z1.14) and even project a 'mask' for one's friends (BGE40, H1.376). The true friend in this sense may also be a traitor to his or her friend – that is leaving the friend behind when one's development raises one's ideal (see D484, the poem that ends BGE, and 'star friendship' at GS279). This notion is also found at Z3.1, suggesting that N's conception of the *disciple* is closely akin to friendship. N frequently calls his readers 'friends', indicating that the function of his writing is to aid in the elevation of others (see BT24, UM3.8, GM3.27).

frog

Frosch. The frog is cold and weak (GS1.345); it comes from the swamp (i.e. is spiritually shallow, dirty) (Z3.7) and sees swamp in everything (i.e. is a pessimist: GM1.1). 'Frog-perspective' is a technical term in representing visual perspective, as in painting, which means viewed as if from below. Thus, such a perspective gives a falsely elevated image (especially of morality or metaphysical values) (BGE2, 1885.40.44).

fullness

See *gift*.

future

Zukunft. The future is the focus of N's attention in thinking about
the real meaning of a healthy, human mode of life and its *ideals*
(e.g. H2.99). This follows from his definition of life that involves
growth or development, and likewise in N's earlier work from the
definition of culture as that which brings about greatness. Ideals
for new possibilities of human life are projects working towards
the future (e.g. H1.245). *Free spirits* have an individual or collective
responsibility for the future of the human (e.g. GM3.14). Thus,
ideals are not to be understood as transcendent or impossible
(H2.114). However, ideals should also not be understood as
a reactive attempt to escape the past or present – if so, then the
ideal would be founded upon *ressentiment*, guilt, self-loathing or
perhaps an *ascetic* relation to what is or was (e.g. H1.249, D71,
the classical and romantic both project a future, but only the
former out of strength: H3.217). Thus, part of the ideal must be an
affirmation of the past and present. Equivalently expressed, only
a healthy mode of life in the present is capable of having a future
in this sense. That is, there are modes of living in the present that
live 'at the expense of the future' (GMP6, 2.12). N attempts to
portray this longing for the future which is without any despising
of the past or present, in Z3.14: for such a healthy and affirming
being, the future and past lie close together. This idea is found in
an embryonic form in UM2.1 (relation to the future is possible only
with a healthily selective memory of the past). One of N's criticisms
of the unbridled historical sense is that it is incapable of having a
future (Z1.14). Similarly, he often accuses modern Europe of living
too fast, living for today and thus abdicating any responsibility for
the future (TISkirmishes39) – and see the various discussions of
cultures that had time, stability and the confidence in themselves
to build a future (H3.190, 275, GS356 – Rome in particular is
N's exemplar here, although see D71). Not surprisingly, a frequent
metaphor for futurity is fertility or *pregnancy* (thus sensuality is
'the future's exuberance of thanks to the now': Z3.10.2).

game

See *play*.

garden

See *plants*.

Gast, Peter

Pseudonym of Johann Köselitz, a close friend of N's from the mid-1870s on. Gast was a musician and composer of modest gifts. He also supported N's writing activity through the most acute phases of his illness in the late 1870s (e.g. taking dictation, correcting manuscripts). After N's collapse in 1889, Gast (along with Overbeck and, later, N's sister Elisabeth) helped manage N's literary estate.

Gay Science, The

Prelude of poetry and four books written in 1881–2 and published in 1882. A new edition was produced in 1887 with a Preface, fifth book and an Appendix of poems. N originally thought of this book as a continuation of *Daybreak*. What is new here is, first, the emphasis on *nobility* and *creativity* and second, the notions of the death of *God* (especially in book three) and *eternal recurrence* (especially in book four) – both of which can be experienced not as disasters, but with the gaiety or cheerfulness as indicated by the title of the book. Book two contains N's most extensive comments on *art* since the early work. Book four ends with the introduction of the figure of *Zarathustra*. The fifth book, titled 'We Fearless Ones', contains many formulations with 'we' and 'our', and is thus an attempt to sum up N's latest thinking on the *free spirit* and the practitioner of gay science, in the context of European modernity.

genealogy

Literally, genealogy means the history of something, with an emphasis on the continuities or discontinuities (i.e. inversions, sublimations) of descent, inward influences or divergences. That is why it is used to describe a 'family tree'. The concept of such an analysis is extremely important for N, although the term itself is used relatively rarely, and in N's published writings is prominent only as the title of GM. Instead, N uses a variety of expressions, such as 'history of development' (H1.16) or 'natural history' (in the title of the fifth chapter of BGE). Several features distinguish N's notion of genealogy from other kinds of historical accounts. (i) The attempt rigorously to avoid anachronism. That is, what N claims is a tendency to assume the validity of a current value and then project it backwards in time (GM1.2, also 2.12). (ii) N argues that providing a history of a value, even one that shows it developing from out of its opposite or from error, is not a critique (e.g. GS345). Genealogy, insofar as it will also give a history of the influence of a value on the health of life, includes such critique. (iii) Genealogy is not 'progress'. Thus, N is able to argue that modern science is not in fact an opponent of asceticism, but its most recent form (GM3.23). (iv) Genealogy includes cross comparisons with other histories, for the reasons N outlines at BGE186 – thus N's late work contains many discussions of Hindu or Buddhist value systems (see especially AC and TIImprovers). (v) The genealogy of some subject will also include a history of the philosophical or scientific attempts to study the same subject (BGE194). Thus, for example, N's discussion of Schopenhauer in GM3. (vi) Genealogy will seek to uncover underlying forces or mechanisms in the development of something, which can then also be seen operative in other histories. For example, the notions of *ressentiment,* internalization, or *spiritualization* are all identified within genealogical analyses, and also employed as explanatory mechanisms in other contexts. (vii) Genealogy, insofar as it is constantly assessing the value for life, will identify future possibilities. For example, the 'opposite ideal' at BGE56, the 'other path' at GM1.16, or the 'reverse attempt' at GM2.24.

Genealogy of Morality, The

Book, mostly written in 1887, and published at the end of the year. Comprises a Preface and three 'Treatises', of increasing length. The *Genealogy* is among the most often read of N's works, perhaps because it is his most academically conventional. (Although one should not ignore the subtitle: 'A Polemic'.) The writing eschews the aphoristic style, the treatises work progressively on clearly stated themes, and by comparison with the books that follow in 1888 the tone mostly seems restrained. The work gives sustained accounts of several key ideas, such as the *slave* revolt in morality, *guilt*, *conscience* and the *ascetic* ideal.

generosity

See *magnanimity, gift*.

genius

Genie, Genius. This is one of the key concepts in early N. For our purposes, the concept of genius has its origins in Kant's aesthetics, and in Romanticism. Kant argues that genius is that quality of an artist by which he or she apprehends and then finds expression for an 'aesthetic idea', a sensory presentation that contains inexhaustible content for thought. Romanticism tended to stress two aspects of struggle or striving, which can be found in an initial form in Kant. First, the struggle of the genius to find adequate expression forms for his or her idea. Second, the struggle of thought to 'catch up' with art – that is of the viewers of art works to understand the work of genius. The genius is thus commonly portrayed as 'tortured' by the effort of expression, and also a solitary and misunderstood figure.

In the early work, N employs genius primarily to refer to something that is not individual, but rather a power of giving transfiguring form that lies in human drives (e.g. BT2, 5). Philosophers, no less than visual or literary artists, could be geniuses in this sense (this is partly because N's understanding of language- and concept-formation stressed the imaginative processes involved). N gets from Schopenhauer the 'Republic of Genius'. Individual instances of genius are particular moments of the genius of an underlying set of drives (that genius is trans-personal is also intimated in Kant). So, even if separated by centuries of time, these individuals have a relationship and carry on a kind of conversation. In them is written the true history of a people (PTAG1, H1.235, H2.408). The aim of all *culture* is to produce genius, so that this conversation might continue. It is on these terms that, at UM1.2, N attacks the 'cultural philistine' (i.e. the leading German intellectuals of his day). In H, N is expressing some scepticism about the artistic genius per se (H1.162), in parallel to his evolving attitude to art generally, though he continues to use the concept to refer to those who create in the domain of ideas. At H1.636, N introduces the notion of a genius of *justice*, who in part reconciles that book's Enlightenment sensibility (scepticism, scientific enquiry) with N's idea that the generation of genius is the function of culture.

In the later work, genius is that which is able to create *values*, new ways of life, and new institutions, beliefs or practices. The concept of genius, rather than being implicitly understood to be positive in some way, is now immoral (or at least amoral) – it is a concept within a philosophical anthropology of the genealogy of culture. Thus, genius is used to describe reactive or unhealthy instances of creation: for example hatred having become genius (TIImprovers4, AC24); or GS354, a description of a levelling, collective consciousness, headed by a rather ironic take on Schopenhauer's phrase 'the genius of the species'. A similar immoral approach is found in N's discussion of the 'two types of genius' (see entry on *feminine and masculine*) at BGE248 (and see GS24). A genius inherits an accumulation of cultural energy, and expends it like an explosive, having only an accidental relation to *milieu*. The genius is a squanderer, giving excessive *gifts*, transforming the cultural landscape. Thus, he or she represents an end point, leaving behind 'sterility and exhaustion' (TISkirmishes44).

Gerber, Gustav

Author of *Language as Art* (1871), which stressed the notion of a series of imaginative translations that occur between sensuous stimulation and utterance. From Gerber, then, N obtains the idea that the mechanism by which sensations become language and judgement is one characterized by rhetorical transformation (e.g. metaphor) – and this is found in N's 'Lectures on Ancient Rhetoric' and in 'On Truth and Lies'.

Germany, the Germans

Having moved to Switzerland as a employee of the University of Basel, N abandoned any citizenship rights and was effectively stateless for the rest of his life. Nevertheless, and not surprisingly, politics, culture and philosophy in Germany were frequent topics in his writings.

Something akin to the modern state of Germany was founded in N's lifetime (see *Bismarck*). Before that, there were a set of separate principalities that had emerged from out of the gradual decline of the Holy Roman Empire. The birth of this new nation, for an ancient people, was accompanied by a strong strain of nationalism (complete with anti-Semitism), a sense of superiority within European affairs (the formation of the new nation had been precipitated by an overwhelming defeat of France), and optimism in the new, highly centralized German state. N found all of these developments distressing. A bitter critique of the current state of German intellectual culture was the topic of N's UM1, and this is continued in the lectures 'On the Future of Our Educational Institutions'. N does the same on a smaller scale in 12 aphorisms starting at BGE240 and again in TIGermans. (See also *newspapers, beer.*) The counterpart to this critique is a concern with the genuine possibilities of German culture (BT23, GS105, BGE240, DP4). This idea ·of a renewal of German culture within modernity is one of the things that attracted N to Wagner. Likewise, his break with Wagner is in part because (to his mind) Wagner had sold out to existing cultural and political powers. Ultimately, N subsumes his hope for German culture (his 'hearty fatherlandishness' BGE241) into the notion of the *Good European.*

giving/gift (also bestow)

Geschenk, Gabe; schenken (bestow). The gift, and the virtue or nature of giving/bestowing, are themes throughout N's working life. The abundance of gifts is a characteristic of the Dionysian. The idea is something like this: scarcity, or the condition of not having sufficient, is a feature of individuality; in itself nature is only endless abundance. Thus, in the Dionysian state, 'freely nature offers her gifts' (BT1). Likewise, Wagner's 'true music' gives 'abundantly' even 'its most precious jewel' (UM4.6). Giving, in N's sense, thus describes someone who has aligned themselves to this abundance, and turns their world into a mirror of their own feeling of strength or beauty – this is something most clearly seen in the artist (H2.173, TISkirmishes8–11), but also more generally (see Z1.22, 2.13). Part of the gift is *communication*; at UM4.6, N claims that such music 'can do nothing other than communicate', because it draws us into the oneness of the real. Nietzsche may drop the Schopenhauerian understanding of this, but he does not drop the phenomenon (see TISkirmishes8–11).

The gift also is characteristic of the 'higher festival' that is the philosopher, who wants to be a 'doctor of the spirit' without even being noticed, certainly without having an advantage or receiving gratitude (D449, 464). Here, N is studying how it is possible for there to be a gift that does not shame the giver or receiver (H3.320: '*to give* is more blessed than *to have*', Z2.9). *Generosity* or *magnanimity* is a virtue attached to the new knowledge and ways of life N is pursuing (e.g. D551). The free spirit has a duty – although it is not selfless – to aid the development of the human. Such a notion of abundant generosity, even up to the point of one's 'going under' (i.e. destruction), is captured in the first two sections of ZP. First, the sun's happiness lies in its giving illumination (ZP1), and then Zarathustra claims to be offering a gift of love to human (ZP2) – with a clear parallel to the love of God culminating in the gift and sacrifice of Jesus. A persistent theme in Z, N further pursues such ideas at Z1.22.1, 3.10.2, 3.12.5, 4.8. Likewise, Z itself is called 'the greatest gift' (EHP4) See *squandering*.

goal, end, purpose, *telos*

Zweck, Ausgabe, Ziel, etc. Goal (or 'purpose', 'task', 'telos' or 'end') means the image of some future state which motivates and guides present behaviour, or which is the function or meaning of some current state. N employs this concept in several different ways.

1   By analogy we can talk about God's purposes with respect
    to the world. For example, in Christianity, God's plan for the
    redemption of humans; or, in Stoicism, the gods as images
    of natural reason. In these senses, purpose becomes nearly
    equivalent to 'meaning' or 'essence'. Any entity (including a
    human being) is essentially defined by the role it plays in the
    divine order of things (see for example 'dependent' humans
    at AC54). It is this meaning that N has in mind when at
    Z3.4 he writes of redeeming things 'from their bondage
    under purpose'. Analogously, morality is felt as something
    imposed upon the human, correcting or improving it; to that
    is counterpoised a moral law given to the human by itself
    (see for example D109, 164). In this direction also are N's
    comments on the love of the earth (reality conceived of as
    immanent), or of the earth having a goal (e.g. GM2.24).

2   A goal can mean the highest achievement of something, or
    the state at which something would arrive were its history
    allowed to play out fully. At BT4, tragedy is the 'goal'
    of both the Apollonian and Dionysian cultural drives.
    Likewise, the Socratic appears to have the goal, through
    education, of 'fathering a genius' (BT15). These are not
    primarily instances of an individual person envisaging
    a goal, but rather of the idea that drives or cultural
    movements might, when viewed on a large enough scale,
    have direction and historical function.

3   Goals are experienced as giving a meaning or value to
    activity. It is this that N has in mind when writing of the
    despair of one who realizes that 'mankind as a whole has
    no goal' (H1.33), or that in itself science is goalless (H1.38).
    Pessimism, nihilism and the later stages of the ascetic ideal
    can all be understood as responses to goallessness (e.g.
    the loss of faith in Christianity or in political or moral
    progress; see for example GM3.28).

4   N frequently saw his own task as proposing a new 'goal'
    to all of humanity (e.g. H1.107, H2.179), and thus a new
    happiness at the having of a goal (Z4.13.17). This new goal
    is towards 'new philosophers' who in turn can envisage and
    deliberately generate the conditions for 'what might be made
    of man' (BGE203). However, N goes so far occasionally

as to suggest that humanity as a whole does have, and always has had, a goal. It just required a more 'rigorous examination' to identify it (H3.189). The most famous instance of such ideas is probably Z1.15 'On the Thousand Goals and the One'. Each type of people or culture has a goal, which is the sustaining and perfection of those virtues that made it into a people or culture. However, only now is it possible to envisage a single goal for all cultures and peoples: the overhuman. N sometimes uses the term *ideal* to express an idea similar to this highest, future goal.

God, gods

In the early work that employs the concepts of Apollonian and Dionysian, the Greek gods are an 'artistic middle world' developed to allow insight into but simultaneously also veil the horrors of existence. They are, then, N's first solution to problem of the peculiarly Greek combination of cheerfulness and pessimism (BT3). The point is generalizable: religious objects of worship are in some way a projection of the needs of a people. In Greek religion, this projection is of health and the affirmation of life; in other religions (Christianity most notably) this projection is of the needs of weakness, illness and revenge. On N's account, more harmful than any theism per se is monotheism. Monotheism represents a detachment of religious beliefs and practices from the life of a people, the mummification of ideals and conceptions of value in abstract concepts, the crushing of the concept of man (and likewise, body, sense, passion) beneath an impossible ideal and thus also the 'premature stagnation' of human development (these ideas are found, variously, at GS143, Z3.8.2, TIReason1; AC16–19, 25). Additionally, in such passages, monotheism is often termed 'Asiatic' in contrast to the Hellenic (e.g. H1.114, Z4.6), bringing the history of religions into line with N's observations about the influences and movements of peoples and cultures. (Importantly, the teaching of *Jesus* himself as described in AC is something quite different.)

The *metaphysical* ground of any positing of the existence of God lies in Platonism in a very broad sense. This means, for example, the positing of another 'world' in contrast to this world of becoming, or the positing of true being as individual and substantial, thinking in terms of subject and predicate logic (thus N's famous claim that 'we have not got rid of God because we still have faith in grammar' TIReason5; see also BGE54). At AC47, N clarifies that his primary concern is not, however, with the issue of whether a God exists or not, but the kind of values necessarily associated with or at the origin of faith: this monotheistic faith is a 'crime against life' (and see TIMorality4, EHDestiny7).

Monotheism is contrasted to polytheism (especially *Greek*) at GM2.23 (and see H1.114). The gods are generally understood as symbols of the diversity of human ideals – and this diversity is itself a healthy thing (H2.220, AC55). Polytheism was a product of the drive to stubborn selfishness (GS143), but also the ennobling of that previously unproductive drive. A parallel historical narrative is outlined in GM2.19: in a primeval period, the gods originated out of fear of the power of ancestors (or nature: H1.111). However, in a later, noble stage of development, this fear was transformed into piety and the gods were projected ideals of one's own noble qualities. Similarly, N argues in BT that it was a multiplicity of Greek god-ideals (Apollo and Dionysus especially) that gave Greek culture its dynamism and its highest achievements. In contrast, the Socratic eliminates this multiplicity and thus prepares the way for monotheism.

Among the most famous of N's ideas is the 'death of God'. By this is meant a number of related historical phenomena: (i) the decline of any real, direct significance of theism (N primarily means Christianity) for European culture – which is to say the increasing secularization of moral, social and political institutions; (ii) or similarly, the rise of scepticism about, for example, the literal truth of sacred texts or the relevance of religious observances, which in turn leads to an increasingly attenuated Christianity (see BGE53); (iii) likewise the rise of avowed atheism; (iv) the increasingly obvious irrationality of Christian beliefs on a philosophical or scientific analysis (e.g. BGE54); (v) the broadly Hegelian concept of the 'evolving god' – that is, the deity as the gradual realization of the absolute in human history and consciousness, which removes any religious content from the concept (H1.238, and see UM1); (vi) what N sees as the rise of a new kind of 'free spirit' who sees Christianity as not simply irrelevant or wrong but positively dangerous to the health and growth of the human (AC47). Importantly, the free spirit is not identified with atheism per se. Atheism, N often contends, is blissfully unaware of both the implications of the 'death of god' (GS125), or of the continuing although indirect influence of religious concepts and values – for example, on notions of human rights, equality or democracy, but also even in science (e.g. H1.131, GS344). If Christianity involves a degradation of man, then the death of God was 'murder', a revenge on the omniscient one who could be 'witness' to human abjectness (Z4.7).

The concept of Dionysus in the later N suggests a new conception of the gods. This is neither the unthinking negation that is atheism (BGE295), nor founded on fear or revenge. 'Even the gods philosophise' N writes (again, at BGE295), suggesting that Dionysus is not a transcendent entity who views the world from outside of it, or who is unchanging. Rather, N's new god or ideal here is a projection of his longing for human development and a heightening of nobility. 'Some god in you' led you to your godless piety, the last Pope says to Zarathustra (Z4.6). Because of this new relation, N terms himself a 'disciple' of Dionysus (TIAncients5, EHP2). Indeed, the idea is sometimes expressed that one must become a god (GS125, Z4.6). This means to align oneself – in affirmation, joy and freedom from shame (Z1.7, 3.12.2) – with the nature of the will to power so as to become an embodiment of this ideal. In EH N ironically uses concepts that refer to Christ in order to discuss this idea. For example, incarnation (EHDestiny1, 2); or the splitting of historical dating into before and after (8). But here, the god become human is not an instance of something that was originally, and remains, somehow transcendent to reality, but 'it is *reality itself*' (5). The Dionysian ideal belongs to the real (it is immanent), and does not come from 'outside' (and see 1887.10.138).

Goethe

Towering literary and intellectual figure in Germany in the late eighteenth and early nineteenth centuries, and one of the few persons in recent cultural life for whom N had virtually unqualified respect. Goethe was resolutely independent from literary fashion – a pioneer of Romanticism in his early work, a classicist later when all around him were Romantics. Likewise, he was independent both from Christian traditions, and from the unthinking atheism of free thinkers. Moreover, Goethe was deeply fascinated by both the zoological and physical sciences. In *Faust* he portrayed the endlessly striving human being, rescued from his pact with Mephistopheles by 'the eternal feminine' (see entry on *feminine and masculine*).

good

See *morality*.

gratitude (thankfulness, etc.)

Dankbarkeit. Gratitude is an important element within N's account of affirmation. In part, the notion comes from Epicurus (e.g. 'Letter to Menoeceus', and see H1.223). Also, in part, it stems from N's analysis of ancient Greek, and other pre-Christian, religions (BGE49, AC16) – where gratitude is in contrast to a religion built on cruelty (BGE55), or on fear and bad conscience (GM2.19). Gratitude is the defining feature of the antiquarian historian, one of the modes of historical remembering and forgetting that 'serves life' (UM2.3). Gratitude is noble (H1.366), and handling gratitude badly is akin to the contempt found in pity (D138). The ability to express gratitude is the work of a mature culture that has a great deal to be thankful for (GS100). Towards the end of Z, Zarathustra realizes that the higher humans are 'becoming thankful' Z4.17.1 – that is, are overcoming their fears and *ressentiment*.

N often expresses his profound gratitude even to those cultural movements or systems of value that, in other ways, he despises (e.g. to Platonic dogmatism at BGEP, to ascetic rejection of life's most familiar aspects at GM3.12, or to the specific illness that is Wagner at WCP). N's immoral attitude to history – arguing that what is called good has an origin in the evil, or vice versa – means that there are few phenomena to be universally condemned. This he sometimes calls *justice*. But in this case gratitude is more than simply a just appraisal, it also includes a concept of fate. If in the present there are new, future possibilities for human development, then the entirety of human history up to that point has made it so. It is in this way that the notion of gratitude is part of *affirmation*, and specifically, *amor fati*.

gravity

See *weight*.

great, greatness

Größe. 'Greatness' is an often used term in N, and in a wide variety of contexts: great individuals, great people, great style, great politics, great health, etc. In the early work, the production of greatness is the task of an authentic culture. (Thus N's attacks on mediocrity in, for example, UM1.) Such greatness is, he claims, an 'aesthetic' or perhaps moral standard, but not ultimately about knowledge (1872.19.37, H1.521); 'mankind grows only through admiration of the *rare and great*' (1872.19.80). Accordingly, life is served by monumental history insofar as it keeps alive the memory of that which 'expanded the concept of man' (UM2.2). Incidences of greatness are like a chain of mountain peaks, indifferent to the ordinary course of history (this comes from Schopenhauer's notion of the Republic of Genius).

In later work, N sometimes uses the term 'greatness' ironically, to refer to those individuals or events that the masses consider great. Thus, for example, in the title of Z2.18 'On Great Events', or the greatness of dogmatic systems in BGEP. What is ordinarily considered great is, closely analysed, normally something that became corrupt long before, and thus more a fiction created by admirers than a reality (BGE269, EHClever10). Indeed, the effects might be dangerous as admirers become 'intoxicated' and destroy themselves or their culture (GS1.28). So, authentic greatness cannot normally be measured by its effects; or rather, the effects to be measured are the enhancement of the human type *in his or her person*. Thus at BGE212, greatness is characterized by its concealment, its invisibility to the masses. N clearly has sympathy with one of his imagined 'patriots' at BGE241, who describes Bismarck as 'strong and insane! Not great!' Other characteristics typically assigned to greatness include fullness or abundance (see *giving*), manifoldness combined with unity (BGE241, see *comprehensive*), and the strength to conceive of reality as it is, to align oneself with reality (EHDestiny5). See also *health, politics, style.*

Greece, the Greeks

As a philologist, N specialized in ancient Greek languages and manuscripts, and the courses he taught (or was at least scheduled to teach) were overwhelmingly on the subject of Greek philosophers, poets or rhetoric. Moreover, both BT and PTAG are books devoted to the study of ancient Greece, and there are several shorter works in this vein too. All the rest of N's writings include passages that take Greek figures – the tragic dramatists, Heraclitus, Epicurus, Socrates and Plato among them – as vital reference points. It is thus not an exaggeration to claim that his studies of the Greeks pose the problems that N's subsequent philosophy is intended to address.

Among these problems are (i) the nature of a unified culture that fulfilled the basic purpose of all culture, which is the production of genius or greatness (e.g. PTAG1); and similarly, a culture characterized by magnanimity and humaneness but without 'modern ideas' such as democratic equality (e.g. GS18); (ii) a mode of cultural life that combines the apparently incompatible attributes of knowing cheerfulness and pessimistic wisdom (throughout BT, and see H1.16, 154, 261); (iii) a healthy or life-affirming type of religion and religious practice (e.g. H1.114, GS302, BGE49, GM2.23) – or, expressed more generally, a positing of ideals that is not a denigration of the real; (iv) similarly, the problem of a relation to the body and passion that is both healthy and productive (GS139).

N criticizes contemporary classicists and historians who read their own values back into Greece (e.g. UM2.6), the image of Greece is valuable to us precisely because of its alienness (see UM2P, H2.218) – even if sometimes N seems to despair of this alienness (TIAncients2, D195). It would be naïve, though, to think that N wished for or believed in the possibility of a return to Greek modes of life. Instead, the future envisioned by BT is of a 'music-making Socrates' – that is, a rebirth of a Greek ideal but under the conditions of modernity. This more complex relation is discussed also at UM4.4, AC59.

guilt

Schuld. N's most famous discussion of guilt is found in GM. There, N gives a psychological history of guilt, tracing it to the notion of debt (i.e. a contractual relationship concerning buying, selling and repayment). Thus, punishment rested upon an equivalence between crime and punishment (GM2.4–8). The feeling of guilt – the having of a 'guilty conscience' – is, N claims, rare among criminals (GM2.14), and is a later historical development. He understands the psychological origin of bad conscience in the turning inwards of those power drives that are forbidden outward expression in a society (GM2.16–17). Guilty conscience is guilty before that power which gives the society its identity and legitimacy – ultimately, a deity (GM2.19–22). Other notable analyses concerning guilt include: (i) D240, where N argues that the guilt of the hero in tragic drama is not the main point, but a later moral interpretation. (ii) N contrasts the 'gruesome paganism' of the Christian interpretation of sacrifice and salvation, with Jesus' elimination of the very idea of guilt (AC41). (iii) N argues that those who suffer need a cause, something that gives their suffering meaning, and something that, in its condemnation or destruction, can serve to anaesthetize that suffering (GM3.15, TIErrors6). The ascetic priest *sublimates* this, saying 'you alone are to blame for yourself'. That is, the ascetic priests turn the *ressentiment* of the sufferer against the sufferer.

habit, or custom

As in English, the German terms here have two meanings that we might want to distinguish. On the one hand, a custom is a tradition, some practice that a society (or some smaller group, like a family) implicitly takes to be valuable and defining of the society. Although a customary or traditional practice is something done regularly, it can be done consciously or deliberately. On the other hand, custom could also mean habit. Habits tend to be associated with individuals rather than societies as a whole, and tend also to be unconscious or automatic types of behaviour. N's claim is that morality is a custom in the first sense (society-wide), but also unconscious as in the second sense. Morality is traditional and habitual obedience to the law (D9). N makes a very similar claim about religious faith (H1.226). In German, the connection between custom and morality is easy to make: *Sitte* means both custom and morality, and the most common word translated as 'morality' is *Sittlichkeit*.

At D149, N indicates all the small ways that those who are otherwise 'free spirits' still follow customs, for the power of morality does not consist in belief, but in obedience. The reasons behind the custom are *forgotten* – probably they had to do with the preservation of the community (i.e. fulfilling the values it considers important to its identity and survival). Perhaps, N speculates, the reasons were only invented later (GS29). Even where one struggles with a moral decision, what is being struggled with is the question of which course of action best accords with some traditional custom. Meditation on the law itself is forbidden, is immoral (H1.96). At D14, N claims that those who did throw off this 'yoke' had to think of themselves as mad – particularly, in the sense of being possessed in the grip of a higher power – in order to feel justified. At GS125, part of N's point is the oblivion of the people in the marketplace. They blithely imagine themselves free of the old customs and beliefs, not grasping how widely and deeply engrained habits are. Indeed, N playfully argues that the feeling of freedom has to do with the fact that we have become accustomed to our 'chains' (H3.10).

The morality of custom has two important consequences. First, it produces a homogeneous type of human, in his or her values and behaviours. N's various discussions of *breeding* and the *herd* belong here. Second, though, it also produces the 'sovereign individual' – the being who has 'become free' and is 'permitted to promise' (GM2.2). Someone capable of entering into contracts according to custom develops the ability to promise, to will across long stretches of time. In fact, habit or custom is not a sufficiently strong term for N's conception here, and thus he talks about the creation of new *instincts*, through punishment and 'internalization' (see *incorporation*). A revaluation of all values, then, is not an intellectual exercise, but the task of living differently, or even the invention of new ways of being human. Our customs are wider than just our moral practices, narrowly defined. For example, our cognitive short-cuts and simplifications are habits (BGE192), including the need immediately to supply a cause for every state (TIErrors4). Part of the meaning of N's call for us to pay attention to the 'closest things' is for an analysis of the innumerable small habits that organize our lives, and the value (or lack of value) they may have. See, for example, the 'history of the everyday' at GS308, or N's discussion of 'brief habits' at GS295.

happiness, joy

The most common German words are *Glück* (happiness, but also means luck), *Freude* (joy), *Lust* (either as joy or pleasure, depending on context). Happiness has been a preoccupation of many philosophers, either as a way of understanding human motivations, or as an element in the characterization of the 'good life'. Two traditions are of particular concern: that of Epicurus during the Greek period, and the broad British tradition of Hume, the Utilitarians and Darwinists.

The British tradition N frequently ridicules, as at ACArrows12: 'people *don't* strive for happiness, only the English do' (see also GM1.10). Moreover, happiness is neither the purpose of existence, nor its natural end (e.g. D108, although see H3.350). To be sure N went through a period during the composition of H in which he understood pleasure and pain to be basic psychological motivations. More generally, however, it is to *perspectives* and the feeling of *power* that N looks for motivations. Moreover, it is for moral reasons that the history of psychology has overlooked feelings of power in favour of pleasure or happiness: the latter types of motivation are more suited to a *herd* morality. From this also follows N's distinction between his sense of happiness and 'wretched contentment' (ZP3, GS338), which he equates with the notion of *narcotizing* (as at GM1.10). Part of the critique of herd morality – and part of the revaluation of all values – will be to transform passions (that previously we tried to narcotize) into joys (H3.37, 350).

In the early work, N sometimes identifies 'happiness' with the goal of culture. The man of 'monumental' history has happiness as his goal but this goal is, more carefully examined, a continuation of the 'mountain chain' of greatness across history. D raises the question of the relation of happiness and knowledge: the 'barbarians' were happier, because they allowed themselves happiness without knowledge, and indeed welcomed deception (and see GS328). We moderns, however, have developed a will to knowledge and can no longer experience such happiness. Accordingly, N speculates that our culture will have to learn to experience happiness and beauty in knowledge (D433, H1.292). This development of a will to knowledge is one reason why modernity cannot simply return to ancient values and ways of life (and see H2.187, GS12).

N's mature conception of happiness is founded in part upon that of Epicurus. In Epicurus, the chief good for human beings is the avoidance of mental or physical disturbances (i.e. anxiety, regret, pain, etc.): *ataraxia*. Such a state would be characterized by quiet, stillness or repose – and this is exactly how N, for much of his career, discusses states of happiness. N explicitly refers to Epicurus at GS45 (the sea imagery is repeated at GS60, 302), and frequently mentions gardens (e.g. H1.591). Such a state is beautifully described in terms of *repose* at Z3.3 and Z4.10. In both cases, what is described is quiet contemplation of the world, with all its *agon*, understood as *perfect* (see EHZ3). That such happiness rests on danger (GS283) and loss may lend it a certain melancholy, or heaviness (e.g. GS278, Z4.1). N rejects happiness as an end or purpose; repose is rather a moment within the *cyclical* rhythm of the life of a healthy spirit.

N develops the theme of 'joying-with' (H2.62, GS338) – being able to experience joy at another's joy – which he claims is a much higher and more rare ability than pity (suffering-with). Although in a sense it is a response to something external, joying-with is not reactive nor is it a petty feeling of power as in pity. The flip side of this is the capacity to make others joyful (see D422, GM3.18). Likewise, N speaks of the joy of appropriation, and the joy of the weaker in being appropriated (i.e. of being made a part of something greater than one: GS118). At D146, N argues that happiness is an enhancement of the feeling of power. If will to power is the nature of living things, and if joy is the enhancement of power, then as N says at H1.292, nature 'rules the whole world through joy'.

N seems to suggest that there are two types of higher happiness. The first, that we have just discussed, is the moment of contemplative repose, which has in view the perfection of the whole. The second is the happiness of he or she who is overfull, the one who bestows (GS326, the happiness of the sun at ZP1 – and see the entry on *giving*). N argues that those who are *noble* simply feel themselves to be happy. They do not have to 'construct their happiness' by negating the the values of their enemies (GM1.10 – and see GS328). This, N says, is an 'active' happiness rather than passive (AC1, GS56). Similarly, N argues that happiness equals instinct, for ascending modes of human life (TISocrates11) – happiness, in that case, lies in being what one is, rather than in such a 'construction' of an image of happiness. Zarathustra is 'lying in a sky-blue lake of happiness' and yet, because happiness is not in itself the purpose, says 'What does happiness matter?' (Z4.1, Z4.20). 'I am striving after my work' he asserts. The happiness of repose and of the overfull are distinguishable states, but are part of a cycle. The full conception of happiness would be a state that is both active and contemplative at the same time, or at least in a healthy relationship. This full conception is what N is trying to capture in Z3.16 – as indeed its alternate title ('The Yes and Amen Song') indicates. Eternal recurrence is here a symbol of the joining in joy of becoming (action, striving, creation, wandering, longing, etc.) and being (Eternity). Woe wants only children – that is wants either the negation of itself, or some changed future. Joy, deeper than woe, wants Eternity. However, this Eternity is imaged as a woman with whom the speaker desires 'children'. That is, the longing for Eternity *includes* a sense of and longing for the future. The *feminine and masculine* symbolism here is not accidental, but rather part of N's attempt to understand the dynamic relationship among drives. There is a similar account of an integrated notion of happiness for the new nobility at GS337. At BGE193 striving and contemplation are integrated, since flying is a state in which ascent is without effort. With this in mind, we can understand why N writes that 'you yourself may be the eternal joy in becoming' (TIAncients5). If I am in the Dionysian state of alignment to will to power, then I will be joyful both with respect to becoming (becoming is expression of power) and Eternity (my joyful contemplation of the immanent perfection of existence is also an expression of will to power, the feeling of being at a height).

hard

Hart. A frequent metaphor in N, hardness stands for the quality of one's character in being indifferent (e.g. to suffering), being severe or cruel (especially to oneself), or being subject to a difficult or dangerous fate (the nature of women is a 'hard law': GS68). Such hardness is part of the independence of he or she who is noble. Hardness is not about cruelty or indifference as virtues in themselves, but rather as instruments for certain goals (e.g. the development of the human).

Hartmann, E. von

A philosophical contemporary of N, whom N initially praises and then gradually distances himself from. N ridicules Hartmann in UM2. Hartmann's main importance for N was as a source of understanding of Darwinism and other topics in natural science.

health

Gesundheit. Among the most important concepts in N, health is key for understanding N's new ideal of human development and also for understanding N's account of culture. Biographically, of course, N was plagued by ill-health from very early on, with bouts of nausea, headaches, eyesight-problems and other symptoms forcing his early retirement from the University of Basel, and orchestrating many of his habits and movements. Accordingly, one might suppose that his concern with the theme of health was a kind of fantasy. This would be a mistake, philosophically, since N does not have a modern conception of health in mind (i.e. health as long and pain-free or unencumbered life), or a normative or universal definition (H1.286).

N's consideration of the concept of health commences in the early 1870s, already playing a prominent role in the opening section of *The Birth of Tragedy*. A classical sense of health is contrasted with a later or modern one – the former a health of strength, energy and abundance (sometimes explicitly associated with Dionysus), and the latter a pale health of abstinence and *asceticism* (BT1, UM1.11). The latter is not health at all, but a degeneration, an imaginary health prompted by a spirit of revenge against genuine health (e.g. AC51). Even the Greeks were not simply 'healthy' in any ordinary sense, but were able to harness sickness for its power (H1.214) – this is a 'higher' health. Similarly, the sickness of the body leads to a moral or metaphysical rejection of body, and this reinforces a weariness and incapacity for any action. One must overcome suffering and thus recognize the health that lies even within what is conventionally called 'sick' (Z1.3). N sometimes uses the concept of inoculation for a health that recognizes the role of a certain excess or danger within the maintenance of that health (e.g. H1.224, ZP3). Health is trans-personal, not just a characteristic of individual organisms; indeed, it is tied in with the problem of *culture*. In a healthy or genuine culture such as pre-Socratic Greece, the practices of history and philosophy reflect back and enhance that health. In a sick culture, they worsen the sickness (PTAG1, UM2.1). Health, in other words, is whatever conditions permit an individual, or a whole culture, to have a sense of and confidence in its own unity, value, and purpose, and a capacity for action. Science in particular requires subordination to 'health doctrine' lest it destroy life (UM2.10).

This concept later becomes the 'great health', a phrase N uses in the late 1880s (GS382, reused at EHZ2; and see GM2.24). The 'great health' brings together a number of other notions that are important for N: it is characterized by *strength, mischievousness, love* and *cheerfulness*, but above all by a longing for new explorations or *experiments* (which, in themselves, might be *beautiful* or might be terrifying) in pursuit of a new *ideal* of the human (or *overhuman*). This new ideal is itself described partly in terms of just this health, so that again health both reflects back and enhances. Such a health is *redemption* – not of man in the eyes of God, but of *reality* or the *earth*. Such a health requires suffering and risk. It is not a state that one *has*, because it involves *cyclically* being lost (it *expends* itself, as part of such exploration, creation or growth, and by going under into the *depths*) and regained (through *convalescence* or *repose*). N interprets his own biography in terms of such alternations of states of expenditure or recovery *within* a greater health (GSP, and EHClever3, 5, Human2, Zarathustra5, Beyond2), for which he must be *grateful*.

heaviness

See *weight*.

Hegel

Hegel was the most influential German philosopher in the opening decades of the nineteenth century. It is unlikely that N had more than a second-hand knowledge of most of Hegel's immense output. N's attitude towards Hegel is initially coloured by the fact that

Schopenhauer considered him to be a charlatan. The attacks on Strauss in UM1 and Hartmann in UM2 are underpinned by the influence of Hegel upon these two philosophers. Even after N's break with Schopenhauer in the mid to late 1870s, this attitude towards Hegel remains. For example, at EHBT1, he says of his own first book that it 'smells offensively Hegelian'. Nevertheless, very broadly speaking, N inherits a key aspect of Hegel's originality. Hegel studied the historical development of ideas, social and political forms, art and morality – and he considered the understanding of the principles of such development to be a key subject of philosophical enquiry. Although there is earlier precedent for this in historicists such as Herder, N's own thought would not have been possible without Hegel. However, Hegel sees this historical development as the progressive unfolding of spirit. By spirit is meant something that is (arguably at least) transcendent to history, or not immanent to the real per se (N calls it a 'pantheism' at 1885.2.106). It is this to which N objects. As far as N is concerned, this is just another manifestation of the old theological idea of the plans or purposes of God, dressed up so as to legitimate the Enlightenment or liberal notion of progress – or indeed still less desirable political notions.

height

See *ascend*.

Helmholtz, Hermann von

Helmholtz was an important scientific figure in the nineteenth century, who made contributions in the study of the conservation of energy, electromagnetism, as well as nerve and sensory physiology. It is the physiological work – an attempt to understand how mind and sensation occur on an entirely physical or material basis – that most influenced N. N employed Helmholtz's broadly neo-Kantian ideas in his own early work (e.g. 'On Truth and Lies'). Later, though, Nietzsche comes to believe that the underlying materialism of this approach is yet another metaphysical dogma.

Heraclitus

Heraclitus was a fifth-century BC philosopher from Ionia. Several famous ideas from Heraclitus are of particular importance for N. First, and most obviously, Heraclitus' conception of *becoming* as the basic character of the real – indeed, much of N's use of river or sea metaphors can be traced to Heraclitus' 'it is impossible to step twice into the same river'. Second, Heraclitus tries to account for becoming in terms of perpetual strife or antagonism between generation and destruction. Even peace or harmony are understood dynamically as equilibria. Again, N's metaphor of time as the *innocent child* at play is a reference to Heraclitus. It is from here that N obtains much of the substance of his idea of *agon*, as well as his notion the *cyclical* relation of opposing drives (e.g. *Apollonian* and *Dionysian*, *feminine and masculine*).

herd, masses, mob, rabble

Heerde. 'Herd' is N's deliberately demeaning term, not so much for the masses, as for the type of human beings that make up the masses. The term is relatively little used until GS; and in that book N sometimes uses the term 'herd' in a more neutral manner (e.g. GS1), meaning human beings insofar as they live communally and depend upon the community. The values of the herd are those that preserve the community. However, also in GS is another theme, which is that of the distinction between the herd and individuals or those who in some way posit 'private' systems of value (e.g. GS23). However, in most people, and even those who are 'individuals', the herd instinct lives on: for example 'morality is herd-instinct in the individual', the 'herd instinct' speaks in our behaviours and consciences (GS50, 116–17, 174, and later GM3.18). By Z, the more derogatory use is exclusive (e.g. ZP5, 9, Z1.15, Z2.4).

In later work, the concept of herd develops further. The idea is that religious and moral systems – in a European context, this means Christianity – have bred a type of human being who possesses uniform drives, needs, values and habits, a relatively passive disposition, industriousness, and the social and political institutions to go with all this. That is, herd instincts are not necessarily the original or basic instincts of the human, but have been bred in, and have become increasingly predominant despite apparent individualism (BGE202, AC3, 42).

The mob, rabble or riff-raff [*Pöbel* or *Gesindel*], however, represent a slightly different notion. An important passage for understanding the difference is AC57, where N praises the mediocre, who have their own excellence and happiness, as opposed to the 'mob' (similarly, see 'peasants' and 'mob' at Z4.3). A herd *can* be a people [*Volk*], characterized by unity, health and strength; mob or rabble, thoroughly degenerate, cannot. N associates mob or rabble particularly with (i) cities (the market: Z4.13.1; thus dirty and noisy); (ii) mass political or social movements (such as socialism: AC57, and see Z3.12.21, TIDestiny1). More generally, mob or rabble emerge from slave revolutions characterized by an instinctive *ressentiment* towards power or nobility: Z2.6, 4.8. The mob is thus irreverent (including with respect to religion: BGE58). It is sick and suffers from life (Z4.13.16, 20), and needs someone to blame (H2.386); (iii) the democratic mixing of classes, races and types (e.g. at Z4.3.1, BGE264). The Voluntary Beggar asks 'What are "rich" and "poor" today! I have unlearned this distinction' (Z4.8). Likewise, N talks of the 'educated mob' at GSP4 – the idea is that even the educated classes have adopted the traits and ideas of the mob; (iv) with pursuing all the more its guilty, forbidden passions, making the passions filthy (Z3.10.2); (v) narrowly egoistic, thus wanting 'to live *gratis*' without giving back (Z3.12.5); (vi) unconditional in judgement (Z4.13.16). Although much of N's observations about the rabble or mob are directed at his contemporary Europe, because of its links to decadence and the slave revolution, he sometimes also uses it as a historical concept (e.g. the 'rabble in Greece': BGE49). The key example is N's analysis of Socrates with respect to his predecessors and to the more noble Plato (BGE190, TISocrates).

hero

Held. The figure of the hero is used by N in two divergent ways. (i) Sometimes, especially in Z, the hero is a straight-forward stand-in for the higher human or *free spirit*. So for example, Zarathustra asks of his young disciple that he does not 'throw away the hero in your soul' (Z1.8). Similar allegorical uses are found at H1.498, H2.401, Z3.12.18. Likewise, N wonders whether it is better to leave the psychology of Plutarch's heroes unanalysed (H1.36) or at least not sceptically treated (H3.20). The 'new nobility' anticipated at GS337 is introduced by way of the hero. (ii) On the other hand, N is often sceptical of the hero, especially as a historical or contemporary person. The hero is a role in a stage play. That is, it is something artificial, a mere type of spectacle (this is a particularly common theme in GS for example GS1, 78, 80, 107), that tells us more about what the audience wants and needs than what a real person has to offer. For example, the *great* historical hero is often a product of a historian's interpretation (D307). One reason why N uses the notion of hero less frequently later is that he wants to avoid being confused with Carlyle and his 'cult of the hero' (EHBooks1).

hierarchy

See *class*, *rank*.

historical sense

By historical sense N means two interrelated things. First, an ability acquired because of diverse cultural inheritance as well as perhaps proper education, to possess understanding of many different historical periods (H1.23, 274, BGE224). Particularly, understanding the values of these periods, and knowing that these values differ from the present because of the fundamental process of becoming (GM1.2, TIReason1). However, while this has considerable value (e.g. H2.179), it is also a wide, indiscriminate (indeed 'barbarian') taste and is contrasted with the narrowness and perfection of noble cultures. At GS337 and again at Z3.12.11, N envisages a new nobility that has overcome the limitations of both of these extremes. Second, historical sense can be understood as a product of a neutral and unselective approach to history. As a result, history appears as a repository of cultures, styles, modes of life all of which are considered equally valid. Under the weight of this repository, a genuine contemporary culture disappears, and instead we live like patchworks of the past. This motif occurs quite often, for example UM1.1, 2.4, Z2.14.

history

Geschichte. 'History' refers to the past and our relationship to it, as well as a particular form of knowledge or study. N's thought, from beginning to end, is historical in both these ways. N's early philological work concerned ancient Greek language and manuscripts; it is thus a specialized form of history, and shares many techniques. His early philosophical work (e.g. BT, 'Homer's Contest', etc.) is an attempt to understand the principles that animated the history of ancient Greece, the metaphysical meaning of those principles and what happened to them in subsequent historical epochs. References to or studies of the histories of Greece, Rome and of Christianity are found in every subsequent book, while UM2 concerns the role that various types of history play in the development of human life and culture. H proposes both a history of the development of thought and a history of moral sensations. Z can be understood as a speculative retelling of the history of European morality were it to have had a different origin. Finally, the concept of *genealogy* (from the title of GM) stands for a broadly historical reconstruction of the origin and continuing implications of key notions within morality. The key idea throughout N's career is that values, forms of life, types of thinking and even the basic structure of world as appearance were not just given, either by God or nature, but have *become*. Thus, the task of understanding or evaluating the nature of values, forms of life, et al. must be a historical one through-and-through. This idea is made methodologically explicit in H (e.g. H1.16). N writes that 'only that which has no history is definable' (GM2.13), meaning that only by thinking ahistorically could one eliminate becoming from the real (TIReason1).

What has become must exhibit both continuity (i.e. for examples, the values we hold now will have 'come from' somewhere) and discontinuity (i.e. they will have been transformed, inverted, distorted or repressed along the way). In both cases, history is significant through its effects. 'The past continues to flow within us in a hundred waves', N writes at H2.223, in the form of inherited values, drives, institutions or beliefs (and see H2.126, D506). Most important are not so much the noisy 'great events' (Z2.18) that are widely held to be meaningful by others (H1.143, N has wars or the rise and fall of nations in mind), but rather the quiet events that constitute real changes (N means the invention of values). N tends to stress discontinuity, since he is interested in the manner in which the origins of values or ideas are misunderstood.

In UM2, N famously distinguishes between three forms of history: the monumental, antiquarian and critical. Each serves life, health and culture by being 'unjust' – that is, by forgetting part of history in order to find meaning in another part. Each also poses a danger if not 'regulated'; for example the *historical sense* (understood negatively) develops because the history we embody is too dispersed, or is mere information. The point is not that one of these modes is to be preferred to the others, but that all three modes are necessary. Although N does not carry on using the terminology he develops here, nevertheless these ideas remain central to his thought. For example, the late idea of *amor fati* bears some initial resemblance to antiquarian history; however, *amor fati* does not rule out either monumental history (and thus action) nor critical history (and thus self-overcoming). In other words, it can be interpreted as a description of what a mode of existence would be that incorporated all three historical modes. Against various types of unfruitful forgetting or misinterpretation, N proposes the employment of history in service of 'true culture' at UM2.10; similarly, he envisions its *just* use by the 'noble' at GS337 or Z3.12.11, someone who has 'experienced history' in himself (D545) prior to making judgements, especially moral judgements.

In addition, N criticizes three other types of historical analysis. First, to the extent there is continuity in history, this is not to be understood teleologically, as if all history led precisely to us. This is the concept of progress (see H2.147, Z3.12.11). (Although, in a twist on Hegelian thought, N does experiment in the late 1870s with the idea that a universally known history (including natural history) would comprise true self-consciousness (H2.184–5, 223).) Just as he was generally critical of the idea of progress, so N is critical of Enlightenment attempts to identify universals within history, such as a single and unchanging conception of human nature. The historical configurations of various nations or periods are intrinsically different (an idea N gets from eighteenth-century historicists such as Herder). Nevertheless, N's conception of history – and of its study – incorporates a number of concepts that arguably are employed universally and are not themselves historical. These concepts include *life, health, instinct, drives* or *will to power* (the basic realities 'behind' historical events; the Apollonian and Dionysian would be early examples); *culture, people, herd, religion, political* institutions (key types of historical formations); as well as *ressentiment, sublimation, spiritualization, cycle* or *decadence* (explanatory concepts of historical change). So, for example, N will talk about several *slave revolutions*, implying that closely analogous conditions and processes are found in otherwise different historical epochs. Finally, N is highly critical of the quasi-scientific or objective approach to history that was becoming dominant in the nineteenth century. Such an approach is at best only an instrument in the hands of a broader and higher approach, one that genuinely serves life and culture. This is made clear particularly at UM2.4, and for example the 'critical historians' at BGE209. Objective history rests upon the assumption that one can and should take up a neutral stance to the concerns of life and culture. But this attempt at neutrality results in the destruction of culture, an inactive pessimism (UM2.5 and see UM3.26), and robs the present of any reason to strive for change (UM4.6). It is on this basis that BT10 and 23 oppose history to myth (and see UM2.7); likewise, at UM1.2, N laments the transformation of philosophy and philology into entirely 'historical sciences'.

Perhaps most importantly, on N's analysis history has meaning only insofar as it generates, in the present, *future* possibilities. For example, at BGE45, N claims that the point of natural history is to explore the 'as yet unexhausted possibilities' of the human. In UM2, all of the three modes of history are opposed to any mere preservation of the present. The task of new philosophers or free spirits is to somehow employ and take partial control of history so that in the future the production of greatness is not left to accident (H2.179, BGE203). What can be learned from the history of Greece, for example, is a possible form of life that is a beautiful and healthy embodiment of tragic knowledge; what can be learned from Christianity is the origin of, and the instruments for the domination of, a number of values that must be overcome if there is to be the possibility of future growth in the human. History can be something that mirrors our contemporary predicament (H1.616, H2.218), helping us to envisage possibilities otherwise

unseen. Nevertheless, history is irreversible. N's admiration for
the Greek mode of life does not entail a belief that one could
return to that mode of life; the problem rather is to generate a
future mode of life that has learned from the Greeks but within
the inescapable conditions of modernity. Thus, for example, the
'rebirth' of tragedy discussed at the end of BT is not the elimination
of the Socratic, but the invention of the 'music-making Socrates'.
It follows that historical understanding itself may face limitations:
indeed, N goes so far as to claim at TIAncients that the Greeks
are 'too foreign'.

holy, Saint, sacred

[*Heil*, and other constructions founded upon it – it is the same root
word to indicate someone canonized as a 'Saint'.] There are two
main issues here. The first is N's account of the nature of the Saint;
the second is N's revaluation of the concept of the holy.

The Saint – either someone canonized, or saint-like behaviour –
is *will to power* directed back upon the self, often *ascetically*, an
instance of great self-overcoming. Insofar as we think morally and
believe in opposites, then the Saint represents a miracle (BGE47).
This 'miracle', N suggests, is simply a misunderstanding of the
nature of apparent 'opposites'. Because of its miraculous quality,
saintliness is ascribed to an external influence (the divine). This
is the 'new power' N discusses at BGE51 (and see the analyses
at D14, 62). At WC3, N argues that for the people saintliness is
needed; for philosophers, though, the saint stops short precisely
at the point where the philosopher's ideal opens. That is to say,
holiness is a misunderstood self-overcoming, the misdirected ideal
of which is ascetic.

Especially in Z, N uses the concept of holiness in a positive
manner, as another way of describing the basic acts of a *healthy*
and powerful will to power, especially insofar as it has taken
the overhuman as its goal. Thus, both the 'no-saying' of the lion
transformation and the 'yes-saying' of the *child* transformation are
termed 'holy' (Z1.1). Similarly, the *ideals* of a people (Z1.15), or
laughter (Z3.16.6, Z4.13.18, 20). Not surprisingly, this revalued
sense of holiness is linked to the divine, in N's sense of the gods
as human ideals; thus, in an allusion to the divine blessing of a

marriage, Zarathustra says 'Such a will and such marriage I call holy' (Z1.20). Insofar as science is a late form of the ascetic ideal, art – in which 'precisely the lie makes itself holy' – is its true opponent (GM3.25) because it deifies life.

home

Heim, *Heimat*. The notions of not being at home, or not having a single home, are alternative ways of discussing the concepts of the *untimely* or the *wanderer*. For examples, see Z2.14, BGE44, GS377. N's ideal of a home is expressed at Z3.9 'The Return Home': it is *solitude*, where one no longer needs to wear masks or 'mix up' one's *language*.

Homer

Assuming that there was a single author of the *Iliad* and *Odyssey* named Homer, he would be a great narrative poet of the early Greek period, and creator of the genre of the epic. Thus, in BT, N contrasts Homer (*Apollonian*) to both the lyric (*Dionysian*) and tragic poets (both drives, and see H2.219). At GM3.25, N contrasts Homer and Plato: the former the deifier of life, the latter its 'slanderer'. Homer is thus an exemplary figure in the Greek attitude to morality (i.e. of what N calls 'master morality': see H1.45), to constraint (H3.140 – see *discipline*), and to the gods as ideals and a Greek sense of happiness (GS302). For this same reason, the rediscovery of the pleasures of Homer is something we owe to our *historical sense*, that which permits us understanding of other cultural systems and values (BGE224).

honesty

The English term 'honesty' is the most common translation of both *Ehrlichkeit* and *Redlichkeit* – the former has overtones of being honourable or noble, while the latter is related to *reden*, to speak, and thus is more akin to truthfulness. More rarely, N will use *Rechtschaffenheit*, which contains the idea of law or right in a legal sense – this is a particularly common word in AC. Again, 'honesty' is a plausible translation, as is 'integrity', and given the context of AC, N probably intends to reclaim from Christianity the concept of 'righteousness'.

N accuses those who espouse morality of being dishonest (even and especially when they tout 'honesty' itself as a virtue; H1.52–3, 65, H2.32, 56, D84, GS319, TISkirmishes42). Honesty, especially honesty towards oneself, is a virtue that can lead to philosophical growth (H3.37, D167, 370, 556). At D370, this honesty means waging an agonistic campaign against yourself and your thoughts in the interests of truth (see Z1.10). At GS110, honesty is part of a speculative account of the genesis of the drive for truth. Zarathustra calls it the 'youngest of the virtues' (Z1.3, see 'On Truth and Lies' and Z4.13.8). N appears to associate honesty with the concept of intellectual conscience, a 'conscience behind your "conscience"' (GS335, AC12). Likewise, the cruelty of intellectual conscience in its ruthless pursuit of truth can be called honesty but, given that the will to truth is only one element within the will to power, this is a bit too pretty and showy a word (BGE230). Such a ruthless honesty carries dangers, however, such as the 'nausea and suicide' mentioned at GS107, the literally bloodless *specialization* of the 'conscientious in spirit' (Z4.4), or becoming 'saints and bores' (BGE227). Honesty is thus in a *cyclical* partnership with art and beauty, as its convalescence, and likewise with *mischievousness* or *laughter*. Honesty is not simply a question of truthfully relating what one knows or feels, but rather a process of critically evaluating these things, for they may be dishonest, the product of errors, misinterpretations, or surreptitious values (e.g. morality – see BGE5). Likewise, honesty is not just an intellectual process, but also a set of practices or *experiments* (e.g. the 'small marriage' at Z3.12.24, even asceticism 'as long as it is honest': GM3.26). Accordingly, honesty as part of one's task is compatible with dishonesty or evasion (e.g. BGE289–90). Eventually, honesty becomes 'instinct and passion' – that is to say, an aspect of a mode of life (AC36).

It is important to realize that honesty in N's sense is not incompatible with a certain inscrutability of the self. The point is made at BGE227 and again at GMP1 (and compare GS335). What is at stake here is an ontological or existential sense of honesty, rather than an epistemological one. For all that *critique* and *interpretation* of morality, religion and psychological states can achieve, knowledge and self-awareness are tools not goals. So, honesty as freedom from dangerous deceptions, values and mistakes, and as the practice or discipline of so freeing oneself, likewise also my health, and the alignment of my mode of life with the nature of life – none of these are the same as 'knowing oneself'. N is a 'riddle', but not one that he feels in the least compelled to solve (BGE281). Instead of self-knowledge, he aims for a 'faith' or 'certainty' concerning himself; N writes that 'the noble soul has *reverence* for itself' (BGE287). 'Reverence' translates *Ehrfurcht*, which has a common root with *Ehrlichkeit* (see discussion above); and thus 'honesty' here means that the noble soul finds itself noble and worthy of respect (see discussion under *veneration*). Similarly, at EHClever9, N claims that the process of becoming who you are involves a certain necessary lack of self-insight, so that the 'governing "idea"' should grow inside. He calls this 'selfishness'. The analogy is with *pregnancy*.

honour

See *veneration*.

hope

Hoffnung. Hope is so easily 'hope for a beyond' – that is, something that positively requires the discrediting of knowledge and reason (AC23) and the rejection of 'this life'. This is N's take on the myth of Pandora's box. Hope alone remained in the box after all the evil had been released; but this hope is not the salvation of the human but rather the worst curse, for it 'protracts the torment of men' (H1.71). As with a projected ideal, a hope is a product of the health of one's mode of life. Accordingly, at GSP1, N describes his illness circa 1880 as patient, severe, without hope – refusing the hope for a beyond that normally accrues to illness. Then, in his convalescence, he is 'attacked by hope'; but now, a hope that is within the compass of what is. This same contrast is found in Z, between 'all those who do not want to live, except they learn *to hope* again' (a hope that rejects life, Z4.11), and 'highest hope'

(Z1.8). The hope for a Dionysian future that N first put forward in BT is one that he has 'no reason to take back' (EHBT4).

Human, All Too Human: a book for free spirits

Originally three separate publications (1878, 1879, 1880), rebound together in 1886 in two volumes with new prefaces. The book is notable for introducing N's aphoristic style; a return to a broadly Enlightenment trust in *reason* and in scientific method; a thorough-going attempt to offer a *psychology* founded on pleasure and pain, which would investigate the history of the development of thought; the concept of a 'history of moral feelings', and key among these the feeling of *power*; some of Nietzsche's most sustained analyses of social organization and *politics*, employing especially the concept of *utility*. To a contemporary readership, the scattered comments on *art* and artists (see especially the fourth chapter of H1) would have clearly referred to Wagner; this book thus marks N's decisive break with his former friend and idol.

human/humanity

N's thoughts on the human per se are too diverse to be discussed in one entry. Despite occasional excursions into a philosophy of nature, the nature of the human is his most constant subject matter. Topics such as *art, morality, religion, history, science, politics* – N's interest in them lies almost exclusively in what forms of human life they express, and what implications they hold for other, possible forms of human life, and thus the relationship to the *animal* or the *overhuman*.

Here, let us focus on the concept of humaneness [*Humanität*, and sometimes N uses *Menschlichkeit* in this sense], by which N means the distinctive modes of excellence – particularly, healthy and noble but highly spiritualized feelings towards others – that belong to the human. A related term in English might be 'civilized'. Such humaneness does not mean that the human is not something to be overcome (ZP3), or that we have made moral progress, or that modes of human life within the modern world are not generally decadent and ill. Humaneness has not arisen for the reasons we believe (e.g. selflessness). Instead, they arise from the action of savage forces (H1.246) or basic errors (GS115). The notion of humaneness is N's attempt to justly judge what human beings have achieved. Good examples can be found at H1.624, H2.231, D81, TIGermans5, EHWC1. Humanity is also a common theme explored in notebook 15 from 1888 (see particularly entries 63, 67, 110, in which the 'true love of humanity' is distinguished from the pseudo-humanity of Christian morality). N expresses admiration for seventeenth-century France who 'loved existence' as a 'place where greatness and humanity are *possible* together' (D191). By the later work (BGE on), N often uses the term ironically (e.g. TISkirmishes37).

I

See *self.*

ideal

Ideal. By ideal is meant some kind of imagined state in which a mode of life is fully lived or a value is fully realized. By its nature, the ideal provokes a longing for it, or a striving so as to achieve it. Or, looked at differently, a mode of life is always associated with an ideal which defines it and towards which it longs and strives. That is how N uses the term 'goal' at Z1.15. Nietzsche uses the term ideal in three distinct senses. (i) An ideal which involves the negation of some aspect of life or of existence more generally. Often, the point of such analyses does not concern the ideal as such, but rather concerns what kinds of life would posit this as their ideal, and what have been the historical effects of the pursuit of this ideal. For example, in GM3, N writes about the 'ascetic ideal', the state in which freedom from passion or even sensation would be achieved. Likewise, the ideal human posited by morality is a tamed beast (TIImprovers). Ideals in this sense are generally targets of N's harshest criticism (e.g. EHPreface2). (ii) Occasionally, N uses 'ideal' to indicate someone's desire for something which is beyond them, mere fantasy, and thus a kind of escape from reality (TISkirmishes32) – it is thus related to 'idealism'. Here, the ideal requires the positing of and probably subordination to some transcendent reality; in this way it is (like the first type) opposed to life and this world. (iii) Ideal as a projection of one's possibilities of health, growth or beauty, which does not require either the rejection of what is, or the positing of a transcendence. Thus, for example, the Greek gods are the 'ideal image' of the Greek mode of life (BT3, and see also H2.99, GS143); or, the ideal of the philosopher that N derives from Schopenhauer's value as educator (UM3.5). N uses the term ideal particularly for his various concepts of future and higher types of human (e.g. GS382). Accordingly, he also sees his philosophical work as proposing this ideal as a 'counter-' or 'opposite' ideal. It is 'counter' to those ideals that are projected by weak or ill modes of life (GM2.23 and 3.23, BGE56, EHGM).

idealism

Kant termed his own thought 'transcendental idealism', and the German philosophical tradition after Kant (e.g. Fichte, Schelling and Hegel) is often called 'German Idealism'. However, N makes little or no mention of these specific meanings. N's usage is also not the everyday sense in English: an idealist as someone who holds unrealistic goals or values. N's use of the term refers instead to any philosophical, ethical or religious doctrine that rejects (as illusory, false, degrading, or inferior) 'this world', one or more of its primary features (especially becoming), and our bodily connection to it (sensation). Parmenides and Plato are the key philosophical points of reference. N's account of idealism thus ties in closely with the notion of *ascetic ideals*. At GS372 the attitude to the senses is key. N offers a critique of modern science beginning in GM3.23. In the following section, he groups together many of his contemporaries – 'pale atheists, anti-Christians, immoralists, nihilists, these sceptics' – labelling them all idealists. They are the last and most spiritualized devotees of the ascetic ideal, because they still believe in *truth*. In this passage also, N refers us back to GS344, which explains why there is an idealism implicit in any appeal to 'truth'.

Idylls from Messina

A collection of poems published by N in 1882, at roughly the same time as he was completing *The Gay Science*. Some of the poems, in a revised form and with completely different titles, were reused in the Appendix to the second edition of *The Gay Science*.

illusion

See *appearance*.

imagination

Various constructions based upon *Einbildung*. Imagination is a very important concept in earlier German philosophy, but in N its function is mostly treated under other headings (e.g. *interpretation, metaphor*). Imagination has two functions, the reproductive and the productive (this idea comes from Kant). The first means presenting an image of that which exists or existed but is not now present. For example, memory involves imagination in this sense; likewise gathering together similar instances under a single *concept*. Productive imagination means generating an image of that which was never and perhaps could never be present. That is, it is akin either to *creativity*, to having sympathy for other's feelings (H1.59), or to generating an illusion or delusion. This last idea is most frequent in N. For example, the lyric poet's subjectivity (BT5), the over-historical age's justice (UM2.5–6), Christian love for enemies (H2.96), the 'higher world' of 'higher feelings' (D33), art in contrast to science (D550), or revenge (GS359). There is a positive use, however, as part of the method N claims as his own, and missing from all his contemporaries, of the 'discriminating, experimental imagination' in grasping problems of value (GS345).

incorporation, internalization

Various terms. To incorporate means to make something that is outside or different from the self, part of the self. This can be literal (food), or figurative (acquiring a new piece of knowledge, experience, value, habit, etc.). The concept is thus related to translation or interpretation (i.e. to bring something within one's sphere of intelligibility), possession, inheritance (i.e. incorporation that happens over generations, see TISkirmishes47), education (see D540), simplification (or reduction, that is to make something manageable), issues surrounding diet or environment, or internalization [*verinnerlichung*]. By internalization N means taking a value or the object of will to power – originally directed to something outside – and applying it to oneself (see GM2.16, GM3.14; see also D104, 248).

The notion of incorporation becomes important fairly early, in N's account of culture. An authentic culture is one of great 'plastic power' (UM2.1). That is, it is capable of encountering what is foreign, perhaps taking it into itself, changing of course, but remaining whole – which means not having that tension between form and content characteristic of German 'culture' (UM2.4). The health of a culture is not its stability per se, but rather its capacity to 'inoculate' itself with change (H1.224). The idea is also applied to individual free spirits in H (e.g. H1.292, H2.228). GS thinks of this process in terms of a generation of new instincts: the making 'flesh and blood' of the values of the creative (GS301), or – where the process has gone too far – making a species fixed, as monotheism threatened to do (GS143).

The essential distinction is between the incorporation *as error*, or the incorporation *of knowledge*. Often incorporation involves simplification – fitting the new into existing categories – or the treating of always different moments of the flux of becoming as identities. Importantly, this is not simply the work of weak or ill spirits. Rather, it is the 'basic will of the spirit' (BGE230, 1885.2.90). However, there is the counter movement of the 'seeker after knowledge' described in that passage. This is the will to multiplicity, to not reducing, not being content with the surface – this manifests itself as a kind of cruelty to one's own intellect (and see GS11). The upshot is the famous idea, found at GS110: 'to what extent can truth stand to be incorporated'. That is, to what extent is it possible to remain healthy, to remain set on the task of the growth of the human type, while at the same time having knowledge (or truth). Or, expressed more ambitiously, what new form of human life can be experimentally discovered for which health and knowledge are not incompatible (see also Z1.22.2). The knowledge N has in mind here is not simply indifferent to life and health – it is not knowledge for its own sake (e.g. GSP4). Rather, the knowledge most difficult to incorporate healthily is precisely knowledge concerning the conditions of health; for example that moral opposites are not really opposite, or science is founded upon a set of basic errors. See *digestion, spirit*.

independence

See *freedom, free spirit*.

individual

Individuum, Einzelne. Individual is meant in two senses. First, in the metaphysical sense in which individual entities (or causes and effects) are separable from each other. Second, in the moral or political sense of individual human beings. N's view of the former is influenced by Schopenhauer. He argued that the primary feature of the *apparent* world was that it was made up of individual entities and events. Within this apparent world, this individualization was presumed basic, along with it the intellectual tools needed to conceive of individuals (e.g. space and time, number, concepts of identity – that is, Kant's transcendental conditions of experience). In contrast, the underlying *will* (the truly real) is a continuous flood of desire and change. Apparently individual things are only momentary manifestations of the will. This Schopenhauerian framework is adopted more or less wholesale by N in his early work, such as BT. In later work, N certainly rejects the dualism of appearance and reality. Nevertheless, he remains convinced that a key feature of the intellect is to 'create' for itself individual, isolated things (e.g. H1.18, BGE4). Thereby, the world becomes subject to naming and concept-formation, both of which involve a blindness to continuities or differences – for no two entities are in fact identical, and the same holds for human beings (UM3.1, H1.286, H3.11, GS335, 1885.34.123, TIMorality6; the idea owes much to Leibniz' arguments concerning 'the identity of indiscernibles').

The narrower meaning of individual is that of the single, separate human being, and its value. In part, N's thinking in this sphere follows from his thinking about entities more generally. Thus, in the first chapter of BGE, the discussion of atomism as a general physical theory leads immediately into 'soul atomism' – that is the soul as single and unique, having a fixed character (H1.41), or the ground of individual human identity (BGE12). N suggests replacing this 'soul atomism' with an account of identity involving 'multiplicity' (and see the comments about friendship at H1.376; also H1.618). There is another contributing line of thought, however, which is N's analysis of the 'herd' or 'mob'. Christian notions of equality before God, and modern democratic notions of legal and political equality make it *appear* as if the political and social domains are made up of autonomous individuals. This, N argues, is wrong on two counts. Human beings may share inherited drives, and also language, customs and values. Within the herd, there are numerically distinct human beings but there are in fact no individuals (e.g. D105). N goes so far as to speculate that in groups, consciousness is collective (GS354). For such modes of human life, the group is more basic than the single person. Equality among individuals is only possible for those not of the herd, and also of equal rank (where 'rank' means philosophical *nobility* primarily rather than social *class*).

It might seem reasonable to suppose that N is espousing either or both of (i) a kind of radical individualism, where individuals are valued for their own sake as truly autonomous; or (ii) libertarianism, where individual rights and freedoms are the basis for any successful and just political arrangement. On these views, collective morality and other ideas (including the scientific) would involve the repression of individuality. Nineteenth-century liberalism and romanticism both espouse versions of the above. N seems to suggest something like this frequently, although generally with the caveat concerning the herd discussed above. Clear examples are to be found at D132, GS143, 335. At H1.94–5, N argues that morality moves from 'crude' individual self-interest to the individual as law-giver, but where these laws tend to favour communal utility over the personal. In other words, the history of morality is neither the creation of, nor the annihilation of, the individual. Rather, it modifies the sense of the individual, and his or her spiritual ability to envisage and pursue certain goals. Likewise at D107–8, where the repression of the individual is certainly lamented, but where it is also clear that the individual per se is not the issue, but rather the 'slow growth' of reason, or the proposing of goals for humanity as a whole.

In the early to middle period, N argues that the function of culture is the production of individual great men (e.g. UM2.6, 3.6, D529). However, the phrase 'individual great men' does not necessarily mean that they will be individuals in the romantic, libertarian sense, but rather that they are representatives of a culture that is more whole and healthy. Thus, at UM4.4, the meaning of tragedy is the struggle of the individual against the 'prevailing order of things', and yet also the 'consecration' of the individual to something higher. That idea of consecration to something higher remains a key theme in N to the end; GS1 names it as the 'species' – the enhancement of the human – and blames morality not now for repressing the individual, but for promoting a certain view of the individual as value in itself, to the detriment of health. N's targets there are concepts of democratic equality, individual rights and the virtues of charity and pity (see also GS356, BGE188, TISkirmishes41). Again, N is neither for or against the individual per se, but tries to understand the role of individuals with respect to historical development (or decay) – this is made particularly clear at TISkirmishes33.

Indeed, N often gives a historical analysis suggesting that the appearance of individuals is *cyclical*, a historical function of human life in its progression. The idea is this: human life grows during certain historical periods without any need for individuals. It is during periods of corruption that individuals emerge as a broadly revolutionary force (the point is made explicitly at GS1 and 23 but is also the subject of many surrounding passages). Once a new, higher plateau of culture is arrived at, the individual again becomes irrelevant (this is the meaning of H3.337). For example, N argues at H1.224 that the strong collective individual is the foundation of culture, but leads it towards 'inherited stupidity' (i.e. towards decadence). In contrast, we have the weak individuals, meaning those who are unable to help bear culture. Such individuals experiment with new cultural forms and are thus both a danger to the existing culture (and subjected to sacrifice H2.89), but also what allows it to develop (compare GS24). Broadly similar historical narratives, outlining a cycle of dangerous individualism with respect to culture, are outlined at GS76, Z1.15, BGE257–8 and 262. The sovereign individual, discussed in GM2.2, is N's most famous discussion of such a phenomenon. This individual 'resembles himself only' (i.e. is not part of the 'making regular' that is the work of morality). He or she has acquired the capacity and right to be responsible and make promises, the having of a long will and the strength of mastery over intervening circumstances. The language is Kantian in flavour (and see also, for example, AC11–12), and certainly presents a part of N's ideal. However, that the terms of this description are so different from GM2.24 suggests that the 'sovereign individual' is by no means the whole of N's ideal (i.e. the overhuman) but rather a stage in the cycle of history. It is precisely the decadence of moral culture that leads to autonomous individuals, who then possess the far-sightedness for the creation of new modes of life that is normally found in only peoples or states as a whole (TISkirmishes39). The task of free spirits, broadly speaking, would be to take this 'natural' cyclical process and make it deliberate, for example by reforming institutions in accordance with the function of the individual (e.g. education, discussed at H1.242). GS371 summarizes the idea by suggesting that individualism as a cultural stage should outgrow itself, leaving 'we incomprehensible ones' as 'no longer free . . . to be anything individual' (and see H2P6, GMP2). N goes so far as to suggest that from the highest Dionysian perspective of health, nothing is 'reprehensible' except the individual (TISkirmishes49).

industry (work)

See *work*.

inheritance

Various terms. N holds what might be called a strong account of biological determinism. Our virtues and vices, strengths and weaknesses, nobility or slavishness, are by and large a family inheritance. This happens through selective breeding, and also through the inheriting of acquired characteristics (a now-discredited concept). For clear examples see Z4.13.13, BGE264, the inheritance of herd disposition (BGE199), or the many generations it takes to produce a philosopher (BGE213, and see TISkirmishes47). This is also the reason why nobility can be built up within a family, or why morality can be a programme for breeding a particular type of human being. Accordingly, N also talks about national or racial types (the Germans, the Jews, etc.). Late in life, he believes his ancestry is Polish nobility (EHWise3). Nevertheless, N has to leave room for the effects of *cultural* institutions. Because such institutions – such as moral customs, religious practices, political and social forms of organization – last across generations, they are an important mode of non-biological inheritance. For examples, see AC44, N's discussion of the ascetic priest at GM3.11 (and see *marriage*). N also does not discount the effect of *education*, and the activities or habits of everyday life (e.g. UM2.3), or *experimental* modes of living, or finally the *incorporation* of truth (Z2.8, BGE231), in modifying, repressing or furthering the inheritance.

innocence

Unschuld. By innocence N means one of two related ideas. First, the lack of any absolutely existing values, purposes or designs, both for human beings, and for nature more generally. For example, it was God's prohibition against eating the apple which created the possibility of humans being in conformity with the law, or guilty of transgression. Adam and Eve were never innocent, even before their transgression, because they were subject to law. Likewise, to the extent that we think Platonically that ordinary things are somehow 'shadows' of Forms, or similarly that things were made according to God's idea of them, then ordinary things are not innocent. Examples of innocence in N include the child stage (Z1.1), the senses or sensuality (Z1.13), perception (Z2.15) or chance (Z3.6). Importantly, innocence chance or accident is not understood in the sense of the random; rather a necessity but not one that follows from some set of independently existing laws.

Second, innocence follows from a lack of freedom, namely the freedom of an individual to follow or break some law. Such freedom would mean that an individual can be held responsible for their actions, as approved of or prohibited by pre-existing values (see H1.99, D13, TIErrors7). In the absence of freedom (in this traditional sense), one is innocent. N's frequent analyses of the nature of the criminal, and of the 'justice' that judges and punishes, employ this second idea of innocence. There is an alternative analysis of the problem of freedom, namely that freedom itself would be the absolutely existing value which stains innocence in the first sense above. This second possibility is why, for N, Kant's moral theory is so important. Indeed, N sometimes writes in strongly Kantian language (e.g. the 'sovereign individual' at GM2.2), incorporating Kant's notion of autonomy but without the notion of a moral law. The conceptual inconsistencies in the relation between free will and punishment are explored at H3.23. By way of contrast, the innocence of acting is discussed at GM2.14–16. It is in a different sense of freedom that N equates freedom and innocence (e.g. 1885.2.206).

instinct or drive

Instinkt; *Trieb* is generally translated as 'drive'. 'Instincts' and 'drives' are two different ways of talking about the basic behaviours of some organism or type. By instinct is meant those behaviours that are regular and predictable, and thus define an organism as to its type. N tends to use the term 'drive' to mean a more or less constant and active movement towards some end, and one that always carries a value (H1.32). N sometimes identifies drives with will to power ('every drive wants to be master': BGE6). Occasionally, he uses the two terms interchangably (e.g. TIErrors5).

N does not provide a systematic typology of instincts or drives, but certainly mentions a great many. He talks about instinct or drives when he wishes to ascribe some apparently virtuous behaviour to organic functions (e.g. instinct for health at H2P2, instinct for life at TIMorality4), likewise some apparently intellectual behaviour (instinctive reaction to fear at GS355, instinct as a form of cleverness at BGE207 – and see BGE3), or when he wishes to reduce the behaviour of an individual to a type (e.g. Luther at GS358). Conversely, habits, broader modes of life, or even knowledge may become instinct (examples include GS11, 361, GM2.2, EHDestiny6). That is to say, part of N's analysis of drives or instincts includes the mechanisms by which they can be created or modified. Accordingly, a key type of decadence is the 'anarchy' of the instincts, in which the instincts are no longer in any way unified by a strong culture or by a noble health. Discussions with these themes can be found at GM2.16, TISocrates9, TIErrors2, TISkirmishes41, AC5.

institutions

An institution is a mode of social organization that embodies and perpetuates a set of values. The most obvious example in N are *religious* organizations, but he also regularly discusses *marriage*, criminal *punishment*, the state (see *politics*), *education*, artistic traditions (UM4.10). Likewise, N speculates on alternative institutions for the *free spirits*. A good example of N thinking about various institutions at length is UM3.6.

interpretation

Several German words can be grouped together here: *Auslegung*, *Deutung* or *Ausdeutung*, *Interpretation*. N uses the concept of interpretation in two ways. First, interpretation signifies the meaning that is given to states, entities or events based upon some more basic set of conditions (e.g. on deeply held values or instincts). Although this concept pre-dates it by nearly a decade, interpretation is thus related to what the later N calls *perspective*. For example, N lampoons Gervinus' 'moral-pathological' interpretation of Shakespeare at BT22, and mischievously speculates that Socrates' moral practices led him to interpret an 'ear infection' as his 'daemon' (H1.126); similarly with artistic interpretation (H2.126), or objective history (UM2.6, BGE38). This idea of interpretation is generalized to the lack of intellectual conscience of all religions (D319). In that passage, N is clearly indebted to the Stoics who also considered affects to be interpretations. An important text in this regard is 'On Truth and Lies' where clearly something like interpretation (or artistic creativity, metaphor) is at work behind all conscious life, use of language or relation to the world. It is from such a universal and fundamental sense of interpretation that N's notion of perspective arises. In BGE and thereafter, N is clearly using concepts of interpretation more or less equivalently to his concept of perspective.

The second main use of the concept of interpretation is as a specific methodological issue within historical, textual or psychological analysis. Interpretation in a strict philological sense would be the reconstruction of texts, establishing dating and authorship, tracing word meanings and making sense of cryptic or fragmentary passages. N's early publications are good examples, but see also his critique of the use of the Greek word *pneuma* in the New Testament (H1.143 see *spirit*), and his critique of the 'Christianization' of the Old Testament (D84, 1887.11.302). What N is doing in such passages relates to the tradition of *critical* hermeneutics. N's views on the desirability or even possibility of such genuinely objective approaches varies (compare for example UM2.6 and H1.132, 134). Also typical of N's thought is attention to the origin and development of language and the use of language. N's frequent interpretation of etymologies should be understood as reflecting the basic idea that language develops out of historically specific forms of life (and in turn helps to perpetuate them). That is, language embodies a set of values by which a people lives, identifies and perpetuates itself. Similarly, the fact that certain old terms or phrases are still in use may reflect aspects of our own mode of life of which we are not aware. A variation on this idea is the famous notion that an interpretation of the Greeks is like a mirror in which aspects of the modern world allow themselves to be seen (H2.218).

Interpretation on the analogy of philology helps us to understand aspects of N's practice as a writer. What does it mean for N to be a poet, or a writer of *aphorisms*? The value of incomplete thoughts (or incomplete expressions of thought) such as those found in poets is not in telling us new ideas, but rather in stimulating a desire for new ideas (D207, GSPrelude23). GM3 is accordingly a model of the kind of interpretation N would expect of readers of his work (see GMP8). N's aim for a certain 'timelessness' in his writing is related to a critique of philology as a historical mode of understanding (D506). Finally, N wishes to be read as a 'good old philologist' would read Horace (EHBooks5) – Horace can express what other languages cannot even express the desire for, N says by way of an explanation (TIAncients1).

These two meanings of interpretation (interpretation as a fundamental process related to perspective, and interpretation as reading on the model or analogy of philology) are related, certainly. It was N's professional training as a philologist that provided him with a sensitivity to and much of the evidence for the phenomenon of interpretation in the first sense. The clearest examples of the relation of these two meanings of interpretation are found in 'On Truth and Lies' and UM1; and see H1.8 or BGE22 where N compares the interpretation of nature in physics with the interpretation of texts in philology.

intoxication

Rausch. N uses the notion of intoxication consistently throughout his career to talk about art. In BT it is associated with the *Dionysian*, and means a state in which individuality is surrendered to the underlying Will. Later, at TISkirmishes8–11, N generalizes further: all art requires some type of intoxication, which 'intensifies' experiences, and is a feeling of strength, fullness or overflow. (See also notes from this period in 1888.14.) At GP1, N talks analogously about the 'intoxication' of his convalescence from illness. Intoxication is thus related to the idea of *gift*.

intuition

The word discussed here is the latinate *Intuition* rather than Kant's *Anschauung*. (N only rarely uses the latter in a Kantian or Schopenhauerian technical sense: for example GS99, BGE33.) In his early work, N employs the notion of intuition to indicate a kind of thinking or awareness that is not – or is not entirely – held within the accepted conceptual limits of a language.) See the 'man of intuition' at 'Truth and Lies' 2, BT4 and 25, and 'The Greek State'. This solves the problem of how a new or independent way of thinking could arise, and also how a way of thinking could arise that understands the origin of language and thought. By the later work, he has decisively abandoned this solution to such problems (see D550, BGE16).

irony

In the everyday sense, irony means to write or speak in such a way as to indicate that what is really meant is different from the surface meaning. N employs such irony frequently as a rhetorical strategy, for example in the pretended disbelief expressed by 'What?' at BGE15. Socratic irony is an important variation: pretended naivete or ignorance in order to draw out a response or initiate a discussion. BGE7 contains examples in its unanswered questions to which, we suspect, N has in reserve an answer. Romantic irony is a concept in the German tradition referring to the manner in which a finite written text can indicate the chaos and infinity of the universe, perhaps by pointing out an author's lack of control over both his or her text and its meaning (N employs something of this idea at GS383, BGE277, 296 and GMP1), or by being deliberately fragmentary or open-ended (see *aphorism*). Finally, at UM2.5, N speaks of a dangerous irony that belongs to modernity, in which it sees itself as a late-comer of 'epigone', and thus is detached from, or over-reflective upon, itself.

Jesus

N's primary concern in this area is with Christianity – a family of religions that has had a profound effect upon the history of Europe. He is less interested in Jesus as a historical figure than with *what was made of Jesus* by the Church Fathers (and in particular by St *Paul*), and what continues to be made of him in the contemporary world. In early and middle period work, this distinction is not yet fully formed, however. So, passages like H1.144 or 235 portray Jesus in a manner continuous with the later Christian tradition. The change perhaps comes in the brief mention at Z1.21, and is complete by BGE (see BGE164, 269). The result is the two-part analysis in AC. First, Jesus himself as something akin to a Buddhist (roughly AC29–35); second, the complete and malicious misunderstanding of Jesus by Paul in order to create a new religion (AC39–47). Thus, when EH ends with the famous 'Have I been understood? – *Dionysus versus the crucified*' (HEDestiny9), the contrast is not with Jesus but with the later, religious figure of the sacrificed god. However, in contrast, see GM1.8 where N emphasizes continuity with the values characteristic of the later period of Jewish history.

Jews, the

The Jewish people and the Jewish religion are both frequent preoccupations of N. This is because both inform the history of Europe. Although N's work would become closely associated with *anti-Semitic* thought, N himself condemned anti-Semitism.

For understanding N, it is worth distinguishing three phases of Jewish history. First, the early period, in which the Israelites represent one of N's archetypes of a strong and great people. This is 'the most remarkable people in world history' (AC24), a people 'firmly attached to life' (D72) and not characterized by an ascetic hatred of the body; 'the moral genius of all peoples' (GS136) and the origin of sublimity in morality (BGE250). Originally, the people of Israel had a 'natural relation to all things', and their Yahweh was a expression of their power and their values (AC25). Second, a later phase in which power is passed to a priestly class who interpret the nation's failures in terms of sin with respect to a divine world order (AC25, GS135); their morality becomes abstract, their religion no longer one related to the needs of a people. The people have become artificial, we might say. The priestly type 'has a life-interest in making humanity sick' (AC24). This is the invention of the Jewish religion as a 'world' religion. Insofar as Christianity represents a slave rebellion (AC27), it is this anti-natural morality that prepared the ground for it (BGE195, and this is the implication of D377). In AC, N traces this later history of the Jews, the figure of Jesus and the various interpretations placed upon him, ultimately concluding that Christianity is a continuation and generalization of his late Jewish religion and morality. The third phase, skipping a couple of thousand years, finds the Jews and Judaism dispersed and stateless in the modern world. They will be instrumental in the formation of a united Europe (D205); they have given to philosophy logic (GS348); and remain the 'strongest, toughest and purest race' (BGE251).

journals, journalism

See *newspaper.*

joy

See *happiness.*

judgement

Judgement is used in two broad senses. First, a type of mental act (*Urteil*), usually the ascription of a property to something ('the pencil is long') or a classification of something ('That is a cat'). Judgement was a particularly key theme for Kant. Second, much more specifically, the defining act of a judge (*Richter*), particularly with respect to those accused of being criminal or sinful (H2.33, GM3.14). See *punishment, criminal.*

N argues that a judgement in the first sense implicitly makes unjustifiable and *metaphysical* claims about the thing judged (1872.19.242, H1.18), for example confusion of *cause* with effect, of relations with the thing related or belief in substance and identity. The demand that judgement be made, or made prematurely, is criticized by N at AC40, 52. With respect to judgement, N presents both his own concept of *justice*, and also the ancient notion of the suspension of judgement (*ephexis* or *epoche*, in the Stoics and Skeptics, see D82, AC52). Philological method demands that one refrain from judgement or interpretation – until all the evidence has been presented and weighed, and thus see AC62. This involves patience, caution, multiple perspectives and the ability not to react to a stimulus (TIGermans6, this last point is another Stoic notion). Interestingly, also in TI, the Dionysian is defined as the inability not to react to any stimulus (TIAncients). That is, the Dionysian achieves just judgement not by *epoche*, but in exactly the opposite manner: through *comprehensive* intoxication, aligning with the world understood as a network of will to power.

justice

Normally *Gerechtigkeit*. Justice has a narrower meaning – criminal, social or political justice – and a more general one. On the narrower meaning, and in deference to Hobbes' version of the social contract, N posits an equilibrium of power and the establishment of law as the origin of justice (H1.92, H3.22, GM2.8, 11). One should compare also passages such as D199, where N speculates that the main role of the state was to sublimate aggressive instincts among those of approximately equal power. Similarly, the noble and active human being invents instruments of justice to sublimate the feelings of *ressentiment* among the people (GM2.11). Where the instruments of power posit an equality of persons – that is something much more than an equality before the law – then this is the 'end of justice' (TISkirmishes48). Similarly, justice as the imposition of the law of God is revenge, not justice (see GM1.14, H2.33).

The more general meaning is that of a just viewpoint – an overall or comprehensive, but not abstract, view that understands the role of each in the scheme of things. Such a justice is active (GM2.11), 'gives to each its own' (H1.636) and is 'love with seeing eyes' (Z1.19). It is a viewpoint that aligns itself with the nature of things, and is thus akin to 'eternal justice' (BT25). In part, the idea is from Heraclitus, where justice is the recognition of the reciprocal necessity of conflict, of the generation and destruction of things. Importantly, however, this justice is not the same as objectivity or disinterestedness (GM2.6, 3.6). This wider notion of justice is also at work in the narrower one: for example, it is the more comprehensive view that disproves the socialist's analysis of property (H1.452). This view is difficult, and indeed the health of individuals and peoples may depend upon limited horizons, on being 'unjust' in certain ways (this is the problem of history in UM2.1). The egoism of the truly noble is just, because this egoism is not the same as a narrow, individual selfishness (BGE265 and see *egoism*). Although the relationship is more clear in English than in German, in defining justice as 'giving each its own' we can hear 'gift' – thus, Z1.19 also talks about being 'rich enough' and N writes 'the noble soul gives as it takes' (BGE265). Thus, above, we saw N talk about the noble and active individual creating justice as a sublimation of *ressentiment*.

Kant

Kant is one of the few philosophers with whom N has a constant dialogue or struggle throughout his career. It is not clear just how much of Kant N read, however; much of his familiarity probably came second-hand by way of Schopenhauer and those contemporary neo-Kantian philosophers that he certainly did read. In the 1860s, N made extensive notes for a thesis on the second part of Kant's *Critique of Judgement*. From this early source, Kantian themes of life, purpose and wholeness are found later throughout N's work, although he rarely makes mention of Kant in this connection. In most of N's work, explicit discussion of Kant's philosophy concerns five other issues:

1   Kant's *critical* study of the foundations of experience. In BT, N thinks of Kant and *Schopenhauer* as investigating the conditions of possibility of science, performing a critique, and thus precipitating a crisis in Socratic thought (BT18; see also UM1.6, 3.3). Here, Kant is a revolutionary figure, and excepting Schopenhauer subsequent German thought is disappointing in its inability even to recognize this fact. The revolution lies in the impossibility of a naïve realism, or in a conception of science and truth that rests upon such a realism. The concept of *causality* is particular important for N in this regard. Much of N's reading of contemporary philosophers of science was of broadly neo-Kantian thinkers such as Lange, Helmholz, Spir or Gerber. Later in his career, N takes a much more sceptical look at Kant's work concerning the foundations of epistemology (BGE11). However, even here he is not questioning the 'revolutionary' aspect of Kant discussed above (see GS357, BGE54). Rather, the point of N's scepticism here concerns the basic concepts Kant used to account for the possibility of experience. N argues that Kant's reasoning is circular (begs the question), and that moreover Kant was not even asking the right question, which is one of *value*. N seems to call for a critique but with different, less empty foundations: specifically, the *will to power* as the condition of the possibility of experience. In other words, N sometimes

understands his own work as a kind of Kantianism but
with a shift towards a more concrete and historically
situated underlying set of mechanisms. (See *perspective*.)
Kant's assumption that the conditions of experience are not
to be understood in terms of value means that Kant was a
great critic (BGE210), but not a 'whole' philosopher in N's
sense.

2 Kant's exposing of the dialectical illusions of transcendent
and especially religious thought. One of the most famous
implications of Kant's epistemology, discussed above, is
that the possibility of experience (and thus knowledge)
has definite limits. Certain kinds of questions, particularly
metaphysical ones such as the nature of the soul, or
the existence of God, are meaningless ('dialectical').
Propositions in these areas can be neither proven nor
disproven. On the one hand, not surprisingly, N approves:
this puts the emphasis both in philosophy and in other
disciplines back onto the world as accessible to the senses.
(See entries on *sensualism, world, idealism*.) On the other
hand, the neither proven nor disproven concept appears to
N as a ploy to legitimate concepts such as *faith* or *freedom*
(AC10), both of which Kant indeed defended against
sceptical attack. Similarly, N argues that Kant's concept of
the intelligible character of things is part of the *ascetic ideal*
(GM3.12).

3 The concept of *regulative* ideas (see separate entry).

4 The moral law and autonomy. Kant argues that the only
way in which the rational will can be both free (where
freedom is a condition of ethical action) and also law-
governed, is if the rational will *gives laws to itself* (is
autonomous). (In this there is something of the Leibnizian
solution to the problem of free will, and likewise the Stoic.)
Moral law presents itself as a 'categorical imperative' –
that is, a command to the self that is not conditional upon
anything else. This structure of self-legislation N finds
compelling, and he employs analogues to it frequently
enough (e.g. the account of promising in GM2). Kant's
assumption, however, is that in the absence of any influence
from my situation or character, 'my' reason is universal,

and thus the laws I give to myself will be the same as any other rational creature. On N's analysis, this would require reason to be transcendent with respect to body, nature and history – Kant's assumption is thus absurd, and the assertion of universality dangerous and destructive (AC11).

5 The beautiful. There are a number of constituent ideas to Kant's analysis of the beautiful, but the most important for N are disinterestedness and *play* (see separate entry). Nietzsche discusses the former idea at length at GM3.6, in relation to Schopenhauer and the ascetic ideal. At best, distinterestedness is a psychological error; at worst, it demonstrates the extent to which the infection of the ascetic ideal has spread to aesthetics, the theory of knowledge and so forth. (See *beauty, taste*.) Nevertheless, a different concept of 'being just' towards things emerges in N. This has its genesis in Kant's notion of 'indeterminant judgement' (i.e. a judgement that is not simply the application of some concept) and in particular Schlegel's use of that notion (see *justice*).

knowledge

See *truth*.

labyrinth

The labyrinth is a standard metaphor for a problem that is both dangerous and bewildering (e.g. H1.291, BGE29, GM3.24). Wagner – because he sums up modernity – is the guide to the labyrinth of the 'modern soul' (WCP). See *Ariadne*.

Lange

Nineteenth-century German philosopher and author of *History of Materialism*. Lange was a neo-Kantian, but looked to the living body, and in particular the physiology of the nervous system, as the seat of the transcendental operations that make experience and knowledge possible. He also offers an appraisal of materialism – in the sense of Democritus and ancient atomism – which he considers the basis of contemporary scientific knowledge but which is metaphysically naïve. Both of these ideas were influential on N.

language

As a philologist, N's primary professional interest was Greek language and literature. Thus, his approach to the nature and function of language is not just philosophical, but also arises from out of philological studies. For example, many of the concepts we know best from the famous essay 'On Truth and Lies' are found in his lectures on ancient rhetoric. In addition, there is a significant influence on N from contemporary writers such as Gerber, who emphasize the importance of language and language-like processes (e.g. metaphor) in human cognition.

We will discuss N's views on language under the following headings:

1 The relation of language to truth. It will be useful to distinguish here between three 'levels' of language, implicitly found in N's discussion in 'On Truth and Lies'. The first are the kinds of unique responses in sounds that are made to 'nervous stimuli'. Even at this most basic level, however, these 'words' are by no means immediately related to the stimuli, but undergo modification, selection, amplification or association. (Later, N often suggests that such transformations already occur in stimuli themselves – there is no basic data [see for example 1887.11.113]. This idea becomes part of the *will to power*.) The second level is the formation of a language for the common use of a group, permitting communication about the needs and values of that group. A third is the development of a system of concepts for understanding, measuring and predicting both the human group and the world around them. Because of this third level, both science and philosophy (in the sense of metaphysics) are possible. The subsequent levels are built upon the preceding ones, through a further series of modifying 'metaphors'. Because of this series of

discontinuities, the world as understood through *any* of these levels of language is not the world as it is (H1.11). Rather, it is now a world that is intelligible, suited to our needs, capable of being predicted and controlled. It follows, therefore, that what we normally call *truth* or knowledge – claims about the world expressed in language as unambiguously and as precisely as possible – is a form of 'lie'. However, this in itself is not necessarily an objection to it (BGE4), for truth might be defined as what is an essential condition of a form of life (1885.40.15). Employing etymological analysis as a method is as least a partial solution to recovering the meaning of some of these transformations (e.g. GM1.4).

2   The relation of language to communication and communities. What we called above the second 'level' of language is one that is shared and agreed upon by a social group. But this agreement is founded upon shared interests, needs and values. Language is thus limited by the way that the group, on the basis of its interests, interprets its world. N's clearest account of this is found at BGE268. By limited N means that it is difficult or impossible to express an idea, or refer to a type of experience, that is not already held in common. Moreover, language in turn forms the human, enhancing this commonness. Within common language use, exceptional human beings will thus be at a disadvantage, because isolated and poorly understood. There is a counter-movement, which is rhetorical or poetic in form: a language becomes 'great' because it enforces upon itself apparently arbitrary constraints of rhyme and rhythm. The tie that these phenomena have to the body (e.g. the relation to dance, or the length of breath – BGE246–7) is another resource for breaking through the limits of the common. During his convalescence, Zarathustra delights in the 'chatter' of his animals, because their naïve use of language disguises the uniqueness of his pain, and makes his 'abyss deep' thoughts into mere sounds (Z3.13). More generally, though, Zarathustra despairs of finding 'ears' ready to hear his new teachings (ZP). The task of *style* for N then is of communicating to those who might be able to

understand – where understanding is not just an intellectual state, but one that also involves coordinated modes of life – while avoiding reaching those who are in some way not ready (GS381). Thus N sometimes talks about having a language 'of my own' (GMP4) or 'our new language' (BGE4, EHBooks1). The point is not so much about a new set of words and concepts that are different, but rather the whole new mode of life and set of experiences that underlie them.

3   The relation of language to concepts and to thought. Generally, thought (moral, scientific or philosophical thinking most obviously) is conditioned by language. As a result, N argues that concepts like substance, free will or atoms are all derived from and held in place by basic grammar (e.g. GS354, BGE20, TIReason5), or even from the phenomenon of concept-formation itself (the third level of language; see H3.11, D115). Similarly, language seems unable to avoid using oppositions (BGE24). Philosophers are caught in the 'web' or 'net' of language (1872.19.135 and then much later at 1886.5.22). This determination is not just in terms of what thoughts are thinkable, but also in terms of *values*: what thoughts are considered valuable. However, between what we called above the first and second levels of language, and again between the second and third, there is a 'gap' that might allow us a kind of thinking that is not restricted by the grammatical functions of language or the metaphysical beliefs and values embedded in higher-level concepts. The essay 'On Truth and Lies' ends with a description of the 'man of intuition', where *intuition* stands for this different kind of thought. In the later work, there are a number of passages that would seem to rely upon this sense of a kind of thought prior to – or at least independent from the systematic nature of – language and more specifically concepts. For example, the lament over 'dying' thoughts at GS298 and again at BGE296; the analysis of thinking in words at GM3.8; the account of Jesus as a mode of life distinct from any contingent set of concepts at AC32; or the way that N talks about the writing of Z at EHZ3. The last cited passage refers us back to Z3.9.

laughter

Lachen. In H, N attempts a psychological account of laughter and the comic: these arise when something happens that is sudden or unexpected – but entirely harmless or indeed nonsensical (H1.169, 213). This is a general account, which includes those everyday instances of laughter that carry no philosophical significance. However, the basic idea is useful in understanding the kinds of laughter that N does consider significant. Such laughter is a release from the kinds of burdensome anxiety or seriousness that either (i) religion, morality or science tries to impose or that (ii) the higher human imposes upon him or herself, for example in the feelings of nausea, responsibility or pity. For example, the transformed Shepherd's laughter having bit off the head of the black snake (Z3.2), the laughter of someone who has realized the narrowness of science (BGE24), the laughter of he or she who can not only 'live bravely' but also 'live and laugh gaily' (GS324), or the laughter of someone who has learned to live without 'metaphysical consolations' (BTA7). In contrast, serious higher humans in Germany 'do not laugh' (GS177). Likewise, see *Lk.* 6.25; Christianity's 'seriousness' – the desperate need for salvation from 'this world' – cannot accommodate laughter.

N's account combines the two great traditional theories of the comic. First, the theory of the sudden release of tension; second, the notion of superiority found in ancient Greek writers (we laugh at those who reveal themselves as beneath us), and which N endorses at GS200: '*Schadenfreude* [delight at the misfortune of others] but with a good conscience'. N's frequent references to mockery also have this meaning. In N, this notion of superiority is found in laughter at sudden elevation (in the sense of the order of rank, feeling of power, noble freedom). Likewise, it is found in the more comprehensive perspective which laughs even at itself 'from the whole truth' (GS1, and see GS383). Thus also the notion of 'Olympian laughter', the laughter of the gods (e.g. UM2.2). Himself mocking, N imagines Wagner having composed *Parsifal* in this spirit of a laughing feeling of being above both oneself and one's work (GM3.3).

Leibniz, Gottfried Wilhelm

Late seventeenth and early-eighteenth-century philosopher. Leibniz's account of the relationship between determinism and freedom may have influenced N, especially in the latter's understanding of fate. Leibniz's idea of *petites perceptions* – perceptions that are both effectively infinite in number and below the level of conscious apprehension – is also important (and is alluded to in many of N's references to waves or the ocean). Leibniz's theodicy (justification of the created world as the best possible) is famously lampooned in Voltaire's *Candide*, but bears some affinities with N's concepts of *affirmation* and *amor fati*.

life

Leben. Life is a very broadly conceived, but nevertheless important, concept in N. Although it might seem obvious that a defining feature of human existence is that it 'lives', N argues that in fact this feature is most often overlooked. The history of philosophy or religion is crowded with concepts such as 'human nature' (the essence of the human as something itself unchanging – for example H1.2), 'immortal soul' (something detachable from the living *body*), mind (even if not detachable from the body, at least not dirtied by its being alive – thus unconcerned by *digestion*, growth, passion, creation or death) or truth (a belief that does not inhabit any particular body; for example UM2.10: 'the man of science . . . who stands aside from life'). Life entails growth, change, death, values and perspectives, conflict or competition, etc., and entails these for the concept of the human as a whole, and for the mind, soul or spirit no less than for the body. Thus at Z2.13 N writes that 'all of life is a dispute over taste and tasting'. Likewise, life as a whole could not be valued because we are participants, not judges (TISocrates2, Morality5, but see BGE205). That is, life exists as *perspective* and there is no viewpoint 'above' those perspectives. At Z2.10 and 3.15, life is personified as an elusive and changeable woman. Human life can be healthy and ascending (i.e. developing towards greater power, health, comprehensiveness, etc.); or it can be ill, decadent or stagnant (see AC6). N often describes the latter using metaphors of death (Z1.9, TIReason1). Even life that is in its value opposed to life (e.g. despising 'this' life in favour of the next life) is nevertheless living – that is, such 'ill' life must somehow serve life. This is a key theme of GM3.

N sometimes uses 'life' in these related senses: (i) Life as meaning the whole of human existence, thus BTForward or 23. Life here is often seen as interconnected, thus the notion of *amor fati* – for example, feeling gratitude to decadent forms of life for their role in making possible health – or the necessity of the 'rabble' (Z2.6). (ii) Life as that which characterizes all living things (e.g. GS26, AC6), or even (in reference probably to Schopenhauer) of existence more broadly (e.g. BT7: 'in the ground of things . . . life is indestructably mighty'). At passages such as BGE9 or GS109 N explicitly disavows this Schopenhauerian view. (iii) Life referring to a particular way of life, belonging to an individual or a group. Examples would include the 'type of life' discussed at TIMorality5, or life as a 'bridge' to some other existence, GM3.11. Similarly, in UM2 N discusses three different modes of history, each of which serves life in a different way.

light

See *night*.

lightness

Leichtheit and similar. Lightness is the opposite of the heavy or burdensome. With the idea of lightness N describes the characteristics of forms of life joyfully aligned to the nature of life: *laughter*, *ascending* or flying, liberated from imaginary external constraints and feelings of *shame* or *nausea*. Because of this symbol's close relation to the notion of *weight*, we will further discuss both under that heading.

lion

See *cat*.

logic

See *reason*.

longing

There are a number of German terms, clustering around the concept of desire. In various contexts these terms receive various translations: *Lust* (desire – but more often simply pleasure, joy), *Wollust* (most commonly translated as lust – also sensuality, voluptuousness), *Sehnsucht* (longing, yearning – and *sehnen*, to long), *Verlangen* (longing), *Begehren* (coveting) or *Begierde* (desire), *Wunsch* (wish, desire, the thing wanted), *Brunst* (sexual lust, as with animals in the mating season). Of these, only *Wollust* and *Brunst* have predominantly sexual meanings. These terms are clearly also akin to *suchen* (which N uses most commonly as meaning to seek, to strive). Longing or desire can be used in a technical sense, to designate a class of basic psychological movements. For example, N begins one of his most famous discussions of will to power with the supposition that nothing was real except 'desires and passions' (BGE36). In Schopenhauer, the underlying will is constantly longing without attainment; such suffering is the root of his pessimism. (The concept owes something to *Epicurus*, also.) Wagner's *Tristan and Isolde* embodies this idea dramatically in two separated lovers and musically in a complex, dissonant chord that is unresolved until the end of the opera (which is also death). As N writes in BT25, what is man if not 'dissonance assuming human form'. N's later conception of longing moves away from these Schopenhauerian roots.

The key distinction for N, from very early on, is between two forms of longing. On the one hand, a longing that demeans both desirer and desired, or which is a kind of escape from the self. So, for example, in Bismarck's great politics, lust after political ends means an abandonment of one's proper sphere (H1.481). The origin of Christianity is described in terms of a lust for control or power, anticipating N's concept of a reactive will to power (D68, and see D204 comparing capitalism). Similarly, Zarathustra makes a theme of the hidden and diseased lust for life that resides even in those who despise life (Z3.12.17, 3.13). This is one of the ideas in GM3, so for example the ascetic priest has the sick longing after pain (GM3.20) because it is a stimulant *to* life. When N, in accordance with the idea of *amor fati*, describes himself as not possessing a ripple of longing (EHClever9), his examples make clear he is talking about such reactive forms.

On the other hand, there is a longing that is not escape, not a longing for something transcendent to the self. Such longing is for the discovery of oneself, a growth or ascending to what one is (see entry on *Becoming who one is*). Thus, for example, eternal recurrence could be experienced as a longing for recurrence (GS341, Z3.16). Again, N's intellectual task to 'think pessimism to its depths' is an 'enigmatic longing' (BGE56) for a new ideal of a mode of life. The notion of longing in this sense is already found in UM (e.g. UM1.2, 3.6). The last cited passage includes the notion that such longing is experienced as a sense of inadequacy or even vague guilt; so, such longing is a form of *distress*, but 'is worth more to us than any pleasure' (D575 – the phrase contains a play on two words with the same root, meaning 'longing' and 'pleasure'). Or, expressed differently and more generally, 'In the end, one loves one's desire and not the desired' (BGE175, and see 1887.11.75). This doubleness of distress and longing as valued becomes a common idea. For example, at GS76, N discusses how the commonality of feeling, language and experience arouses both a new nausea and new longing (and see Z1.8, Z4.11 with the concept of the 'great despising'). All love and marriage is bitter, but (rather than a cynical or pessimistic viewpoint) this is part of the longing for the overhuman (Z1.20).

Lust (or sensuality) in a sexual sense is one of N's most famous revaluations of values. He attempts to overcome the hatred of lust by the preachers of death (Z1.9) – that is by Christians and moralists alike – who are preachers of death precisely because of the value of sensuality for the growth (or even the preservation) of life (see Z3.10). Indeed, the revaluation of *Brunst* is complete in Z, as its use to mean animal sexual lust at Z1.13 and Z3.10.2 becomes the ultimate expression of the affirmation of life in Z3.16, with its refrain 'how should I not lust after eternity?'.

love

Liebe. The concept of love is among the most complex in N. We should begin with the ancient reference points, which include

Parmenides positing Eros as the first born of the primordial goddess. That is to say, the striving of different things towards their unity is a mythical counterpart to the oneness of being. This notion is also cited in Plato's *Symposium*, another important source (see *beauty*). There, Plato provides an account of the relationship between love, beauty and wisdom. That in turn forms the basis for Plotinus (a Neoplatonist) talking about love as the movement of lower orders of being towards the higher. Love (both in its spiritualized and in its sexual sense) is an organizing principle of reality for Greek and Latin thought, and not something that requires a transcendence or a 'world beyond'. It is this Greek idea that N adopts, and the central ideas are the same whether he is talking about sexual love, spiritualized love (e.g. *friendship*), love of an ideal, or love of self.

Love is unconditional trust, and only this trust makes possible *creativity* (UM2.7, D216). In one sense love is shielded within illusion, but this only means that the 'blissful' and 'overflowing' truth of love is opposed to the truth of rational enquiry (1872.19.103, and see AC23). Thus, love provides a clear vision of the self (and of the self's defects) and of the higher self towards which love strives (UM3.6). Accordingly, much later, N describes an aspect of his method as a 'loving and cautious neutrality' (AC36). It is a kind of neutrality with respect to the multiplicity of values and perspectives, but *not* with respect to the development of the human. Likewise, what is to be loved in others, or in human beings, is what can be hoped for (GS272). It wants not the object but what can be made of the object. Thus N's surprising praise of 'to love man *for God's sake*' (BGE60) – only the impossible transcendence of the Judeo-Christian God is a mistake, since otherwise it is the same notion as Zarathustra's love of man for the sake of the overhuman. Likewise, great love does not want to be loved, 'it wants more' – that is it wants the striving and the ascending (Z4.13.16). Indeed, 'one loves one's desire and not what is desired' (BGE175, 73). (However, see the beautiful lament at Z2.9, describing the solitude of the philosophical giver as an unrequited lover.) Love is constant, longing for the ever higher, ever more comprehensive. It could not in principle be satisfied, not because its object is impossible (as in love of God), but because its ceasing entirely at any given plateau would mean it ceasing to be love. So, great love in its longing overcomes 'even forgiveness and pity' (Z2.3), while on the other hand a 'foolish love' is the great danger of the lonely (Z3.1).

N employs the concept of love as an attitude or mode of being responsible for creativity and the growth of the human. What happened subsequently to the ancient period, N argues, is a four-way split. On the one hand, Eros was made evil by Christian morality (D76) – the only love not overlaid with sin is pure love, that is love for God. Thus, for example, marriage has to be sanctified by God. Such love is no longer immanent, but transcendent and founded upon a denigration of 'this world'. Second, the predominant sceptical or pessimistic mood of science renders love (in N's sense) impossible. Thus N contrasts the attitude of love – its defining illusion and its trust – with reason and science, both of which (whatever other virtues they may have) are infertile. Third, the hate of the slave revolution that was early Christianity transforms itself in to the love of God for man (GM1.8) – not as the negation of that hate, but rather its fulfilment – such that God sacrifices himself out of love of the 'debtor' (the sinner) (GM2.21–2, TIImprovers4). Likewise, hatred of the self manifests itself in an illusory 'love of neighbour' (Z3.11). Similarly, N discusses the figure of Jesus as insatiable in *demanding* love (Z4.13.16, BGE269). Fourth, on the other hand, under the 'pressure' of the above value judgements, we have the sublimation of the sex drive into love understood as a *passion* (BGE189, which TIMorality3 calls 'a great triumph over Christianity'), and this must be of noble origin (BGE260). Only a noble individual would feel the distance between two people ('the deadly hatred between the sexes': EHBooks5) as something desirable, and devote themselves whole-heartedly to the overcoming of that distance. In love, I joyously affirm the existence of someone who is essentially defined as different from me (D75). Thus Zarathustra 'goes under' [the expression means to die] to deliver his message, out of love for human beings, bringing them a gift (ZP2–3, 2.3). (See also the discussion of 'love as fate' at WC2, and H2.280.)

lust

See *longing*.

Luther, Martin

Luther was not the only major figure in the Protestant Reformation in the sixteenth century, but N pretty much identifies the two. For N, Luther represents a peasant's mistrust of the *contemplative* life (D88, EHCase2). Also, he represents a misunderstanding of the victorious, noble scepticism and tolerance of the Roman Church (GS358) which was, in N's view, no longer Christianity but the spirit of the *Renaissance* (H1.237, AC61). N sums this up in saying Luther belonged to the North, the church he attacked to the *South*. Finally, Luther represented a German's desire to be commanded, to exhibit unconditional obedience (thus N posits a relation between Luther and Bismarck's authoritarian state: D207). Luther also produced a translation of the Bible into German, which had enormous influence on the modern German language (see BGE247), and many of N's comments about him have that as their topic.

Machiavelli, Niccolò

Politician and political philosopher in early-sixteenth-century Florence; he is known especially for *The Prince.* Machiavelli's influence on N is centred on two ideas. First, Machiavelli reinforces N's view of the immoralism of all moral and political practices. See 1887.9.145 which outlines the presence of *will to power* from the top to bottom of political spectrum. Second, the concept of *virtù* which is we might say Machiavelli's revaluation of the concept of *virtue.*

machine

Maschine, most often. N recognizes the machine as a key feature of modernity (UM2.5), especially in its connection with industrialized labour (H3.218, 220, 288, and several entries in notebook 1879.40), which category includes modern *scholarship* (Z2.16, BGE6). The machine metaphor gives us unity (in the *Socialist* movement, or in a *democracy*), but without self-control (i.e. it leads to excessive behaviour), autonomy or the capacity for *creation*. The machine notion is also characteristic, since Descartes, of the modern physiological understanding of living organisms (AC14) – although N's early study of Kant's *Critique of Telelogical Judgement* means he is suspicious of this kind of reductionism as anthropomorphic. Likewise, thinking of the cosmos as a machine is anthropomorphic (GS109).

madness

Wahnsinn, Irrsinn, etc. N uses the concept of madness in several different ways. First, the madness or apparent madness of those who break deeply held moral conventions, insofar as they have no way of understanding their own law-breaking, except perhaps as the influence of the divine (D14 – and see Plato *Phaedrus* 265a). This is not simply an appearance of madness to others (though it might be a mask) but also to oneself. The criminal, capable of the act but not capable of understanding or accepting the image of his act, suffers from 'madness after the deed' (Z1.6). Although his tongue is in his cheek, N discusses the relationship between the criminal and the mentally ill at D202. More generally, the appearance of madness rests on any individual who does not recognize the same values, who is untimely, or who has far-reaching insights (thus the 'madman with the lantern' at GS125, or the task of knowledge being 'an insane task': BGE230). The point is made most clearly at GS76. Interestingly, N uses the concept of inoculation here: 'where is the madness with which you must be inoculated?' (ZP3, and see H1.224).

Second, the madness of types or groups (BGE156), whose mode of life has deviated from alignment to the world as will to power and thus to what N calls 'health'. (Indeed, N will often just speak of illness in these contexts, rather than madness.) For example: (i) those whose 'bad conscience' leads them to project a transcendent God as judge and executioner of their guilt (GM2.22, and see Z1.3). Similarly (ii) the 'madhouse air' that surrounds diseased forms of humanity whose shepherd is the ascetic priest (GM3.14). (iii) The madness of pessimism or nihilism understood as end rather than transitional states (Z2.20). (iv) Those whose need for revenge leads them to posit the social and political ideal of equality (Z2.7). In all these cases, madness consists of the positing of a disastrously anti-natural set of values, which in turn only exacerbate the original condition.

magnanimity (or generosity)

Grossmutigkeit. In D, this designates one of the virtues that N studies in connection with the noble. It thus supersedes *benevolence*, which was a frequent object of study in H. Magnanimity is a feature of *nobility*, one that modernity has not lost and may even excel in (D199, 556 and also GS283). At the end of the first edition of GS, N identifies a certain lack of magnanimity, a certain need for revenge, even in Socrates and then writes 'We must overcome even the Greeks!'. As a virtue of the future, N associates it with both courage and a 'supreme arrogance' (D551). It is a feature of a 'great thinker' who, perhaps with embarrassment or laughter, 'offers himself and his life as a sacrifice' (D459, see 449). Similarly, D547 connects it with the important notion of 'What do I matter!'. Ideas of self-sacrifice in higher natures recur at GS3, now in connection with a certain absence of pragmatic reasoning: 'reason pauses' (and see GS49). At Z2.13, magnanimity is associated with gracefulness and with *beauty*. For a further discussion, see *gift*.

marriage

Ehe. Marriage is one of the social institutions to which N gives considerable attention. Marriage *should* be the place where the opportunity to form the future (the having and raising of children) is given careful consideration (Z1.20, TISkirmishes39), where the productive *agonistic* relationship of two people is fully realized and thus also a key place where the *feminine and masculine* drives can work together. Thus, on a symbolic level, the achievement of tragedy by the Apollonian and Dionysian drives is termed a 'marriage' at BT4, while Zarathustra's affirmation of eternal recurrence is a love and marriage to eternity (Z3.16). The philosopher, who contains both drives within him or herself, is thus typically not married (GM3.7). Unfortunately, modern marriage does none of these things. By 'marriage for love' N means marriage as the legitimation of sexual attraction through its blessing by God. This is the worst reason for marriage for its consequences serve none of the above ideals (H1.379, 389, D27, 150–1, Z1.20, TISkirmishes39), and because it makes of chastity and *sensuality* opposites (GM3.2). Marriage for sexual attraction, then given the stamp of approval by the state and church, makes the partners unprepared for commitment (Z3.12.24), and even ruins the institution of the mistress (BGE123).

Marx/marxism

See *socialism*.

mask, disguise, role and related ideas

Maske, among other cognate terms. The notion of mask, wearing a disguise, or playing a role are all significant components of N's thought concerning society and social behaviours. Everyone will have a sense of him or herself (which of course is not necessarily a true assessment), plus a sense of how they want others to view them (the mask he or she wants to wear), and finally there will be the various ways in which others in fact do view him or her (the mask he or she in fact wears – see for example UM3.3, GS365). Those who are rich or famous have a need to project a mask of their (false) spiritual nature (H2.310, D469). The various self-deceptions that lie at the origin of metaphysics or morality are also related to the adopting of a mask that cannot then so easily be removed. As sociological observations, these are interesting enough. Their philosophical importance lies in N's understanding of:

1   The mask's relation to personal identity. Why must we assert there has to be an identity behind the mask? N often suggests that identity – in the sense of a stable knowledge of oneself – generally occurs from the exterior *in* (GS52). N likewise talks about the way in which a friend, or the mirror provided by historical study, is a necessary detour to self-knowledge. Again, every profession begins as a role to be played, before it becomes an identity (H1.51, see GS356); most people borrow their ego from the perspectives of those around them (D105); and dissimulation is older than truth ('On Truth and Lies'). N, in misogynistic moments, asserts that some 'beautiful women' are all mask. However, the men who desire them

for this reason are necessarily also only playing the role
of the lover (H1.218, 405, GS361). Similarly, we have
analyses of the relationship between whole cultures and the
historical masks they wear (UM2.5, BGE223).

2   The mask's role in philosophical method. N often discusses
the use of various kinds of masks or disguises to protect
the philosopher, to preserve his or her solitude and distance
from others. This is a particular theme in BGE (see BGE25,
40, 270). However, this must not be understood as simply
a defensive gesture. When 'the Wanderer' surfaces from the
depths in BGE278, he calls for 'Another mask! A second
mask!'. That it is a 'second' mask means that the journey to
the depths was itself *already* a mask. The *wanderer*, the one
who is *comprehensive*, means to take up a series of roles.
In N's case, this means philologist, psychologist, historian,
poet, Zarathustra, etc. – and these are *both* strategies of
self-defence, and strategies of engagement with properly
philosophical problems and tasks. Similarly, N discusses the
concept of the 'actor' and whether it is not the main clue
to the nature of the artist and even the 'prehistory of the
genius' (GS361). It should be remembered that N's original
interest in masks likely stems from ancient Greek theatrical
practices. The actor exhibits 'falseness with a good
conscience', and an overflowing of dissimulation (GS361).
This is exactly how N describes elements within his account
of *creativity*. (See also the will to deceive and be deceived at
BGE230, the disguises of the philosopher at GM3.10, and
H1.51–2.) Again, there is an element of mask or role play in
N's accounts of writing and teaching (e.g. D469, or Z4.1).
This whole discussion is related to the concept of the 'noble
lie' which N gets from Plato (see for example GM3.19).

3   The mask also protects others, and is thus part of N's
account of *humanity*, or the avoidance of *shaming*.
For example, see H3.175, D469. Likewise, the need of
'profound spirits' for masks also entails that it is humane
to 'respect the mask' (BGE27). Zarathustra and the
Soothsayer both wipe the expression from their faces, to
disguise both their thoughts and also the fact that they have
seen the thoughts of the other (Z4.2).

masses [*die Masse*]

See *herd*.

master

See *slave, noble*.

mathematics

See *number*.

matter, materialism

Materie, Stoff. To a great extent, nineteenth-century science was materialistic. That is, it posited both matter as the basic nature of the real, and the movement and interaction (force) of matter as the basic means of explaining physical phenomenon. Materialism thus promised a single type of solution to everything from the problems of the movements of stars and planets, to the nature of life and human thought. Broadly, N follows Lange in arguing that materialism serves a certain *regulative* function without our having to ascribe metaphysical truth to its basic claims (see for example GS109: 'matter is as much of an error as the god of the Eleatics'). N also finds the lack of given meaning or purpose within a materialistic universe (as in Epicurus) useful for combating theistic and moral conceptions of the universe. For N's specific criticisms of materialistic ideas, see *atomism, causality, becoming, metaphysics*.

Maya

The phrase 'veil of Maya' is employed in *The Birth of Tragedy* to designate the world of *appearances* considered as a mere illusion (or, which is not at all the same thing, appearance). N gets the phrase from *Schopenhauer*, and he in turn from Hindu thought. Analogous ideas are found in pre-Socratic thought, and certainly in Plato. Moreover, Plutarch reports the inscription for the veiled statue of Isis (or perhaps Athena) at the ancient Egyptian city of Sais reads: 'I am all that is, was, and shall me. No mortal has ever lifted my veil' (see GS57), and this was an important eighteenth- and nineteenth-century motif.

measure

See *number*.

memory

See *forgetting*.

metaphor

A metaphor in its narrow meaning is a figure of speech that identifies two things that are, in their surface meanings, unrelated. It thus implies some kind of analogy between the terms. The original Greek meaning of 'metaphor' suggests a kind of movement, a transposition from one thing to another. The notion of metaphor has a looser meaning for N, which is any identification of things (whether in language or not), and where there needs to be no implied analogy. Thus in 'On Truth and Lies', N designates each stage of the 'translation' of sensation to image and then to word as 'metaphor'. Again, in BT, the chorus of satyrs is a metaphor for the 'original image of humankind' (BT8). There is an important difference between these two examples, however. In the former, N's point is that because of the metaphorical transformations, what we call truth is nothing like what we think it is. Communities agree on a set of fixed metaphors that seem to serve them; science or philosophy is still more precise, but there is no way back from our concepts to the sensations from which they arose, and still less to whatever caused those sensations (see 1872.19.228). In the passage from BT, however, metaphor is one of the means by which poetry tries to be 'the unadorned expression of truth'. The idea is not that poetic metaphor is some kind of mystical insight, but rather than it strives to do some justice to *intuition* by being creative rather than falling into the trap of believing in concepts (which are simply forgotten metaphors). After the early work, N rarely talks about metaphors per se. However, the concept, in something akin to its function in the earlier work, may still be on N's mind (see EHZ3). More often, he employs the language of symbol or *allegory* in order to understand the poetic functions of language.

metaphysics

'Metaphysics' is used in three senses by N. First, as a philosophical enquiry that uncovers, or finds some other mode of awareness of, the basic nature of reality. This usage contains a certain optimism about metaphysical enquiry and is mainly found in the early work (e.g. BT4, 16, UM3.4–6). Second, as a way of interpreting the nature of reality that belongs to a way of life, a basic drive, a religion, or a people – for example, we can talk about Kant or Schopenhauer's metaphysics, knowing that these are not just sets of beliefs but are projections of the philosophers' unconscious needs (BGE6, GM3.6–8).

Third, and most commonly, metaphysics is any attempt to understand the world as it appears in terms of some 'true' world characterized by being (rather than *becoming*), stability, identity and *number* (rather than fluidity and singularity), order or law (rather than *chance, innocence*, or the action of unique forces), the possibility of *truth* in the sense of correspondence (rather than *perspective*), *freedom* (rather than necessity or, again, chance), transcendence (what is beyond the world, rather than immanent to it), *reason* (rather than *instinct* or drives), idea or *spirit* (rather than *body*), or *will* or *purpose* (rather than chaos). Metaphysics in this third sense is always error, and much of N's work is concerned with refuting these errors. But more important than any refutation is N's examining of the conditions that led to belief in them (e.g. the need to make the world intelligible, or the need for a transcendent basis to certain values), and the implications that follow such belief. These implications are, most broadly and generally, the negative value of metaphysical beliefs for the development of the human type. This third usage is found quite early in N's career (e.g. UM1.7), but becomes predominant from H on (e.g. right up-front at H1.1 and throughout that chapter; and see BGE2, GM3.24). Metaphysical errors will at one point have been, and may continue to be, necessary for the perpetuation of life (e.g. BGE4), making N's philosophical attempt to revalue them, 'dangerous'. Metaphysics in the third sense is generally also metaphysics in the second: that is, such understandings of the true world will generally be related to the historical needs of groups.

method, procedure, strategy

Methode, Verfahren, but often implied. By method is meant a set of principles according to which valid philosophical (or scientific, historical, etc.) enquiry can happen. In N, the principles of his enquiry include, first, as radical and thorough a sense of *becoming* as possible, such that forms of life, values and concepts are understood to grow and develop out of each other. Thus, at the beginning of both H and BGE, N stresses that opposites are only apparent. Accordingly, N designates his philosophical project as a 'history of the genesis of thought' (H1.16) or as 'genealogy' (in GM). Second, objectivity or neutrality re-understood not as the absence of any perspective, but either the perspective of human health, or as the multiplicity of *perspectives*, or a *comprehensive* view. Thus, the philosopher 'has no right to be single in anything' (GMP2). Moral problems only become visible when one compares 'multiple moralities' (BGE186). See also 'modesty' at AC13, and *wanderer*.

From the first two principles follows a third: that the philosopher must not judge a phenomenon on the basis of some historically specific criterion. At any given time, a set of 'convictions' – some of which may even go unnoticed – are assumed to be just true, common sense or natural. *Metaphysical* ideas concerning identity, substance, number or causality are obvious examples, but N claims these also hide moral judgements. Genuine method must seek to free itself from such convictions (AC13, H1.635). For example, N accuses 'English psychologists' at GM1.2 of assuming the validity of a certain contemporary moral view, and proceeding to understand the history of morality from that perspective. Or, again, he argues against the assumption that the origin of something and its later function must be the same (GM2.12). Methodologically, this is closely related to the Stoic or Sceptic notion of suspending judgement. This N claims is the characteristic virtue of 'the great, incomparable art of reading well' (AC59) which he identifies with *philology.*

The fourth aspect of N's method involves an immanent understanding of both the nature of things and the processes by which they develop. That is, a psychology or physiology that can do without 'metaphysical intervention' from that which is understood to be transcendent to the real (H1.10). A related principle is N's version of 'Occam's Razor', by which we mean two things. First, the attempt should be made to account for the whole of life (or even beyond, into the inorganic) as a single system (e.g. the human domain does not present a special sphere divided from the animal); second, to do so with as few explanatory mechanisms as possible (BGE13, 36). The *will to power* is N's proposal for a basic and universal explanatory mechanism. Finally, fifth, the most important issue is not the truth of beliefs but rather their *value* for the health and development of human beings. For example, the 'value of the will to truth' at BGE1, or the value of pity (GMP6). Even method itself must be evaluated in this way (thus N's critique of objective history).

midday, noon

See *night.*

milieu

See *closest things, condition.*

mind

See *spirit.*

mirror

Spiegel. The mirror is a conventional metaphor for that which represents-back-to, with a greater or lesser degree of distortion. For clear examples, see H1.132–3, H2.218, Z2.1, BGE207. Another feature of the mirror is that it exhibits visual form without other sensory properties. Thus, N's notebook 1872.19 contains a number of entries in which N explores the human understanding of the world in terms of form using the mirror as an analogy (see especially 153).

mischievousness, rogueishness

There are a number of different terms N uses here to describe a quality of spirit who is iconoclastic, cheerful, holding things in a degree of contempt, wilful in a way that may seem arbitrary or inconsistent, willing to use irony and trickery. Thus, Socrates at H3.86, Montaigne at EHClever3, the cat-behaviour in the poem at Z4.14.3 (see also Z3.3, 4.17), the whole of GS (so N claims at EHGS), and Zarathustra is called a 'rogue' several times (e.g. Z4.2). Similarly, all becoming seems to Zarathustra like the impulsiveness of gods (Z3.6). Along with, for example, *foolishness, laughter* or *wandering*, this is or rather can be a feature of those *experimental* modes of life of the *free spirits* (see D432).

mob

See *herd*.

mockery

See *laughter.*

modernity

Depending upon the context, N defines the 'modern' in one of several ways. In an important sense, the modern begins with

Socrates in ancient Greece. The historical narrative given in BT, and again much later in TI, is that Socrates represents a break from the earlier more noble and healthy period, and the advent of a certain broad, metaphysical way of understanding reality, the dominance of plebeian tastes and values, and an optimism in logic and science and their capacity to effect progressive change. Alternatively, N sometimes identifies modernity with 'modern ideas' – equality, democracy, human rights, a kind of naïve atheism or practical indifference to religion (see BGE58), etc. – and thus modernity begins with the Enlightenment and French Revolution. N argues that socialists, anarchists and industrious democrats all have the same underlying set of values (BGE202). Finally, one of the truly distinctive characteristics of modernity is that it is the end-point of several thousand years of religious, moral and social values that have imploded. Modernity would then be identified with pessimism and nihilism, with exhaustion (WC5) or decadent instincts (TISkirmishes39), the impotence of the *historical sense*, and a culture with no sense of future (e.g. UM3.4) – and see EHBGE2. 'Insofar as it is not weakness but power', however, our modern being is 'hubris', N argues. He means a dangerous pride towards nature insofar as we dominant it through technology and with concepts like 'matter', towards God by refusing the need for reality to have eternal purpose, and towards ourselves insofar as we *experiment* with ourselves (GM3.9, and see Z4.15).

moment

See *eternal recurrence*.

money/wealth/poverty

See *work, socialism, class*.

monotheism

See *God/gods*.

moods

See *affects*.

moon

Mond. The moon shines by reflected light; its radiance is characterized therefore as *passive*, and relatively dim and cool. The moon is a symbol of the supposed *objectivity* of the *sciences*, and the associated *disinterestedness* of *scholars* (Z2,15). (See also Z3.2.)

morality

Moralität, Sittlichkeit, Ethik. Morality – what is it, how did it originate, and what does it mean in terms of the development or health of the human – is clearly among N's most important subjects. Although the most famous and influential treatments of morality date from late in his career, the theme begins very early, and in characteristic ways. Here, we will briefly discuss the development of N's account of morality, and then treat the later (from the 1880s) account.

Already in BT, N claims that Euripides' new tragedy – one that essentially misunderstands the nature of tragedy – is motivated by a non-Dionysian 'morality' (BT12, 24). That earlier and later tragedy and art should be differentiated by an entirely different understanding of morality is an easy-to-overlook aspect of N's account. N thus posits an all-important historical change in morality that occurred in the Ancient world (and see UM3.2). This idea becomes increasingly prominent in later N. At UM1.7, he accuses David Strauss of not being consistent in his pursuit of the moral implications of Darwinism – that is, of not treating the human being as 'a creature of nature and nothing else'. Again, this concept of the unnaturalness of morality continues into the later N. Morality is not served by the modern obsession with history; morality in fact consists of resistance to the 'tyranny of the actual' (UM2.8). There is a distinction in that passage between (i) a morality that involves a certain complacency or comfort, espoused by the 'legionaries of the moment', and (ii) a morality that serves the future of life. Although N will shortly change terminology (N is reluctant to describe Zarathustra in terms of a 'morality' at all), nevertheless that same distinction is at stake in passages such as ZP5 and Z2.14.

N's thinking at the time of H was influenced heavily by Paul Rée, with whom he was working closely and whose *The Origin of Moral Sensations* appeared in 1877. In H, N analyses morality in terms of egoism (H1.133), but this is an egoism that belongs primarily to a community and has utility for that community; its mechanism is the establishing of custom, that is automatic responses (see H1.94, 96, H2.89, H3.44). The German word '*Sitte*' means custom in the sense of both tradition and habit, while the clearly related term '*Sittlichkeit*' means morality. The second chapter of H1 is entitled 'On the History of the Moral Sensations', a subtle variation on Rée's title and one that stresses the importance of history for N's thought in this area. Much later, in GMP4 and GM1.2, N recounts in an exaggerated fashion his intellectual distance from Rée. What N accuses Rée of doing (in a way that associates him with 'English' moral theorists, those working in the wake of Darwin) is taking a contemporary moral value (specifically altruism), assuming naively that it is ahistorical in character. This, N argues, ignores precisely the point he was making in BT and UM3, that our moral concepts have undergone at least one revolution (the 'slave revolution' at GM1.7) and are not historically continuous.

Morality takes centre stage in N's thought from D (with its subtitle: 'thoughts on the prejudices of morality') onwards. Here we find N's evaluation of morality as the weakening of the human (see D132, 164), which should remind us of UM2.8, discussed above, and of the discontinuous history of morality already found in BT. Likewise, D moves away from the cynicism of H (morality is a fraudulent ideal, based on the 'all too human' ground of egoism). Thus all three volumes of H end with something of a sigh, while D culminates in a series of aphorisms willing the reader towards new ways of living. In short, D pursues the project not just of a critique but an *overcoming* of morality. Similarly, at D103, N argues that this cynical view of human moral behaviour (here, attributed to La Rochefoucauld) is incomplete. Instead, N posits that it is possible to be honest, to genuinely believe in moral principles and be motivated by those beliefs (at GS44 he adds that the belief or value invested in the principle is probably more important than the principle). It remains the case, however, that these moral principles are false. The more important and interesting level of deception lies in the explanation of these beliefs. This is a move from a dismissal of morality as 'all too human' to a deeper analysis of its surreptitious relations with other beliefs, values or modes of life. This move is characteristic of N's later work. It also permits N to imagine a form of life that was *honest* not in the conscious sense, but in an existential one, aligned to the nature of life. This would be the overcoming of morality.

In N's later work, morality is a species of *values*. Values are a basic affective feature of any living thing. Values are also our principal tool for the interpretation of reality (GS114, see *perspective*). We could call all values 'moral' insofar as they are normative. However, N often reserves the term 'morality' for a system of values that does not recognize the existence or even possibility of other systems (BGE202). N argues that universalizing morality and monotheistic religions are linked. Moral values in this sense are characterized by being universal, abstract, ahistorical; they are ultimately related to the ignoble and democratic (see D164,194, GS335). Rather than resisting this illegitimate universalization, philosophers with their 'rage for generalisation' (H2.5) tend to make it worse. On the other hand, relativism – the idea the no morality is binding – is 'equally childish' (GS345). This is because relativism assumes the possibility of viewing values from the outside, or of living without values; also, relativism jumps too easily to a nihilistic conclusion about the lack of values.

Morality bears some relation to the conditions of preservation of a historical people; the conditions that led them to grow into the people they are. Moral value is thus the solidification of those types of people or types of acts that had utility. Morality is thus the 'herd-instinct in the individual' (GS116), that is a residue in the form of customs of a long historical period. It follows also that morality must involve, in one way or the other, the repression of the genuinely *individual* (BGE198), who is seen as evil, criminal or dangerous. Individual variations on morality (e.g. the various moral systems of the philosophers) are to be understood in the same way – as a 'sign language' of the basic needs and feelings of that philosopher (BGE187). As a set of principles of preservation, morality is *ipso facto* set against further growth or development, and still more against any 'going under' (i.e. the destruction of the people's identity). Morality thus at least serves to fix the concept of man. However, N argues, continual growth and development is part of the nature of life; thus a moral system of this type can be understood as unnatural or anti-life. Groups under the sway of morality tend to lose any relation to the future; they become 'comfortable', decadent and thus endangered from within and without. This is one of the ways that morality has built in to it a process of self-overcoming (H3.114, BGE201).

On N's analysis, modern morality is the product of a 'slave revolution', which is a negation or inversion of the values of the masters or the *nobles* (BGE195, GM1.10). This serves as a manner in which the weak (those who are either literally or figuratively slaves) can express their will to power, albeit in a reactive way: *ressentiment*. *Ressentiment* is the state of a will that cannot act outwardly, nor can it create values from out of itself, but achieves a positing of values only as an act of revenge. Morality is a programme for breeding weakness, oversensitivity or illness into human beings, or of 'domesticating' the human (TIImprove1–5, TISkirmishes37). The herd is bred to obey (BGE199). In this, Christianity is particularly culpable, because one of its chief moral values is *pity* (or compassion), which functions as a mechanism for preserving in existence those who are ill. Part of this breeding consists of the development of the human who can promise, which in turn leads to the phenomena of guilt and bad conscience (this is the account given in GM2). In this breeding process, morality contradicts itself: the mechanisms it employs to create moral human beings are, by its own standards, immoral (TIImprove5). N famously contrasts slave or herd morality with (i) the barbarian 'blond beasts', those who impose their power on populations and set up the first states (e.g. GM2.17 – see *animal*); (ii) the 'noble' Greeks or Romans, inheritors of those barbarians, or in general those who are the masters against whom the slave rebelled (D131, BGE260); and (iii) individuals of strength and distinction (Cesare Borgia being the most notorious name N mentions: TISkirmishes37, BGE201) who arise as exceptions within the Christian era. In the present or future, herd morality is also contrasted with the *free spirit*, and ultimately with the *overhuman*. The absence of relation to the future in itself is 'unnatural', against life. This is exacerbated when morality becomes the product not of a historical people, but of some group wishing to claim and maintain power (priest class – GM3.11, AC51, 55). Morality here is entirely artificial, and this artificiality goes beyond the misunderstandings of nature and life that are involved in all morality. At best such a morality serves life only by providing stimuli to an exhausted form of human life (this is the theme of N's treatment of asceticism in GM3).

Morality, especially in the Christian era, and even more so in the modern period, values altruism or unegoistic acts. N's strategy in H is to demonstrate a consistent reduction of moral acts to *egoism* (and see D133, GS119). Either a thoroughly unegoistic state is psychologically impossible (and thus morality involves a falsification of reality), or it is possible but is founded upon weakness rather than strength – in any case, it leads to disastrous consequences (and thus its supposed utilitarian value involves a falsification). In general, morality is founded upon a series of errors and self-contradictions (TIImprovers1, 5). These errors include belief (i) in free will, (ii) in the possibility of purely selfless acts, (iii) in the identity of different acts in different situations, (iv) in the possibility of self-knowledge, (v) in human beings being essentially different from animals. *Pity* (or compassion) is one of two central virtues of Christian morality. Moreover, on N's analysis, it is actually egoistic in nature, and more significantly demonstrates contempt, lacks shame and multiplies suffering (D134–5). The same is true of the other key virtue, selflessness (or neighbour love) which is not a product of a kind of divine, saintly strength (the overcoming of one's selfishness) but of weakness (the inability to have and maintain a self) (EHWise4); or alternatively, a misinterpretation of the cruelty involved in self-discipline and self-formation (GM2.18). Because these virtues are in some way impossible to attain, a concept of sinfulness and of the despicable nature of the human in general or the body in particular develops, which could only be overcome by the grace of a transcendent God (or the sacrifice of a God) (D87, Z1.4). Asceticism develops as a practice the explicit aim of which is the radical repression of the body, in order to prepare for 'another existence' (GM3.11). These developments also should be classified as in some way unnatural or against life. Moral concepts despite having been propped up by religion nevertheless survive the death of God, without our realizing their untenability (e.g. TISkimishes5). Likewise, moral values creep into practices that are not obviously moral in nature, such as scholarship generally (GS345), natural science more narrowly (BGE14, 22–3), or philosophy (BGE6). Morality thus has an afterlife, difficult to eliminate, even when its original ground is taken away or becomes suspect (GS125).

The overcoming of morality involves several aspects. Above we introduced the idea of morality's self-overcoming; part of this is that morality serves as a training in discipline, yielding strength and creativity (BGE188). Likewise, both the development of bad conscience and asceticism contribute to this overcoming (GM2.24, GM3.12). Again, the moral notions of equality and democracy have contributed to a mixture of biological and cultural types, and this too creates opportunities (BGE223–4). In brief, N's account of a new morality (if we should call it that) is not simply a rejection of the old, as if one could ever simply dispense with one's historical conditions. Rather, it is a product of the previous morality, and even employs that morality as an instrument. Much of N's writings on morality, from H on, could be termed a *critical interpretation* of moral phenomena. This means, N insists, raising morality as a problem, rather than taking contemporary moral values and seeking to refine, explain, justify or extend them. As part of the *revaluation* of values, N asks: what is the value of morality (GS345)? What N means is threefold: first, what errors or contradictions does a moral system contain, which undermine it as a system of values (for example, its dependence on a psychologically implausible account of freedom)? Second, what hidden, underlying values does a system of morality pursue (e.g. the maintenance of priestly power)? Third, how does a moral system relate to the values that stem from life itself (health, growth, etc.)?

If the above analysis results in our thinking differently about morality, then this in turn may result in our feeling differently (D103). That is, we move from recognizing the dangers in our current values, but still being devoted to those values, to devaluing or *revaluing* them. Given that values are key component of our intellectual life by which we constitute the objects of our experience, the thinking part of the 'self' is not essentially different from the feeling part. Thus, once a thorough thinking differently becomes possible, feeling differently is just a question of time. Similarly, N talks about the way a consciousness of the will to truth as a problem will gradually lead to the perishing of morality (GM3.27). The chief question, then, is how such a thorough-going 'thinking differently' is to be possible. In addition to the critical interpretation discussed above, a process of comparison of moral systems, identifying differences of value (BGE186), is important. Let us provide a few important examples of what this feeling differently might mean. It will involve a removal of the bad conscience that morality has attached to egoism or to unfree action (D148), and likewise a transference of bad conscience from guilt about matters immanent (the body) to a guilt about any dependence upon the transcendent (GM2.24, and see Z3.10 and the 'three evils'). Similarly, the morally derived concepts of equality and democracy have given a bad conscience to any consciousness of or desire for *rank order, nobility* or the *pathos of distance* (BGE263), and one must learn to think and feel differently here, too. Finally, one must not interpret selfishness as self-preservation, as the pursuit of one's gain or comfort. The higher selfishness N is after involves the willingness to 'go under', that is for one's self to be lost in its devotion to future values (and, ironically employing the golden rule, willing to sacrifice one's neighbour too: D146).

Famously, at the beginning of Z (Z1.1) N distinguishes between the 'lion' and 'child' stages of the spirit. The lion is capable of destroying values – capable of critically interpreting them, thinking and feeling differently – but is not capable of creating new values, like the child stage. Rather than passing on to the creative stage, the lion could just as easily find itself trapped, as if critical interpretation were an end in itself (cynicism), as if no morality could be binding (relativism) or have genuine value (pessimism). The most dangerous of these kinds of traps is *nihilism*. N offers a portrait of a 'hero' in such traps at Z2.13. These traps are the ultimate outcome of morality's self-overcoming. What is required is a different, active or productive strength that can set up a new ideal. Again, this ideal emerges from out of the condition in which we find ourselves (it does not come from nowhere). Thus N argues at both BGE56 and GM2.24 that a new ideal requires a thorough thinking-through and destruction of previous ideals. The new ideal is alignment to and affirmation of life. N uses the notion of *pregnancy* often to explore this creativity, and its connection to future forms of human life. In this connection likewise, N speaks of *eternal recurrence* and *amor fati* as either mechanisms that might achieve such an affirmation, descriptions of or tests of it (EHClever10, EHZ1). Likewise, N uses the concepts of *great health* and *overhuman* to indicate what a form of life capable of such alignment and affirmation would have to be.

morning

See *night*.

mother

See *feminine and masculine*.

motive, intent

Motive, or cognate expressions. Deontological ethics, such as Kantianism, tends to see the intent as most important when judging an action. N charts the rise of such a theory from out of more ancient alternatives, such as the type or character of the agent, or a focus on consequences (BGE32). Motives, or beliefs in motives, are an important moral fact (D103, GS44). However, N suggests that the determination of acts generally has more to do with habits or unconscious drives (D129, GS335) than with conscious motives that we seem free to choose. Moreover, a type of action that was originally designed for the utility of a community eventually becomes custom (H3.40, D9). See *morality, noble, will*.

mountain

See *height*.

multiple, manifold

Various terms. The concept of the multiple has an important but not always easy to discern role in N. First of all, it is an aspect of meaning. At BT10, N claims that the true Dionysus manifests as multiple figures. Much later, he argues that Wagner's multiplicity comes from the Hegelian notion of Idea and its infinite meanings (WC10). One source for this analysis prior to Hegel might be Kant's *Critique of Judgement* (section 12), where the beautiful excites a play of cognition without coming to an end in a definite concept. Another important source would be the Neoplatonist idea of emanation of the One into the multiple, which in turn informs the tradition of negative theology. Although the early N might have been willing to take this Platonic (and Schopenhauerian) notion seriously, it is clear that by the late work he sees it part of a romantic obsession with the transcendent and ineffable. Note that Dionysus refuses names for his virtues at BGE295 not because they fall short (as in negative theology) but because they are too pompous.

Second, the multiple is a characteristic of ignoble modernity. Today, we exhibit tolerance which means we allow a multiplicity of concepts to be possible or valid (H3.230), rendering their multiplicity harmless and unproductive (TISkirmishes19). The German soul is 'manifold' (BGE244) because of its mixed origin; and with this manifoldness comes the mixed blessing of the *historical sense* (although compare 1887.9.119). Zarathustra rejects the multiplicity of scholars at Z2.16, by which is meant both the scholar's objectivity or refusal to judge, and the manner in which his or her methods are assumed to be applicable to any number of circumstances. The image of their 'nimble figures' is reversed in BGE186: precisely that ability to apply a method anywhere makes it crude and insensitive to just those subtle differences of values that N wants to discover.

Third, the multiple as a positive characterization of the philosopher and the philosophical method. Multiplicity here is a description of the philosopher as *comprehensive*, a *wanderer*, and his or her view being informed by many *perspectives*. Such multiplicity is not a dissolution of identity (which is N's objection to the second sense above), but rather a 'wholeness in multiplicity' (BGE212). See especially H1.618, BGE61, 230, GM3.12, EHClever9. N attempts to formulate the basis for these notions under *will to power*.

music

See *Wagner, Schopenhauer.*

myth

Mythus. The notion of myth is particularly significant for the early N. Myth is the means by which a culture becomes unified – specifically, myth is the projection into the Apollonian domain of images of the unity of the underlying Dionysian Will. See especially BT15–16, 23, UM4.8, H1.261. Later uses of the concept tends to be sceptical, meaning 'stories we used to believe' (e.g. BGE21).

names/naming

See *language.*

Napoleon

On N's interpretation, Napoleon represented an older stage of French or European culture – one that was stronger, with a longer will, more masculine and war-like – and was the antithesis to the French Revolution and the 'modern ideas' that animated it (TISkirmishes44). He was a form of continuity with the Renaissance (GS362), 'last sign pointing to the *other* path' that modernity could have taken (GM1.16). The phenomenon of Napoleon prompts also reflections upon the cult of the hero (D298, the reference is partly to Carlyle), and to the herd's need for someone capable of command (BGE199).

narcotic

Narkotikum, or related such as *Opiat, Beruhigungsmittel.* Narcotic is one of N's most common descriptions for any belief, act, habit or indeed substance (e.g. alcohol) that eases suffering, promotes *comfort,* or in some cases temporarily stimulates the exhausted. Religion, broadly speaking, is a common 'art' of narcotizing, and does so for example by reinterpreting suffering as something good or useful (H1.108, TIGermans2). Similarly with virtue (Z1.2, BGE200; see *Epicurus*); modern scepticism (BGE208); Wagnerian music (H3.170, EHH3). Most generally, any essentially passive or weak type will experience its happiness as rest and quiet (GM1.10). However, N speculates that *ressentiment* is born of an attempt to anaesthetize a suffering through some strong affect (i.e. through a sudden emotion) by attaching guilt for suffering to some external agent (GM3.15). The ascetic priest then renders this harmless by directing the supposed guilt for suffering back onto the sufferer. Narcotizing should not be confused with *intoxication*.

nationalism

Nationalism is a political view that ascribes great value to the identity of a people with its homeland and with its nation or state. N objects to nationalism for several reasons: first, its conception of the unity of a people is generally imaginary, backwards looking or a device in the interests of a few (see H1.475, EHWagner2; see *culture*); second, it sustains this conception by the exclusion of others (the Jews, for example [H1.475, BGE252, where N wryly suggest expelling the anti-Semites instead], or the French [UM1.1]); third, the nation or state is exactly the wrong mechanism for bringing about cultural unity and certainly for bringing about cultural greatness (Z1.11, BGE241). N opposes nationalism to his notion of the 'good European'.

naturalism

See *nature*.

nature

Natur. In the philosophical tradition, 'nature' is generally distinguished from the human sphere of culture, society, politics and ethics. 'Human nature' is thus that part of the human that is prior to or independent from any particular culture. In religious or ethical thought, such a conception of nature is often accompanied by a denigration: that which is 'natural' in man (passion, sexuality) is to be avoided or repressed (e.g. H1.141, GS294). Thus human value lies either in what has become civilized or cultured (a repression of the natural) or that which is supernatural (freedom, justice and relation to God). For example, see the end of H3.22 where N analyses punishment as being akin to (one conception of) the 'state of nature'. Even the Stoics, who unusually prescribed acting in accordance with nature, did so because they interpreted the natural world as essentially ordered and rational (see BGE9) – that is to say, they began by anthropomorphizing nature.

One of N's most common themes is the collapsing of this distinction between the human sphere and nature (e.g. 'we ourselves are nature' H3.327, or love 'translated back into nature' WC2 – and see BGE230). This idea yields the title of chapter five of BGE, 'The Natural History of Morality'. This is a form of 'naturalism' – the claim that everything that exists falls under a single set of explanations, and thus there are no supernatural influences, nor discontinuities between the human and the rest of nature. Even the apparent distinctiveness of the human has a natural explanation (e.g. UM3.5). Similarly, one of the key ideas of GM2 is a natural account of the arising of one of the most distinctive of human traits: the capacity to feel guilt. On the other hand, at TIMorality4 and also in the title of that chapter, N contrasts 'naturalism' in morality with the 'anti-natural'. By the latter he means virtually all the moral systems there have been. N is using 'naturalism' here in a different and rather odd sense. In fact, N uses this term quite rarely, and most often in a quite different sphere of thought – namely, to refer to particular artistic styles (e.g. Euripides). We need to distinguish between (i) moral values which are presumed to have their explanation in nature (in social, psychological or physiological processes). On the other hand, there is (ii) the accord or lack of accord of those values with the health and advancement of life – for which reason the values might be 'anti-natural'. This distinction allows us to give a natural explanation of those moral systems that are 'anti-natural' in their values. 'Naturalism' here does not just mean a type of explanation, but rather a moral system whose values are in some way aligned to nature. This is what is meant by a 'return to nature', but in a way distinct from Rousseau and later Romantics, at TISkirmishes48. N sometimes stresses a link between his concept of nobility and that of alignment to nature (D423, 502). Accordingly, the saint's powerful asceticism is natural (it is the expression of will to power) but as a mode of life embodying values it is 'anti-nature' (BGE51, GM3.12). In a similar spirit, at AC24, N discusses how slave morality began as a denaturing of the Jewish people by their priests. The values now espoused were in direct contradiction to the 'ascending movement of life'. The Jewish people became, we might say, 'artificial'; and much more so the Christians who followed (AC51).

N's moral naturalism, however, is not a simple one. For example, it is not the case that proper morality could be simply 'read off' from nature (e.g. as, arguably, Aristotle does once he settles on a *telos* for the human). That would yield a universal morality of the type that N decries at TIMorality6. Relatedly, N asserts that to 'naturalize' the human must also mean the discovery of a new, 'redeemed' nature (GS109). Nor is it the case that this naturalism is compatible with some reduction of moral behaviour to a set of underlying causes, as if a psychologist could read a person like a geologist reads a cliff-face. At TISkirmishes7 N accuses psychologists and artists of a kind of naturalism in this sense; and this subjugation to nature is akin to the leech at Z4.4. It follows that an awareness of the 'naturalness' of the human is far from the end that N has in mind. Naturalization is not primarily a type of understanding or way of analysing; it is a way of living. In EH, for example, N goes to great lengths to sketch out his own life practices, where and how he lives. The purpose of this is not to recommend a way of life, but to show what it might mean for a way of life to be aligned to the nature of life as life manifests itself in this or that individual (i.e. 'its fatefulness' EHWise1). N's free spirit must joyfully affirm naturalization, and thus also be cleansed of the feeling of being 'goaded' by *either* the belief that 'man is only, or is more than, nature' (H1.34, 107; see also nobility at D502). The suggestion is that most of those who espouse naturalism do so intellectually, but without having genuinely experienced its meaning, and without incorporating the idea into their lives and bodies.

nausea, disgust

Usually *Ekel*. If life is growth and self-overcoming, then the response to that which inhibits these processes, and does so necessarily (i.e. as part of the overall *economy* of life) is a literal or metaphorical nausea. Accordingly, Zarathustra's disgust at the thought of the necessity of the rabble (Z2.6, also Z3.13), or his overcoming of disgust at Z4.8. But also, for higher humans and free spirits, there is the nausea at the present, at the recognition of the state of humanity, its degeneration and possible further degeneration (BGE203, EHWise8, thus the 'great disgust' at Z4.10, GM2.24).

necessity

Notwendigkeit. N offers a critique of the way necessity has been thought in philosophy and in science. Most importantly, N does not see necessity and chance as opposites or as incompatible. Only from a particular analysis of law would they be so: namely, necessity as that which follows natural law, chance somehow escapes it. N argues this conception of law is an anthropomorphism: we think of natural laws as existing separately and governing natural occurrences on an analogy with how national laws are created and exist separately, and then govern human behaviour (BGE22, 1887.9.91). Chance and necessity must be *redeemed*, or made *innocent*. N also describes a process – something like aligning oneself with the world as *will to power* and loving one's place within the economy of life (*amor fati*) – which is a becoming necessary (Z3.12.30, BGE56, EHClever8). This is related to the task of the free spirit of assuming comprehensive responsibility for the future of the human.

need

Bedürfnis. Schopenhauer – ultimately following Kant's analysis of the natural dialectic of pure reason – formulated the notion of 'metaphysical need'. By this is meant that human beings have a need for meaning, explanation, purpose, and what is historically called *metaphysics* (also religion) was invented as an attempt to meet this need. N follows Schopenhauer here, although not his underlying explanation. In N, this need extends much further, and finds its way into science, morality and politics (e.g. the 'atomistic need' at BGE12). This need is what makes *nihilism* so extraordinary a phenomenon and what makes *asceticism* so easy to misunderstand. N concludes that the latter is not actually an instance of an overcoming of the metaphysical need, because it is still a willing, in this case, willing nothingness (GM3.28).

neighbour

Nachbar, or similar. Christian morality is full of references to neighbours – the last two of the Ten Commandments, certainly, likewise the 'golden rule' is expressed in terms of the neighbour at Lk. 10.25–28. On the one hand, N treats such ideas as an instance of slave morality, rooted in dissatisfaction with the self, and emphasizing a false equality among individuals, as well as an equality before a transcendent law (God). Accordingly, there are in Z many formulations concerning the neighbour (e.g. Z1.10, 12, 16, 3.12.21). On the other hand, N does have his own version of the 'golden rule', which is found in D146: for higher goals, sacrifice your neighbour as you would yourself (see also Z3.12.4). To the morality of the neighbour, N contrasts *veneration* of the self, *magnanimity,* and the concept of the *friend* (Z1.16).

neuter/impotent

See *fertility.*

newspapers

Zeitung is founded upon the word *Zeit* – time. A newspaper is 'of its time' and only 'for today' and nothing else. Newspapers become for N a symbol of much that he finds repellent about nineteenth-century Europe: its focus on the present at the expense of the *future* (i.e. the opposite of N's own *'untimeliness'*) (UM3.4, 4.6); its indiscriminate accumulation of information and its *representative* quality (at Z1.11 and 3.7, the newspaper is made of that which cannot be *digested*); its reinforcement of comfortable habits and domesticity (UM1.9, 1.11, 2.9, BGEP, BGE208); its frivolous love of petty *politics* and insignificant battles (UM3.4, H2.321, BGE208); and finally the poor or improper use of language in such publications (BT20, 1873.27.28). Included in this category – and especially in what we just called the 'representative quality' – are other kinds of journals that specialize in the popular presentation of intellectual, cultural or scientific affairs.

Nietzsche Contra Wagner

Short book from 1888, gathering lightly edited selections from N's previous publications, all concerning *Wagner*.

night and other times of day

N employs a large set of symbols clustered around day and night. These symbols include light and dark, noon, midnight, twilight, morning, dawn and pre-dawn and shadow. To a great extent, N draws on the traditional meanings of such symbols. These meanings are part of a cultural inheritance that extends back to the ancient world. For example, day or light is life, knowledge, reason, but also action; night is death, ignorance, passion, madness/chaos, but also rest and contemplation. Similarly, dawn is creation, youth or beginning (as in the title of D), while twilight or evening is tiredness, age or an ending (as in the title of TI). Plato's allegory of the cave famously uses sunlight and shadow to depict the relationship between appearance, knowledge, and that which makes possible true knowledge. Likewise, light is an important symbol in Judeo-Christianity, from the first lines of Genesis, to light as understanding at Psalm 119; to Jesus as the 'light of the world', the bringer of salvation and life (e.g. Jn 8.12). Not surprisingly, many of N's usages come from Wagner, for example the yearning of day giving way, in the night, to passion and death (*Tristan and Isolde*); and TI's title is itself a twist on Wagner's *Twilight of the Gods*.

However, N's use of such symbols is often idiosyncratic or at least modified by the context. We shall have to content ourselves with a few important and indicative examples. In BT, the light associated with *Apollo* (god of the sun) picks out clearly demarcated individuals and unambiguous surfaces; while *Dionysus* dissolves such identities and surfaces. There, light is protective illusion, while darkness is the reality of the Will (e.g. BT9). At ZP1 and

Z1.22, however, light is the condition of giving, light overflows in its generosity, seeking takers for its happiness or its wisdom. This though is also a lonely condition, and Zarathustra longs to be darkness (Z2.9). The 'great noon' (or 'midday') signifies the point where the accumulation of knowledge and insight has reached its high point (Z1.22.3), shadows (the various aspects of the self, or my feeling of distance from past or future selves [see TITrueworld]) are at their shortest, it is a point of ripeness or readiness (Z4.20) and thus, perhaps, it is now possible to move towards incorporating that insight, making a new, integrated human instinct. Fore-noon is the time for contemplative study (GM3.8, ZP9). Noon also signifies a turning point, the fire of destruction of an old order (Z3.7). In Z4.19.7, the day is identified with 'woe' – with that which longs and strives for change – while the night is 'joy' which desires only itself and in itself, all things eternally. 'Deep midnight' is the point of highest joy. Likewise, though, high noon is such a point of joy, stillness and perfection (Z4.10, H3.308). This symbolic complexity is acknowledged at Z4.19.10, and in the context of these passages each is perfectly intelligible. A similar symbolic tension arises within a single passage at GS343: the death of God is both a sunset – the end of a long day of trust, faith and certainty and the beginning of doubt – but is also a dawn – 'finally our ships may set out again'. In the symbolic realm, too, there are no real or absolute *opposites*, but rather the ebb and flow of perspectives.

nihilism

Nihilism is a state of culture in which nothing of values remain. Although the issue of a falling away of values, and the paralysing effect this might have, was a concern of N's since early in his career (e.g. the analysis of historicism at UM2.1 and 8), N only becomes preoccupied with the term nihilism in the mid-1880s. Nihilism is a key description of the condition of contemporary Europe for N. N speculates on various responses to nihilism – whether ever greater *comfort* and *narcotizing* are pursued, whether nihilism is simply lived with in a kind of grim determination, whether some form of the *ascetic* ideal is followed, or rather whether nihilism itself is overcome in some way, perhaps in a value-creating project. Indicating the importance this concept held for him, in GM3.27, N announces a project entitled 'The History of European Nihilism', to be part of the proposed book *The Will to Power*. Several longer notebook entries appear to be plans or sketches of this, or other projects featuring an analysis of nihilism (e.g. 1885.2.131, 1886.5.71). The second of these passages, which was written in June 1887, argues for two types of nihilism. Originally in the ancient world, nihilism occurred as a kind of thorough-going pessimism: the world is huge and dangerous, without purposes, suffering is everywhere and in itself humanity is nothing. This first type of nihilism (elsewhere N denies that this is a true nihilism: 1885.2.127) is what gave rise to Christian morality as its 'antidote'. In a modern Europe where one no longer feels constantly threatened, a second nihilism has a different origin: precisely that we no longer believe in the first antidote and also can no longer believe in *any* antidote (i.e. we have become more mistrustful of there being any meaning in 'evil' or in existence itself). GS346 is a good example of this general position, but the idea is found also at H1.34 and 107.

Significantly, it was Christianity itself that brought this about, as it reaches its utmost conclusion in five ways. (1) A morality of equality and pity (and indeed a set of institutions designed as if to breed the human in accordance with these two values) creates a flat, 'herd' condition. This is echoed in recent political history (the rise of democratic institutions, abolition of slavery, rights of women, rise of socialism), all of which results in the lack of any 'redeeming class' (1885.2.131). In such circumstances, there is no longer anything to will, nothing for the reactive will to react against – N calls this a kind of exhaustion (GM1.12, 3.13). Moreover, nihilism as a psychological condition can be a kind of disappointment, a consciousness of wasted time, subsequent to the critique of values (1887.11.99).

(2) The cruelty involved in subordinating oneself to God – itself an attempt to achieve a feeling of power – reaches its pinnacle, which is the sacrifice of God to nothingness (BGE55, GM3.28). In other words, nihilism is motivated by the desire to feel power over oneself, but cruel self-destruction is a mode of will to power that has no future – that is, which cannot create new values or forms of life. (3) Christian values provided a means of valuing the human – created in God's image. The rejection of these values entails a disgust or hatred of the human with and by itself, without also offering a way to overcome this disgust (GS346, GM2.22,

1887.11.99), for example by the appearance of a higher type who might restore faith in the possibilities of the human (1887.9.44). On the basis of (1) and (2) we can see that nihilism is related to pessimism; N sometimes writes as if nihilism is an extreme pessimism (1887.10.22, 192). Similarly, *romanticism* involves a comprehensive and reactive rejection of values and world, and thus tends towards nihilism; and likewise the nihilism of Russian authors Dostoyevsky and Turgenev rests on a 'need for faith' (GS347, see BGE208), and is thus to be understood as a reaction to the historical falling away of beliefs.

(4) Christianity involved a belief in truth, but also a scepticism, such that truth becomes more and more difficult to establish (1885.2.127); taken to its conclusion, this becomes the predicament of the 'shadow' in Z4.9. Alternatively, nihilism might begin by investing value in a 'true world' that is beyond appearance and becoming; because value is defined in this way, the dissolution of the concept of the true world leads to nihilism (1887.11.99, BGE10). This development is also found in science, in two forms. First, the empty, mechanical interaction posited by Laplace (see *causation*); the problem is that the meaning of things does not belong to the order of cause and effect. N's concept of will to power is an attempt to provide an account of becoming and interaction that does not necessarily result in such arid meaninglessness. Second, N sees a radicalization of the same Kantian, critical turn that he discussed in BT18, one which digs into the very conditions of possibility of science. N's notion of *perspective* is an attempt to arrive at a broadly neo-Kantian position but one that neither falls back into metaphysics (as he accuses Kant of doing, and see BGE10) nor falls forward into nihilism.

(5) A universalization of moral values involves at least a partial rejection of life (here, characterized by abundance, difference, growth), but the eventual abandoning of these values generally remains a rejection of life (AC7; GMP5). See AC11 where for this reason Kant is called a 'nihilist'. Christianity, N goes so far as to say, was already nihilistic (AC58). This is analogous to contemporary historicism (a constant object of criticism by N throughout his career): reducing all values, institutions and other forms of cultural to historical descriptions robs the present of an authentic culture and future, and means that forms of culture are borrowed randomly from history (see Z2.14).

On a few occasions, N writes about nihilism as something indicating great strength, something 'divine' (1887.9.41, and see BGE10). In part, this is to indicate that a certain self-overcoming must be involved in the thorough-going scepticism of (4) above, or in the cruelty described in (2). Moreover, in part this alludes to the manner in which nihilism can become active, a nihilism of the deed (1887.11.123). We might classify some anarchists in this manner, but N is likely referring instead to the activity of self-overcoming, having the strength to destroy values and not simply replace them with others taken from elsewhere (1887.9.35). However, such nihilism still lacks the strength to create new values. In that last cited passage, N contrasts such activity with passive nihilism (e.g. Buddhism, or the nihilism of exhaustion, and see 1888.14.174). Considered as active nihilism, nihilism is not simply a regrettable cultural condition, but rather a necessary phase in the growth of the human type. Such a phase is itself overcome by an affirmative mode of life, capable of creating value for itself out of every moment of its existence.

noble (also aristocratic)

Noble (*vornehm, edel*) is an extremely important concept in N, which covers a great deal of conceptual territory. Its importance is highlighted by N entitling the last and longest chapter in BGE 'What is noble?' In his earlier work, N tends to use *edel*; in his later work, *vornehm* becomes more common. The primary meaning of both for N is not some political or social order (i.e. the 'aristocracy' – there are a number of other German terms employed for this meaning: *Geblüt, Aristokratie, Adel*). Rather, it refers to 'higher' types of human being. A given aristocratic order *may* be noble; the order is a consequence of (and perhaps only a faint echo of) nobility in this more fundamental sense. At best, aristocracy is a system of selective breeding for noble traits (see for example the discussions at D198, 201, BGE257). In the following, we will discuss the following inter-linked characteristics that N assigns to the noble: insight, justice, magnanimity, capable of bestowing, dancing, singular, having a sense of order or rank, active, 'natural', health, wholeness, concern for the future, and dialectically related to barbarism. Many of these ideas have their own entries also.

Early in N's career, the noble refers to those who are most sensitive to 'the burden of being' and thus most require illusion as salve and stimulant (BT18, similarly at UM3.3). Nobility is then associated with insight into the Dionysian nature of things, but also full participation and awareness of the Apollonian. Nobility also means a certain wider perspective, and thus above all a sense of justice (UM2.6) which (in this context) means having a sense for what is great or important in the present or the past, with respect to the proper functions of culture (see also Z3.12.11, GM2.11). This insight and sense of justice is reflected in N's discussion of tragic experience at UM4.7: we return from the tragic view more noble, meaning redeemed from those affects that follow from an over-individualized or fragmented view of the human. So, for example, we are now more 'benevolent' – the *magnanimity* of the noble is a common theme in N (e.g. GS3). From this it follows that the noble must avoid shame – thus, they would rather assume the guilt than the punishment (GM2.23), which preserves the feeling of power; and above all perform the most merciful of all acts to the weak, which is not to highlight that weakness and bring them to shame, as would pity (Z2.3). N thus attempts to describe the noble virtue of giving (Z1.19, 3.12.5, 4.8, BGE265) – a giving that does not demean and which enables reciprocity.

The link between the noble and justice continues in a modified form in H. Greek religion is 'noble' because it is founded upon a just sense of the worth of human beings (H1.111, GM2.23). Similar points are made at H1.366 and 440: abstracted from the religious context, nobility means dignity (a sense of one's worth, and the worth of one's equals) even in obedience. At H1.637, the free spirit's sense of justice and need for constant change or at least flexibility of perspective does not allow him or her to become a dogmatist; thus, the free spirit is constantly a 'noble traitor' but without any guilt. A related idea is that the noble does not attain to the heights or depths (of passion, stimulation, self-release), but exhibits something like a Greek sense of moderation or restraint (H2.397, D201, BGE284). Similarly, the noble has the strength to be capable of *not* reacting, of suspending judgement (TIGermans6). Nobility is characterized by a certain ease that comes from reserves of strength and from confidence; N sometimes describes this in terms of dance (TIGermans7).

That which is noble is also, however, concerned with the exception, with singular values. Accordingly, the most noble things have no impression on the 'masses' (UM2.9); the scientist is more noble because the problems he or she pursues are not widely considered valuable (H2.206). Despite this exceptional taste, the noble has a desire and often ability to *communicate*; in this way, the noble is an instrument of cultural (and ultimately, human) development (see BGE268). Noble justice considered as a valuing of equality is possible, but only among a ruling class (H1.451) – justice here means equality for those who are equal. However, it is typical of the noble to believe that their exceptional ways of valuing things are or should be widely shared. Thus, surprisingly, the noble is intrinsically unjust in that it mis-measures the majority of human beings (GS3, 55), attempting to raise them to its own level. The universality of the genuinely free is a noble ideal. A higher nobility would be one that has brought about the situation where it was indeed noble to be the 'champion of the rule'. In other words, where the dignity attached to the human was one genuinely shared by all. Many religious or political beliefs have perished by espousing this ideal of equality too soon, with the result that all that is achieved is an equality of slavery. In contrast, nobility 'breathes power', and is constantly feeling its power (D201). But again there is no reason in principle why this must be a privilege of the few. (That is N argument at this stage, at least, but perhaps not later: see BGE257 for example.) For the present, only the noble may be given freedom of spirit, for the time has not yet come for a universal equality (H3.350). Likewise, at least for the present, the human realm is characterized by an *order of rank*: those few who are noble feel their distance both from each other and especially from all the others (the 'pathos of distance'); related concepts are *solitude* (BGE284), *reverence* and *cleanliness* (BGE263, 271).

The noble is characterized by activity rather than reactivity (i.e. not acting in response to some external standard). Indeed, even the idealism of Plato is 'noble' in this regard, in that it demanded mastery over the passivity of the senses (BGE14). The exceptional nature of noble values also belongs here – they are not borrowed from the masses, and do not arise primarily through a calculation of what will preserve either an individual or the masses (see also BGE190). Thus, nobility is contrasted with slavery, where the slave is defined as the one who is not capable of self-command

(GS1.18). Because of this active valuing and production of values (see BGE260, GM1.2 and 7 onwards), the noble has an unflinching certainty about him or herself, and 'self-reverence' (BGE287). See also the concepts of rule or control as used in Z1.22, TISocrates9, EHWise4, 6.

A further significant quality that N ascribes to the noble is something like a naturalness, but in an anti-Stoic sense, as here nature means being attuned to one's drives rather than controlled by reason (GS1.3, and see GM1.10, TISocrates5). Likewise, at D502, he writes that the noble person experiences passions as wild nature, and their own normal state as 'tranquilly beautiful' nature. At GS1.294, nobility means not having fear of oneself, not understanding what it would mean to despise one's nature according to some other, external, standard. This naturalness is clearly related to the making-noble through tragedy which is discussed at UM4.7: one is thereby released from artificial individuality and has an appreciation of the whole. N also describes this idea using the concept of health (e.g. GM3.14), specifically that health that involves a freedom to express the values that stem from one's unimpaired life. The noble is a whole being, and one with a whole or comprehensive perspective. Thus, the beautiful description at GS337 of the first of a new aristocracy taking on the whole history of grief and still rising to greet the dawn. That latter notion of greeting the dawn is an important idea in its own right: the noble person has concern for the future (see Z1.8, 3.12.12).

By way of contrast, however, in BGE N pursues the idea that nobility has a tendency to stagnation (this is an apparent reversal of the idea expressed in H1.637). That is, nobility insofar as it is the expression of a culture brought to perfection, has a very definite *taste*, and resists further change (BGE224). Thus, in this passage, the historical sense arrives as the destruction of that narrow taste, and the facilitating of new cultural development. In other words, N is suggesting a kind of productive historical dialectic between perfected culture and 'barbarism' or 'corruption'. This becomes explicit at BGE257–8 and 262, although these discussions primarily concern 'aristocracies' in the specifically sociopolitical sense, and thus are perhaps not about nobility more generally (see GM1.11). N's analysis, then, may be that at moments of corruption the quality of nobility passes from the community of the aristocrats to the dangerous individual – and then, in the formation of a new cultural order, back again. Nobility, in other words, concerns itself with the future in the sense of the advancement of the human; at various historical stages; however, this function might lie in an aristocracy, but at other stages the function might belong to barbarians or revolutionaries. This would account for why the chapter on nobility in BGE ends with a stress on the future: for example, the description of the philosopher 'pregnant with new lightning' (BGE292) and the figure of Dionysus who 'tempts' the human to further advancement (BGE295).

north

See *south*.

nose/smell

See *sensation*.

notebooks

N wrote more or less constantly, and kept a long series of notebooks which together make up more than half of the Colli-Montinari *Kritische Studienausgabe*. In addition to these notebooks, the *Nachlass* also includes a number of never-published essays (such as the famous 'On Truth and Lies in an Extra-Moral Sense'), a nearly complete book (*Philosophy in the Tragic Age of the Greeks*), public or University lectures, and an extensive correspondence.

As one might expect these notes comprise thoughts and reflections, drafts or plans of works he hoped to publish, fragments of poetic or dramatic works, and often extensive notes on the reading he had been doing. Some entries are only a few words, others are pages in length. Use of the notebooks for scholarship is invaluable, but one needs to take care. Many ideas here are expressed in a hurried, fragmentary and compressed fashion – even in comparison to the aphoristic style N uses in publication – such that interpretation is difficult. Moreover, ideas in the notebooks that do not then also appear in published writings were (we must assume) left out for some reason. *The Will to Power* was an early, often very misleading, collection of notebook entries, presented as if they were more than notes. It would seem prudent to give most weight to (a) notes that are clearly restatements or elaborations of published ideas; (b) *Nachlass* pieces that are more or less complete essays or short books, since these too would have been worked on over a period of time; (c) and perhaps also notes that represent ideas to which N returned more than once (i.e. did not just immediately abandon). An example of the latter are the various attempts to prove eternal recurrence using principles of cosmology; because notes working on this appear over the course of several years, we can at least have some confidence that he took the *attempt* at such a proof seriously. The notebooks are also useful as they often contain first drafts of passages in the published works; this allows the scholar to observe N at work crafting his prose writing.

number

Number is the basis for any *scientific* understanding of *nature*. Number is employed to measure space and time (distances and durations). Likewise, number permits one to interpret qualities as quantities (e.g. 1872.19.66), for example power as a quantity of force, and thus again measurement. This leads for example to the absurdity of putting the world of *values* onto a set of scales which Zarathustra does in a dream (Z3.10, and see TISocrates2). N occasionally writes about the measurement of power, in terms of its effectiveness (thus Z3.10.1, or TISkirmishes8). Similarly, power is talked about in terms of quanta (e.g. GM1.13, 1887.10.82, 1888.14.79, 105). This parallels the expression '*unusquisque tantum juris habet, quantum potentia valet*' from Spinoza's treatise on politics, which N frequently cites. However, N comments also that power is felt qualitatively and only *interpreted* as a quanta (1885.2.157, 1886.5.36). The role of measurement in all values is developed in more detail at GM2.8. Number is also closely related to identity (H1.19) or to logic (TIReason3, 1884.25.307). Number as identity or logic permits one to designate something in terms of its type (e.g. a basic type, a species, or a cause or effect), or its *unity* (as a molecule, or living organism). In all these ways, number is for N an enormously useful error, one ultimately founded upon our assumption that we can arbitrarily divide up, and separate, the flux of reality or experience (H1.11), or to take up a particular *perspective* on value and assume it to be universal and fixed.

objectivity

See *truth, perspective, method.*

Oedipus

Probably the most well-known of Greek tragic heroes, and the subject of two tragedies by Sophocles. Oedipus is a symbol both of the greatness of human mind and action (see D128; he defeats the Sphinx by solving her riddle, the answer to which is 'a human' [see BGE1], and he solves the mystery of the murdered King) and of the impossibility of escaping fate (by attempting to avoid it, he makes it happen). Oedipus' self-inflicted blindness is also an important symbol for N (e.g. BGE230).

opposite

Gegensätz, Gegenteil. One of the basic principles of traditional logic is the law of non-contradiction. This states that a proposition and its opposite cannot both be true. N argues that whatever validity such a law may have in the domain of pure logic, it cannot be applied to values, or even to the state of being true. H1.1 and BGE2 both argue that there is no reason in principle why apparently opposite states or evaluations could not have developed out of each other. This could happen across a historical span: N's two most famous examples are the development of the concept of evil from out of the noble concept of good (see GM1), or the development of our notion of truth from out of errors ('On Truth and Lies'). Or, it could be a vertical relationship of an act and its real motives: what according to one moral perspective is the good act of *pity* is grounded in motives that same perspective would not call 'good' (selfishness, power, cruelty).

On the other hand, N does sometimes use the principle of non-contradiction in his own reasoning, as at GM3.11. Moreover, he very frequently relies upon a series of oppositions: illness and health, slave and noble, decline or growth. Finally, he uses the concept of 'opposite' in a special sense. For example, at BGE44 he talks of 'we opposite men'; likewise, there are instances of a positing and pursuing of an 'opposite' or 'inverse' ideal at BGE56 ('the opposite ideal') or GM2.24 ('inverse attempt'). In each case, what is meant is a revaluation of existing values such that the new values (and ways of life, and ideals) will be directed to the health and development of human life rather than to illness, degeneration or stagnation. In other words, the validity of an opposition is dependent upon that of the *perspective* that employs it, and the strategic use to which it is put.

Orient

See *Asia*.

overcome

Überwältigen, *Überwindung*, etc. The former is sometimes translated as 'overpower' or even 'dominate'. To overcome has several broad meanings in Nietzsche. (i) To be overcome, especially by music – N uses this idea in identifying and ultimately criticizing the Wagnerian understanding of art (UM4.7, H3.170, D142, 255); (ii) overcoming in the sense of to repress or *narcotize* a feeling or drive – N's frequently made accusation against morality is that it demands this, producing tiredness, weakness or illness (D9, 500, Z1.2, BGE61). (iii) An overcoming could be evidence of an awesome strength, but one that is unproductive, or even destructive. Examples of this would include passages like BGE14, 211 or 'despotism' at GM2.20. The whole phenomenon of the *saint* might usefully be placed in this category. (iv) His most familiar meaning is to encounter a resistance to one's movement, where 'movement' is a very broadly meant, and yet for that movement to continue and perhaps even be strengthened.

Within that fourth meaning, though, are several subtle variations. This resistance could be external (e.g. another person, a group, idea or institution). A good example is the use of religion by certain free spirits as an instrument to overcome resistance to their rule (BGE61). Or, it could be internal (e.g. a value one holds, an idea one believes in, a habit one has acquired). For example, at Z3.3, Zarathustra must overcome himself in being able to express and affirm eternal recurrence (and then overcome also the pity for the higher men in Z4). Again, at Z2.13, beauty and goodness are the restless powerful (those who are sublime) overpowering themselves. N tends to emphasize the internal, though even then he uses metaphors pertaining to external resistances, such as battle, warrior, etc.

As we noted above, 'movement' is meant to cover a great deal of conceptual ground: from simple organic survival and growth (GM1.13), to being able to carry on as a living being (BT21), achieving an insight or alteration of value, all the way to the overall growth of the human as a type (ZP3, BGE257). Overcoming is often used as a very general and basic function of life (Z2.12), with the emphasis there on continual risk. This foundational notion of overcoming has it roots (at least in N's later writings) in the *will to power* as relational. For example, at BGE117, N notes that the overcoming of an affect is not a *will* (not a conscious choice on my part, and not something separable) but the action of another affect (and see 1888.14.93). Moreover, that life should strive to thrive and grow (in whatever is the relevant sense of these terms) is why overcoming is associated not only with a movement continuing, but being strengthened or enhanced in the process. The idea of overcoming in that fourth sense is related to the *agon* and its role in N's understanding of cultural growth. Thus, at H2.274, N contrasts 'woman' as the achievement of human development while 'man' is the sum of what that development 'had to overcome'. Overcoming is there practically synonymous with advancement. Similarly, at GS283, N writes of those 'preparatory human beings' who will view all things in terms of what in them must be overcome, in order to further advance the human type. Important in self-overcoming is often the concept of a strict *discipline* or practice, as with the Jesuit order at H1.55.

Most often, N uses the expression to signal a philosophical 'movement' that overcomes something both spiritually (i.e. at the level of ideas and books) and bodily (insofar as ideas will have been internalized as values, habits, dispositions, etc.). Such an overcoming would involve critique, but also a discipline designed to alter things at the physiological level. For example, N talks about overcoming metaphysics (H1.20), morality (BGE32, including that morality which insists on certain types of self-overcoming: 1887.11.300, EHClever9), one's own time (i.e. the values and beliefs of one's time, and the self-overcoming of the internalization of these into one's modes of life; see UM3.3 and GS380), or the world (i.e. a particular way of conceiving or experiencing the world [BGE14, 257]).

overhuman, *Übermensch*

This famous, indeed infamous term could also be translated as 'superman' or 'overman'. Over- is preferred to super- here because it permits us to see clearly the relation to overcoming or 'going under'; while -human is preferred to -man because, despite N's undoubted prejudices, it is nevertheless impossible on his account for there to be human development without both genders. N's use of this term may have been inspired by Lucien's *hyperanthropos*. In fact, N employs several different terms and phrases for what is a closely related cluster of concepts. For example, 'Zarathustra' is used in this way (i.e. not so much as a character in a narrative, but as a type) at GS342, TIFable, and EHZ1; 'new philosophers' (BGE2) or 'experimenters' (BGE42); 'philosophical physician' at GSP1.2; and also 'Dionysian' (EHZ6) – this list does not include passages of sustained description but without an over-arching label, such as GM2.24. The term overhuman is used in Z, and although it is used rarely thereafter, does not disappear (see 1887.10.17, AC4, TISkirmishes37, EHBooks1).

In all these cases, what is at stake is a further development of the human type, physiologically, culturally and spiritually. The overhuman should be thought of not as an end point, a final evolutionary stage or a new fixed species. Any state of the human that refused further growth would, by that very fact, not be the overhuman ('Life is an instinct for growth', AC6). Rather, the overhuman is a perpetual ideal of human development, continual self-overcoming. The overhuman is thus a way of talking about the 'ideal' discussed in such important passages as BGE56, GM2.24 or GS382. Importantly, although one could not simply 'be' the overhuman, this ideal is not unobtainable. It is not set out beyond 'this world' or 'this life' (like virtue or grace in the Christianity of St Paul, or in general a traditional notion of the divine – see Z2.2). Thus, the overhuman will appear terrifying or evil, precisely because he or she does not involve a negation of reality (EHDestiny5). Likewise, it is not something that demands a rejection of any of life's essential characteristics (as does the ascetic ideal). Instead, N defines it as the 'highest constitutional excellence' at EHBooks1, and frequently links it to his notion of 'great health' (GM2.24, GS382 which is quoted at length in EHZ2). This is to say, the overhuman is a mode of human life that is most aligned to the nature of life, and capable of living (which can mean expending or 'squandering' itself, or also 'going under') as an affirmation of life. The concept of the overhuman, thus, is linked to other notions that involve such affirmation (*amor fati, eternal recurrence*). What N frequently calls the *free spirits* are 'preparatory' human beings – those who have recognized and understood this new ideal and are in process of freeing themselves from that which binds them to the current state of humanity.

pagan

See *God, gods.*

pain

See *pleasure, affect.*

Pascal

Seventeenth-century French philosopher and mathematician. Pascal's late, unfinished work *Pensées* is important for N in several ways. First of all, it is written in aphorisms or fragments (although it is not clear that the final text, for which these were the unfinished and partly unsorted notes, would have taken this form). Second, rather than simply setting out its ideas and arguments, it seems to adopt a set of strategies the purpose of which is to guide the reader rationally towards the questioning of reason. On this particular idea, N sees Pascal as representing the final stages of Christian thought, the long suicide of reason (BGE46). However, this notion of a strategy of writing the purpose of which is to in some way effect a change in the reader is something recognizable in N. For N, Pascal is 'profound, wounded, monstrous' (BGE45), but rather than something that is behind us, just such profundity is a necessary stage within modern thought. This is because, as Pascal thought, reason is indeed corrupted, although not by original sin (AC5). Therefore, as corrupted, we cannot simply use reason as a neutral or pristine instrument.

passion

Either the Latinate *Passion*, or *Leidenschaft*. The meanings of these two terms overlap, but only the former also has a religious meaning in the suffering of a Christian martyr. More generally, a passion is an *affect* so strong or violent that one loses self-control. Sometimes, N uses the term more broadly to indicate a fundamental psychological mechanism (e.g. BGE36). Much of N's analysis focuses on the misunderstanding – even the repression – of passion. This analysis thus forms an important branch of N's more general analysis of the history of the valuing of the body. N argues that neglect of, and failure to understand the affects has created a situation where passion is feared (H3.37). For a clear example, St Paul's attempt to eliminate all passion except for the passion for God, is contrasted with the Greek sense of passions as divine (GS139, see TIMorality1). A similar point is stated in terms of nobility at D502. Similarly, he reads Schopenhauer's theory of art as specifically a quieting of sexual passion (GM3.6).

Instead, the passions could be joys (and see the title of Z1.5), divine or beautiful. This point is elaborated at TIMorality1: N argues that passions have a 'stupid' and destructive phase, and the attempt to annul the passions for this reason means in turn that we never attain to the 'spiritualization' of passion. By 'spiritualized' is meant that the stupid and destructive aspects are overcome insofar as the passion is employed within the spiritual interests of an individual or a people. N's examples there of spiritualized passion are *love* and hostility (see entry on *agon*). The ugly and clumsy passions normally exhibited by the Germans are, only sometimes, elevated to beauty (GS105). The chief target of that analysis of 'ugly passions' is Wagner and those he influenced (WC6). Moreover, passions could be instruments harnessed for 'good spiritual works' (H3.53). Such 'works' would include philosophical or scholarly pursuits (TIGermans3), and thus N's complaint about modern scholarship is that it lacks passion (AC9). N also argues that passion is intrinsically transient. Thus, to expect passion to endure – as love (spiritualized sexual passion) is believed to do in marriage – is a falsehood. However, though false, it is still an elevation of the human insofar as the human at least now values passion (D27).

pathos

See *affect*.

Paul

On N's account St Paul is the key member of the early founders of Christianity for turning the life and teachings of Jesus into an organized system of values. N gives a psychological account of Paul, suffering distress over the impossibility of fulfilment of Jewish law, seeing in Jesus an opportunity for revenge against the law. See D68, AC41–7.

people, folk

Volk. A people is a group corresponding to a unified culture and way of life (UM1.1, H2.170). In his earlier work, N conceives of his own project partly as the 'resurrection' of the people, and in this is influenced by Wagner (BT24, UM4.8). Such a resurrection particularly involved reformulating a unified mythic system. Later, N prefers to understand this unity as one of valuing; so a people is defined partly by the morality of custom it has generated to preserve itself, and partly by the prohibition of the customs of its neighbours or enemies (GS43, Z1.15). At AC11, N writes 'A people is destroyed' when it confuses its own values with some abstract or universal sense of values. Indeed, at Z1.22.2, Zarathustra suggests that his disciples, insofar as they value and live differently (they 'withdraw to the side'), will form a people. People is to be distinguished from the 'herd', and the 'rabble'. A people is not these, because it assumes higher and lower strata (thus also we should not understand the state as a projection of the people: H1.450, Z1.11). A people finds its full expression only in its greatest individuals (PTAG1, 1872.19.1, BGE126 – and see also the contrast between the peasants – remnants of a prior people – and the educated at BGE263). A people, unlike the herd, is not necessarily opposed to experimentation and development (AC57). The Jews of the old testament were a people (GM3.22, AC11), but Christians are an artificial assemblage of races and classes (AC51).

perfection

Vollendung, Perfektion; etymologically, both mean something completed. Perfection has two related roles in N. First, as a way of discussing the idea of the classic, and thus also of the relationship between previous cultures (Greek and Roman most obviously) to contemporary aspirations (H3.125). Our *historical sense* provides us with understanding and insight of the values of the past, except into instances of cultural perfection (BGE224, Z4.13.15). Second, perfection is a way of describing one moment in the cycle of states that make up a healthy and ascending mode of life (this is how N employs the concept at Z1.18, 3.3, 4.10, WC1). It is the moment that N also discusses using the ideas of *repose, beauty* (or *art* more generally, as at 1888.14.47) and the *feminine*. These two ideas come together at TISkirmishes19. There, beauty is the mirroring back of the sense of perfection held by a human way of life.

personality

See *Character*.

perspective

Perspecktive, or cognate expressions. The notion of 'perspective' is used earlier in his career in the informal sense of 'having a view'.

However, a more technical concept of perspective is important throughout the later N.

Perspective involves an analogy with vision. In human psychology, perspective arises from interpreting the subtle differences between images in the two eyes (or differences in size and arrangement in a single visual image); these differences are signs of something's distance away from us. There is not a direct observation of distance, but at best an indirect inference. N's idea here could be fruitfully compared with that of Berkeley in *A New Theory of Vision*. In the history of painting, perspective is the art and science of making things on a flat canvas appear near or far, with respect to an implied viewing angle. The object itself (the flat canvas), has nothing to do with the objects or events depicted. In this case, the implied perspective is achieved by a set of visual signs which, in themselves, have nothing to do with nearness. N accounts for his own specific use of the concept by making explicit reference to these practices (e.g. GS162, BGE2), or more often still, implicit references to perspective in its various optical senses. Accordingly, N sums up his concept of perspective at GS354: there is no direct access to the truth of things. Rather, we become conscious of (or we experience) not things but only 'signs' of things, where those signs have long been agreed upon by the human community, and codified in language, institutions (e.g. the perspective involved in a legal institution, such as the designation of something as a 'legal entity'), accepted values (morality) and habits.

What is the origin of such 'signs'? N's answer is supposed utility. That is, the human becomes conscious of those things that are, and only in that way that they are, considered to be favourable or disadvantageous for the survival and thriving of a community. In other words, the key attribute of any thing that we become conscious of is its *value*. What N means by 'perspective' is that human experience is irreducibly founded upon evaluation. Accordingly, perspectivism is not exclusively or even primarily an epistemological concept (concerned with the nature or conditions of knowledge). That something is *taken* to be knowledge – that is held to be true – may be very important; whether or not it actually is true, much less so and possibly a nonsense. These values could be obviously moral (thus the perspective that a people has towards its heroes or its law-breakers, or that a religion has towards those who pursue or resist its ideals) or less obviously so (e.g. concepts in physics: BGE14). Perspective is thus the basic condition of all life (BGEP). In addition, N speculates that religions begin with interpretation or perspective, but not one that is allied to the concrete life of some *people* (i.e. to values that have some non-religious utility), but is rather in some way artificial (see GS353, AC51).

However, this way of expressing the concept of perspective again makes it sound as though (i) in themselves, the sensations or perhaps nervous stimulations that I have (prior to conscious 'interpretation') are in themselves value-neutral; moreover, (ii) the objects of my experience are 'out there' and likewise value-neutral. The first of these would amount to something like phenomenalism, the second a naive realism. N definitely rejects realism in this sense. N does write like a phenomenalist fairly regularly, although usually with the caveat that we could not on principle have access to these sensations (e.g. D119, GM3.12, 1887.11.113, TIErrors4). Indeed, even the apparently basic affects of pleasure and pain are interpretations (GS127 and see H1.108). Such a critically limited phenomenalism is not overcome by any appeal to original evidence of phenomena, then, but rather the cultivated ability to move between perspectives, gauging what is at stake in the differences in their evaluative constitution of things (see for example H1P6, GM3.12, EHWise1). Expressed as a general aporia, this idea is found at D243: if the 'mirror' is our consciousness or thinking, then neither it, nor things (whether we mean sensations or their causes), can be grasped as such.

Whether or not we should interpret N as a phenomenalist, the key issue here has to do with N's concept of the *will to power* as a basic principle of life. Also at stake is whether, in any given passage, we think that by 'life' N means a particular form of human life (a people, say) or some undifferentiated sense of organic life that humans share with animals and plants. Because the will to power is not just a characterization of consciousness, but a characterization of the human body, including its sensibility, perspective is found 'all the way down'. Neither the world, nor my sensations, exist as in themselves, and are subsequently interpreted. At D119, N raises this as a question: are our experiences, in themselves 'nothing'? Repeatedly in the notebooks, N extends the concept of the perspectival beyond phenomenalism. There, he argues that the world – perhaps even the inorganic – exists as perspectival (1885.34.120, 36.20, 2.148–51,1886.5.12, 1888.14.184) and famously 'there are no facts, only interpretations' (1886.7.60, BGE108). Arguably, at least, this more radical concept of perspective is not just found in the notebooks, but also at BGE14, 22, GM1.13.

pessimism

See *Schopenhauer, nihilism.*

phenomenon

See *appearance.*

philology

The study of the history of language, and of the appropriate reconstruction and interpretation of texts. N was trained as a philologist, specializing in ancient Greek manuscripts, and produced several significant publications in this area. However, at the beginning of 1870, N gave two public lectures on music and tragedy. From these it was already clear that he had a strong inclination to a more philosophical, less formally academic, way of thinking and writing. This alternative mode eventually resulted in *The Birth of Tragedy*, which some saw and not without reason as a declaration of war against traditional philology. N's relationship with philology remained ambiguous. On the one hand, for example, in the 1886 preface he regrets not tackling *The Birth of Tragedy* as a philologist (BGEP3); again, at EHBooks5, N hopes for an audience that will read him 'as good old philologists read their Horace'. On the other hand, N's comments about the severe limitations and indeed the truncated humanity of *scholars* abound. Certainly, N remained interested in the philological themes of the nature of *language* or *style*. Ultimately, we should see philology as exemplary of a method that has patience, and does not rush to judgement, as discussed at H1.8, DP5, AC52 – although this is not the same as what is normally called 'objectivity' (UM2.6, GM3.12). In other words, N takes philology as a model for generalizable *method* of the interpretation of phenomena.

Philosophy in the Tragic Age of the Greeks

Book manuscript written by N in the early 1870s but never published. It comprises a series of short studies of the pre-Socratic philosophers. It is an invaluable source not only for N's account of *Greek* thought, but also for his image of the philosopher with respect to possible modes of life and authentic *culture*.

philosophy, philosopher

N uses the terms philosophy and philosopher in two senses. He does the same with 'sage' [*Weise*] and 'thinker' [*Denker*]. First, pejoratively, to designate most of what is called philosophy in the past and present. Here philosophy is typically metaphysical in nature – that is, unknowingly using, treating as justified and as universal, the most basic errors – and usually also following the traditional moral and religious categories. For clear examples, see UM3.8, D427, Z2.8, BGEP, 6, AC12. Second, positively, to characterize the free spirits of all periods, and especially 'of the future'. Good examples can be found at H1.235 (there writing of the 'sage'), H3.267 (now the 'thinker'), BGE2, 42–4, 203. The philosopher in this second sense encompasses a number of qualities: *freedom* or independence; the capacity for *irony*, *foolishness* or *laughter*; *nobility* and overflowing *strength*; *comprehensiveness* (which includes the ideas of the *scholarly*, *scientific* and *critical*); moments at least of great *health* and therefore also illness or *exhaustion*; a willingness to *experiment* or be *cruel*, even and especially to the self, as part of the process of creating new *values* and ways of living; assuming *responsibility* for the *future* of the human; a *joyful* alignment to the world understood as *will to power* and to the fatefulness of one's place within it (*eternal recurrence, amor fati*). This 'fatefulness' is emphasized at BGE292; thus the gods, in the loving of their fate, also philosophize (BGE295). Philosophy is always something personal, an unconscious though *spiritualized* confession (BGE6). However, the key question is: does this personal projection happen out of weakness – that is out of a reaction, or a need to relieve distress – or strength and 'riches' (GSP2)?

physics

The root of the word is the Greek *phusis* meaning 'nature'; physics thus shares its etymology with *physiology*. For particular topics, see *nature, atoms, number, matter, force, science.*

physiology

Physiology is the science studying the *body* as a part of *nature* – thus the etymology in Greek *phusis*. Physiology studies the form and function both of the body's individual organs and their interrelations such that the body forms something like a system. The physiological studies that interested N the most were those concerning the physiology of the senses and nervous system – that is, which related the body to *experience* and to *thought*.

piety

See *veneration.*

pig (or swine)

Schwein. As in English, general term of abuse for a coarse (thus the phrase 'pig-German' at 1885.37.4), lustful and greedy animal. N often evokes the story of Circe who turned most of Odysseus' crew into pigs. Their repentance is an instance of pigs *worshiping* chastity – that is converting the opposite of oneself into an object of the highest *value* (1882.3.1.217, GM3.2). Similarly, the pig takes *revenge* on filth in a way akin to *cynicism* (Z3.7) or in a way akin to a *metaphysical* hatred of *this world* (e.g. hatred of the body) (Z3.12.14). To the whole opposition between lustful and *ascetic* (pig and *saint*), N contrasts the *beauty* of self-restraint, giving oneself *measure* (1884.25.348, 26.167). Like the *ass*, the pig is also a figure of indiscriminate taste (Z3.11.2).

pity, compassion, sympathy

Usually *Mitleid*. This word is also frequently translated as 'compassion'. *Mitgefühl* (usually 'sympathy') is sometimes used in this sense; likewise *Erbarmen*. N takes pity/compassion to be a key virtue espoused by Christianity (see for example Mt. 9.36, 2 Cor. 1.3–4, 1 Jn 3.17). It is also an important concept in Schopenhauer's ethics: compassion in the sense of sharing another's suffering is the recognition that our separation from one another as individuals is only an appearance; it is therefore literally unegoistic (GMP5, AC7, and the figure of the Soothsayer at Z4.2).

N argues that pity is, in fact, immoral by its own definition. That is, the feeling of pity or an act associated with it is not unegoistic, and is very often based upon the petty feeling of power or superiority one gets with respect to the weak or needy, a cruel need to highlight another's helplessness, a simplification of a unique suffering to a type, or upon a need to share one's own suffering. N's most sustained discussion is at D132–7. See also H3.50, D224, GS13, GS338, Z2.3, BGE222. He further argues that pity is, in fact, counter-productive. This in one of three senses, which are often discussed together. Either the person pitied is a born sufferer (from the beginning broken, perhaps suffering from existence itself), in which case coming to his or her aid is prolonging that suffering. Or, for the sake of the growth of the human, the sufferer represents a diseased type that should be allowed to perish. That is, pity or compassion is protracting the period of human stagnation, creating perhaps a pathological sensitivity to pain, and perhaps even leading in this manner to *nihilism*. Finally, by doubling suffering, and initiating a cycle of petty feelings of power, pity is 'infectious' (AC7). For discussions see BGE62, GM3.14, AC7, TISkirmishes37. For all the above reasons, feeling pity for one's friend is particularly delicate (Z1.14).

For the 'free spirit', pity remains a dangerous temptation, a seduction to deviation 'from my path' (GS338). For free spirits, pity is generally directed to 'higher humans' – those who have broken new ground or pursued new values, but who ultimately fell victim to environment, success or their own weaknesses. Z4 is a narrative of Zarathustra's being tempted by pity for a string of such 'higher men' – satirical portraits of Wagner, Schopenhauer and Jesus among them – and allowing them briefly to distract him from his true 'children' (see also GS289, BGE269). The free spirit exhibits also a different kind of pity for the lost opportunities for the development of human beings per se (BGE225). N there distinguishes between Christian pity for the created being (here meaning a human type that has ceased its development), but a higher pity for the creator in whom suffering can be productive.

Pity, along with fear, is also part of Aristotle's famous account of the function of tragedy: to evoke pity and fear and thereby purify them. N comments on Aristotle's theory many times (e.g. BT22, H1.212, GS80, AC7, TIAncients5). The consistent objection is that Aristotle shows complete misunderstanding of Greek tragedy – and thereby also of the nature of art more generally. Tragedy is, for N, the highest instance of aesthetic play and of affirmation.

plants, garden, trees, etc.

Plant or garden metaphors are used by N in a wide variety of ways, here are six of the most common: (i) A reference to the Garden of Eden (thus apples, serpents, fig leaves, etc.) or other mythical gardens or paradises (e.g. Z3.13); (ii) a reference to the garden of Epicurus – that is a place of sanctuary, quiet and friendship (D174); (iii) a metaphor of the jungle or the tropics, meaning lush, dense, rapid and untamed growth (e.g. BGE197, 262); (iv) metaphor of the tree (e.g. Z1.8, GS371), and its roots (hidden sources), dangers (lightning), height; (v) flowers or fruits, usually meaning the outcome of a process (e.g. H3.189, GM2.2), the end of some particular historical stage (EHTI2), or the moment of ripeness (Z4.10); (vi) a metaphorical reference to the methods of horticulture (GS87): see the discussion of self-cultivation (D560), pruning as a form of discipline (TISkirmishes41), transplanting (UM2.2), picking ripe grapes (Z3.14).

plastic

See *form*.

Plato

N's relationship to Plato is complex. On the one hand, of course, Plato's theory of forms is the archetypal world-denying and 'world beyond'-positing philosophy, with enormous influence both on subsequent philosophy, science and on Christianity. Plato is thus a 'coward in the face of reality' (TIAncients2). On the other hand, Plato is more *noble* than Socrates (BGE14, 190). Thus N often speculates that he was ironic throughout (1885.34.179, 195), had a secret and sphinx-like nature (BGE28), and himself employed the 'noble lie' that he describes in the *Republic*. That is to say, Plato's idealism in fact stemmed from a magnificent health (GS372), one that found its feeling of power in mastery of the senses (BGE14). Other ideas from Plato with which N works include the account of *love* and *beauty* in the *Symposium*, the structure of the state described in *Republic* (see D496), the account of *thumos* (spiritedness – see entry on *spirit*), and the relationship between action and knowledge of the good (H1.102, BGE190).

play

Spiel. The three most important reference points for N's concept of play are Heraclitus, Kant's aesthetics, and the fact that in German as in English, 'play' also means what is presented in a theatre. Play as in spectacle, that is something that can be treated as *merely* something to be watched, is a common idea (e.g. BGE56, 218, AC6). The idea is that an entire course of history is understood as observed with a kind of ironic detachment founded upon height or distance in nobility or rank. (See *tragedy*.)

Heraclitus writes that time, or the creator, is a *child* building with, then scattering, his playthings (see BT24). Change, *becoming*, and all that we might call *purpose* or order – all these are play. Importantly, though, the concept of spectacle is linked here: it is the ironic detachment of one's height – even with respect to oneself – that makes it possible to achieve a *happiness* understood as higher play that is not simply opposed to work (H1.611). Likewise, making it possible to handle great tasks as if they were play (EHClever10, 1888.18.16). The philosopher as child, when he or she becomes disappointed and discards the old concepts (toys), will have to invent new playthings (BGE57). Likewise, when Zarathustra says that 'woman is the most dangerous plaything' (Z1.18), it is play in this sense that is meant: that is the 'great task' of bringing feminine and masculine drives together so as to determine a future.

The Kantian meaning is found in a quotation from Goethe than N cites at BT22. Tragedy was not only a play (in the sense of a drama) but also 'aesthetic play'. Aesthetic play is a reference to Kant's aesthetics, as developed in his *Critique of Judgement*. In an encounter with something beautiful, Kant argues, the judgement is neither determinate (i.e. employing a single, definite concept), but neither is it simply unrelated to thought. Rather, he describes it as a play within our capacity for thinking – play in the sense of a kind of back and forth movement which is not serious because the activity is the important thing, not the end product. Goethe's idea is that, for the Greeks, even tragedy could be something not serious – disengaged from the world of morality and scientific understanding. N's discussion in BT of the 'middle world' of Apollonian images is his development of this idea. More generally, to the extent that for N the Greeks represent a high point of human development, this capacity for play is an important reason why.

pleasure

Lust (pleasure or joy), and *Freude* (also joy, or satisfaction) are the most common terms, also *Vergnügen* (pleasure), while the adjective *angenehm* (pleasant, agreeable; for example a pleasant sensation) is more than frequent enough to deserve mention. *Freude*, *Vergnügen* and *angehehm* are especially common in H and D (*Vergnügen* is a common expression in N's correspondence); while *Lust* is used more evenly throughout N's career. At BT2, 16, H1.98 (among other passages), the first two are used interchangeably; likewise at for example H1.103, *Lust* and *Vergnügen*. Therefore, it seems reasonable, as a first approximation, to treat all these terms (and there are others) as denoting similar concepts. If anything, *Freude* has a spiritually elevated connotation, and is often the outcome of a particular, conscious activity of some kind (it is the word in Schiller's Ode, on which Beethoven based his ninth symphony). *Vergnügen* is generally used to describe the pleasure I feel as an effect of doing or observing something (e.g. H1.91, 157). *Lust* can be used more generally. Moreover, *Lust* and *angehehm* are N's preferred terms for basic psychological states or underlying motivations of action.

Documenting all the various ways that N employs this concept (or concepts) would be an enormous undertaking. Let us be satisfied with three. First, N's version of the old problem in aesthetics – how can an audience enjoy depictions of suffering in tragedy? – is answered in terms of the reciprocal dependency of two sources of pleasure. The first is the pleasure in semblance, in beautiful forms; the second is the pleasure in the ecstatic Dionysian, the reunion of all things. Tragedy is a pinnacle of artistic achievement because it permits the second, along with the corresponding insights of the Dionysian, while neutralizing with the first the terror associated with the destruction of the individual. Although N's account changes, broadly speaking this relationship remains a theme throughout.

Second, the idea that pleasure and pain (or their anticipation) are the key and perhaps the only motivation in human psychology is an old one, with roots in ancient Greek thought; in modern thought, Hobbes is often read in this way, and Bentham certainly is. In contemporary philosophy, this is called 'psychological hedonism'. N holds something akin to this view in his early and especially in the middle period (e.g. 1872.19.84, H1.18, 97). Much of H is concerned with the various ways in which pleasure is sought and found, and how these explain social, cultural or moral phenomena (H2.119 is a good example). By the time of *The Wanderer and His Shadow* (H3), however, he seems to have moved on (see H3.12). Certainly in D, N's attention turns to drives as basic principles of psychological motivation, and pleasure and pain are seen as derivative phenomena founded upon prior evaluations (compare D38 with H1.32; and see also GS127, BGE225, AC11).

Third, pleasure (here generally *Lust*, and usually translated as joy) is associated with the will to eternity (Z3.15.3, and this sequence is repeated starting Z4.19.3). In this same passage, the 'Soothsayer' (Schopenhauer's pessimism) dances with pleasure (Z4.19.1) indicating the overcoming of such pessimism by such a will to eternity. Only a life healthy, growing, aligned to and thoroughly affirming the nature of life itself, could experience the thought of eternal recurrence in this manner – that is, with joy rather than either indifference or despair. At Z3.15.5, Zarathustra talks of the joy in seeking, the 'seafarers' joy'. The idea is that, again only for an aligned life, a noble form of pleasure is found in a kind of *longing for* (rather than attaining to). In this context, that means *experimenting* with the forms and practices of life as part of the development of those forms of life (and see 1887.11.75). See *happiness*.

poetry

Dichtung, Poesie. N was not a prolific poet, but he certainly considered this aspect of his work important. H1, GS and BGE include substantial poems or collections of poetry as either the first or last chapter, while Zarathustra not only includes several major poems but many sections are intended to be *dithyrambs*. More broadly, many prose passages are more poetic (tonally akin to lyrics, odes, laments; and employing poetic language) than strictly philosophical. N encourages us to think about the intellectual tensions between his philosophical prose and the poetry (as in the poem in Z4.14 with the lines 'mere fool! mere poet!', or the lament that he did not 'sing' in writing BT: BTA3). This is because the 'poets lie too much' (Z2.17). This has both a narrower and a broader meaning. Narrowly, it is a discussion of the figure of the poet, his or her petty needs and employment of the arts of deception to fulfil them. More broadly, as N discussed in 'On Truth and Lies', the origin of our metaphysical and religious views of the world lie in poetic transformations of sensation. In this tension lies a reference to Plato's account of the relationship between poetry and knowledge (see both *Ion* and *Republic* – see H2.32). However, also in Z2.17, Zarathustra says 'But Zarathustra too is a poet'. This too has a double meaning: first, that like all humans, one lives and speaks on the condition of certain errors, whether they are acknowledged or not. Second, however, that a 'transformation' of poetry is possible. In H2.99 (and compare H2.172), N urges poets to aid the future development of the human by imaginatively producing 'a beautiful image of man', but without leaving 'this world' behind. Similarly, N wishes that the poets would be '*seers* who tell us something of the *possible*' (D551). This idea is a development of the relationship between poetry and mythology developed at UM4.9. The purpose of poetry, then, is not philosophical knowledge but that other, more important aspect of philosophy: the task of creating and pursuing values. Thus Zarathustra says 'I now speak in allegories' (Z2.17). See *allegory, metaphor, language*.

politics, state

Politik. Political organization tends to be a symptom rather than a cause of things, on N's analysis. Thus, he scornfully writes that it is a joke to think that the problems of existence could even be touched by politics (UM3.4). Similarly, at GM1.6, N argues that superiority or *nobility* of soul determines political superiority. In other words, a political organization is neither necessary nor perhaps even helpful in the generation of such superiority. Indeed, an 'ideal' state would be a disaster for such an end (H1.235), and the greatest cost of politics is the time wasted by talented individuals (H1.481), the sapping of energy that could otherwise have been devoted to *culture* (TIGermans4). Culture and the state are incompatible ambitions. Within the state, also, *education* necessarily becomes corrupt, turning citizens into state functionaries, and making all the classes feel that their advancement is gift of the state (H2.320). Nevertheless, N does have a vision of a changed or reformed modern state, one that for example knowingly employs *religion* as its instrument (H1.472), and which is founded upon a meritocracy (H2.318).

The *free spirit* or new philosopher is generally in some way above or remote from politics. However, there are important passages where N suggests that intervention in the affairs of the state becomes necessary even for these select few (UM2.2, H1.438). In his later work, N talks about a 'great politics'. Now, this is a concept N gets from *Bismarck*, but revalues. In early and middle period work, he critiques the very idea (H1.481, D189, Z.1.11). N singles out for criticism the manipulation of the people – indeed, the destruction of them as a *people* – while pretending to be their mouthpiece. For the later N, however, 'great politics' means the task of free spirits or good Europeans – and the strategies or instruments employed in that task – of taking 'comprehensive responsibility' for the future of humankind. This includes both the critique of existing values, the generating of the conditions for future greatness, and having the 'time' to envision 'millennia hence' (1885.35.45, 47, BGE208, EHDestiny1, and see the Romans at AC58).

positivism

Nineteenth-century positivism is a development of empiricism. It emphasizes that all knowledge is founded upon the data or facts of experience, that knowledge consists of generalization of this data into descriptive laws – not explanatory laws, laws which would have to refer to some reality beyond those facts – and that the verification-procedures of all knowledge are those developed by the sciences. The key figure is Auguste Comte, who extended this scientific approach into sociology (the study of human interrelations and social structures). In the middle period work, N's thought is often close to positivism. The contrast there between science and metaphysics (e.g. H1.10) is straight out of Comte, as is the claim that psychology is ultimately a branch of natural science (e.g. H1.1). Neo-Kantian philosophers, such as Lange, offer a critique of positivism, which is that it simply assumes the distinction between appearances and things in themselves, but without giving an account of the nature of those mechanisms by which the data of appearance come to be data, or laws come to be formulated. That is, without giving an account of the constitution of what Kant calls 'experience' (see 1886.7.60). Such considerations lead N to his notion of *perspective*. Another objection to postivism, one more difficult to understand, is its filthiness and its mish-mash of concepts, the objection N puts in Ariadne's mouth at the end of 1885.37.4 (see also BGE10, 210). Notice Ariadne is pointedly playing with the thread from the labyrinth, an echo of N's earlier phrase 'guiding thread of the body'. The point is that such a way of thinking doesn't offer any ideals, any future; knowledge of the body is thus contrasted with the value and future possibilities of the body. Thus, 'sensualism' is a *regulative* hypothesis (BGE15).

possession/property

See *work, socialism, class*.

possibility

See *actuality, future*.

power

[*Macht, Kraft*] *Kraft* is often used interchangably with *Macht* –
and this includes in the technical sense of the latter as will to
power (e.g. BGE13; for *will to power* see separate entry). The terms
also overlap with how N uses the term 'energy'. Depending upon
context, both could reasonably be translated as power or force,
and *Kraft* perhaps even as energy. Where he is speaking of political
power, or power recognised by laws or institutions, N generally
uses the term *Macht*. Where the issue is to do with physical power
(in the body, or in a mechanical analysis of a physical system) N
tends to use *Kraft*.
The concept has the following broad meanings:

1 The most common usage is to describe the capacity of a thing
   or event (for example, a drive) to bring about a significant
   change in something else. Thus, the power of the Dionysian
   (BT2), the folk song at BT6, the Dionysiac vision at BT8 (and
   see the parallel accounts at TISkirmishes9–10), or Euripides
   (i.e. the Socratic drive – BT12). Similarly, the power to repay
   exact retribution (H1.45 – an early version of the distinction
   between master and slave morality), likewise H1.99 where
   this is part of a narrative concerning the founding of a state
   (see also the equilibrium of power at H3.22, 26, 190). Other
   examples include: in pity the power to harm or at least look
   down on (H1.50 – this is an important aspect of N's account
   of pity throughout his writings); the power of a 'new pride' to
   overcome inhibitions against new interpretations of the moral
   (D32); the lion's power to create freedom (Z1.1); Zarthustra's
   teaching of eternal recurrence is 'above his power' (Z2.22), or
   'all evil is the best strength' (Z3.13.2), the power to approach
   the highest problems (BGE213) or the power of appropriation
   (BGE230).

2 A subclass of the first meaning would be explicitly political
   or military power, as for example the new German state at
   TIGermans1, 4.

3 Knowledge or faith distinguished from the power to bring
   about action (D22); relatedly, the intellect superficially and

easily envisages possibilities that are beyond the power of action (D125). These are to be located within N's discussion of action in distinction from contemplation (see *action*).

4   Power is something felt, and it is this feeling of power that is important as a sign of health or a motive for action (H1.50, 103, D42, BGE230. TIErrors5);

5   In the sense of energy, that is, the capacity to do something but without a specific end (H2.226, D111). Thus also power can mean one's capacity for action that might be invested in this or that direction (e.g. Z1.5). Similarly, we free spirits are the 'heirs of all that power' accumulated in the struggle to overcome previous cultural forms (BGEP, and see 253, 262, TIGermans1, Skirmishes44). These are closely related to N's frequent metaphor of *tension*.

6   Physical power in the body, as in dance (BT9) or in the character of the aristocrat (D201 – and see N's comments about the power available to a race that has 'become pure' at D272); similarly, at BGE36 N uses *Kraft* to talk about what would otherwise be called mechanical efficient force.

7   Great or overwhelming power is often a key or even defining character of something, whether nature in its truth (BT8), that which was considered divine by the Greeks (H2.220), the surplus of power that is unconcerned by apparent loss (H3.34), the meaning of cheerfulness (TIP), or the Dionysian as 'excess of power' (TIAncients4).

pregnancy (and birth, etc.)

Schwangerschaft, or figurative allusions. Pregnancy and birth are common metaphors in N's writings, standing broadly for *creativity*, care of the extended self and the possibility of contributing to the *future*. There are all manner of mythical and cultural allusions in these metaphors; Plato's Socrates being a 'midwife' is an important one. To the possibility of pregnancy, N contrasts the lack of *fruitfulness* of various modern types or institutions (e.g. UM2.3). D552 is a beautiful passage which employs pregnancy as a metaphor for creative thought. There is, N says, no more 'holy' condition than pregnancy. If thought is a manifestation of the state of the body, then the state of being pregnant with thought transforms how traditional notions of willing or creating are to be understood. One simply does everything for the benefit of 'that which is coming to be within us'; it is an 'ideal selfishness'. Similarly, at D177, N contrasts 'the profound speechlessness of pregnancy' with the modern need to be continually involved in or comment on events. N uses very similar language later at EHClever9, in describing 'how you become what you are'. There he adds that there is and should be in such pregnancy a lack of self-knowledge. Z3.14 is a portrait of the 'great yearning' of that which is pregnant for the 'vintner's knife'. The soul's pregnancy awaits the coming of *Dionysus*, that is a divine ideal of new human possibilities. Similarly, Zarathustra says 'for the creator himself to be the child, newly born, he must also want to be the one giving birth [*Gebärerin*], and the birth giver's pain' (Z2.2, and see H1.107). In other words, pregnancy is an allegorical account not just of creativity, but also of *self-overcoming*. Obviously, the metaphor of pregnancy also evokes the notions of *feminine and masculine;* fruitfulness involves the co-presence of both these drives.

prehistory

In ordinary English usage, prehistory means events, and the study of these events, dating from periods prior to written or oral recorded history. Such events would have been perfectly 'visible' then; it is just that today only indirect evidence remains for them (e.g. archaeological evidence). Sometimes, N uses the concept in this sense (e.g. H1.45, D31). Alternatively, the term is used to designate a set of prior events that are used to explain or justify something in the present (H3.24, D71, AC42). At GM2.3, for example, N discusses the cruel 'prehistory' of the human ability to remember and thus make promises. Finally, the concept can mean the set of essentially invisible developments or psychological states that eventually produce some visible state or disposition – for example, at D312, dreams are manifestations of a primal, animal 'prehistory'. Similar usages are found at GS335, 348. N sometimes uses the term 'atavism' or an equivalent to designate the reappearance of the primitive or prehistorical in the present (e.g.

H1.42, GS10, BGE20). AC 57 provides an important observation: if a law permits its own prehistory to be known, then it loses its 'imperative tone'. This, of course, is one of things N intends to bring about through his 'genealogy' of morality.

preservation

See *utility*.

priest

Priester. N's writings are full of references to priests – either individuals (e.g. Paul or Luther as failed priests), orders (e.g. the Jesuits) or types (the priestly class, the ascetic priest, etc.). See especially entries on *ascetic, religion, the Jews, Christianity*.

primitive/savage

See *prehistory*.

progress

Various terms. There are two principal images of historical progress that N criticizes. The first is the Hegelian narrative concerning the historically progressive unfolding or actualization of *spirit*. The second is the Enlightenment idea that rationally reformed political and social institutions will achieve advances in the areas of *morality* and *justice*, while scientific advances will improve the comfort and security of all. These reformed institutions normally include some kind of representative *democracy*, widened or universal enfranchisement, human rights and universal *education*. N sees such 'modern ideas' as symptoms of modern decadence or corruption, and our over-sensitivity to suffering (BGE201, TISkirmishes37). Importantly, it is not that N claims little has changed or could change – that is the argument used by philosophers such as Pascal (reason itself is corrupted by sin) or a satirist like Swift (human nature is depraved, whatever rational institutions it finds itself in). N's question is rather whether the change genuinely represents improvement (AC4). In his middle period, N certainly does talk about progress of a sort (e.g. 'the temperate zone of culture' at H1.236). But even in H, he is sceptical of progress in either of the above two senses (H1.24). However, progress is something that may *now* be possible; in the just cited section he writes 'men are capable of *consciously* resolving to evolve themselves to a new culture' (and see GM2.12).

Protestantism

See *Luther.*

psychology

N sometimes conceives of his work, or a key part of it, as psychology. For example, H35–8 argue that whatever the merits of psychology – understood as the investigation of moral sensations and affects – as something a healthy and happy individual should pursue, it has now become necessary. This notion of the possible danger of psychology, along with its importance as 'queen of the sciences', is found again at BGE23. In EH, N extols himself as a psychologist 'without equal' (EHBooks5) and Zarathustra is the 'first psychologist of the good' (EHDesitiny5). Psychology achieves this importance because it permits us to understand moral feelings (or any feeling of value) not as founded in universal reason, in divine laws or in the nature of things, but rather having emerged from a long history of 'human, all too human' drives and habits. Up to now, psychology has like the other sciences rested upon moral prejudices, which is why for example it suffered a 'shipwreck' in trying to understand the phenomenon of the saint (BGE47), and why the psychologist should mistrust even his own first thoughts (GM3.20). Such mistrust means that, following the example of positivism, psychology is a science achieved primarily through the observation of others. Occasionally, N writes as if psychology should be subordinated to physiology (e.g. GM3.13).

punishment

See *criminal, justice, innocence.*

purity

The German word for 'purity' (*Reinheit*) has a close connection to the term usually translated as *cleanliness* (*Reinlichkeit*). Please see also that separate entry.

In earlier work, N employs the concept of purity in a fairly conventional manner, to mean something that has had anything extraneous or added-on removed. The last paragraph of UM3.3 is a good example, with its gloss on the idea of untimely (also D272). A similar point about Schopenhauer is made at the end of UM3.7, and there purity is an aspect of solitude (see also BGE61, EHWise8). In later work, N *revalues* of the concept of purity (in this, he is not dissimilar to the Renaissance humanists that he discusses at BT19). In H, purity acquires a moral character (H1.46, 237, H3.20); this moral character is not above a kind of immoral psychological analysis, but this is not the same as a cynical devaluation of purity as a sham. Purity, that is, requires analysis, but not simply dismissal. GS139 gives us a particularly clear instance of revaluation, as N observes different practices leading to different concepts of 'purity'. At EHWise8, N claims that the whole of Z is a 'dithyramb to solitude . . . to *purity*'. But a dithyramb is a hymn to a divine ideal. Solitude and purity are not, then, just states of being away from other people or their influence, but moments of growth or advancement with respect to the Dionysian. At Z3.4, Zarathustra says 'O Heaven above me, you are so pure! So high! That is what your purity is for me, that there is no reason-spider or – web.' Purity has become purity *from* purposes, origins, from any transcendent creator or destination, but then also purity *for* 'Godlike accidents' and ascent. That is, for the independent growth of life. Purity is a description of the condition of being aligned to life and capable of affirming. See *innocence.*

purpose

See *goal.*

qualities and quantities

See *number.*

rabble

See *herd.*

race

Rasse, but also *Kaste,* etc. Of all the aspects of N's thought, his analysis of race is probably the most disturbing for modern readers. This is in large part because of the reception of N after he lost control of his literary estate, and then after his death. The lauding of N by eugenicists in the early years of the twentieth century, and then by the National Socialists in the 1930s, casts a long shadow over his work. Like N's misogyny, it is not difficult for the apologist reader to dismiss his discussion of race as conventionally nineteenth century (but see *anti-Semitism*). N clearly holds that races are intrinsically different forms of human life. That is, N dismisses as naïve and wishful thinking the 'modern idea' that racial differences are irrelevant. Therefore also he argues that the mixing of races (either socially or genetically) creates problems, since these forms of life are likely incompatible (e.g. BGE208). Importantly, he also tends to associate race with national identities. Thus, he will talk about the Germans, French or ancient Greeks as a racial type. This is not because N is naïvely unaware of the complex history of migrations; rather, he claims that races are constantly evolving, and a nation or a people achieves itself as a race (D272, BGE200, GM2.20). Taken as a whole, he argues that these races or identities have distinctly different characters – this may be in their attitude to religion, morality or art for example. The point of such an analysis is not to enhance nationalism but rather the opposite. The various races in Europe, including the Jews, are fragments of a whole, and only as a whole does Europe have a future (UM3.4, H1.475, see entry on *Europe*). The mixing of races may create difficulties, but is ultimately necessary.

rank, order of

Rang. Rank, or 'order of rank', is N's most common expression for the differences of *nobility* or *health* between individuals, types, or nations (D198), drives within an individual (BGE6), or among things and not only among humans (BGE219), or philosophical questions (e.g. GS273). At H1.107, the phrase is used simply to mean a range of differently evaluated things, but is already used in N's typical manner at H2.362. It is a deliberately old-fashioned or aristocratic concept (thus N complains that 'we no longer have rank' because we have money: D203). N takes the idea of rank to be a natural one (i.e. it is the most straightforward or honest expression of will to power; see for example GM3.23, AC57, and *class, animal*). Thus religious or modern ideas of *equality* are in some way unnatural or decadent (BGE62). Likewise, the ascetic ideal misinterprets rank, and also universalizes its own place at the top of rank order (GM3.23). The having power over someone of higher rank is important in N's analysis of *cruelty* (GM2.6). Concepts associated with rank include *reverence, taste, distance* and *height*.

reason

Vernunft. In its modern usage, reason means either (i) a cause or justification of something ('Give me a reason why I should do that'); (ii) evidence for something ('The reasons we have for thinking that X is the case'). In German, the term *Grund* (ground) is normally used for these first two senses. Finally, (iii) our capacity to use various types of evidence to arrive at conclusions (thus the verb 'to reason'). Logic, in modern usage, has come to mean the set of formal tools that can be legitimately employed in reasoning (in the third sense).

An essential historical precedent within German thought is Kant. For Kant, the term reason is primarily meant in the third sense above, as a 'faculty'. In Kant, there is both a theoretical reason – which concerns itself with governing the concepts of experience – and a practical reason – which is the rationality of the free will. Reason has a certain autonomy or independent activity. Kant talks about the 'needs' of reason – above all its striving for completion in its reasoning – which in turn leads us to dialectical illusions (the belief that reason can achieve insight beyond the horizon of possible experience). This sense of reason having a life or will of its own, which in Kant is primarily metaphorical, is taken much more literally in N (in part, this is the influence of Rousseau). Socrates, then, is the 'overfertilisation of logic' (TISocrates4), reason issues 'commandments' (D96). For N, once created, reason takes on a life of its own, whether in the form of the history of metaphysics, or (in a more limited but more successful manner) in the form of science.

In N, reason has two sides, best explained at Z1.4. The body is the 'great reason' and its tool and toy is the 'small reason' that we call mind or spirit. This involves at least two claims. First, all the senses of reason above, including those of Kant, are secondary phenomenon, conditioned by the life of the organism. Second, that the 'small reason' never lacks a relationship to life. Even where it 'despises' the body and rejects life, this is still the action of life (this idea is developed most fully at the end of GM3). Indeed, precisely where the small reason falls into its greatest errors (e.g. in treating that which is similar as identical) and thus denies the most basic principle of life, namely becoming – this error is necessary for life (e.g. for its preservation: see GS111, BGE3). Moreover, these essentially arbitrary rules are an important aspect of the training of thought (see H1.265, TIGermans7, and *discipline*). Nevertheless, part of N's task is the critique of philosophical reason and logic. Thus, for example, the chapter in TI entitled '"Reason" in Philosophy'.

The 'great reason' of the living body does not in itself contain universal values. The great reason creates values, and thereby gives names and purposes to things. However, this great reason is not the natural reason of the Stoics, nor the eternal emanation of the One as in Neoplatonism, nor the divine plan of God, nor again the history of absolute spirit as for Hegel. This projection of reason to a domain outside the course of becoming is, for N, a basic error of metaphysics. Indeed, all these serve to 'devalue the only world there is, – to deprive our earthly reality of any goal, reason or task!' (TIDestiny8). The 'great reason' is *will to power*, which always exists as multiple or as a network of power relations. Thus, at Z3.4 Zarathustra speaks famously of the liberation of things from purposes – that is, from some cosmic sense of reason. 'In all things, one thing is impossible – rationality!' He then adds

'A little reason, indeed' – in other words, local instances of order (individual organisms and their societies), or temporary and provisional creations of value by living things.

The history of reason and logic is a history of self-overcoming. These errors upon which science is based serve life for a time, but then outlive their usefulness, and even become degenerate and dangerous. Such degeneracy is discussed concerning topics such as marriage or education, which ought to be restored to their 'rationality' (TISkirmishes39, 41). Thus ascetic philosophy is 'a violence and cruelty to *reason*' (GM3.12) and Pascal represents the slow 'suicide of reason' by Christianity. The idea is related to the self-overcoming of science in Kant and Schopenhauer that N discusses at BT18. This overcoming might lead to pessimism or *nihilism*, or it might lead to a new and more comprehensive small reason, one that is more aligned to the nature of the great reason, which can look down with laughter at the small reason of others, and use it as *its* tool and toy (see *free spirit*). Accordingly, N sometimes uses reason in a positive sense, as at D96, or 'my *restored* reason' at TIErrors2. It is a particularly common theme in EH, where N casts himself in the role of someone whose instincts are not essentially ill, not essentially opposed to what he had earlier called the 'great reason' (e.g. EHWise6, Clever9).

redemption

Erlösung. The most important precedent behind N's use of the concept of redemption is the Christian meaning. Christ's life and death, and the believer's faith, constitute a redemption of the human from sin (e.g. Col.1.14, Heb. 9.15). On N's analysis of the logic, the guilt of sin against God was so great that only the sacrifice of a God would cleanse it (GM2.21, and see H1.132). As a psychological achievement, N writes 'let us honour "redemption" in the great religions'. It is a genuine method of self-hypnosis, the highest good for those who are sick and suffer; it is the attainment of Epicurus and Schopenhauer's ideal (GM3.17). However, N employs a non-religious concept of redemption from early on (see for example the human as the redemption of the animal in nature at UM3.5). There are three key ideas. First, art 'redeems' (UM4.7, WC2) from excess of knowledge or from heavy burdens (and indeed redeems redemption: WC3). Second, reality insofar as it has been denigrated in value by religion and metaphysics, is redeemed by N's thought (GM2.24; see *innocence*). Third, the past – which seems to escape the will, that is we cannot 'will backwards' – is redeemed by the thought of eternal recurrence. That is, the affirmation of recurrence is equivalent to willing that which is already past (ZP4, Z2.20, and 'redeem the graves' at Z4.19.5).

Rée, Paul

A friend of N's from the early 1870s through 1882, when their friendship collapsed because they were rivals for the affections of Lou Salomé. The two were particularly close during the time N was writing H, when Rée too was working on quasi-evolutionary accounts of the history of moral psychology. Later, N dismisses Rée for being, like the English moralists, ahistorical in his thinking (GMP4 and GM1.2).

Reformation

See *Luther.*

regulative

Regulativ, or cognate. In Kant, the ideas of pure reason have no legitimate constitutive function – that is, they cannot produce knowledge of things – but do have a vital regulative function. By this is meant that the ideas guide the activities of the understanding in some direction without any presumption that the endpoint could ever be reached. For example, the beginning of time is impossible as an object of experience or knowledge, but seeking to push our understanding of states further and further back in time is valuable scientific enquiry. N uses something like this Kantian concept of the regulative, especially in the years 1884–6 (also see UM3.3). Phrases like 'regulative hypothesis' or 'regulative fiction' are common. The rather breathless series of notes at 1886.7.4 shows N taking the concept of the regulative from Kant and, indeed, using it against Kant.

N's intent is clearly to try to understand why concepts such as matter, will, truth, number or sensation seem difficult to eliminate from metaphysical or scientific thought, and are indeed useful there, despite the fact that only the naïve continue to believe in them as anything but errors. For example, this is how N talks about sensualism – meaning accepting that sensations are straight-forward data, whether this means data as a kind of thing-in-itself (as in positivism) or as the direct effects of an external world on our sensory organs (as in classical empiricism and naive realism; see BGE15). This is 'regulative' because such sensualism is contradicted by will to power, and yet the pursuit of our thoughts and feelings back through sensations, to the body and from there to the body's relation to the physical environment is the condition of possibility of the science of physiology. Mechanistic materialism at 1885.34.247 is said to be a 'regulative hypothesis' for the very useful process of understanding the world in terms of 'sight' – that is in terms of stable entities occupying space and being in motion. See other examples at GS344 and 1885.35.35. This idea of a regulative function is not an entirely new departure in N's thought, since it is obviously related to how N discusses the 'concept' in 'On Truth and Lies' – that is, as an 'artistic' construction of something simple and fixed, which in turn makes knowledge possible. Moreover, something analogous to the regulative is at work in the second part of Kant's *Critique of Judgement*, concerning which N proposed a dissertation way back in the 1860s.

religion

Religion, along with morality, is probably N's most commonly pursued topic. However, the strands of his thinking here run in so many different directions, that it is best to discuss them many under different headings (e.g. individual religions such as *Christianity*, the more specific topic of *God or gods*, and likewise *asceticism, ideals* or *morality*). Here, therefore, we will deal just with a few important general issues. In N's thought, a religion is an institution, and more fundamentally a mode of life. It is thus either coextensive with a people, or governs a kind of artificial people created for their own purposes by a priestly class (AC24–6). It likely believes itself to rest on some form of devotion, generally to a God or gods. However, the gods are projections of human values, and positing them as existing separately from the human thus creates a cosmic endorsement of those values (GS353). When N discusses religion, he is most likely referring to one of the following (and normally it is clear which): (i) Christianity; (ii) Judaism, especially during the period narrated by the Torah; (iii) Greek polytheism; (iv) either Hinduism or Buddhism; (v) prehistoric religions generally. What these have in common, if anything, is the very broad definition given at the start of this entry. What they certainly do not have in common is either a commitment to monotheism (and thus opposition to Roman tolerance: BGE46), a *metaphysics* that posits true being and transcendence, or an intrinsic relation to morality (see 1885.2.197). The history of religions in Europe (N is speaking primarily of Christianity) presents two dramatically different effects. On the one hand, by way of its metaphysical commitments and its morality, religion in Europe is a system for the *breeding* of weakness, for perpetuating illness, and for the repression of *nobility* or *greatness*. On the other hand, the recognition of this fact through philosophical *critique* and through science, and the *overcoming* of these commitments and moralities in ourselves, would not have been possible without the *discipline* fostered by Christianity. Thus, N insists on a *gratitude* towards religion.

N himself explicitly disavows founding a religion in any conventional sense (EHDestiny1, and see D542), but that does not rule out a conception of the gods and of piety towards an ideal (which might be termed the *overhuman*, or *Dionysus*) that satisfies the 'religious instinct' but without a theism (BGE53, and see 1886.3.13). Aware of the quieting and organizing effect of religions, political states – and later the *free spirits* – can use religion as an instrument for non-religious ends (e.g. H1.472, BGE61). In other words, for those who take in hand *comprehensive* responsibility for the ends of humanity, religion can be employed to serve the development of the human.

Renaissance

The Renaissance ('Rebirth') refers to a historical period, centred in Italy in the fifteenth century, which in a number of broad cultural ways is a departure from Medieval modes of life and thought. It was only in the nineteenth century that German historians invented the term; and a key figure in defining this period was N's Basle colleague Burckhardt. N frequently mentions the Renaissance or figures within it such as Raphael, Machiavelli or Cesare Borgia. N's understanding of the Renaissance is of a period when culture attempted to shed a religion-derived morality, and live according to the principles of power, health and nobility (see GM1.16, AC61); the Renaissance pursued greatness, and therefore was also dangerous and a squandering of power (TISkirmishes37, 44). The Reformation is the counter-movement, by means of which 'The Germans have robbed Europe of the harvest, the meaning, of the last *great* age' (EHWC2). Importantly, in the earlier work, N has a rather different notion of the Renaissance as a rebirth not of Greek antiquity but of the 'Alexandrian-Roman' (BT23). Thus, music in the centuries immediately after, he argues, represented a more positive 'counter-renaissance' (H1.219 and see UM4.10), rescuing music as an art of the people rather than as something scholarly and aloof.

repose/rest

Various terms. Throughout N, there is a frequent contrast between motion and rest, action and contemplation, or turbulent change and still beauty, or even masculine creation and feminine pregnancy or care. He frequently uses notions of repose, rest, stillness or quiet for the latter states. In BT, N employs the distinction between Dionysian and Apollonian to understand how these states could all be characteristics of the Greeks.

One key way of understanding the notion of repose is as a substitute for an end state. A *cycle* of states is part of the character of life, which grows or becomes, reaching a new state at which it plateaus, temporarily weary and gathering its strength, before growing again. There is no end state at which point a task is done once and for all (H1.471). Likewise, N describes a 'vision of happiness' is a serenity that has no relation to work (H1.611), that is no relation to an end product. However, this lack of an end state should not at all lead to pessimistic or nihilistic conclusions about the necessary imperfection of the world. So likewise the *wanderer* has no destination (H1.638), but sometimes 'relaxes quietly beneath the trees' and contemplates the perfection of what is (see also H3.308,

Z3.12.18, BGE44). The beauty of the plateau point is a symbolic image of the perfection of the whole. The idea is expressed most famously and beautifully at Z4.10. There, Zarathustra lay down beneath a tree, the 'world became perfect', before he rushes off again in pursuit of the 'cry of need'. Importantly, all these passages take place around *noon*. Here, noon symbolizes both a high point, neither climbing nor descending, but also a point of transition into a new phase of activity. In a narrower context, N makes the same point about art, which makes the connection to the Dionysian and Apollonian in BT all the more clear. Genuine art is either of great repose or great motion (H2.115). Art does not exist for the struggle but for the 'intervals of quiet' when we 'comprehend the symbolic', refreshing the viewer (UM4.4). This sense of tiredness should be contrasted with that discussed under the entry *exhaustion*. See GS376 where N makes this distinction.

representation (Vorstellung)

See *appearance*.

republic of genius

See *genius*.

responsibility

Verantwortlichkeit. N treats of the concept of responsibility with respect to a number of other topics. First, the analysis in GM2 concerning the development of the capacity to promise is explicitly an account of the 'origins of responsibility' (GM2.2). In other words, the creation of stable societies was not just about imposing laws, but rather inculcating habits and breeding types who could enter into contracts. Second, in connection with the notion of free will, he talks of the responsibility (or lack thereof) of the *criminal*, and also the instinct to assign *guilt* and punish in those who judge (see *innocence*). Third, he discusses responsibility in the sense of who makes us who we are, where does our fate come from. N's argument, obviously, is against assigning concepts of *purpose* or plan to reality (see *accident*). Here, we should compare TIErrors8 with Skirmishes38. The former passage argues that no one is responsible for us, including us (understood as individual or autonomous agents), in the sense of bringing us about as a purpose or for a reason (see also H2.386). However, the latter passage suggests that the appropriate response to this is not to relinquish a sense of responsibility (particularly this would mean to fall back into the herd – that is why N stresses 'distance' immediately thereafter), but to assume or create responsibility (see also the much earlier UM3.1). That leads us to the fourth important use of the concept: *free spirits*, or philosophers of the future, have and accept a 'comprehensive responsibility' for the future of the human (BGE61, 212, GM3.14). This is both in the sense that they are key raw materials for future human types, and in the sense that self-awareness of historical processes has reached a point where such individuals or groups can consciously employ other types, institutions, even morality itself, as instruments towards such future ideals.

ressentiment, revenge

N discusses the phenomenon of revenge (*Rache*) throughout his career. To begin with, N tends to discuss revenge as a psychological topic, being clear to distinguish types of revenge that are thoroughly reactive and founded upon fear, from those that are active, noble or even 'benevolent' (see H3.33, D138, 205, and later GM1.10). However, an analysis of revenge as specifically a foundation of religious or moral values develops at about the same time. The discussion of St Paul at D68 and Christianity at 71 are both significant developments in N's thinking concerning revenge. At D202 N analyses the need to punish in terms of revenge, and this becomes an important theme also in his later work. The mature conception of revenge is the reactive feeling towards that which is noble, by an individual, a slave class, or a subordinated priest class (Z1.12, 2.7, GS359). Then, from GM on, N uses the French word *ressentiment* as his preferred term for this (e.g. GM1.10, 3.14, AC24). Insofar as revenge, real or imagined, creates a feeling of power – even in the absence of action – it functions either to invert power relationships or at least make everyone appear to be 'equal' (Z2.20). At Z4.7, N assigns the death of God to human revenge at its shame – revenge, that is, at the witness who was omniscient and could see into men's hearts.

revaluation (of all values)

Umwertung (aller Werte). Late in his career, N employs this phrase to designate a large-scale project he intended (e.g. EHTwilight3). He considered AC to be the first volume of this larger work. However, the idea of revaluing, in the sense especially of showing the importance of values or feelings denigrated by the moral tradition, was a preoccupation much earlier.

By a revaluation of all values, N means offering a critique of the system of inherited moral or religious values and institutions as to their relation to the health and ascending development of human life. The analysis of *pity* is a particularly clear and prominent example of this. Likewise, *marriage* is a traditional institution that N revalues. In addition, one must offer the same kind of critique of metaphysical beliefs, which implicitly contain values within them. One of the infrequently noticed features of the famous passage at TITrueWorld is that the metaphysical and epistemological issues arising with respect to the true world are, at each stage, linked to values and obligations. Obviously, a frequent upshot of these various critical analyses is that a value is in some way dangerous or destructive (e.g. it is founded upon *ressentiment*, and is inimical to the overall health of the human). It may also be that the object of the value is entirely imaginary (the value placed on altruism or free will, for example). The most common outcome of revaluation is that what is valued is something genuinely important within the *economy* of human life, but our understanding of it must change. Both pity and marriage, mentioned above, are examples; clear further examples would be N's discussion of 'hostility' at TIMorality3 (see entry on *agon*), and the 'three evils' at Z3.10. In all these cases, something like the object valued when reinterpreted from the perspective of the health and development of life, is discovered to have a positive role. A final aspect of the revaluation would be *incorporation*. That is, the new values must not just be intellectually apprehended, but brought into institutions, ways of life, and ultimately into the habits and dispositions of individual bodies.

revenge

See *ressentiment.*

reverence

See *veneration.*

riddle

Rätsel. The riddle is a significant motif in N; among the many allusions N makes (including the Old Testament: see Judges 14), there are two principal allusions. First, Oedipus defeats the *Sphinx* by answering her riddle – and the answer is 'a human being'. The riddle thus stands here for human intelligence and daring, and also suggests that the human is the answer to the riddle of existence (see BT4, 9). Second, there is a riddle competition in Wagner's *Der Ring des Nibelungen* (second in the Ring Cycle), in which the dwarf Mime is terrified by a particularly fateful riddle. Again, riddle answering is about daring to know the most difficult and hidden truths. Thus, uncovering and answering riddles is a metaphor for the new philosophy (see for example BGE57, GM3.24). Zarathustra asks a riddle of the brave seamen in Z3.2, the answer to which is not the human but the overhuman or at least Zarathustra himself.

right

Recht. There are two issues here. First, is the concept of rights, as in 'human rights' or 'equal rights' – a way of conceiving of morality or justice within a social-political sphere. N's account of rights, as is his conception of justice conceived more broadly, is founded upon the equilibrium of powers (see H1.93, D112). There could be no equal rights where there is no rough equality of power: so, for example, between men and women in matters of love (GS363). The notion of equal rights then, universally applied, is a 'poisonous doctrine' (AC43). This leads us to the second meaning, which is the notion of 'having' a right to something, which for N means noble or strong enough for such possession to have significance for the overall health of the human. For example, Zarathustra asks 'show me your right and your strength' to be a creator (Z1.17, and see BGE202, GM1.2). N writes that the ascetic priest's 'right to existence' stands or falls with the ascetic ideal. That is, the value of such an ideal justifies the existence and role of the ascetic priest. This, however, is a form of legitimation from outside – much as a religious priest received authority by being the mouthpiece or agent of God – it is thus a form of weakness and not 'having a right'.

ripeness

Reif, and cognate. 'Ripeness is all', Shakespeare writes (*Lear* V.ii). This image of ripeness as the opportune moment, the moment when everything is ready to change is a common one in N. Thus, an exhausted or decadent age is 'over-ripe' (H1.141). Ripeness is also the moment or plateau of a stillness and perfection, thus the ripe grapes at Z4.10 (see 4.18.6). The idea here is that this pleasure at the moment of perfection is also a longing to be harvested (for the 'vintner's knife' – and see Z3.14), which means to move on to other tasks; while unripeness (Z4.18.9) is a suffering that wants to remain so that it can become ripe. These two aspects of longing – the longing to die, the longing to live – are brought together there in the idea of *eternal recurrence*. See also *pregnancy, time.*

river

Fluß. The river (and indeed water more generally) is a standard image of continuous change, and thus the non-self-identity of things, at least since Heraclitus' 'it is impossible to step twice into the same river'. And indeed N employs the image in a more or less direct reference to Heraclitus (H1.14, Z2.12). The image of river can also stand for the constant movement towards some outlet of drives or desires. This (earlier in his career) N identifies as the will in broadly Schopenhauer's sense (UM4.2) and (in later work) with *will to power* (e.g. Z2.6). Moreover, the river, waves or ripples are the movement of history, with respect to all of which individuals and their conscious beliefs or choices are more or less incidental (H2.394, GS360, Z2.12). Similarly, this river of the dominant forces of history may crush those who have potential for nobility or human greatness. Accordingly, Zarathustra offers himself to his disciples as a 'railing' to help them gain their feet, but refuses to be a 'crutch' (Z1.6).

role

See *mask*.

Romanticism

Historically, romanticism is a loose movement of thinkers and artists dating from the late eighteenth century through much of the nineteenth. It was widely dispersed: although its intellectual roots lay to a great extent in Germany (the *Sturm und Drang* movement, and many of the philosophers of post-Kantian idealism, especially Schelling), there were significant romantic trends and figures in every European country, and in the United States. Typical themes of romanticism include a valuing of *individual* emotional life, *sensation*, spontaneity and *imagination* (the figure of the tormented, perhaps *heroic*, artistic *genius* is common); a rejection of the *Enlightenment* attempt to understand human life and nature in terms of *matter* and physical laws; likewise a rejection of the neoclassical notions of order or harmony; a belief – but not necessarily a conventionally religious one – in a transcendent, spiritual domain. Because romantics often condemned the West for its various values, romanticism typically borrowed heavily from the non-classical past (especially the Medieval period) or from the Orient. Such impassioned rejection of the existing order also led to an association with revolutionary and nationalistic movements.

Although he could not help but be influenced, N's attitude towards romanticism was deeply sceptical. For example, although N created figures such as the free spirits, philosophers of the future, Zarathustra or the overhuman, he stressed many times that they should not be thought of in terms of the heroic. Thus, for example, at GS370, N distinguishes between a suffering from a superabundance, or an impoverishment, of life; most romantics confuse these and eventually fall into the latter category. Again, N freely borrows ideas and images from the past and from other 'exotic' cultures, but also attacks his contemporaries for their *indiscriminate* borrowing (e.g. D159). Although N's political thought is strongly opposed to the states and political, moral or religious systems of his day, he has little sympathy with any of the revolutionary movements either (although see BGE256). N often accuses romanticism of a wholesale rejection of the present, a determined pessimism, and thus a kind of reactive sensibility (e.g. H2P5, GS380). Although N certainly criticizes Enlightenment-inspired attempts at physical reductionism, his response is not a simple rejection of the Enlightenment per se (D197), nor any kind of transcendent spirituality. This latter point is one of N's most common lines of attack on Romanticism: that it tends to fall back on religious ideas that, however unconventional they may be on the surface, reflect the same rejection of the world and the same moral prostration before a transcendent being as Christianity (see BTP7, H2P2, and see H1.110). See also *irony*.

Rome, the Romans

N's conception of the Romans goes through a substantial change as his critique of Christianity picks up steam. In BT23, Rome is a perpetuation of the Socratic-Alexandrian culture which misunderstood and all but eliminated early Greek culture (and see BT21). By D, however, N's more familiar theme of Rome versus Christianity has emerged (D71). This idea is found again, and with much less ambiguity, in the late work (e.g. BGE46). Rome, N argues, was a civilization that had time and confidence, that could plan a future (AC58), and employ art in the 'grand style' and indeed turn that style into 'reality, truth, life' (AC59). Rome thus provided for a '*solidarity* in the chain of generations forwards and backwards, to infinity' (TISkirmishes39). The Christian slave revolution robbed Europe of these, just as the Reformation robbed them again after the Renaissance. (Note that these are characteristics N had ascribed

to all great cultures [e.g. UM2, H3.190, 275], but not initially to
Rome.) In TIAncients, N claims that Rome is our primary model
of style, because the Greeks are just too 'foreign'.

Rousseau

Eighteenth-century Swiss philosopher, most famous for his inversion
of the social contract theory developed by Hobbes or Locke. Rousseau
argued that the apparently 'rational' institutions of civilization –
and property in particular – were primarily responsible for the
enslaving of human beings, and that the original state of nature
was characterized by goodness and freedom. Rousseau was hugely
influential, on political ideas and events from the French Revolution
to other political reforms or revolutions thereafter (see UM3.4), and
on concepts of nature and the 'primitive', especially those found in
Romanticism. While N could agree with something in Rousseau's
analysis of the corrupting nature of institutions and certain forms of
reason, he vehemently objects to Rousseau's understanding of nature
as without struggle or *agon* and a good without evil (H1.463), or
the moral idea of equality (TISkirmishes48). Rousseau's 'fanaticism'
is thus in the party of the Revolution and not the Enlightenment
(H3.221, DP3).

sacrifice

Opfer. The concept of sacrifice is important within N's analysis
of both pre-Christian and Christian moralities. For example, the
ascetic sacrifice of one's self is part of the full analysis of the morality
of custom (D9, 18). And in turn this informs N's claim that 'the
Christian faith is a sacrifice of freedom, pride and spirit' (BGE46).
The difference is that the sacrifice in Christianity is reactive, born out
of fear and guilt. The Christian conception of sacrifice progresses to
nihilism – the 'sacrifice of God himself' (BGE55, see GM2, AC41). In
N, that pre-Christian and noble sense of sacrifice becomes important
(see D146). For example, it is a part of method: 'These English
psychologists . . . trained themselves to sacrifice all that is desirable
to truth' (GM1.1). Likewise, the Dionysian experience is one of the
will to life rejoicing in sacrifice of its highest (TIAncients5).

sage

See *philosophy*.

saint

See *holiness*.

Salomé, Lou Andreas-

Russian-born psychologist and novelist with whom N and his friend Paul Rée have an experimental relationship. She turns down N's proposal of marriage in 1882 and, partly because of interference from N's sister, the relationship breaks down completely by the end of that year, along with N's friendship with Rée. In 1887 she enters into an open marriage with Friedrich Andreas. Salomé becomes an important intellectual figure in her own right, writing one of the first books on N in 1894, and being closely associated with many psychological and literary movements in the decades to come, including collaborating with Sigmund Freud.

scepticism

Scepticism in an everyday sense means a suspicion concerning the apparently true or widely believed. Philosophically, it means the claim that certain types of knowledge (of an external world, for example, or of a transcendent world) are impossible. N claims he is dispositionally sceptical (GMP3) and that scepticism is a dominant characteristic of modernity. However, most notably at BGE208–10, N contrasts two forms of modern scepticism. First, the 'poppy' of scepticism caused by exhaustion or decadence of the instincts – a scepticism that simply isn't strong enough to say 'yes' or 'no' to anything. Second, however, is a 'manly' scepticism, which constitutes one of the few really positive things N has to say about German culture. This is a form of scepticism that does not narcotize and forbid one action; it is the 'tough will to undertake dangerous journeys' of the spirit (see also H1.633). He is thinking of the tradition of critical hermeneutics and philology, Goethe, and to some extent also of contemporary Neo-Kantian thinkers such as Helmholz or Lange. The latter may only be 'critics' (as defined at BGE210) but are referred to at BGE10 as 'sceptical anti-realists' repelled from either modern positivism or materialism. This idea of the philosophers of the future as sceptics culminates in a fine passage at AC54: '[G]reat spirits are sceptics'; N adds 'convictions are prisons' and the great spirit is free of them.

Schiller

Philosopher, poet and playwright (see H2.170) of the late eighteenth and early nineteenth centuries, who worked closely with Goethe in Weimar. Schiller is – almost as much as Schopenhauer or Wagner – N's constant intellectual companion in BT. The concept of 'naïve poetry' informs N's account of Greek art (BT3); also Schiller presents a more profitable account of the tragic chorus than Schlegel (BT7). More generally, the idea of competing drives that arrive at a synthesis comes from Schiller's *Aesthetic Education* letters. This idea orchestrates the whole of BT, albeit with different drives and a different context. In his later work, N's infrequent mentions of Schiller are critical (TISkirmishes1, WC8).

scholar, scholarship

Gelehrte. By 'scholarship' N means the careful, narrow and apparently disinterested investigation which was becoming the norm in the natural sciences as well as in the human sciences (e.g. *philology, history*). By 'scholars' he means the type of people who can and do pursue scholarship. N himself, of course, was a talented scholar of philology, and received a prominent position at Basle at a young age. However, under the influence of Schopenhauer and Wagner – both of whom were in various ways deeply critical of scholarship and the typical activities of universities – N gradually abandoned scholarly publishing. BT is written in a deliberately unscholarly fashion; the implicit claim is that scholarly work is incapable of genuine cultural insight or productivity. UM takes up this theme and makes it explicit (see particularly UM2.6 and 3.6).

The claim that scholars are dry and unproductive (symbolically and perhaps literally emasculated) is an old cliché, but one that runs throughout N's later work. Passages such as H3.179, GS366, Z2.16, TIGermans3 are typical. Scholarship is an extension of the *ascetic ideal* (GM3.23), of *democratization* (GS348), of industry (BGE58), *specialized* so as to never achieve a *comprehensive* view (BGE204–5), grown into a cramped little 'corner' (GS366). Scholarship is thus opposed to the philosophy of the future, although the latter must also make use of – and sometimes wear the *mask* of – the former (e.g. GS381, and this is the overall theme of BGE part six, see EHUntimely3, BTP3). Metaphorically, then, scholarship is one of the places to which the *wanderer* wanders (see the beginning of Z3.7).

Schopenhauer

The young N was heavily influenced by Schopenhauer, whose work of several decades previously was gaining in popularity. At least in part because of Schopenhauer, the following ideas found their way into N's early writings: presentation as *appearance*, in distinction from the *will* as the underlying reality; the contemplation of *art* as quieting of the individual will; *music* as direct encounter with the will; pessimism; atheism; the significance of Eastern thought, especially Hindu philosophy. Their mutual admiration for Schopenhauer was one thing that linked N to *Wagner*.

In fact, notes from the late 1860s show that N was already not uncritical of Schopenhauer. Importantly, N's view of Schopenhauer even at this early stage was that he had in some way betrayed the Kantian legacy by claiming to have identified the thing-in-itself as will. Schopenhauer, N argued, had to adopt the language of appearances (e.g. causality) in order to describe the will (which was supposed to be transcendent to such concepts), falling into a contradiction. Later, N comes to recognize this kind of bind as not something that could be solved, but rather the condition of philosophy (BGE22). By the mid-1870s, Nietzsche had thoroughly revised his view of Schopenhauer. The third *Untimely Meditation* was devoted to Schopenhauer, but surprisingly does not much present or discuss his philosophy, but rather his character and cultural significance. N's later assessment of Schopenhauer is summed up in GS99. Instead of the insights that belonged to Schopenhauer's 'higher culture', his German followers (including Wagner) enthused over his 'mystical embarrassments', including 'the nonsense about pity'. BGE204 adds that Schopenhauer's 'unintelligent wrath' against Hegel robbed later German culture of everything that was genuinely positive about their *historical sense*. GM3.5–7 provides a psychological interpretation of Wagner and Schopenhauer's aesthetics (see also TISkirmishes22, and the hilarious account of the *Ring Cycle* at WC4). Schopenhauer's ethics of *pity* played only a small role in early N, but is frequently attacked in the later writings (e.g. AC7). At TISkirmishes21, though, N insists that Schopenhauer was the last great German figure, the last who is a 'European event'. Schopenhauer's pessimism is now identified with the phenomenon of *nihilism*, a 'total depreciation of the value of life'. The character of the Soothsayer or Prophet in Z is clearly Schopenhauer, challenging Zarathustra with the concepts of pity and pessimism. Overcoming the enervating effect of that pessimism, and passing through the 'test' of pity, are both key themes in Z.

science

Historically, the German term *Wissenschaft* has a broader meaning than the English 'science'. While in English the word has the 'hard' or 'natural' sciences as its primary object, in German any discipline having to do with knowledge is a science. Thus, when N talks about 'science' he means not only physics, biology and physiology but also history or philology. N's analysis of the nature of science varies dramatically across his career, and indeed is often taken to define the stages of that career. During the time of BT, science is taken to be the consequence of the Socratic cultural drive, which by N's period had finally reached the end of its run and was undercutting its own foundations. The result would be the rebirth of a tragic understanding of the real. N asks 'what is science for *at all* if it has no time for culture?' (UM1.8), and thus N attacks particularly the idea of a fully scientific history (UM2.4).

By the mid- to late 1870s, however, N's disenchantment with Wagner (and thus with the revolutionary project in art and culture) had precipitated a rethink. H begins, for example, with the idea of a 'chemistry of concepts and sensations', and goes on to define sciences as 'the imitation of nature in concepts' (H1.38). N himself enters a 'scientific' or 'positivist' phase, embracing scientific methods – indeed, in the figure of Voltaire, embracing the Enlightenment generally – as the weapon against the true enemies of healthy culture: morality, religion and romanticism (e.g. H1.37, 244). This sense of science remains important for N, as we can see from AC47–9. There is an emphasis on the procedures or methods of science, as well as the psychological history that accounts for the development of these procedures (H1.634–5, H2.215, GS300). An important issue here is the autonomy of science; or equivalently, the question of what interest is served by the will to knowledge (this, after all, was a theme of BT). N initially argues that science is not an end in itself – nor in itself does it possess a *telos* – and so ideas of utility or just the 'joy of knowledge' need to be added (H1.38, 128, H2.98). It is something new, N then adds, that science should want to be more than a means (GS123) – and this autonomy of science is both opportunity (GS7) and danger (see BGE204). The praise of the scientific spirit continues in D and GS (e.g. D36, 270, GS293), along with the discussion of the purpose and autonomy of science. One should compare H1.128 with Z4.15. A typically Nietzschean distinction arises between a science that takes its motivation from fear or the desire for comfort, on the one hand, and a science of dangerous journeys and futures. This distinction is also the point of BGE204 and 253, which discuss the relative 'rank' of science and philosophy, or a science that knows and a science that creates.

Stylistically, Z would have been an odd vehicle for a scientifically minded philosophy. It is difficult not to see its composition as N's return to a mythic and poetic mode of pursing philosophical issues. Z thus marks the transition to the third and final phase of N's work. In the later work, the critique of the metaphysical foundations of science becomes prominent. A key idea here is that science stands on moral ground (GS344), and its belief in truth makes it the most spiritual descendent of the ascetic ideal and not its opponent (GM3.23–4).

sea

Usually *Meer* or *See*. The sea or ocean is another water symbol in N, and thus stands for flow, becoming, undifferentiatedness (as in the famous Schopenhauer passage used at BT1, and see D314). See particularly the endless seeking of the waves at GS310, and also see *river*. In addition, the sea has at least seven further symbolic meanings in N. First, an image of hidden, perhaps unified, profundity of the self (UM2.6), where hidden drives or fragments of one's personality reside (Z2.13). Second, representing the mute profundity of nature (D423, GS60), or a depth to be explored (H1.291, Z2.15, BGE278). Third, the sea represents a dangerous journey, likely one of discovery (the reference is to mythic characters such as Odysseus or Jason, as well as to the ocean-borne age of exploration, see UM2.10, D575, GS124, 343, 382, Z3.2.1, BGE23). Fourth, a kind of stillness or repose embodied in the 'patient game' of the endless waves on the surface (H2.249), or the smooth seas could be a cultural plateau of perfection (BGE224, WC2), or absence of longing (GS45, EHClever9). Fifth, a place of origination, for example from out of which land creatures ventured (ZP2, Z3.1). Sixth, that which isolates, perhaps a refuge from noise (D423 – and see EHD1 – Z1.11). Seventh, the flood (e.g. Z2.5) a reference to the biblical story of Noah.

seduce, tempt

Verführen, while *versuchen* is to tempt, although also to *experiment*. In N, this concept has two distinct meanings. First, to seduce or tempt is to lead astray, to cause (at least partially) a deviation from a task or goal. Much as Jesus was tempted by the devil in the desert (Matthew 4 and Luke 4), or Faust by Mephistopheles, so the Soothsayer seeks to 'seduce' Zarathustra to pity for the higher humans (Z4.2, and see GS338, BGE41). Similarly, the philosopher's relation to knowledge specialization may be seduced by being a dilettante or amateur in the domain of knowledge (BGE205). Not surprisingly, N claims the whole of the Gospels employ morality as a technique of seduction (AC44, GM1.8). The actor – N generally has Wagner in mind – is a born seducer, leading others to feel or believe things but without being a genuine representative of them, and without self-respect (WC3, Z4.15, TISkirmishes48, and see BGE205). What, though, if the one who seduces is not a mere actor, but a genuine ideal? Then, we have the seduction by 'another ideal' as at GS382, or Dionysus as the 'genius of the heart . . . born pied piper of consciences' (BGE295 – N may be referring to Plato's account of rhetoric in *Phaedrus*). In other words, the function of a higher ideal is its seductive power, that makes us long for it and seek or strive for it.

self

N employs an array of terms to discuss what we might otherwise call 'the self'. Although there are differences among them, they do not form a clear taxonomy. They include:

(i) The 'I' *(Ich)* or subject *(Subjekt)*. In traditional thought, the 'I' is that which does things, or to which things happen. N insists both that such a conception of freedom and causality is mistaken – the I is not a potential agency separate from the act, nor is the I something that 'has' its thoughts, sensations or feelings the way a box has contents. Moreover, equally mistaken is the supposed unity of the 'I' (see BGE16–17, 54, GM1.13). The 'I' is also identified with the historical emergence of the individual from the herd (Z1.15–16). N sometimes uses 'subject' and 'soul' interchangeably (as at GM1.13).

(ii) The 'heart' *(Herz)*, used conventionally to mean the emotions or passions, especially with respect to the emotions such as love or compassion, and also especially when these are considered as active rather than reactive (e.g. Z2.7, BGE87, AC50).

(iii) The 'soul' *(Seele)* is very often used critically in a religious or metaphysical sense, especially concerning the distinction between body and soul. For example, H1.5, or 'the soul is just a word for something about the body' at Z1.4. Thus, N is critical of any idea of an immortal or 'simple' (in the metaphysical sense, that is single, indivisible) soul (e.g. BGE12). Yet, Zarathustra says that even now the earth is free for 'great souls' (Z1.11) – that is, not standing in need of the grace of God. The soul is the part of the self that might be elevated, precisely to the extent that we do not see elevation as being with respect to the body. Soul is used sometimes when a state of perfection has been attained, as at Z3.14, 4.10 (and see TIMorality3). Soul is also used to mean something like character or personality (H1.34, H2.126), especially if aspects of this are hidden from view (Z3.13.2). Thus, the 'internalizing of man' forms what is later called the 'soul' (GM2.16). Soul is the most common German translation of both *psuche* and *anima*.

(iv) The 'spirit' (mind, but also forms of desire), see *spirit*.

(v) The 'ego'. N tends to use this expression when he is talking about the interests of the self – thus in contexts where he is talking about *egoism* or altruism in morality, or disinterestedness in aesthetics.

(vi) The 'self' (*Selbst*). At Z1.4, Zarathustra suggests this as meaning the body as a whole, insofar as it is an organization with some unity of purpose and function, incorporating 'mind', 'spirit', 'soul', etc. 'Self' is also used in discussions of *egoism* (i.e. 'selfishness').

Not surprisingly, the notion of the self broadly speaking is important in a host of other themes in addition to those above. For some of the most important connections, see *overcoming, action, contemplation, incorporation, becoming oneself, despising, honesty, individual, mask.*

sensation, senses, sensualism

Empfindung, most commonly. In certain contexts, this could also be translated as 'feeling'; for a discussion see *affect*. This term should not be confused with *Sinnlichkeit;* see *sensuality*. 'Sensualism' is not a term N uses often, but it does occur in particularly important places, as we shall see. N links it both to empiricism and to positivism. A provisional definition of sensualism would be the idea that sensation is a primitive and pure form of data that cannot be further investigated. N famously analyses the role of idealism and asceticism in philosophy and culture more generally; the nature of the senses has to play an important role in such an analysis. However, just as N's analysis is not unambiguous (he does not simply reject idealism or asceticism), so his account of the senses will be likewise.

N's most sustained meditation on the senses and on sensation is found in the notebooks from Summer 1872 through to Spring 1873. See especially 1872.19.149, 156, 159, and 1873.27.37, 77. The key ideas here begin with sensation as the limit of our knowledge both of ourselves and our world. That is, asking what sensation is *of* (what is the thing-in-itself) is absurd, for the world, our body and our mind are all encountered first as sensation. (Sensation is, so to speak, akin to a thing-in-itself.) However, to simply reduce all of cognition to sensation is true but trivial, for it ignores all the intervening levels of interpretation. All of these ideas are found also in the famous essay fragment 'On Truth and Lies'. In itself, N seems to suggest, sensation (more specifically, nervous stimulation) is neutral, it just is; interpretation according to values and needs occurs later. During this period, N is responding to his avid reading of certain broadly neo-Kantian philosophers and scientists, such as Lange, Gerber, or Helmholtz, as well as the influence of the positivism of Comte. This type of thought is what Zarathustra means, at Z2.2, by thinking 'your senses through to the end' (repeated at TIReason3). The problem of how to understand the representation of space and time on this basis is addressed by the cryptic fragment 1873.26.12, sometimes referred to as the 'Time-Atom Fragment' (there may also be some influence of N's reading of Boscovich in that passage). Curiously also, N speculates that the inorganic realm also might be intelligible in terms of sensation (1872.19.149); that is, that attraction, repulsion and impacts of materialistic physics could be understood in this way. (At 1873.26.1 this idea seems to be attributed to Empedocles.) This mode of thinking looks forward to the notion of *will to power*, understood as a basic metaphysical concept.

A few years later, N's meditation on sensation resurfaces as the 'chemistry' of sensations and concepts proposed at H1.1 (N pursues the idea through the first chapter of H1; see for example H1.18.) Chemistry is the appropriate analogy because it deals with combinations and arrangements of things (atoms in molecules in the case of chemistry, sensations and concepts in the case of N's proposal) without having the authority to ask about the nature or origin of the things themselves. N seems unsure as to whether to consider *pleasure* and pain as the most basic of sensations. The traditional reason for making such a claim is to understand how sensations – in themselves conceived as neutral effects of external simulation – lead to action. Once N discovers the concept of *value*, he believes that he has a solution to this problem, without resorting to pleasure and pain as basic sensations. At D117, the senses 'measure', and the context makes it clear that N means this in the sense of 'interpret' or 'value'. Likewise, at H3.12 N can claim that pleasure and pain are the consequence of certain anthropocentric vanities. These ideas too lead eventually to the concept of will to power: the feeling of power is simultaneously a feeling directed to something (e.g. something that resists power and needs overcoming) and a value.

Because of the bond between sensation and value, the overcoming of atomism – which N considers the last relic of an idea of substance – is also the 'greatest triumph over the senses' (BGE12). The point is repeated at BGE14, and contrasted to a 'noble' Platonic mode of thought, which resisted the senses. Which sensations or groups of sensations carry value is a determinant of the order of rank within a society (BGE268). However, that first chapter of BGE also contains a limited endorsement of sensualism – that is the broadly empiricist notion that the data of the senses are the only data (BGE11, 15, and see 1881.11.194) – at least as a 'regulative hypothesis'. This is the most valuable fruit of the eighteenth century, passed on into the nineteenth by Kant, N says at 1885.34.116 and again at DP3. In TIReason1–3, N's thought seems to return to his treatment of sensation in the 1870s. Here the discussion focuses on the traditional problem that the senses portray a world of change and becoming – philosophers such as Parmenides and later Plato reason that the senses must be deceptive for this reason. N argues that the senses do not lie, but this seems to take us back 15 years to sensation as a value-neutral substrate to experience. Thus N writes at 'We have science precisely to the extent that we have decided to accept the testimony of the senses' (TIReason3). Here his reasoning is Epicurean, although obviously N rejects the atomistic theory that underlies Epicurus' epistemology. Sensation is in and of itself true simply as a physiological event (see TIErrors4). What Epicurus calls opinion arises when we judge sensation, without adequate 'testimony'. (Descartes makes the same move in *Meditations*.)

So, we have a tension, observed in BGE and TI, between sensualism in a radically empirical sense (in which sensation is in itself true and could be nothing but value-neutral), on the one hand, and the inseparability of sensation and value (in which sensation occurs immediately as valuation or interpretation – in other words, is *perspective*), on the other. This tension in N's thought is never fully resolved, but other passages suggest a way forward. First, at 1885.37.4, N has Ariadne rebuke him for his positivism, calling it 'snout philosophy'. Ariadne here represents a Greek approach, pre-modern and pre-scientific to be sure, but a lover and beloved by Dionysus and thus capable of human advancement and greatness. Likewise, at TISkirmishes7, N decries the 'working from nature' of those French psychologists who elsewhere he calls 'positivists' (1885.35.34) – it is only for those of a 'factual' nature, not for artists. Then, in BGE15, N very carefully calls sensualism a 'regulative hypothesis', but not a 'heuristic principle' – that is, not a principle by which one should learn or teach. Given N's lifelong tirade against education that destroys youth rather than makes possible greatness, this distinction is important. In other words, whether sensualism should be thought of as naïve and metaphysical, or not, is not in the end the most important issue. It is plebian, and carries antagonism towards any advancement or even health of the human. It is a method in the sense of a strategy and 'one must know *who* one is' (TISkirmishes7).

sensuality

Several terms might plausibly be translated as sensuality, among them *Wollust, Sensibilität* and *Sinnlichkeit*. By 'sensuality' we mean sensation or feeling insofar as immediately connected with affects, especially overwhelming pleasure, and thus especially in a sexual context. There is an important connection with the notion of *sensation*, because sensuality is generally considered a sub-class of sensation more generally. (N sometimes discusses the two concepts together, making the distinction difficult.) Thus, N discovers that the moral or religious reasons for hating sensuality are often found together with the epistemological or ontological reasons for distrusting the senses (e.g. in asceticism at GM3.24, or Plato at D448). In turn, the rejection of the senses is part of the rejection of both the human body (as something dirty, sinful, holding back the immortal soul) and 'this world' (of matter, becoming, illusion).

Sensuality and sex are made sinful or shameful because of the denigration of body and the real.

Nevertheless, at Z1.13 Zarathustra claims there is a difference between the 'innocence' of the senses, and the 'bitch sensibility', which is 'cruel' and 'shallow'. Although the term used changes to *Wollust*, the same point is made at Z3.10.2. As the imagery suggests, part of the point is that the simple animalistic element misses what is important about sensuality. However, another point being made is that, once it is made sinful or shameful, sex becomes a 'guilty pleasure' – that is pleasurable in part precisely because it is forbidden. See the poem at Z4.16 for a comic European moral posturing on the subject of sex. In contrast, notice how in Z3.10.2, innocent sensuality brings together in the now both the future's 'exuberance of thanks' and the past's 'reverently preserved wine'. Sensuality thus becomes an important *allegory* of the redemption of time through eternal recurrence. The matter is pursued at greater length at GM3.2, where N writes that there is 'no necessary opposition' between chastity and sensuality, and that every 'good marriage and every genuine affair of the heart' is 'beyond this opposition'. Also beyond it are the genuine spiritual needs of the philosopher, who avoids sensuality because of his or her higher, dominant instinct and not because of weakness or fear (GM3.8). The distinction within sensuality is found – though with modifications – in a distinction between Southern and Northern sensuality at WC2 (and see WC5). N's critique of Wagner focuses on the last opera *Parsifal*, which represents an antique Christian *asceticism* towards sensuality (GM3.3, and see H1.217). The relation between rejection of sensuality and asceticism is a key theme throughout GM3, and see D109.

sex

See *sensuality*.

shadow

Schatten. See also *night*. As a symbol, there are a vast number of important precedents. For example, in the underworld of Greek and other mythologies, the dead are imagined as 'shades' or 'shadows'. There is a similar usage in Pindar's *Pythian Odes* viii (human beings are 'dreams of a shadow'; N cites this in 'The Greek State'). Shadows are changeable and deceptive appearances in Plato's allegory of the cave. That Platonic notion is found also in the New Testament, for example James 1.17. The shadow is something incomplete, and thus perhaps prophetic of completion. This is how Paul uses the symbol to describe religious law at Col. 2.16. Given N's focus on Paul's relationship to the law in D and again in AC, this passage is important.

N uses the symbol of shadow in at least five, often overlapping ways. (i) First of all, shadow as a relation to the powerful: either under the sway of something, or as a kind of image cast by the powerful. So, Europe under the shadow of Socrates (BT15) or the saint (H1.143); the shadow of God, or belief in God (e.g. GS108); to live in the shadow of one's deed (i.e. guilt, or perhaps the idea of having outlived one's ability to act – see Z2.13, see *criminal*). The shadow is also the image cast by one, outside of one's control and visible to all. So Zarathustra vows to rein in his shadow at Z2.18. Similarly, N portrays the philosopher as a shadow, shying away from the bright light of fame, power, and from his 'time' (GM3.8). (ii) shadow not as the dispensable opposite of light, but as equally necessary for things to be beautiful, clear or understood (e.g. H3Dialogue, Z2.7); (iii) shadow as prophetic, as an anticipation of some future, as per Paul in *Colossians* (and see the shadow of the death of God at GS343). So, for example, N uses Michelangelo's – and in turn the neo-Platonist's – idea of art as the shadow of the divine (Z2.2, 2.22). The combination of this meaning with the first yields the notion of noon as the moment of shortest shadow (TITrueworld) – that is, the moment at which there is the least being over-shadowed by the past, and the least being only a shadow of the future. See *night*. (iv) shadow as burden, weight or seriousness, thus TIPreface or the appearance of the Soothsayer at Z4.2 (and see H3.7). (v) Shadow as death or a state not far from death (GS278, EHWise1) – this may be because of the deadening effect of insight, as seems to be the case of the Shadow's aimless nihilism at Z4.9, who is rendered thin and weak.

Shakespeare

N considered Shakespeare to be a great poetic genius, but for slightly unusual reasons. Shakespeare's works contain so many ideas – especially moral observations – that other plays seem empty. However, the works may be less theatrically effective for this reason (H1.176). Likewise, Shakespeare stands in a 'barbarian' tradition with respect to European theatre, and thus it takes a rather decadent *historical sense* to be able to appreciate him (e.g. H1.211). Only Shakespeare's own *nobility* could have made his portrayals of Brutus and Caesar possible (GS98, EHClever4), and thus N concludes that the plays were probably written by Bacon. The account of Hamlet at BT is repeated briefly at EHClever4, which also makes clear Shakespeare's importance for N's own use of the figure of the *fool* or clown: 'how much must one have suffered, to be compelled to play the fool!' Like all Dionysian, tragic poets, Shakespeare is not a moralist condemning his characters because of their faults, but rather celebrates life through the lives, and destructions, of great individuals: 'it is an adventure to live!' (D240).

shame

Scham. At GS275–7, N seems to sum up his whole new conception of virtue in terms of shame, indicating the concept's importance to him. At H1.100, N attempts a definition of shame in terms of one's encroaching on or defiling a mystery – something worthy of reverence and forbidden, and thus that should not be looked upon, defiled through proximity or touch. His examples are religious shrine, Kingship and the soul of the other. We can extend N's account by analogy to the defiling of an ideal. In 'The Greek State', work is understood to be shameful, because work shows lack of reverence towards or defiles one's own nobility. Modern people honour knowledge, and know better, and yet are 'not ashamed to call themselves Christians' (AC38). Pity brings shame because the pitied person is, thereby, shown to be weak and dependent. Zarathustra feels shame – importantly, he does not feel pity – before the Ugliest Man at Z4.7. The latter, though, is the 'murderer of God' because 'His pitying knew no shame'. God is the absolute witness, 'God sees into every heart' (TIMorality4). The believer is thus constantly in a state of shame.

Encroaching on what is hidden in another's soul – especially a noble soul (thus in his or her investigations, the philosopher should 'respect the mask': BGE27) – brings shame to both parties. However, Dionysus is the ideal of reverence for the self, the body and the earth. The nakedness of his body and soul then defiles nothing. Dionysus is thus the ideal of a being without shame (Z2.21, BGE295). Accordingly, Zarathustra 'must yet become a child and without shame' (Z2.22), and the higher humans must not be ashamed of their failures, but 'play and mock' (Z4.13.14). N sometimes expresses this in an intriguingly different way: because reverence for the body and the earth is not defiled by nakedness, the gods will need other masks than clothes (BGE40 and see GS77).

sheep, also lamb, shepherd

Schaf. The sheep (and lamb) is the most commonly referred to herd animal in N (although see also *cow*). The sheep is a conventional symbol of something timid and weak (BGE201), and in need of guidance and care. Thus also N's references to the biblical imagery of the shepherd (see Pss. 23.1 and Jn 10; and in N see GM3.15, Z1.2). The priests, as shepherds, are criticized for taming or domesticating humanity – that is, for creating this weakness and need to be guided and protected. The lamb resents the bird of prey (especially the eagle) above it, and this is a metaphor for *ressentiment* (GM1.13). The sheep is the herd aspect of humans, as opposed to the divine (Z4.14.3).

sickness

See *health, convalescence.*

sin

See *morality.*

slave

Sklave. Most of the societies that N writes about – ancient Greece and Rome, of course, but also some more recent European states – were slave-owning. The democratic movement in Europe and elsewhere calling for the liberalization of institutions were essentially directed at slavery, in all its various guises. A slave can be defined in N's terms as someone who thinks and acts as part of a group (a herd) – that is, according to a principle or source of command external to him or her *qua* individual – and thus who does not have command over themselves (see also GS18). N would agree with Marx that workers in a capitalist state, regardless of its democratic pretensions, remain slaves in a closely analogous fashion, and are perhaps even worse off (H1.457) – and N would add that so are the owners and state representatives (H1.283). To be sure, many or most of these modern instances of slavery may be 'slavery in a higher sense' (AC54). Nevertheless, it follows that democratic and socialist movements are (i) self-deceptive, replacing one type of slavery with another; (ii) dangerous, in so far as promising things to the masses that could not in principle be delivered; and (iii) seeking to annul the only thing that gives slavery meaning (the existence of nobility or higher types).

The early N insists that Socratic/Alexandrian culture requires a slave *class* (BT18). The point is expressed in just this way partly as a sop to Wagner and his residual revolutionary ideals. Later, N clarifies that *all* higher culture demands this (BGE259, AC57 – the idea is already found in 'The Greek State'). The key condition is that those who are *noble*, and who directly or indirectly rule, must have leisure and must be able to assign values and duties to themselves. Both ruler and slave are contrasted (as Plato does in the *Republic*) with a military class (both literally and metaphorically understood) whose nobility lies in obedience (Z1.10). The most famous use of the concept of slave in N is in 'slave revolution' (see Z4.8, BGE195, GM1.8–10). Both Jews and many early Christians spent much of their history enslaved, and N argues that this played a key role in developing their value systems. The idea is that a system of morality arises founded not upon the active positing of values, nor upon the needs of life and human development, but upon the desire for revenge (or '*ressentiment*') against the rulers. The result is an 'inversion' of noble morality, so that what was formerly good (in terms of noble values) becomes bad or even sinful, and what was formerly bad (again, in terms of noble values: the condition of being enslaved, impoverished, weak or ill) become the characteristics of those who will 'inherit the earth'. In this connection, N interestingly contrasts Epictetus (a stoic philosopher who was, for much of his life, a slave) and Christian attitudes (D546). Importantly, this slave revolution happens as the result of the fervent of a priestly class, who envisage that revolution as their opportunity for power with respect to the noble (GM1.6–7).

sleep and wakefulness

Schlaf, Wachsamkeit. N employs the metaphors of sleeping and awakening in a fairly conventional symbolic sense: to sleep meaning to be unaware and unconcerned, and wakefulness as being aware or acting. Thus Zarathustra is 'awakened' but travelling down to the sleepers (ZP2); the free spirits' 'task is wakefulness itself'; or Rome awakened in the Renaissance, only to fall asleep again (GM1.16). Among the relevant allusions are the minor Greek deity Hypnos who is the brother of Thanatos (death), Mk14.41 ('Are you still sleeping? Enough! The hour has come!') and Eph. 5.14 ('Wake up sleeper, rise from the dead'). See *exhaustion, narcotic, repose.*

snake

Schlange. The snake is sometimes seen as filth, or stupid *cruelty* either in a psychological sense or in a metaphysical one (H1.236, H2.62, Z2.15). At Z1.19 the meaningless cruelty of the adder's bite is transformed by Zarathustra's reaction. The idea here concerns how human relations are dominated by a cycle of *revenge*, in turn founded on an unwillingness to give up one's petty *pride*. Other subtle meanings are at work in the snake, especially the following three. (1) The snake or serpent as the Old Testament figure of evil (GS259, BGE202, Z4.9, AC48), thus putting the traditional concept of good at odds with knowledge or insight. (2) The snake shedding its *skin* (D455, H2P2, D573), a symbol of the necessity of renewal or growth; and thus also skin becoming akin to the concept of *mask.* (3) The *Ouroboros*, the snake biting its own tail forming a ring (BT15). This in turn means either science and logic destructively realizing their own limits (BT15), or *eternal recurrence* (ZP.10, Z1.22, Z3.2). See also Plato's *Timaeus* where a similar notion is used to describe the self-sufficiency of life as a whole. The snake is sometimes contrasted with the *dragon* as a great or superior snake (H1.498, Z1.19). The rattlesnake occurs a few times, a figure that relies upon the contrast between the childlike sound of the rattle and the poisonous animal itself (WC3, Z2.21) – thus a metaphor for those who act an innocent part.

socialism

N frequently refers to socialism, as one of the many 'modern' political ideas or movements that are symptomatic of a degenerating culture; it is closely akin he argues to democratic equality. He argues, conventionally enough, that socialist abolition of private property is a serious attack on the rights of private persons (H3.285). Also, socialism is synonymous with the expansion of state control upon the lives of citizens. Indeed it 'outbids all the despotisms of the past', it aims at the 'annihilation of the individual' by reducing it to an 'organ of the community' (H1.473).

Socrates

Socrates gives his name to the Socratic (one of the three cultural drives in BT) and is also its most obvious representative. Cultural productions of the Socratic are above all *logic* (from its beginnings as *dialectic*) and *science*. The Socratic is characterized by *optimism* (in the possibilities of knowledge), a certain contempt for appearance per se (and thus the urge to correct or *improve* it), and a stubborn belief in the original reality of individual, unchanging *forms* (e.g. Plato's forms). This latter point puts it in opposition to both the *Dionysian* and the *Apollonian* (for that latter never loses the awareness that forms are illusions). Importantly, the Socratic does not just compete with or struggle against the other drives, it denies them as misunderstandings. Through its influence on *Euripides*, the Socratic brings about the suicide of *tragedy*. N argues that the Socratic is the birth of *modernity*.

In later writings, Socrates remains an important reference point, but a deeply ambiguous one. At times, Socrates is seen as a potential counter to Christian moral thought (H3.86). an intoxication with new types of thought that break the hold of custom (D544), or the exhaustion of ancient culture (BGE212). In 1888, N's view of Socrates returns to a view more akin to BT: Socrates as a *decadent*, seeking a kind of totalitarianism of reason and the destruction of that which enhances life (TISocrates1–12).

solitude

Einsamkeit. Solitude is used both literally and figuratively. Literally, in the kinds of personal practices N favoured – smaller towns, mountain walks, the seaside, and a small group of close personal friends. Figuratively, solitude links to several other ideas. They include: (i) *Distance* – those who are *noble* understand themselves as isolated from others, even of their own rank. (ii) *Untimeliness* – free spirits and new philosophers will be the bad conscience of their age, will think, live and value differently, and will thus in this sense be alone (GS50, 117). Zarathustra is more alone with uncomprehending crowds than in his mountain cave (Z3.9). (iii) Spiritual *pregnancy* is something solitary and quiet, especially to be contrasted with busy modern lives (D177, 440, GS338, Z1.12, BGE25). Importantly, though, such solitude is not simply an escape, or an individual spiritual project (see UM3.5). Zarathustra *cycles* through periods of needing solitude (as contemplation or convalescence) and going in search of disciples. (iv) the solitude or loneliness of bestowing (D464, Z2.9; see *gift*).

Sophocles

The second of the three great Greek tragedians. Sophocles made some important innovations to the conventions of *tragedy*, which N analyses at BT14 as being already the beginning of the end of tragedy as a significant cultural form. See *Oedipus, sphinx, riddle*.

soul

See *self*.

south

The distinction of European cultures into South (*Süd*) and North (*Nord*) is hardly original to N. Of particular importance for N, though, are the different relationships to Christianity and the Church, because of different attitudes to *sensuality* and to *health*. In this regard, N discusses the different relationships between individual and herd in the South (GS149); a constitutive relationship to Africa (WC2) and the Orient (GS291, 350); the Southern Church in contrast to Luther's Reformation (GS358). The distinction is also operative in N's account of modern music and its function (e.g. BGE255, WC3, EHClever7).

specialization

See *scholar, education*.

spider

Spinne. The key attributes here are the spinning of a web – something artificial, nearly invisible, ensnaring and yet also fragile – and the spider hiding at the centre, killing vampire-like by sucking blood. Given the many references to the circular shape of the web, N must frequently have had orb-weavers in mind, the most common of which is the *Kreuzspinne*.

In association with Greek mythology, where the fates 'spin' out the world and destiny, the spider in N is the 'world spider' (H2.32). More particularly, the spider and its web can thus stand for concepts, which capture and organize sensations (OTL1, D117); or habits that constrain us without being noticed (H1.427); systems of ideas or practices (both religious and philosophical: D130, GS358, AC17–18) and which in the end offer no real support (UM2.9). The spider sits in the centre and drains the life out of things (BGE209, AC11, 17, and see 1888.16.58). *Kreuzspinne* occurs with two distinct meanings: one evoking the Christian symbol (Z3.8.2), one apparently referring to the tale that these spiders unspin, eat and respin their webs every day (UM2.9). The most famous use of 'spider' in N is as part of the introduction of eternal recurrence. In both GS341 and at Z3.2.2 the spider is on that short list of things that recur. This beautifully brings together several of the above meanings, most obviously the world-spider and the continually respinning *Kreuzspinne*; in addition, though, much of the burden of eternal recurrence is the recurrence of that which opposes life (the cross, the vampire), and the same errors and delusions (web of concepts). N often uses the idea of 'net' with much the same meaning as 'web' here.

Spinoza

Seventeenth-century Jewish-Dutch philosopher, who was also a significant early figure in critical biblical studies. Spinoza's concept of monism – that mind and world are two aspects of a single substance which can also be called Nature or God – is an enormously important notion within the history of thought. Although N of course rejects the theological dimension of this idea (which has become so attenuated as to be meaningless anyway: GS372), his thought too has such ambitions. In addition, N admired the rigour of Spinoza's denial of free will, and his restoration of what N called *innocence* to human action (GM2.15, and see letter to Overbeck, 30 July 1881). Where Spinoza goes wrong, N thinks, is in including the idea of self-preservation as key among the mechanisms within innocent action (BGE13, GS349), and in the famous geometrical method which says more about the psychology of Spinoza than about philosophy (BGE5).

Spir, Afrikan

Half a generation older than N, Spir was a Russian who emigrated to Germany and then to Switzerland. Spir was a Kantian in his sense of philosophy as a rigorous science and of an absolute difference between reality and appearance. Reality is understood in a Parmenidean fashion as unchanging self-identity; the empirical world is characterized by becoming and is therefore illusory. Insofar as our cognition is a necessary falsification of the empirical world of becoming (our sensations are mediated), the laws of thought (above all the principle of identity) are our first clue to the nature of the real. Spir's most innovative idea is that time as becoming is not simply illusory, but real. The human, thus, is caught in a bind between becoming and being. N read Spir frequently throughout his career, and was influenced by Spir's analysis of the way cognition deals with becoming (analogous to the analysis in Schopenhauer), and the anti-realist and anti-empiricist implications of that analysis (see particularly PTAG). However, N saw no reason to agree with Spir that reality should also be understood in a Parmenidean manner – this, for N, was a surplus metaphysical assumption.

spirit

N employs the word '*Geist*' often, but its conceptual content is not immediately obvious. Broadly, '*Geist*' as a word N inherited has two meanings. First, mind or consciousness. Thus, Hegel's title *Phänomenologie des Geistes* used to be translated as *Phenomenology of Mind*; while Marx uses the term to mean 'having to do with the intellect'. Second, spirit as collective identity and direction, as in the expressions 'team spirit' or 'spirit of the age' (a straight-forward translation of *Zeitgeist*), or 'spirit of music' at BT16 and 'spirit of science' at BT17. This supra-individual sense is also part of the meaning in Hegel (who in turn gets it from the Neoplatonists).

Luther used '*Geist*' to translate the Hebrew '*ruah*' in the Old Testament (as in 'the spirit of God' at Gen. 1.2); *ruah* as 'breath' also meant thought or knowledge, and also word. Luther likewise used *Geist* to translate the Greek '*pneuma*' in the New Testament (as in 'holy spirit'). N occasionally uses *Geist* in an echo of these senses (e.g. Z3.16.3 or 4.13.20). N considered the writers of the New Testament to have had poor knowledge of Greek in the way that they used *pneuma* (WC9). *Pneuma* meaning *wind* or *breath* always had a physical sense, not a supernatural one, in earlier Greek usage and even in the Stoics. N comments that spirit belongs to the body and is thus always only quasi-spirit (Z2.17). Thus its use in rhetoric means a phrase of one breath. A remnant of this physical meaning is present, but rare, in the New Testament; see Jn 3.8 or Acts 2.2. Moreover, the New Testament usage also moves *pneuma* towards the intellectual and operative. Thus, the

Holy Spirit is what allows man to comprehend something of God (Jn 14.17) and through which God has agency in the human, thus speaking in tongues or prophecy (Lk. 1.67). Accordingly, calling God 'spirit' is already a step towards unbelief, since it places God outside the world (Z4.18, and see AC14). However, Luther might also have been making a mistake in German: the etymological sense of *Geist* is of excitement, perhaps anger or fear. Thus, the term *Geist* is arguably more akin to the Greek *thumos* than to *pneuma*; and indeed, the standard English translation of *thumos* is 'spiritedness'.

It is after the first phase of his career that N's distinctive use of the concept of spirit commences. Spirit, then, is certainly mind and consciousness, together with the tools of knowledge (e.g. logic, reason). However, these intellectual faculties function by simplifying, giving form and incorporating. Spirit is a mechanism of life and its need for the feeling of growth or power (BGE230). Thus, although it means intellect and consciousness, we must not think of these as merely passive or representational (see 'over-spiritualization' at AC20). Rather, spirit is more fundamentally the capacity (of an individual or a people) to have a wider or further view and envision possibilities, perhaps on a grand scale, which envisaging is also a *longing* for these possibilities, and an acting towards or achieving them. At Z2.8, N uses the image of a ship's sail as pregnancy, driven by the 'spirit'. Accordingly, there is a linkage between spirit and genius (AC29). Thus, the 'spirit of revenge' is a foolishness that has acquired spirit, that is which has become aware of what it believes to be the source of its pain, and now pursues its revenge as a global enterprise. The spirit of science is a longing for *complete* knowledge, though it only be knowledge of something small and narrow (e.g. Z4.4). The *free spirit* is a spirit that longs for and acts towards ideals that are different from those of his or her time. The German spirit has become coarse and shallow (i.e. abandoning its former gift for intellectual matters) but more importantly the spirit is growing 'meek'. That is, becoming *merely* intellectual, petty, representative, concerned only with today, and thus not also a longing for ideals (TIGermans1–3). Spirit is a manifestation of life, but 'cuts into' life (Z2.8). That is, spirit is the means by which life is capable of destruction or growth. Life becoming aware of itself or having knowledge of itself either kills action (as at BT7, Z3.12.16, BGE230), or overcomes itself to the enhancement of life.

Relatedly, *cleverness* is connected to spirit, the capacity to deceive, bide one's time, and to use various circumstances as instruments towards one's ends (AC14, and see Z1.4). At times, N suggests that this is the primary meaning of spirit (TISkirmishes14). A usage more Hegelian is found, for example, at Z2.6: even the rabble is spirited, meaning that the rabble is an essential element among life's instruments. For 'spirit of gravity' see *weight*.

N uses the term 'spiritualization' (e.g. at TIMorality1–3) to describe the process by which some passion initially operating 'blindly or 'stupidly'' becomes more far-sighted, refined, thoughtful or even clever in its actions. A blind and urgent drive overcomes its mere destructiveness, and need for direct satisfaction, and becomes a *longing* and perhaps creative. N's two examples here are love and hostility (he also pursues the examples of justice at BGE219 and cruelty at 229 and GM2.6). At BGE189, N describes this with the concept of *sublimation*. At GM3.24, the spiritualization of the ascetic ideal means both that the ideal has become 'intellectual' and lost any apparent reference to the senses or the body, but *also* that thereby it has cunningly acquired a new way of expressing and enhancing its power. Spiritualization can also mean internalization – something originally external that has become part of one's identity – as with the battle between noble and slave morality (GM1.16).

Also, N regularly uses the French word *esprit*. The word means liveliness (especially in sociability), wit, cleverness, and N uses it in this sense at D193 or 524. In such cases it is often used particularly to describe a certain way of being a philosopher, as at EHBooks2 and Wagner4. Its lightness or ease is a characteristic of the noble (explicitly at GS103, but implicitly often). Although sometimes *esprit* carries for him the same meaning as *Geist* (e.g. at H1.203); sometimes also, it has a meaning more like spirit's opposite where spirit might be taken to mean intellectually strict and overly serious (GS82).

squandering

Vergeudung. Already by the late nineteenth century, it had become conventional to describe *health* in terms of long life and lack of pain, and also self-preservation as the goal of individuals or species. N argues against both. 'Mankind as a whole has no goal', N argues (H1.33). To be sure, N also argues that the goal of *culture* is to produce greatness (in the earlier work) or that the goal of *free spirits* is to heighten the human type (in the later work). However, these goals do not necessarily involve longevity, *utility*, preservation or even *happiness*. *Will to power* expresses and discharges itself (BGE13); it is overfull and exists to give away (see *gift*). Thus, although the individual often needs to 'conserve', or take care of him or herself in the interests of spiritual pregnancy (BGE41, EHClever9), this is strategic (N sometimes calls it *cleverness*) and not an end in itself. Accordingly, N distinguishes between noble *egoistic* values and those of utility (GM1.2), and observes the wastefulness and indifference characteristic of the Renaissance, 'the last great age' (TISkirmishes37). Moreover, the wastefulness (the absence of an economic rationality or balance) of nature is not a local phenomenon. Against Malthus and Darwin, N argues that nature is characterized by abundance (BGE9, TISkirmishes14) and competition for resources is the exception and not the rule.

state

See *politics*.

stillness/quiet

See *repose*, *perfection*.

Stoicism

N sometimes seems to identify what is valuable about ancient Rome with Stoicism (H3.216): brave, tough, insensitive. From the ancient philosophical tradition, N obtains above all the concept of the *innocence* of actions, the lack that is of genuine blame or *guilt* (H2.386). Thus again this is a Roman virtue in contrast to early Christians who could only live out of hope for the forgiveness of sin, and through *ressentiment* (D546). However, Stoicism can also be an affectation, a disguise (GS359). Roman Stoicism is contrasted with Greek Epicureanism at GS306. The former is the mode of life suited for those who live in violent and changeable times; the latter is the mode of life suited for those with work of the *spirit* to do (compare also the 'idealists' discussed at D546). N thus has qualified admiration for Stoicism as a way of life. On the other hand, he ridicules Stoic metaphysics (e.g. the rationality of nature at BGE9).

strength

The distinction between strength (*Stärke*, and sometimes *Kraft*) and weakness (*Schwäche*) is among the most famous and frequent topics in N. Individuals, types or peoples can be 'strong' or 'weak'. Slightly confusingly, we cannot separate the conception of strength from those of *power* or *energy*, and those entries should be consulted. We will deal briefly with four key features.

1 Independence is the capacity to not simply be one of the herd of one's historical age (BGE29). So, the strong has the ability to be just, in the sense of not simply assuming the validity of a current set of values (UM2.6); and overcomes his or her time (GS380) as well as overcoming any 'romantic' untimeliness or suffering from one's time. Related to this notion is that of having a future, or being responsible for a future. Thus, at Z1.17, Zarathustra asks him or her who would create a future through children to 'show me your right and strength for that'. This idea of independence evolves into the notion of *affirmation* or *amor fati*. These are modes of life to which 'accidents' can no longer happen (Z3.1), who are 'strong enough that everything has to turn out for the best' (EHWise2). Weakness then is dependency, lack of creativity, lack of future or *ressentiment* towards events. See entries on *freedom* and *free spirit*.

2 Having the strength for knowledge. In knowing, N argues, one becomes conscious of one's strength (H1.252). At BGE39, N famously talks about the 'measure' of 'the strength of a spirit' being how much truth one could 'endure' (and see the similar notion at EHDestiny5).

More generally, N claims that the most spiritual people are the strongest; they find their happiness where others would find their doom (AC57), strength is thus associated with a certain asceticism with respect to knowledge, the willingness to take on trials and burdens. Weakness, by contrast, would be either a refusal of knowledge or a cowardly preference for illusion and error. (Importantly, illusion and error can also be characteristics of strength, but as instruments rather than ends.)

3 Similarly, strength characterizes the ability to tolerate the negation involved in scepticism or *nihilism*. Thus, N talks about the one who has the strength to destroy values and not simply replace them with others taken from elsewhere (1887.9.35), to not need extremes of belief or action (1886.5.71.15); or has strength for renunciation of peace, comfort and purpose (GS285); again, the noble has the strength to be capable of *not* reacting, of suspending judgement (TIGermans6, 1888.14.102).

4 Strength is the ability to overcome not only internal but also external obstacles, to have power over something. There is no freedom or unfreedom, but only stronger and weaker, N argues (GS118, BGE25). Strength is not only exhibited but also built through 'wars and victories' – that is through the *agon* (GM2.24). Strength, however, does not necessarily mean greatness (BGE241).

struggle

Ringen is most commonly translated as struggle, there are other cognates. Often N uses this word to designate the important notion of *agon* (e.g. H1.141, H3.122, GS13, Z1.1, BGE262), for which see separate entry. Here, we are interested in a different meaning: to have difficulty with, to exert oneself, to sweat. The sweat of struggle is associated with industrial labour (H3.266, 1881.16.23), but above all with working for some other master, reactively, without genuine self-love and without affirmation. There is thus a consistent contrast between such heavy exertion and the lightness of great accomplishment – and especially later in

N's career, with the accomplishments that involve *amor fati* or the love of recurrence.

For example, in 'The Future of Our Educational Institutions' 1, N writes of how many must work and struggle for *Bildung*, for the sake of a few who will attain greatness. Likewise, in the second lecture, he writes that one must struggle to learn language well, so that one might grasp how lightly and freely it is used by the greatest poets. At GM1.14, N writes of those who sweat while talking of 'love of one's enemies', meaning that such supposed love hides both a terror of, and enslavement to, those enemies. The spirit of gravity imposes burdens, makes humans labour and sweat and claims that the burden is necessary to life (Z3.11.2). At Z2.22, Zarathustra sweats as he is unable yet to be the teacher of eternal recurrence; similarly, at Z4.2, Zarathustra's characteristic lightness and jesting turn to sweat at the prospect of pity. The contrast between the lightness of Bizet and the sweating *seriousness* of Wagner is made at the beginning of WC1 (and see 1885.37.10 where this point is generalized to all Germans). Finally, in speaking of punishment, N advises that there is something demeaning and certainly counter-productive about a struggle that reacts, and does not result in enhancement (GS321). That passage contains an implied contrast between two senses of struggle: the reactive, enslaved or destructive, and the productive (*agon*). There is a conceptual link here between this idea of exertion and two famous passages in Z: 'On the Three Transformations' (Z1.1) in which the lion must become a child, and 'On the Sublime' (Z2.13) in which the hero has not yet learned stillness and beauty. At EHClever9, N writes of his own tranquillity and lack of struggle, as that with which he is *pregnant* slowly comes to term (compare Epicurus on ease and struggle). Such lightness or ease is often characterized as instinctive, as opposed to the deliberate (conscious, reflective, rule-following, dialectic) which are in turn types of struggle (TIErrors2).

style

Stil. The most obvious issue of style is N's own writing – on that broad topic, see the entries *aphorism, communication, language, metaphor, allegory*. In fact the concept of style extends well beyond N as a writer. A few key observations: (i) There is a traditional distinction between style and content – the same meaning can be expressed in many different ways. This N rejects. If anything, the content is less meaningful, since our thoughts are generally superficial expressions of our *drives* and their relationships. Style is what gives us insight into these. In his discussion of Schopenhauer's style, style is a question of honesty (UM3.2). Thus, N defines style as the ability to communicate a state (H3.88, EHBooks4). (ii) The unity of style is the sign of an authentic culture (UM1.1), and therefore modernity with its *historical sense* borrowing styles and modes of life from all over history is the least authentic culture. (iii) Although there is no one law of style (because there are different states and modes of life), to the extent that one has achieved a unity akin to that of culture, one will have a unity of style – namely, the 'great style' (ACP). The 'great style' characterizes the finest Roman cultural products (AC58–9); it does not please, it 'commands' (1888.14.61). (iv) Style is a kind of discipline or constraint. Life at court corresponds to a law of style (GS101); and the strong spirit will 'give style' to their character, force it under one 'taste', and indeed take pleasure in this self-imposed law (GS290). Wagner's 'great style' is a lie (WC1) because Wagner thought he could dispense with the 'higher law' of style (WC8).

sublation

'Sublation' is the now-standard translation of the term *Aufhebung*, as used by Hegel. The German word has two meanings, both of which are meant in Hegel: (i) a raising up in the sense that something is preserved or even purified and (ii) a cancelling out. Especially in H, N frequently uses the expression where clearly only the second of these meanings is intended, as if attempting to reclaim the word (e.g. H1.133, 457, H2.75, H3.22 and see DP4, D248). In such passages, 'cancellation' or 'abolition' are appropriate translations.

sublimation

'Sublimation' translates *Sublimierung*. In chemistry, the term means to pass from solid to gas state without transitioning through the liquid state. Metaphorically, it means for something to bypass its 'natural' motion/place/direction, and 'leap' to some new one, especially one considered more 'rarefied'. N uses the concept to mean a drive or passion that has been diverted, so as to discharge itself in an apparently different way. For example, the herd's instincts for revenge are sublimated into virtues. In principle this could happen consciously or deliberately (D202), but more often is surreptitious. That is, it appears as if the original drive simply disappears (H1.1), or that its new object always was its true object (e.g. 'good actions are sublimated evil ones': H1.107; sex is sublimated into love: BGE180; cruelty into tragic pity: GM2.7; or the ascetic priest changing the direction of *ressentiment*' at GM3.15). N explains sublimation, at least in part, by pointing out that not all 'drives' or 'forces' have a direction or meaning – that is have a 'natural' outlet – and thus another, much weaker force, can be the one to supply that direction (GS360). Freud obtains the idea from N and it becomes a key concept within psychoanalysis.

sublime

Erhaben. The sublime is the overwhelming, terrifying or monstrous. As an aesthetic category, the problem has always been to understand how such an experience – in essence, the ugly – could be in any way pleasurable or even tolerable. N defines the aesthetic sublime at BT7 as 'the terrible tamed by artistic means', and he primarily means by the Apollonian. The sublime in modern music is the presentation of the ugly (H1.217); the ugly are advised to 'put the sublime around you, the mantle of the ugly!' (Z1.10); Wagner is parodied for being incapable of beauty: it is 'easier to be huge than to be beautiful' (WC6). The most important passage is Z2.13. Here the heroic, turbulent seeker after knowledge is termed sublime, because he or she still despises, and like the earlier 'pale criminal' is overshadowed by the 'deed'. In other words, this knowledge has not become productive or fertile, the sublime one has not aligned him or herself with the world that knowledge has revealed. 'When power becomes gracious and descends into the visible: beauty I call such a descent', Zarathustra says. The passage ends with a reference to Ariadne: when the hero (Theseus) leaves, she will be approached by the 'over-hero' (Dionysus).

suffering, woe, etc.

Leiden (suffering) forms the root of both *Mitleid* (*pity* or compassion) and *Leidenschaft* (*passion*) – thus N often treats these three ideas in conjunction.

Following on from Schopenhauer's pessimism – in which the restless will is forever unsatisfied and thus forever suffering – the concept of suffering is central in N. It is the awareness of life by the Greeks as essentially suffering and without resolution, and yet their 'cheerfulness', that generates the problem of the early work. Even after N ceased to be strictly Schopenhauerian, the problem of suffering never goes away (nor does the broadly Schopenhauerian idea that *art* is the relief of suffering). N's conception of modern humans is that we are over-sensitive to suffering, and obsessed with its relief (e.g. H2.187, BGE225, TISkirmishes37) – and thus for example utilitarianism or liberal institutions, or art conceived of as a *narcotic*. To this he contrasts the 'discipline of suffering' (BGE225), suffering as that which gives strength and finds means. Suffering makes *noble* (BGE270), and those capable of greatest happiness are also vulnerable to the greatest suffering (GS302). The noble free spirit, however, does not suffer necessarily (BGE62), that is does not suffer from reality itself (AC15) – that would mean 'you are a piece of reality that has *gone wrong*'. Nor does the free spirit suffer out of discontent or guilt. This is how N describes the internalizing process by which 'bad conscience' was developed (GM2.16), but not his description of the 'fruit' of this process, the 'sovereign individual' (GM2.2). At worst, one should suffer not from humans but from 'the human' (Z4.13.6) – that is from the pettiness and lost possibilities of the human type thus far (e.g. AC8). The overcoming of suffering in the noble free spirit happens through joy in fate and *eternal recurrence* (Z4.19). Accordingly, also, Zarathustra says at the end of Part Four, 'my suffering . . . what does that matter! Am I striving then for *happiness*? I am striving for my *work*!' (Z4.20).

sun

Sonne. For discussions of light and times of day, see *night*. The sun is an image rich with mythic and philosophical content. Of particular importance for N is Apollo as the sun god, allowing N to develop his concept of the *Apollonian* art drive in the first few sections of BT. Also, the 'allegory of the sun' in Plato's *Republic* – there, the sun is the 'beyond being' that allows the forms to become visible to the human intellect. N plays in complex ways with Plato's concept. At the beginning of Z, Zarathustra leaves his cave and greets the sun. Here, however, the sun is the symbol of a *wisdom* that has grown 'overrich' and needs to *give* away (and see Zarathustra's staff at Z1.22). The book ends (Z4.20) saying Zarathustra 'left his cave, glowing and strong, like a morning sun coming out of dark mountains'.

superman

See *overhuman*.

sweat

See *struggle*.

symbol

See *allegory*.

sympathy

See *pity*.

system

System. N abhors the idea of systematic philosophy (such as he is found especially in Hegel). By this he means a type of thinking that constructs an understanding of the whole of reality in terms of a single set of interconnected principles. Such an approach is hubristic and in bad taste, for one thing (GS373); moreover, it assumes that becoming is just the distribution of being across time. Even Hegel, an exceptional philosopher of history, sees the whole of history as the emergence of spirit. System thus kills thought and reality. If there are systems in philosophy or theology, N argues, it is because of the kinds of metaphysical errors which human life had to develop (BGE20, TISkirmishes5). In other words, reality (including human beings) may be systematic in the sense of being fully interconnected and *necessary* (e.g. TIMorality6). The idea of *eternal recurrence* seems to follow from this, and likewise N's frequent use of the concept of *economy*. But this is a system without being 'governed' by principles or laws (BGE22). Moreover, philosophy is within that system, and not contemplating it from outside. Arguably, of course, N himself offered such a system, based around *perspective* and the *will to power*. However, such an interpretation of N's thought might have difficulty understanding concepts such as *accident, innocence* or N's account of *causation* and *law*. In any case, one way of understanding why N writes in *aphorisms*, employs poetry, narrative, parody and *irony*, is to avoid being taken as a systematic thinker.

taste

Geschmack. In both English and German, this is a traditional term for broadly aesthetic judgements. An equally traditional problem is whether taste is simply subjective and relative to each of us, or whether there is a 'standard' of taste (as Hume puts it). N modifies this problem. To be sure, there is a standard, but it is not to be understood (as Hume and Kant do) on an analogy with objective knowledge. Good taste is the noble way of valuing itself and its world (BGE224); that is taste is a question of the values that are part of a particular mode of human life (GS39). As opposed to the relativity of taste (as found in the maxim 'there is no disputing about taste') Zarathustra says 'all life is a disputing about taste' (Z1.13). Thus N admires unity of taste, insofar as it is active (GS290). It follows first that historical or cultural changes in taste are more important, because they are more closely related to the underlying form of life, than changes in beliefs. It also follows that we moderns, with our *historical sense*, whatever other merits we possess, will have taste against us (BGE224). The ascetic priest has ruined health and therefore also ruined taste (GM3.22, TISkirmishes32, WC5). Indeed, in some sense we have no taste at all (not even bad taste), we don't even know what we like: H2.170 (and see the figure of the ass at Z3.11). Thus also good taste today will be *untimely*.

teach/teaching/teacher

See *education, communication, gift.*

teleology

See *goal.*

tempo, rhythm

Tempo (*Tempo*, and cognate) and rhythm (*Rhythmus*) are key aspects of *style* for N. Style is not simply a superficial phenomenon, but relates to the underlying mode of life and its characteristic states or feelings (BGE28, and see EHBooks4, EHZ3). Thus, for example, N complains that in contemporary writing there are 'rhythms that do not dance' (BGE246), of the dangers in Wagner's blending of rhythms (H2.134), and that his own tempo will be difficult for others to grasp (BGE28). The various paces that N believes characterize his own life and work vary – sometimes deliberately slow and cautious (DP5), sometimes 'presto' (BGE213, GS381) – precisely because they relate to the various *cycles* of his underlying life (GS376, and see Z4.1). All this contrasts to a modern life that is unrelenting in its hurry (UM3.4, H1.282, TISkirmishes39).

Rhythm also receives analysis in terms of the constitution of thought from more basic sensations. In 1870, N had what he then considered one of his greatest insights (see letter to Rhode, November 1870). In ancient Greece, metre (i.e. poetic rhythm) was understood more in terms of duration and interval, than in terms of emphasis or 'beat' (which is our default modern conception). This also means, in Greek poetry, a disconnect between rhythm and the surface meaning (because emphasis is used to guide a reader to the important words). Rhythm is the imposition of form onto the real – it is thus a way of falsifying (H1.151), of compelling (GS84). In music, the early N ascribes harmony above all to Dionysus, but rhythm to Apollo (BT2). Rhythm is thus the manner in which becoming is ordered and understood in terms of measurable space and time (1872.19.153, 1873.26.12; the idea is reinforced by N's reading of Dühring in 1875, see his notes at 1875.9.1, 1885.38.10, and see *Chaldini*).

temptation

See *seduce.*

tension

Spannung. An image – based often on the analogy of a bow – of stored or dammed-up energy or force, awaiting sudden release and direction, either in an individual or in a whole culture. For examples, see Z2.1, BGEP, EHClever3. There is also a tension between two contrary forces (UM4.7, TISkirmishes37).

thing-in-itself

Ding an sich. A Kantian concept. If that which appears is mediated in some way by our cognitive processes – in terms of form (space and time), sensation and conceptual content – then the 'thing-in-itself' is that which appears as it is, without cognitive processing. (For the *appearance*/thing-in-itself distinction Kant also uses, in what for our purposes is the same way, phenomenon/noumenon.) For Kant, the limits of our knowledge are the same as the limits of our experience, and therefore the thing-in-itself is an unknown. *Metaphysics* in a negative sense is defined as the attempt to know the thing-in-itelf. N sees this problem as vastly more widespread than Kant, with metaphysical nonsense of this type at the heart of *morality, religion,* and *science.* N's most famous account is TITrueworld.

thought

See *spirit*.

Thus Spoke Zarathustra

In four parts (the first with a Prologue), all written between 1882 and 1885. Each part contains some 20 separately titled sections. The first three parts were issued publicly, as separate volumes. The fourth was only circulated among friends, and was only made public in 1892. In form, the book is akin to a novel concerning a sage named Zarathustra, and with a definite narrative concerning his discovery of his philosophical voice and strategy (part one), his struggles coming to terms with the notion of *eternal recurrence* (parts two and three), and in part four his temptation by pity for the *'higher men'*. In style the whole book is designed to read like an ancient sacred book (complete with *dithyrambic* poetry), its tone varying often rapidly between the philosophically reflective (albeit with greater use of imagery and symbol than is usual, even for N), prophetic, satirical or parodic, lyrical, and hallucinogenically gothic. The fourth part contains a greater preponderance of the comic and parodic. The book contains some of the most sustained discussions in N's published work, of *time* (including *eternal recurrence*), the *will to power*, being and *becoming*, and *affirmation*. The book also contains many passages intended to communicate those new experiences and feelings that N believed would be typical of a human being like Zarathustra.

tiger

See *cat*.

time

Zeit. Time is central to a number of concepts in N. Here, we will list them, directing the reader to other entries. (i) The reality of continuous *becoming*; (ii) the *cycles* and forces of *history*; (iii) the concept of the *eternal* (and see the Republic of Genius or Oligarchs of the Spirit at *genius, free spirit*) and especially *eternal recurrence* (and the latter as a *redemption* of time); (iv) relatedly, the concepts of *fate* and especially *amor fati*; (v) the notions of *tempo* and *rhythm*; (vi) *life* as essentially growth or *overcoming*, and thus being *future*-oriented as opposed to a stagnant present with its *work* and *newspapers*; (vii) N's critique of, but also use of, the concepts of *purposes* and *goals*; (viii) the moment (see *eternal recurrence, beauty*); (ix) the analyses of memory and *forgetting*; (x) the notion of being *untimely*; (xi) the idea of *becoming who one is*, or spiritual *pregnancy*; (xii) finally, a whole host of time metaphors, especially the times of the day or seasons of the year (e.g. noon, midnight – see *night*).

tradition

See *habit*.

tragedy

A key topic from the beginning of N's career right to the end. In N's early work, tragedy represents the high point of ancient *culture*, and was produced by the coming together of two distinct cultural drives, the *Apollonian* and the *Dionysian*. Essentially, tragedy permits insight into Dionysian truth, while also being shielded and rendered communicable by beautiful illusion. This shielding means the transformation of *pessimism* into *cheerfulness*. Tragedy is not then a cultural or artistic event among others, but a philosophical event. Tragedy becomes a marker of the essential difference between earlier Greek culture, and later Greek, or Judeo-Christian, cultures (e.g. D172, GS135). Significantly, N generalizes this notion of tragedy to describe his philosophical attitude as a whole (see 1872.19.35): he imagines a philosopher who is able to observe the truth of the human condition as if on a stage, and remain cheerful (H1.34). The last third of *The Birth of Tragedy* discusses the possibility of a renewal of tragic experience within *modernity*, essentially by way of *Wagner's* art. That position is then restated, with alterations, in UM4, especially sections 4 and 7. In D, N uses tragedy to describe an alternative affect to modern *pity* or *guilt* (D72, 178). In his latest phase, N often identifies tragic feeling with the Dionysian (in his later use of that term): the joyful *affirmation* of *life* even in its destructive phases, and indeed celebrating itself precisely through *sacrifice*, destruction and *suffering* (TISkirmishes24, Ancients5, EHBT3).

transformation, transfiguration, metamorphosis

Verwandlung, Verklärung, etc. N normally uses these terms in one of three ways. First, as an equivalent expression to *sublimation*, or at least to other changes of object or meaning undergone by concepts, values or passions (H2.288, GM1.4, GM3.8). Second, something like idealization: a god should be the ideal image of a transfiguration and affirmation of world (AC18), or music should be world-transfiguring, that is it should permit the experience of new valuations and perspectives (EHWC1). Third, a revolutionary change in a person or culture, where because of a shift of values a whole different mode of life has been entered (e.g. eternal recurrences would 'transform and possibly crush you': GS341; in tragedy, members of the chorus 'seeing oneself transformed before one's eyes' (BT8); 'Zarathustra is transformed, Zarathustra has become a child' (ZP2, and see Z1.1). Importantly, transformation relates to possibilities that are already 'within' us, rather than a discontinuous leap (e.g. 1888.14.151); see *becoming oneself.*

translation

See *language.*

truth

Wahrheit. Right from the beginning, N works on the concept of truth – and not just its nature, but also its *value.* That is to say, although the classic epistemological questions of what is truth, and how is it possible to attain (or how, if at all, is knowledge possible), are important for N, they are generally discussed in the orbit of questions of the value of truth (e.g. BGE34). By this is meant truth's role, real or perceived, in the preservation or advancement of human being.

N takes it for granted that the history of European philosophy predominantly employs a correspondence theory of truth. A statement is true if its content corresponds to the factual arrangement of things. One could quibble about details. For example, what is meant by correspondence – is it some form of image-of, for example? – and likewise about what 'things' are – sensations?, things that appear, or true being, such as the Forms? But these quibbles do not amount to the real problem, which is that correspondence is never more than a secondary phenomenon. In its place, in the famous essay 'On Truth and Lies', N proposes a notion of truth that bears considerable resemblance to that of his contemporaries, the pragmatists. We call truth those statements, beliefs, ideas or ways of doing things that 'work'; that is, which accomplish what we need and expect them to accomplish. N grounds this utility in the preservation of human communities: things are held to be true that are believed to be a condition of survival (e.g. GS354). N thus argues that the phenomena of truth is *moral* from the beginning (see 1872.19.175, 177). (The pragmatists, in contrast, thought of this utility primarily in terms of solving practical problems or predicting experimental results.) Our sensations are manifold, in a continuous flow and without ever twice being exactly the same (the example of the leaf that N uses is straight from Leibniz). Our language and concepts then amount to several layers of interpretation, or 'artistic' reconstruction, of these stimuli so as to present for us the world of our experience. (N's ideas here are neo-Kantian, and owe much to the work of Gustav Gerber in particular.) Once our world is presented in this manner, then for the first time truth as correspondence is possible. It is only because we have systematically forgotten the original metaphorical acts that we believe the flow of ever-unique nerve stimuli is properly understood through the use of language and general concepts. Moreover, this same forgetting allows us to believe that truth is or can be rigorously independent of individual or collective values (safety, survival, growth, etc.), when in fact it is those underlying values, combined with centuries of custom, that explain the 'drive for truth' (and see BGE24). Once a 'drive for truth' is established in the modern world, it is irreversible because it is a characteristic feature of modernity's *will to power* (D429). Importantly, although the language of forgetting sounds negative and something that should be reversed, N does not think that one could simply 'remember' how truths came to be formed, either as an individual or as a scientific investigation, because the metaphorical quality goes all the way down into basic physiology. Moreover, even if one could remember, this would be dangerous in at least two ways. First because these truths are related to preservation and survival. Second, because *not knowing* is a condition of being able to act and achieve things. 'Knowledge kills action' N writes at BT7, by for example disclosing the futility of action.

The three key ideas in the 'Truth and Lies' essay – that truth is a moral phenomenon, having to do with society-wide sense of self-protection; that language and concepts do not understand the world so much as produce an understandable world; and that the ultimate basis of our experiences (here, the nerve stimuli) are unknowable – continue to be important aspects of N's work. However, they do undergo important modifications. In particular the idea of the self-preservation of a social group gradually becomes incorporated into the notion of *will to power*. Preservation is only one means to expressing power, and not always the best expression. In other words, the 'value' that grounds our sense of truth may involve precisely the leaving behind of a given social order. Later, truth is rethought as *perspective*. If reality is will to power, then perspective is not a *view on* reality, but a characteristic of reality itself. N suggests that truth as correspondence is not just a hopeless ideal – because the real ground, the 'true world' is unknowable – but an absurd and degenerate one. It is degenerate – meaning here in some way opposed to the interests of life – because for example it tries to remove the vital *agonistic* character from inquiry (see D507, and GS373). Thus also, the refusal to abandon the ideal of truth marks contemporary science out as an advanced form of the *ascetic ideal* (GM3.24). N famously forms the wry hypothesis that 'truth is a woman' (BGEP1). The point is partly that truth is something elusive and coy, but much more that truth is not the kind of thing that could be 'won' by the dry dogmatism of scholarly science or philosophy. Moreover, the traditional conception of truth is absurd: at the end of 'How the true world finally became a fable' in TI, N writes that with the abandonment of the true world we also must abandon the idea of the apparent one. The notions of truth and appearance are mutually dependent, and truth is possible only if we posit a 'true world' for it to correspond to.

A higher mode of existence would be one that could *affirm* its world as will to power – N suggests a similar idea already at UM3.4 and there calls it a 'truthful' existence. This affirmative existence would require in addition at least three things relevant to the concept of truth: first, abandoning the degenerate striving for grand metaphysical explanations that take one beyond this world or life, and instead being 'good neighbours to the closest things' (H3.16, and see D44). Similarly, in an echo of Epicureanism, at Z2.2 Zarathustra tells us that our 'will to truth' should be for what is 'humanly thinkable'. Second, the affirmative existence would be affirmation of the *multiplicity* of perspectives and interpretations (D130, BGE2, 22). Thus, N sometimes argues that 'conviction' unto martrydom is a positive refutation of truth (AC53). Third, such an existence would require the strength to face insights that demand quite other values and thus, in effect, demand one's destruction. For example, at BGE39 N famously talks about the 'measure' of 'the strength of a spirit' being how much truth one could 'endure', before being destroyed, transformed or rendered incapable of action by a surplus of knowledge. Thus also eternal recurrence is the greatest 'weight' GS341; see BGE59. Implied in this last idea would appear to be a distinction within truth. Truth/knowledge conceived as the correspondence of a judgement to reality is impossible – in the strict sense – except within the horizon of those basic metaphysical errors which constitute any such reality. However, truth/knowledge in the sense of insights into the inter-relationships of perspectives and their value is possible. So, in BGE230 N distinguishes between a will to simplification or to surface, and the will of those who strive for knowledge. But this distinction, he goes on to argue, is not all it would seem: it does not entail that truth and knowledge are phenomena distinct from nature (i.e. from perspective), and thus somehow neutral with respect to the needs of life (i.e. both are will to power). Not knowledge of things in themselves, but rather knowledge of the differences among perspectives – the relations of power and value and the overall *economy* of power and value – is the goal of N's method (GM3.12). Accordingly, N writes that the drive to knowledge has now proven itself to be life-preserving (GS110) – N has scientific and technological innovations in mind. But such knowledge only occurs within the framework of a set of broad metaphysical and moral errors. 'Dangerous' truth is something else. To what end is such seeking after knowledge, N asks; the first sentence of BGE231 answers: 'Learning changes us.' In other words, this dangerous and sometimes cruel seeking after knowledge has its value in being part of the *experimental transformation* of the human (see GS324). Importantly, this transformation may occur in the self, but does not originate there. N explicitly rejects the Cartesian paradigm that inner, conscious knowledge is both the most secure type and also the basis for all other knowledge (BGE16, 281, GMP1, EHClever9). Our 'familiarity' with ourself is part of the barrier, N suggests, since it is of a kind (i.e. habits of simplification) with those errors that prevent genuinely new knowledge (GS355). The kind of comprehensive or just insight N has in mind takes the self as only a moment within the historical development of the human, knowable only indirectly and moreover only as such a moment (see the delightful passages at H2.223 and D243).

twilight

See *night*.

Twilight of the Idols, The

One of N's last works, written in 1888 and published the following year (after his mental collapse in January). *Twilight* is often seen as a useful and concise summation of N's late thought. The beginning and end of the book mark a return to an aphoristic style, while the middle contains a series of short essays on *Socrates*, *metaphysical* and ontological errors (including the justly famous section 'How the true world finally became a fable'), *morality*, and *Germany*.

unconscious

See *consciousness*.

unity, wholeness, all

Einheit, Ganzheit, Alles. These notions appear in a number of different contexts, and always in a contrast with that which is fragmented, partial or arbitrarily assembled. Frequently, and conventionally enough, the model is the unity of the living organism (thus N combines the idea of whole with the notion of life at UM2.4, 4.4, WC7). The contrast could be between (i) a whole or authentic *culture* and cultural decadence or fragmentation (as in UM1.1 or 2.4, Z2.14, WC7; see *historical sense*); (ii) a genuine type as opposed to something corrupt or decadent (e.g. UM4.3, D403, BGE257) (iii) a whole or *comprehensive* image of the nature of the world, as opposed to one that is partial or specialized (e.g. UM3.3); (iv) whole human beings in contrast to those who are fragments because they cut themselves off from something – negate an aspect of their past, their fate, their context. N writes, 'a person *is* in the context of the whole' (TIErrors8). A key example are the human fragments at Z2.20 who are unable to *affirm* all aspects of their selves and their world, and thus in themselves are unable to redeem time (see also 3.12.3, H2.177); (v) the philosopher of the future, who not only has 'wholeness in manifoldness' (BGE212) in terms of knowledge or insight, but has *incorporated* that knowledge and therefore exists *as* that knowledge. This is the figure of Zarathustra, who 'feels himself to be the *highest type of everything that exists*' and who himself is 'the eternal yes to all things' (EHZ6). That is, Zarathustra is a mode of existence that is aligned to and utterly affirmative of the real. This last concept is found frequently in N's later works, for example when N writes that we philosophers have 'no right to be single [i.e. to treat things in isolation] in anything' but should rather be 'witnesses to one will, one health' (GMP2); likewise, in N's praise of Goethe's belief that 'everything is redeemed and affirmed in the whole' (TISkirmishes49).

universality, generality

Universalität, Allgemeinheit. Normally, this concept means one of two things: (i) a feature of some proposition such that it is true everywhere and always; (ii) an operation that tries to use a 'locally' true proposition to understand the everywhere and always (universalization or generalization). N is primarily concerned with the second of these, with philosophers of all types and their 'rage for generalisation' (H2.5). Thus, in the fields of *history* (UM2.6), *religion* (i.e. monotheism, and see Z2.4), *morality* (BGE198, 202, AC11) *politics* and *culture* ('universal concepts . . . the mere sound of words': UM4.5, and see *democracy*) or the *ascetic ideal* (GM3.23) he identifies and critiques the attempt to universalize some observation or value. In contrast, N proposes his concept of the *comprehensive* human being, who has aligned him or herself with all that is and the nature of all that is. For such a human, 'self-knowledge will become universal knowledge with regard to all that is past' and similarly, 'universal determination with regard to all future humanity' can be found (H2.223).

untimeliness

Unzeitgemäss. The concept gives the four Untimely Meditations their title, but is found in various forms throughout his writing. By the untimely, N means two things. First, his own awkward relation (and that of others like him) to his age. N is not only critical of this or that aspect of contemporary European culture or politics – this is presumably a perfectly ordinary phenomenon – but holds in 'sovereign contempt' (EHUntimely1) the key *values* that underlie them. So, UM1 begins with N rejecting the whole verdict that public opinion gives about the Franco-Prussian War; while UM2 similarly begins with a wholesale rejection of the contemporary pride in its approach to history. It follows also that N expects to be poorly understood (e.g. Zarathustra's failures in the market place in ZP, EHPreface1); his philosophy belongs to the future (thus, for example, the future nobility at GS337 or the 'new philosophers' at BGE2). Second, the sense that this very untimeliness is integral to any possibility of changing these values. For example, N's immersion in the culture of ancient Greece – a much more alien place than historians normally claim – gives him a kind of leverage with respect to the present (UM2P, H2.218). Such untimeliness may also consist in seeing historical processes as a whole or *comprehensively* (H1.616, and see the concept of the supra-historical in UM2), rather than from a single *perspective*.

Untimely Meditations, The

Series of four long essays written and published between 1873 and 1876. Nietzsche had various plans for additions to the series, but these were abandoned in favour of *Human, All Too Human*. The four are 'David Strauss, the Confessor and Writer'; 'On the Uses and Disadvantages of History for Life'; 'Schopenhauer as Educator'; and 'Richard Wagner in Bayreuth'. The topic of the first was prompted by *Wagner*, and is an over-zealous attack on Strauss – an influential, and broadly Hegelian theologian and historian. The real target, though, is more broad: the failings of contemporary German *culture*. The second is a bit more sedate, an influential study of the roles *history* plays in cultural development and health. The third is only nominally about *Schopenhauer*, being more concerned with the nature and purpose of *education*. Despite N's increasing suspicions of Wagner, the fourth is only subtly removed from hagiography. It contains some substantial reflections on the function of *art*, and an important restatement of Nietzsche's ideas concerning *tragedy*. In EH, N claims that the real subject of these last two is himself.

use/utility

Benutzung, and similar. N argues that a society develops the various institutions, words, concepts and values it does because these either are, or are believed to be, useful to that society – either in terms of its survival, its identity, its having a great future or its feeling of power. For example, the origin of *justice* is an 'enlightened self-preservation' (H1.92). Versions of this account, broadly speaking, can be found in 'On Truth and Lies', throughout UM2, and at H3.40, D19, GS354, BGE32, 201. Notice, however, that the things that could be deemed useful are quite varied, and may even be at odds. It is a different context, but at BGE13 N insists against Darwin that self-preservation is not the most basic goal of an organism. Thus, N also insists at D37 that what utility we discover for something likely has little to do with its historical (or prehistorical) origin (this notion of a disconnection from origins is an important theme of D). The kind of utility that is found in the title of UM2 is quite different from that which N discusses in 'On Truth and Lies', and different again from that which the utilitarian philosophers employ (for other examples of such differences see D360 or BGE190). Judging by the narrow utility of self-preservation, the one who questions existing values, or creates new ones, will be dangerous, and thus criminal or evil. Not surprisingly, sometimes when N employs the notion of utility he means it only in this narrow sense – so, at BGE260, only slave morality is utilitarian.

Another sense of 'use' is found at TIMorality6 and BGE61. Namely, the notion that we free spirits or 'immoralists' have come to understand the overall 'economy' of things. In this system, even that which is diseased life is nevertheless necessary for the whole, and indeed can be used to further our quite different purposes.

value

Wert. Value is a fundamental concept in N. Let us assume with N that *life* is a continual process of growth, or that *will to power* is something akin to a continual striving for power with respect to something else. Then the first and key attribute of any encountered entity or process is its value. That is, any entity is encountered as something beneficial to life or will to power (a comrade, a tool, a resource, a place to rest, etc.), or something that resists them (enemy, barrier, problem) or perhaps just irrelevant. That valuing is a function of life is also the reason why the value of life per se cannot be established – TISocrates2; but also because there is no alteration in the total economy of value – 1887.11.72.) The process by which value is assigned is evaluation. Such evaluation, especially if active (the values will not be borrowed from others or from traditions) as opposed to reactive, is *creative*. The value that I 'assign' something will be different from the value that another assigns. Thus value is *perspectival*. Now, it is convenient to talk about 'assigning' value or 'evaluation' as if the thing valued exists in a value-neutral way prior to any evaluation. However, the function of the concept of perspective is to indicate that value essentially creates the thing (GS58, Z1.15, and the idea is already found in 'On Truth and Lies'). The world exists as valued; or, if we consider (as N sometimes does) the term 'value' as too subjective or anthropomorphic, then we would change this to the world exists as power-relations (implicit at 1887.11.73). This is N's version of Kant's analysis of the conditions for the constitution of objects of experience.

A moral value is the attribute assigned, usually by a group or institution, to a whole class of things (especially types of behaviour or character-types), apparently concerning their 'goodness' or 'rightness' but actually, on N's analysis, concerning their relationship to life or will to power. *Morality* may have risen in an essentially utilitarian way – these are the values by means of which a people came to be a people, and survived as a people. Alternatively, morality might be the means by which a certain sub-group achieves and maintains its power (N's prime example is the priest class [see GM3.11 or AC55]). It is 'moral' insofar as it carries a universality (the group does not think that its values are perspectival, but rather holds them as normative), and therefore effectively sets up an image of the human being *as he or she should be* (TIMorality6). Values form an inter-connected system; it follows that any attempt to envisage new forms of life would have to involve a *revaluation* of all values. The 'revaluation of all values' is the most famous of the titles for the huge project that N set for himself in 1887–8 (see GM3.27) but never completed, although he considered AC to be its first volume.

veneration, reverence, honour, piety

[*Ehre* (honour), *Ehrfurcht* (veneration, reverence), *Pietät* (piety) are the most common] (*Ehrfurcht* is often translated as just 'respect', but this truncates much of the German word's meaning.) This ensemble of terms is an important part of N's analysis of religion (very broadly speaking). Here, though, it is not a question of the familiar critique of Christianity, its origins and implications. In fact, and perhaps surprisingly, only very rarely does N use these terms in the context of that critique, and often then negatively (e.g. the first Christians could have learned something about reverence from the 'despised "heathen peoples"': GM3.22). The first, camel transformation of the spirit (Z1.1) is reverent; later at Z2.8, Zarathustra adds that the lion stage has 'broken his reverential heart'. That is, one has moved on from an emotional dedication to a critical or sceptical stage. But that stage too must be overcome (and see the comments about the reverence in despising and despairing at Z4.13.3), and a revalued order of rank established that is founded on the nature of the real. Thus, with these concepts N is trying to understand what is *noble* and *healthy* in religion and related phenomenon; specifically, these terms designate those forms of life that are in alignment with the order of *rank* (BGE263, and see H3.260). For example, piety and reverence express what is valuable for life about antiquarian history (UM2.3); 'reverence for each other' describes genuine marriage (Z1.20); 'honour' and reverence are key aspects of N's account of 'master morality' at BGE260; likewise, 'the noble has reverence for itself' (BGE287, see ACP); and reverence for the 'ambiguous character' of the real is the good taste of science (GS373). N describes his relationship to Dionysus as 'reverence' (BGE295).

virtue, *virtù*

Tugend. A virtue is an aspect of one's character, habits or more generally one's mode of life that is considered excellent or more generally valuable – especially where that value is *moral*. By contrast, a vice is such an aspect, but counted a defect (it is a disposition to immorality or sin). N does discuss the virtues of free spirits or new philosophers (e.g. D556, *courage* at Z4.15, *honesty* at BGE227, 'spiritualized' or 'intellectual' *cruelty* at BGE229–30), but even when the names are the same, these virtues will be different in meaning from those of 'our grandfathers' (BGE214). Moreover, he revalues the whole traditional concept of virtue so as to show that they rest on (i) 'vanity and egoism' (things that would traditionally be considered vices: H3.285); (ii) what is imposed for the end of common utility but is great harm to the individual (GS21, automatism and self-denial: WC11, GM3.8); (iii) on moral narcotization (Z1.2) or a moral sense of punishment and reward (Z2.5). In any case, as traditionally conceived, the attainment of virtue is impossible (D87, see *Paul*). The criticisms clearly parallel those of *morality* more generally. Accordingly, N's own concept of virtue will have to be cleansed of any conventional morality (H3.212, and see 1887.10.110). The result is what he sometimes jokingly calls 'moraline-free' virtue (AC2, EHClever1). This in turn is identified with the notion of *virtù* – the qualities of a ruler capable of maintaining power and achieving greatness – as found in *Machiavelli*. One's virtue is essentially unique rather than something imposed upon the self from without (GS304, Z1.5, AC11), it is the excellence of the specific active role one plays – that one *is* – in the overall advancement of the human type (see also Z2.5).

Wagner Case, The

Short book from 1888, summing up N's late opinions concerning Richard Wagner. The title should be understood as treating Wagner as if he were a case study in some medical or cultural disease.

Wagner, Richard

Wagner is an important and innovative German composer, primarily of opera. He also wrote widely disseminated works on aesthetics, culture and politics. N was a devotee of Wagner's music from early on in his life, and became a close friend of the Wagner household. By the mid-1870s there were tensions between N and Wagner, and a break in their friendship shortly thereafter. N may have been infatuated with Cosima Wagner (Richard's much younger wife, and the daughter of Franz Liszt), and continued to write letters to her until his mental collapse.

For N of the early 1870s, Wagner represented the possibility of a renewal of German – and more broadly, European – culture. Wagner's past as a revolutionary (he had been involved in the May Uprising in Dresden in 1849) attracted N, and he saw Wagner as continuing to be a revolutionary figure, but now in a cultural and spiritual domain beyond mere politics. Wagner and N both admired *Schopenhauer*, considering him a renewal of German philosophy in general, and particularly believing in the significance of Schopenhauer's understanding of *music* as the direct 'voice' of the *will* (an idea Wagner put to work particularly in *Tristan and Isolde*). Also, N saw Wagner's operas which were built on broadly Germanic *myths* or stories as a way of bringing genuine cultural unity to the new German state – creating a *people* – which otherwise had only naïve nationalism.

By the mid-1870s, N believed that Wagner had failed as cultural revolutionary, perhaps had never been one at all, but was only an *actor*, and was in any case in thrall to nationalism, the political elite and anti-Semitism. Later still, with his last opera *Parsifal*, Wagner committed the unforgivable: he became a Christian. Nietzsche's later works are rich in direct or lightly veiled comments – mainly attacks – on Wagner. These include the character of the Sorcerer in TSZ4, GS368, GM3.2–5, *The Case of Wagner* and *Nietzsche Contra Wagner*, EHClever5–6, and EHCase1.

wandering

Wanderer, and cognate terms. Wandering, or the figure of the wanderer, are important elements within N's system of philosophical metaphors. Relevant mythic or literary allusions are plentiful and include: Cain's punishment for killing his brother is to wander the Earth without home (Gen. 4:12); the 40 years during which the Israelites wandered the wilderness; Odysseus' wanderings while trying to return home after the Trojan war; the Wandering Jew is a Medieval legend of a man who is doomed to wander until the second coming of Christ; Odysseus-like tales of sailors perpetually wandering the seas are common in modernity (e.g. Coleridge's *Rime of the Ancient Mariner*); and of course there are both Wagner's *The Flying Dutchman* and also Wotan disguising himself as a 'wanderer' throughout *Siegfried*. However, in these precedents, arguably including the last, the wandering is a kind of punishment or forced upon the sufferer. In N though, although perilous (e.g. H2.21) the wanderer is imagined more positively. N writes that we are 'noble traitors' to all convictions, without feeling any guilt; likewise, in the wanderer 'there must be something wandering that takes pleasure in change and transience' (H1.637–8). The wanderer has achieved some degree of freedom or independence, and thus his or her wandering is symbolic, because no idea or life practice is a permanent 'home' (e.g. 'spiritual nomadism': H2.211, D452, BGE44). This symbol becomes a series of narratives concerning wandering in Z (e.g. Z3.5, 7, and see *shadow*). Wandering is thus related to the ideas of *comprehensiveness*, height or ascending (e.g. the ability to look down from above onto European morality: GS380), the ability to compare values and *perspectives* (e.g. BGE260), and *untimeliness*. Wandering is also meant literally for

N, since for most of his working life he rarely spent more than a few months at a time in any one place.

war

Krieg. War (or the warrior) is a frequent motif in N, normally used metaphorically to mean any *agon* (contest or struggle), including within oneself (BGE200), between *friends*, against philosophical problems (EHWise7), or within cultures (e.g. TISkirmishes38). N's account of the role of real war or real peace in the regulation of cultures is found in passages such as H1.477, H3.187, 284.

watershed

See *eternal recurrence.*

weakness

See *strength.*

web, net

See *spider.*

weight, heaviness, gravity

Schwer, or sometimes *Gewicht.* Weight, heaviness or gravity has two main symbolic meanings: (i) That which burdens or is felt as a burden, leading either to a test of one's strength, or to a need for stimulation to escape exhaustion; (ii) that which prevents any upward movement, that is spiritual growth. It is opposed to *lightness, flying, bird* and *ascending* most obviously, but also *laughter, overcoming* and *gratitude.* The two clearest usages of these symbols are found in Z. First, the camel is the initial transformation of the spirit at Z1.1 (and also Z3.11), and it wishes to take on itself all burdens as a test of its strength. The camel thus represses its passions, denies itself comfort, satisfies itself with unproductive forms of knowledge – it is *ascetic*. Only the next transformation, the lion, is able to confront and overcome all this burden. The second usage is the 'spirit of gravity' (or 'spirit of heaviness'), found throughout Z (e.g. Z1.7, Z3.2.1, Z3.11, Z4.17.1). The spirit of gravity is any idea or form of life characterized by seriousness, that is by the notion that the important things or tasks are always burdens or otherwise difficult (e.g. moral rectitude or knowledge), and generally imposed from without (e.g. from God, from nature, from the pre-existing limitations of mind or body). Indeed, for the spirit of gravity, human life itself is a perpetual burden (perhaps of duty, sin, unrelenting desire or sensuality). This weight is an intrinsic condition of life (it may even be despised or nauseating) and must be accepted, not escaped. The spirit of gravity is also characterized by deliberateness in thought and action – as opposed to being instinctual (e.g. TIErrors2) – and thus a *struggle*, plodding. These burdens may be imposed by religious practices, but ironically it is also the task of religion to comfort those so burdened (GM3.17). This comfort serves a purpose, but does not address the underlying sickness.

Rather than being genuinely imposed from outside, 'only for itself is the human a heavy burden' (Z3.11). As suggested by the figure of the camel at Z1.1, taking on burdens is the first step towards being liberated from them. Thus, the eternal recurrence is the 'greatest' weight (GS341), and it takes much of the narrative in Z for Zarathustra to first express and then incorporate this heavy burden. Likewise, Zarathustra seeks those of the 'great despising' (ZP3), that they might in the end shed that burden. What modes of life might lead to such lightness? N links lightness with several other important symbols. For example, one needs the patience of being *pregnant* with new possibilities, and this also means love of oneself (Z3.11). This idea is found also at GS380, along with the overcoming of one's own time as it is incorporated in oneself. Also, new *ideals* or hopes – for different, 'higher' forms of the human – make the spirit of gravity retreat (Z4.17.1). In that same passage, N mentions *gratitude* (which links to the later idea of *amor fati*), and finally the ability to *laugh* even at the self. At BGE193, N writes about a dream of flight, an upwards without *struggle*. Such a new ideal of lightness would bring with it a new sense of happiness. Importantly, this ideal is also of a downward without 'condescension and humiliation'. That is, in accordance with N's notion of *overcoming*, it is not simply that the heavy burden is just removed, but rather that the meaning of (the way of valuing) something has been altered so as to no longer be experienced as burden.

wholeness

See *unity*.

will

Wille. As conventionally understood, my will is my determination to act in some way. So, a 'free will' would be a determination to act which is not itself determined. Schopenhauer makes three very important modifications to this conventional idea. First, the motive for acting, the determination to act, and the action itself are not actually three things – they are aspects of one, underlying thing which Schopenhauer just calls 'will'. Second, will is encountered by means of feelings (or affects), which are distinguished from the elements of cognition (i.e. the presentations of appearances, namely sensations and thoughts). Third, 'my' will is not mine at all, but is an individuated appearance of will, which is the thing in itself behind all appearances. That is, will is understood as a broad, metaphysical account of the true nature of reality. In his early work – especially BT – N follows Schopenhauer's analysis fairly closely. So, for example, the Dionysian is the drive to leave behind appearances and individuality and ecstatically sink back into the original oneness of the will. Later, though, he is openly critical.

At H2.5, he accuses Schopenhauer of over-generalizing and making metaphorical the notion of will, and projecting it onto 'all things in nature'. Similarly, at GS127, N claims that the conventional notion of will mentioned above was always a model for cause and effect in nature (see also TIReason5), and Schopenhauer simply 'enthroned' this belief. We had to believe in will as cause, lest the ego 'vanish in the multiplicity of change' (1887.9.98). He argues that pleasure and pain, rather than being immediate affects of the will, are products of the 'interpreting intellect'. BGE19 accuses Schopenhauer, along with other philosophers, of over-simplifying the will, treating it as a unity. They fail to see in it a conjunction of sensations, thought and affect, particularly the affect of command, and also failing to see that he who 'wills' must be both commander and commanded (and thus will and action are far from the same). 'Free will' now means the affect of commanding, that is, of having the power to command; unfree will the affect of being commanded. Similarly, 'willing liberates' (Z2.2) insofar as it redeems the burden of time past (Z2.20), and creates new values in the future. Will is always characterized as a particular mode of expression of *will to power*. Will in the conventional sense is an affect of the relations among centres of will to power. Thus, sometimes, when N writes 'will' he in fact means his technical concept of will to power. However, often in speaking about will N is emphasizing the particular state (strong or weak, healthy or sick) of the will of a people, a group or an individual (e.g. Z1.11, GS347, BGE208). Likewise, will can refer to a particular instance, or series of instances, of willing. For example, Zarathustra's will 'strides' forward and is 'unchanging' (Z2.11); likewise, he wishes to teach a 'new will', namely 'to will this path that human beings have walked blindly' (Z1.3; this passage is similar to BGE203). This change of emphasis between will to power and will is, explored metaphorically, the difference between the character of the waves, and a wave (GS310). Finally, the highest will to power may manifest itself in *beauty* and stillness, which is in fact the 'unharnessed will' (Z2.13).

will to power

Wille zur Macht. The will to power is N's proposal for the fundamental basis of the real and of becoming, to replace concepts such as substance, atoms, mechanical conceptions of force or cause and effect, and psychological notions of will or motive. This concept is a product of the 1880s, but elements of it are certainly found earlier. The relevant conception of power begins to appear in H1.446 (with its analogy between political power and natural power) or 595 (where the feeling of power is given an important and quite general explanatory role), and is fully formed by D112–13 (and see GS13). Power is not simply a social or political concept of influence or the having of certain rights; nor is it a physical concept of brute strength. Rather, more basically, power designates an *evaluation* and a corresponding striving. Thus, power comprises (i) the various ways that an entity (a person or a people) has of giving itself *value*, that is to say of positing itself as an entity, of being distinct from others, and of having and maintaining an identity (Z1.15, 2.12); and (ii) the various ways that entity has of being in relationship to others, of sensing and acting out differences of value (Z2.12). By the time N achieves this concept of power, he is already thinking of it in terms of a 'striving' (D113). And this means that (i) if power is not felt to be on the increase, then it must be decreasing (stasis situations may be of significance, but are always temporary); and (ii) power is always relational, it is a power *over*. This latter idea is particularly significant, for it suggests that the will to power could not be thought of as a being (thus the term 'entity' above is merely a shorthand), something with a quality inherent to it, since its constitution is originally relational. Thus, N argues that the will to power needs resistances (1887.9.151, 11.77). Equally, it follows that the notions of struggle or *agon* are not accidental features of will to power – that is under certain conditions the will to power experiences agon – but rather essential features.

The notion of will obviously owes something to Schopenhauer's concept of the will – the will as the single thing-in-itself, 'behind' appearance and individual entities, as perpetually striving and suffering in its perpetual striving. This concept N used readily in early work such as BT, although never entirely uncritically. It is productive to compare N's critique of Schopenhauer on the will at H2.5 or GS127. On N's later conception of will, the unity of will is a methodological simplification at best. In fact, the will to power is not an original unity but more akin to a multiplicity – more specifically, will to power is a field of power differences and relations. Moreover, will to power is not an abstract universal phenomenon of striving, but at each moment is something concrete or determinate and possessing a kind of direction: it is a will for this or for that. The concept of will in psychology is (as in Schopenhauer) abstract because it is assumed to be something prior to having its content, its 'where-to' (1888.14.121). That is to say, the will to power is always relational by being intentional (though by no means necessarily conscious). It constitutes its 'object' for itself, and *also* takes up an attitude towards that object, through value (where value is understood very generally). This 'attitude' could be a striving for power over, or defence from; or feelings of *ressentiment, veneration, pity* or *shame*, etc.; or also the elaboration of a philosophy that interprets the world as the 'most spiritual' will to power (BGE9).

The later N claims that pleasure and pain are interpretations of stimuli, and this is one criticism of conventional conceptions of will in which the will is understood as acting on pre-given feelings or expectations of pleasure and pain (GS127) (i.e. I feel pain, and then decide on an action to relieve it). Because will to power is essentially evaluation and interpretation it is not will in that ordinary sense, but a more fundamental process. Because of intentionality (constituting both object and attitude-towards), N claims that will to power can be understood neither as being nor becoming, but rather as pathos or affect (1888.14.79, 121, see GS13). There could not be will to power and then also a *feeling of* the will to power (because then we would need to posit some other type of entity that feels). Will to power is in itself already affect, and the primary affects are either ascending or weakening power. This analysis owes something to Schopenhauer – for whom motive, will and action were all aspects of the same underlying will – but does so without thinking of will as thing-in-itself or as a oneness. The full concept of will to power is essentially a further elaboration of these ideas of power as evaluating and striving into a broad explanatory device both in the domain of individual and social psychology (BGE23), and also down to the level of organs, cells and perhaps even the inorganic (BGE36 – will to power in nature is the 'pre-form of life'). N suggests that the physical concept of *force*, or of a 'something' (an atom, perhaps) subjected to or exerting a force, is devoid of sense without the will to power (1888.14.79).

There are a number of passages in which N seems to suggest that will to power is not an absolutely basic account of either psychology or inanimate reality. For example, BGE44 talks about a will to life being elevated, but under certain conditions, into an 'unconditional will to power'. Likewise, at TIA3, the will to power is said to be the Greeks' 'strongest instinct', suggesting other instincts both then and now. (See also 1887.11.55, 138, GM3.18.) At other locations, and in apparent self-contradiction, N is explicit about the role of will to power as just such a fundamental account (e.g. 1885.36.21, 31, 38.12 – the famous passage about the world as a 'monster of energy' – 1887.11.96, 1888.14.79). At BGE36, N is explicit in this way, although the whole passage is framed as a hypothesis. The hypothetical manner in which the will to power as a basic principle is expressed here might not be caution. Rather, in accordance with the concept of *perspective*, hypothetical or *regulative* modes of thinking might be part of what the will to power means (see *longing*). (The hypothetical manner in which eternal recurrence is introduced at GS341 could be understood similarly.)

An important distinction with will to power may help resolve this contradiction or indecision: namely between active and reactive. By active is meant that the will to power is the source of its interpretative acts and evaluations, and by reactive is meant a will to power that reflects values 'borrowed' from its environment, either in imitation (GM3.14 where this is described akin to infection), sublimation (i.e. a change of object for the will; for example GM3.15) or negation (GM1.10). Such a distinction would allow us to interpret, for example, the 'unconditional' at BGE44 as entailing a distinction from a reactive will to power, rather than a distinction from something that is not will to power. Similarly, claiming that the will to power was the Greeks' strongest instinct might be a way of claiming that the Greeks as a culture were in some way aligned to and celebratory of the will to power as active (see *agon*), and not constantly in a state of dishonesty and self-deception. Again, see the end of AC16, where N describes how a god might represent a people's reactive will to power, too weak to will values. Another possible clue is a further distinction within will to power, namely that between N's symbolic use of *feminine and masculine*: beauty, stillness, *perfection*, on the one hand, and destruction on the other. Only together do these two modes of will to power permit the creation of new values; separately, they yield quite distinct forms of life and culture. So, Zarathustra desires that the sombre heroes of knowledge become beautiful, and this means to 'unharness' their will (Z2.13). He sometimes sees these two modes as in a *cycle*.

The will to power has a complex but important relation to a number of other notions in N, some of which have not been mentioned already above. For example, it relates to *eternal recurrence*, since the point of eternal recurrence seems to be a kind of 'test' of a mode of life aligned to and affirmative of existence as will to power. Additionally, it allows N to discuss and defend the concept of *perspective*, which N sees as a preferable concept to interpretation because it does not imply a standpoint that is *not* perspectival. Will to power relates to the notion of *life*, since life will be a particular mode of will to power (though perhaps not the only one: 1888.14.121). At BGE9, N distinguishes between nature as 'indifference as power' and life which is essentially something that differentiates. It follows that even were we to accept that will to power was a universal account of the real, this is not the same as a simple conflation of the animate and inanimate (again, see the idea of a 'pre-form' of life at BGE36). Will to power as life differentiates, holds itself separate (e.g. the organism as an independent system). Finally, will to power pertains to N's account of *morality*, since moral values (especially including those that are presumed to be selfless or unegoistic) will be revealed as disguised modes of will to power.

Will to Power, The

A large collection of excerpts from N's notebooks, edited by N's sister well after his mental collapse. The title and organization were based on one of the many plans he formulated for a future book (see GM3.27). It was useful for many decades as the only available collection of N's notes, and until relatively recently the only one in English. However, the book can be misleading in that it – by selection, organization and omission – crafts a certain image of N's late thought. Specifically, this image is one designed to fit more comfortably with Elisabeth (and her late husband's) own political views, including German *nationalism*, far right-wing politics and anti-Semitism.

wisdom

Weisheit. One should of course bear in mind that in Greek, 'philosophy' means 'love of wisdom'. The following comments also apply to *Weise*, the 'wise one' or 'sage'. Wisdom is a word used in two quite different senses by N. First, it designates what N believes *philosophy* should and could be (BT18; throughout Z, for example Z1.7, 2.1; EHP4). In Z, Wisdom is the personification of Zarathustra's lover, who closely resembles life (Z2.10), and who also brings Zarathustra and life closer together (Z3.15). One of these personifications of Wisdom is used as the interpretative object of GM3. Second, however, it refers to what philosophy usually is – that is, 'no friend of wisdom' (BGE212). Such wisdom is a 'hiding place' for those who are exhausted and close to death (GS359, TISocrates1), or perhaps a pose for the ascetic ideal (GM3.14, 26).

woe

See *suffering*.

woman and man

See *feminine and masculine*.

work, industry

Arbeit, *Werk*. Both are usually translated as 'work'. *Arbeit* is narrower, meaning one's job or employment, with an overtone of labour. *Werk* is more general, meaning a task one has set for oneself, or the achievement of that task (e.g. an artwork) – Zarathustra says, at Z3.3, 'I am at the middle of my work'. ZP presents a nice contrast, between the discussion of *Arbeit* in ZP5 and the tight-rope dancer's *Werk* in ZP6 (and see *purpose*). Roughly speaking, N defines 'work' in the sense of labour (and thus usually *Arbeit*), as any effort spent on a task that is either unrelated, or only indirectly related, to one's own goals. By indirectly related we mean, in a modern context, working for money which in turn permits the purchase of necessities, luxuries or leisure. Consequently, there is relatively little difference between pre-modern slaves and modern workers – in the ancient world, work was shaming ('The Greek State') while in the modern world work without pleasure is ignoble

(GS42). If there is a difference, it is worse now for the workers (H1.457). Contemporary industrious culture, which is always in a hurry, sees a saving of time as its only virtue, and promotes every person as an independent economic agent, infects every aspect of human life from science to art (UM1.8, UM4.8), religion (BGE58) and relation between the sexes (BGE239). The goal of culture, which is greatness, is forgotten. The arts are complicit in this (H3.170), and have become little more than stimulants, narcotics and relievers of boredom (TISkirmishes30); likewise, the 'blessing of work' is one of the mechanisms employed by the ascetic priest (GM3.18). N fears this industriousness will also infect the contemplative life (H1.282) – soon, it may only be with 'bad conscience' that we can 'take a walk with ideas or friend' (GS329).

The exploitation of the modern worker is condemned by N not on straight-forward socialist grounds, but rather (i) on the ground that capitalists are not, and could not be, leaders of vision and refinement, who a people might naturally want to follow (GS40); (ii) the relation to time in an industrious culture means that the worker has no idea what to do with his or her leisure time, and becomes bored (H1.611, H2.47, GS42 – and this is the point of Z3.12.22); (iii) factory or other machine-based or impersonal work in particular consists in the obliteration of the individual and of an individual's pride in their production (H3.288, D173, EHUM1), and likewise also a distinctive pride in those who own the products; (iv) to the extent any notion of individuality remains, it is the ability to play any role (GS356); (v) workers are 'accomplices in the current folly of nations' – that is the desire to produce and consume goods without limit – and no modification of their working conditions will change this. N interestingly suggests workers should just leave and colonize other parts of the globe (D206).

Aside from that exploitation, the happiness of the many lies in *specialization* and in work; the happiness of the few elsewhere. To tempt the many with a different form of happiness is both cruel and counter-productive (TISkirmishes40). The health of both groups is necessary for the health and growth of all. Importantly, N treats both the middle-class (scientists, state functionaries, artists, etc.) and the 'fourth estate' of factory, agricultural or mining workers, as belonging to the same group, the 'many' or the 'mediocre' (see Z2.16 for example). This then leads to his condemnation of further and higher education, particularly the essentially vocational or specialist training that is started too early (see TIGermans5, EHH3). As does Plato, N sometimes talks about a third class, for example the 'warriors' of the understanding at Z1.10, who like the lion cannot create new ideas or values but can advance and defend them. He is obviously not talking about the military literally, but about a higher type of scholar, or a preparatory type of free spirit.

world

Welt. 'World' can be used to mean the way in which things appear and are valued at some historical point: our present world, or the Greek world. However, like his use of the term 'earth', N uses 'world' primarily to emphasize reality without metaphysical falsifications, and their accompanying overvaluation (if, for example, we think of the world as a creation of God and part of divine purpose) or undervaluation (if we think of it as changeable, illusory or mere matter). For a few clear examples, see H2.99, GS109, 344 and BGE36. Similarly, Zarathustra teases those who believe in a real world behind the apparent one, he jokingly calls them 'back-worlders' at Z1.3 (a pun on 'back-woods', that is a hick, yokel, bumpkin). N provides a famous summary of his view of the intellectual history of 'world' at TIWorld. Since the concepts of the 'illusory' and 'real' worlds are reciprocally dependent, when 'the true world is gone' so is the illusory world. GS346 takes the idea further, refusing to see the human as somehow not 'of' the world. See also *nihilism* and *truth*. World is also a key concept in Hegel and later Hegelian thought: world spirit is the totality of history understood as the progressive realization of spirit. N lampoons the grandiose tone of such ideas at UM2.9.

yearning

See *longing*

youth

See *child.*

Zarathustra

Ancient Persian religious figure, better known in the West by the Greek version of his name, Zoroaster. Zarathustra was, N argues, the first thinker to conceive of both the human and natural worlds in moral terms, as a struggle between good (or true) and evil (or false) forces. Therefore, reimagining Zarathustra as an immoralist (in Z) is a way of rewriting, as it were, the origin of European religion and culture. N identifies Zarathustra – in his highest moments of insight and affirmation – with the concept of *Dionysus* (EHZ6). The name Zarathustra may have etymological connections with several concepts found in Z, such as 'gold' and 'camel'. The Greek transcription was sometimes taken to mean 'pure star'.

GUIDE TO FURTHER READING

Nietzsche's writings

Cambridge and Stanford are each putting out more or less complete editions of N's writings in English. Vintage, Penguin and Hackett also carry more than one of the works in good editions, while the Blackwell *Reader* and Kaufmann's *The Portable Nietzsche* are the best choices among single-volume selections. Beware, though, of inexpensive or public domain reprints of the early translations, which can be misleading or severely edited down. The standard German editions are the Colli and Montinari sets from de Gruyter.

Selected secondary reading

What follows is a deliberately brief selection of major publications in Nietzsche studies. In addition, bear in mind the many helpful commentaries on individual works from Bloomsbury, Edinburgh, Routledge among others.

Allison, David B. (2001). *Reading the New Nietzsche*. Rowman and Littlefield.
Ansell-Pearson, Keith (2009). *A Companion to Nietzsche*. Wiley-Blackwell.
Babich, Babette E. and Cohen, Robert S. (eds) (2010). *Nietzsche and the Sciences*. 2 vols. Kluwer.
Brobjer, Thomas (2008). *Nietzsche's Philosophical Context: An Intellectual Biography*. Illinois.

Clark, Maudemarie (1991). *Nietzsche on Truth and Philosophy.* Cambridge.

Conway, Daniel W. (1997). *Nietzsche and the Political.* Routledge.

Diethe, Carol (2013). *A Dictionary of Nietzscheanism.* 3rd ed. Scarecrow.

Gemes, Ken and Richardson, John (2013). *The Oxford Handbook of Nietzsche.* Oxford.

Hill, Kevin (2005). *Nietzsche's Critiques: The Kantian Foundations of His Thought.* Oxford.

Hollingdale, R. J. (1999). *Nietzsche: The Man and His Philosophy.* 2nd ed. Cambridge.

Jensen, Anthony K. (2013). *Nietzsche's Philosophy of History.* Cambridge.

Kaufmann, Walter (1980). *Nietzsche: Philosophy, Psychologist, Antichrist.* 4th ed. Princeton.

Leiter, Brian (2002). *Nietzsche on Morality.* Routledge.

Montinari, Mazzino (2003). *Reading Nietzsche.* Greg Whitlock (Trans.). Illinois.

Moore, Gregory and Brobjer, Thomas H. (eds) (2004). *Nietzsche and Science.* Ashgate.

Nehamas, Alexander (1985). *Nietzsche, Life as Literature.* Harvard.

Parkes, Graham (1994). *Composing the Soul: Reaches of Nietzsche's Psychology.* Chicago.

Poellner, Peter (1995). *Nietzsche and Metaphysics.* Oxford.

Richardson, John (2008). *Nietzsche's New Darwinism.* Oxford.

Safranski, Rudiger (2002). *Nietzsche: A Philosophical Biography.* Norton.

Schacht, Richard (1995). *Making Sense of Nietzsche.* Illinois.

Schrift, Alan D. (ed.) (2000). *Why Nietzsche Still?* California.

Young, Julian (2010). *Friedrich Nietzsche: A Philosophical Biography.* Cambridge.

INDEX

This index provides pages references only for the most significant passages, with a main entry (if there is one) in **bold**. If a concept is ubiquitous (e.g. 'morality') only the main entry is given. Please also consult the cross-references found in the entries themselves.